THE DYNAMIC FREE SPEECH CLAUSE

The Dynamic Free Speech Clause

FREE SPEECH AND ITS RELATION TO OTHER CONSTITUTIONAL RIGHTS

Timothy Zick

OXFORD
UNIVERSITY PRESS

OXFORD
UNIVERSITY PRESS

Oxford University Press is a department of the University of Oxford. It furthers the University's objective of excellence in research, scholarship, and education by publishing worldwide. Oxford is a registered trademark of Oxford University Press in the UK and certain other countries.

Published in the United States of America by Oxford University Press
198 Madison Avenue, New York, NY 10016, United States of America.

Library of Congress Cataloging-in-Publication Data

Names: Zick, Timothy, author.
Title: The dynamic free speech clause : free speech and its relation to other constitutional rights / Timothy Zick.
Description: New York, NY : Oxford University Press, 2018. | Includes bibliographical references and index.
Identifiers: LCCN 2018003874 | ISBN 9780190841416 ((hardback) : alk. paper)
Subjects: LCSH: Freedom of speech—United States. | United States. Constitution. 1st-10th Amendments. | Civil rights—United States.
Classification: LCC KF4772 .Z415 2018 | DDC 342.7308/53—dc23
LC record available at https://lccn.loc.gov/2018003874

9 8 7 6 5 4 3 2 1

Printed by Sheridan Books, Inc., United States of America

Note to Readers

This publication is designed to provide accurate and authoritative information in regard to the subject matter covered. It is based upon sources believed to be accurate and reliable and is intended to be current as of the time it was written. It is sold with the understanding that the publisher is not engaged in rendering legal, accounting, or other professional services. If legal advice or other expert assistance is required, the services of a competent professional person should be sought. Also, to confirm that the information has not been affected or changed by recent developments, traditional legal research techniques should be used, including checking primary sources where appropriate.

(Based on the Declaration of Principles jointly adopted by a Committee of the American Bar Association and a Committee of Publishers and Associations.)

For Katie and Jackson

Contents

Acknowledgments

THIS BOOK IS the product of several years of thinking about the manner in which freedom of speech and other constitutional rights relate to one another. I have shared many of the ideas in this book with various colleagues, friends, and neighbors. I would undoubtedly miss some of them were I to try to list them all. However, I would like to extend a special note of thanks to the following faculty, friends, and colleagues who read and commented on portions of the manuscript or the principal ideas presented in the book: Joseph Blocher, Ashutosh Bhagwat, Neal Devins, Rick Garnett, Tara Grove, John Inazu, Randy Kozel, Alli Larsen, Greg Magarian, Melissa Radtke, Neil Richards, and Alex Tsesis. I am also grateful to participants at workshops at Notre Dame Law School, Richmond Law School, and William & Mary Law School, where I presented some of the book's ideas.

I am indebted to William & Mary Law School for providing financial and other forms of support during the research and writing of the book. Specifically, I would like to thank my Dean, Davison Douglas, for naming me the 2016–2017 Cabell Research Professor of Law and for approving a research sabbatical during the 2016–2017 academic year. I would also like to thank the College of William & Mary and Joseph Plumeri for naming me a recipient of the Plumeri Award for Faculty Excellence in 2017. I would not have been able to complete the manuscript without this generous support.

Although the manuscript is original, some of the concepts and ideas discussed therein have appeared in my previous publications. These include the following: Timothy Zick, "Rights Dynamism," 19 *U. Pa. J. Cons't L.* 791 (2017); Timothy Zick, "Rights Speech," 48 *U.C. Davis L. Rev.* 1 (2014); Timothy Zick, "Professional Rights Speech," 47 *Ariz. St. L. J.* 1289 (2015); and Timothy Zick, "The Dynamic Relationship between Freedom of Expression and Equality," 12 *Duke J. L. & Pub. Pol.* 13 (2016).

Preface

THIS IS A book about relationships between the Free Speech Clause and other constitutional rights. Rights are formally manifested in constitutional text, through the words in provisions such as the Free Speech Clause, the Equal Protection Clause, and the Second Amendment. Of course, rights are much more than formalized bits of text. Since they are not self-defining, rights are the product of interpretations—by judges, commentators, civic organizations, and the public. We know what rights mean, and what they protect, in part owing to how individuals invoke and exercise them over time.

Rights sometimes act as "trumps." They prohibit governments from doing certain things, such as abridging the freedom of speech or depriving liberty without due process of law. But rights are also very potent rhetorical tools. They are a means of arguing about power, liberty, and the relationship between the two.

This book's protagonist, the Free Speech Clause, is a right in all of these different respects. The clause has been defined with reference to judicial precedents, practices, and commentaries. In some cases, it operates as an effective trump on governmental action. The Free Speech Clause, and the freedom of speech it protects, are also powerful rhetorical tools. They are frequently invoked by Americans, to defend freedom of thought, communication, criticism, and inquiry, but also to advocate for the recognition or expansion of other constitutional rights.

What has generally been missing from the study and understanding of constitutional rights is their critically important *relational* dimension. Rights do not exist or function in isolation from one another. They interact and associate with one another. In the course of these dynamic intersections, relationships among and between rights are forged, old synergies are rekindled, new synergies are discovered, and conflicts between rights sometimes arise. Constitutional rights are not static, formal, and inert conceptions. Rather, they are dynamic, active, and interactive constructs that draw energy from one another and affect one another's meanings and means of enforcement. Thus, in order to fully understand the Constitution's rights provisions, we must attend to their relational dimension.

This is the perspective from which the book examines a variety of intersections between the Free Speech Clause and other constitutional rights. The Free Speech Clause is perhaps the most "social" provision in the Constitution. As a right, an activity, and a form of rhetoric, freedom of speech has intersected frequently with a number of constitutional rights. Some of those intersections occur as governments seek to regulate private and public discourse about constitutional rights. In terms of what might be thought of as "case studies," the book focuses in particular on the Press Clause, Assembly Clause, Petition Clause, Free Exercise Clause, Equal Protection Clause, Due Process Clause, and Second Amendment.

The Free Speech Clause has been invoked and used to facilitate the recognition, exercise, and enforcement of these and other constitutional rights. All constitutional movements, whether they have concerned equal protection, religious free exercise, reproductive rights, the right to bear arms, or other liberties, have relied heavily on the Free Speech Clause and free speech rights, arguments, and principles. The contemporary recognition and meaning of these and other constitutional rights can be traced directly to their frequent interactions with the free speech guarantee.

As the book emphasizes throughout, the influence moves and flows in more than one direction. Contemporary understanding of the Free Speech Clause owes much to its frequent interactions with other constitutional rights. Thus, the Free Speech Clause's central principle of neutrality, as well as its robust protection of freedom of thought, inquiry, and publication, have been significantly influenced by dynamic intersections with other constitutional rights. The book examines both what the Free Speech Clause has done *for* other constitutional rights, as well as what intersections with these other rights have done *to* the Free Speech Clause.

The rights relationships examined in the book have often been both complicated and complicating. Owing to its power and magnetism, the Free Speech Clause has facilitated and abetted other constitutional rights in a number of ways. However, it has also diminished or even supplanted some of the rights it has encountered. In some important respects, freedom of speech has eclipsed rights that would benefit from substantive development on their own terms. For example, the Free Speech Clause has taken on functions relating to press, assembly, and other rights that have stretched and contorted its scope in ways that have undermined the pursuit of democratic goals. The Free Speech Clause has also been copied and imitated in contexts where adopting a free speech framework may have adverse effects for both freedom of speech and other rights.

A central premise of this book is that we can learn a great deal about our rights, and our system of rights, by studying them relationally. One thing that the intersections between freedom of speech and other constitutional rights highlight is the value of having a pluralistic system of constitutional rights. A relational study demonstrates how rights can facilitate one another through overlapping synergies and functions. But it also shows the danger in allowing any one right to dominate or eclipse others through textual or conceptual expansion.

With respect to the Free Speech Clause, this book serves as neither ode nor elegy. Freedom of speech justifiably occupies an elevated status among the American people, its officials, and its institutions. However, studying the manner in which it has related to and associated with other constitutional rights can provide a healthy dose of realism about the Free Speech Clause and freedom of speech. If the constitutional project is ultimately about preserving individual liberty, we will need to harness the great potential of a dynamic Free Speech Clause to facilitate that end, but will also need to check its power to subordinate and obscure cognate rights provisions.

[Freedom of speech] is the matrix, the indispensable condition, of nearly every other form of freedom.[1]

The entire system of constitutional government presupposes [expressive] freedoms in a way that it does not, for example, presuppose the right to be free from prosecution absent grand jury indictment.[2]

INTRODUCTION

Free Speech and Non-speech Rights

THE FIRST AMENDMENT'S Free Speech Clause is perhaps the most recognized and discussed provision in the entire United States Constitution. Countless books and articles have extolled its virtues, analyzed its doctrines, and criticized its exceptional coverage. We have an impressive body of scholarly and other commentary concerning our Free Speech Clause. Further, although their general power of recall with regard to the Constitution is not very strong, Americans are far more likely to recognize the free speech guarantee than any other right in the Constitution. Judges, lawmakers, and the American public all revere the Free Speech Clause—so much so that some have characterized their affection as a form of free speech "idolatry."[3]

For all that we know—or think we know—about the Free Speech Clause, there are still aspects of its influence and authority that are not well-documented. One thing that has generally been missing from our consideration of the Free Speech Clause is an appreciation of its *relational* character. As the opening quotations suggest, in very important respects, the Free Speech Clause is an antecedent or foundational right. It has significantly influenced the recognition and development of a wide variety of other constitutional rights. Further, its frequent contacts with other rights provisions have left indelible marks on the Free Speech Clause itself. Thus, we ought to pay close attention to not just what the Free Speech Clause has done *for* non-speech constitutional rights, but also what its interactions with those rights have done *to* the Free Speech Clause and to free speech.

The Dynamic Free Speech Clause. Timothy Zick.

For a variety of reasons, this relational perspective has not received close attention from scholars, courts, and the public. One reason might be that in American legal education, as well as in our constitutional discourse more generally, there is a tendency to study, teach, and debate constitutional rights as if they are isolated provisions.[4] In many law school classrooms, we teach separate units or even entire courses on freedom of speech, freedom of the press, religious liberty, equality, and due process of law. Academic expertise also tends to reside in discrete silos. Thus, we have free speech, religious liberty, and equal protection scholars. The public seems to view rights in a similar way. Constitutional rights are reported on and discussed as if they are confined to particular textual provisions and have little or nothing to do with one another (i.e., "free speech" rights, "Second Amendment" rights, or "free exercise" rights).

We ought to reconsider this general orientation toward the Free Speech Clause, and toward constitutional rights more generally. In many respects, the constitutional rights that Americans enjoy today are a product of their interactions, intersections, and conflicts with other constitutional rights. Most recently, for example, the Supreme Court recognized a right to marriage equality that is rooted in the connections between the Equal Protection Clause and Due Process Clause.[5] Owing to its capacious language and the ubiquity of communicative activity, the Free Speech Clause is the Constitution's most *social* rights provision. Its influences, both positive and negative, are felt across the spectrum of constitutional rights. As we will see, interactions between the Free Speech Clause and other constitutional rights are part of a broad, diverse, and dynamic process in which constitutional rights are discussed, invoked, exercised, enforced, and interpreted.

The book examines relationships between the Free Speech Clause and other constitutional rights provisions. These rights come into contact with one another in a variety of ways. Governments frequently regulate discourse about non-speech constitutional rights. Those regulations implicate both the Free Speech Clause and the right that is or might be discussed. The Free Speech Clause has also actively intersected with a variety of "non-speech" constitutional rights, including the Assembly Clause, Press Clause, Petition Clause, Free Exercise Clause, Equal Protection Clause, Due Process Clause, and the Second Amendment.[6] This list is hardly exhaustive. There are many other free speech/non-speech relationships the book might have explored, including interactions between the Free Speech Clause and the right to vote, and the intersection between the Free Speech Clause and constitutional privacy. The relationships selected for discussion and analysis highlight the principal roles and functions that the Free Speech Clause performs with regard to the recognition, enforcement, and interpretation of constitutional rights.

These roles and functions occur as part of a dynamic process of interaction between and sometimes among constitutional rights. As some scholars have observed, many of the Constitution's rights provisions share textual and historical connections.[7] Some also overlap in terms of their substantive coverages. However, more frequent and dynamic interactions also occur—most frequently in the courts, but also in regulatory environments, scholarly venues, and public forums.[8] These interactions are the central focus of the book.

Americans revere the U.S. Constitution, in part for the constitutional rights it enshrines. They discuss and analyze rights frequently—too frequently, according to some critics. The free speech and non-speech rights discussed in the book have been the subjects of countless books, articles, and commentaries. However, this book's approach is unique. It does not focus on a single right, for the purpose of establishing its status, scope, or substance. It does not, for example, offer a "correct" interpretation of the Free Speech Clause, the Press Clause, the Free Exercise Clause, or the Equal Protection Clause. Instead, the book closely examines the interactions between freedom of speech and non-speech constitutional rights—including the processes that brought the rights together and the actions that have affected their recognition, interpretation, and enforcement.

This approach to constitutional rights does not ignore substantive concerns. Rather, it examines those concerns in the context of specific rights relationships and, more broadly, in the context of a dynamic system of constitutional rights. The book does not offer an overarching theory of the Free Speech Clause. Instead, it addresses normative concerns about the appropriate functions of the Free Speech Clause as it affects or influences the recognition and enforcement of other constitutional rights. One of the book's conclusions is that answers to many normative questions about constitutional rights can be discovered only through a careful examination of interactions between the Free Speech Clause and non-speech constitutional rights.

Constitutional Rights

In a general sense, this is a book about constitutional rights. Thus, it is appropriate to begin with a general conception of these rights. James Madison once worried that constitutional rights would operate as mere "parchment barriers."[9] His view, which was shared by many others at the time of the Constitution's founding, was that a list or "bill" of rights would be both unnecessary and ineffectual. Of course, constitutional rights would later become far more than mere "parchment barriers." Indeed, in some circumstances, they have come to operate as effective *trumps* against certain governmental actions.

However, constitutional rights are much more than textual restraints or legal "trumps." Rights are relational and dynamic constructs. As Professor Jack Balkin has observed, "[r]ights are not simply a fixed set of protections that the state affords or fails to afford. Rights are a terrain of struggle in a world of continuous change—a site of ongoing controversies, a battleground where the shape and contours of the terrain are remade with each victory."[10] As Professor Balkin has also noted, constitutional rights are "a form of discourse, a way of thinking about the needs of social order and human liberty in the context of a changing world."[11] Further, because they are contested and constantly being reshaped—through invocation, enforcement, and discourse—constitutional rights are "moving targets."[12]

This book treats the subject rights provisions as active participants in, as well as products of, a process that includes a variety of social, political, and legal influences. The book's use of phrases or short-hands such as the "Free Speech Clause," "freedom of speech," or simply "free speech"—not to mention "equal protection," "free exercise of religion," etc.—are intended to capture this broad conception of constitutional rights. The rights clauses of the Constitution contain specific language, but they embody broader concepts and principles that have been discovered, in part, as a result of the sorts of intersections the book chronicles.

Many of the constitutional rights Americans enjoy today are products of these kinds of interactions, collaborations, and conflicts. Contemporary understandings of the Fourteenth Amendment's Equal Protection Clause can be traced in part to that provision's interactions with the Due Process Clause and the Free Speech Clause.[13] As noted earlier, in *Obergefell v. Hodges* (2015), the Supreme Court held that the Fourteenth Amendment's Due Process Clause and Equal Protection Clause combined to protect a right of marriage equality.[14] The Court observed that these two clauses are "connected in a profound way, though they set forth independent principles."[15] Viewing the clauses in relation to one another, wrote the Court, "furthers our understanding of what freedom is and must become."[16]

Incidentally, the Court also noted the special role that the Free Speech Clause played in the process leading up to recognition of the right to marriage equality. Writing for the majority, Justice Anthony Kennedy described how "new dimensions of freedom become apparent to new generations, often through perspectives that begin in pleas or protests and then are considered in the political sphere and the judicial process."[17] The majority characterized its opinion as a single, but important, decision point in the long process by which marriage rights had been debated in various venues. This public discourse, which is facilitated by an established Free Speech Clause framework, was part of the process of self-government as it pertains to marriage equality.

Many rights relationships have developed or unfolded in a similar manner. For example, as discussed in Chapter 4, current understandings of the First Amendment's Free Exercise Clause are a product of its interactions with other rights provisions—including the Free Speech Clause and the Assembly Clause. As discussed in Chapter 6, the roots of the constitutional right to abortion can be traced to protections afforded by the Free Speech Clause and the First Amendment's freedom of expressive association. These intersections are perpetual and ongoing. Existing rights relationships are always developing, and new rights connections are constantly being forged. For example, as discussed in Chapter 7, courts and scholars have recently proposed that the Second Amendment's "right to keep and bear arms" be modeled on Free Speech Clause doctrines and principles.[18]

All of these relationships, and others, demonstrate that constitutional rights are much more than isolated textual trumps, occasionally invoked and activated to resist governmental encroachments. Rather, free speech and non-speech rights are part of an interactive, pluralistic system of constitutional rights.

Rights Dynamism

Interactions between free speech and non-speech rights occur in a process the book refers to as "Rights Dynamism."[19] As explained in Chapter 1, Rights Dynamism focuses principally on courts and judicial processes, where rights are invoked and their meanings are formally adjudicated. However, the process also involves an array of nonjudicial influences and participants: activists, civil society organizations, legislatures, agencies, scholars, the press, and the public all contribute to a process that brings free speech and non-speech rights into frequent contact with one another.

With regard to most of the rights relationships discussed in the book, the process of interaction began quite early—during, or in some cases prior to, ratification.[20] Ratification dynamics, including debates in state conventions and Congress, established important links between freedom of speech and non-speech rights. Later, adoption of the post-Civil War Reconstruction amendments, as well as the twentieth century judicial process by which fundamental rights were "incorporated" against the states through the Due Process Clause of the Fourteenth Amendment, were also critical events for these relationships. Reconstruction and incorporation dynamics altered the enforcement and meanings of constitutional rights, including freedom of speech and non-speech rights such as the right of assembly, freedom of the press, and free exercise of religion.

Although the book acknowledges these important historical relations, it focuses on more contemporary interactions between free speech and non-speech rights. In particular, it focuses on contacts and connections that began in roughly the middle of the twentieth century. This is when the Supreme Court began in earnest to develop concepts and doctrines relating to fundamental constitutional rights, including the Free Speech Clause. During this period, the Free Speech Clause became a crucial mechanism for debating, recognizing, and enforcing non-speech constitutional rights.

The Antecedent, Mediating, and Magnetic Free Speech Clause

The Free Speech Clause is this book's protagonist. As indicated, the book will explore both what the Free Speech Clause has done *for* non-speech constitutional rights and what has been done *to* the Free Speech Clause as a result of its interactions with these rights. In studying why and how constitutional rights interact, there are several good reasons to focus on the Free Speech Clause.

First, as the opening quotations suggest, the Free Speech Clause is in important respects an *antecedent* right. Free speech protection is a necessary condition for the recognition of non-speech rights. This is true in terms of both the Free Speech Clause's pre-communicative and communicative dimensions. The clause protects the formation of thoughts, beliefs, and ideas, as well as the gathering, investigating, and distribution of information. These activities are both central to the exercise of freedom of speech and necessary to the recognition of non-speech constitutional rights.

In the United States, as elsewhere, long periods of public debate have been a prerequisite for the formal recognition of constitutional rights. This was true with regard to the original Constitution and the Bill of Rights. As Professor Akhil Amar has observed, "[t]he Constitution itself came to life in a land teeming with free speech."[21] Proponents and opponents of the proposed Constitution had opportunities to discuss and debate the scope and merits of constitutional powers and rights without unwarranted governmental interference. In this fundamental respect, each of the non-speech rights examined in the book is the product of the recognition and exercise of free speech rights.[22]

Antecedence is not, of course, why the Free Speech Clause appears in the amendment that is numbered first in the Constitution's Bill of Rights. That was an accident of history. However, its antecedent nature does help to explain the Free Speech Clause's "firstness," in terms of its status and importance in American constitutional democracy. Simply put, without the right to form thoughts and actively communicate them to some audience, it is impossible to imagine the system of constitutional rights Americans enjoy today.[23]

This is not the same thing as claiming that non-speech rights could not exist without an American-style Free Speech Clause. Indeed they do, in many parts of the world. However, in the United States, constitutional rights have a unique relationship with the Free Speech Clause. That relationship is defined, in part, by the Free Speech Clause's importance to the recognition of other constitutional rights.

Second, the Free Speech Clause provides a framework for *mediating* public discourse about constitutional rights and constitutional liberty. Among other things, this mediating framework requires that governments grant access to public places for the purpose of communicating and assembling with others, prohibits censorship and suppression of speech based on content, protects rights to organize with others for expressive purposes, and invites debate on public issues that is "uninhibited, robust, and wide-open."[24]

This mediating framework ensures that both proponents and opponents of equality, abortion, free exercise of religion, the right to bear arms, and other rights can freely communicate their thoughts and ideas with respect to the scope and meaning of constitutional rights.[25] In this sense, the Free Speech Clause is critically important to the post-recognition development, maturation, and expansion of constitutional rights.[26]

Generations of Americans have benefitted from this Free Speech Clause mediation. As Professor Balkin notes, "rights and rights discourse are continually invoked by people and by groups to further their ideals, interests, and agendas."[27] Reconstruction Republicans and abolitionists vigorously resisted restrictions on freedom of speech and press, in part because they knew governments would attempt to interfere with both the recognition and exercise of equal protection rights.[28] In the modern era, advocates of racial and other forms of equality have also made effective use of free speech rights to facilitate constitutional equality rights—as have proponents of abortion rights, religious freedoms, and Second Amendment rights.[29]

Third, the Free Speech Clause is a uniquely *magnetic* rights provision. Many rights intersect with one another, textually and in other respects. However, owing to its capacious language ("Congress shall make no law abridging the freedom of speech . . .") and the sheer prevalence of communicative activity, the Free Speech Clause covers more cultural, political, and legal ground than other rights provisions. It intersects with more rights, and on a more frequent basis, than any other rights provision in the Constitution.

As Professor Fred Schauer has observed, partly for this reason, the Free Speech Clause exhibits a strong legal and cultural magnetism.[30] Litigants, scholars, and the public are all especially drawn to it. As a consequence of this attraction, the Free Speech Clause is frequently invoked, litigated, adjudicated, and debated in close proximity to other constitutional rights.

Free Speech Clause magnetism is an important aspect of the dynamic interactions between free speech and non-speech rights. As noted, it has precipitated interactions between free speech and non-speech rights. The allure of the Free Speech Clause has also generated comparisons and analogies between free speech and non-speech rights. More insidiously, as discussed below, the gravitational pull of the Free Speech Clause has resulted in a form of expansionism that subordinated and supplanted certain non-speech rights.

Expansionism, Opportunism, Borrowing, and Conflicts

The Free Speech Clause is the book's protagonist, but not always its hero. Although freedom of speech and non-speech rights have related to one another in some powerfully synergistic ways, they have also experienced significant complications and tensions. These less constructive aspects of free speech/non-speech relationships will be a focus throughout the book.

Perhaps the most serious and troubling complication is the Free Speech Clause's propensity toward textual and conceptual expansionism. Partly as a consequence of its magnetism, the Free Speech Clause has effectively colonized constitutional territory that rightfully belongs to non-speech guarantees.[31]

Consider the current status of the Free Speech Clause's textual cousins: the Assembly Clause, Press Clause, and Petition Clause. As discussed in Chapter 3, the Supreme Court has not decided a case based on any of these distinctive rights in more than three decades. They have all been collapsed into a "Free Expression Clause" that is based almost entirely on free speech doctrines and principles. The Free Speech Clause has swallowed up the information-gathering, publishing, associational, and access rights that are more naturally the province of the assembly, press, and petition guarantees. Thus, information-gathering and publication are protected so long as they are "speech"; only assemblies formed for "expressive" purposes are protected under the First Amendment; and the presentation of grievances to Congress and other governmental institutions is activity now governed by the Free Speech Clause.

Expansionism highlights a critical point about the book's focus on the Free Speech Clause. A reader might fairly ask: Haven't *other* First Amendment rights, including the right of assembly/association and freedom of the press, also been important to the recognition, enforcement, and interpretation of non-speech rights? Of course. However, as indicated, the Free Speech Clause has largely subordinated or supplanted its neighbors or cousins. The fact that we treat these distinctive rights as components of a generalized "Free Expression Clause," a provision that is not actually in the Constitution, is a singular manifestation of the Free Speech Clause's dynamic power.[32]

Other non-speech rights have suffered a similar fate. As explained in Chapter 4, the Free Exercise Clause has been partially supplanted by the Free Speech Clause. In the early 1990s, the Supreme Court drastically limited the coverage of the Free Exercise Clause.[33] However, even before that occurred, proponents of religious liberty had already strategically turned to the Free Speech Clause. They argued, often successfully, that religious activities—including worship itself—are properly treated as "speech" covered by the Free Speech Clause. Moreover, they convinced the Supreme Court that religion constitutes a point of view or perspective for purposes of Free Speech Clause analysis. As a result, some commentators have raised questions regarding the "redundancy" of the Free Exercise Clause.[34]

As the Free Exercise Clause example shows, expansionism is partly the result of strategic choices by litigants to frame their constitutional grievances in Free Speech Clause terms. There are significant rhetorical and doctrinal advantages associated with invoking the Free Speech Clause.[35] However, Fred Schauer and others have expressed concerns that litigants may be overusing or even *misusing* the Free Speech Clause. In particular, critics argue that litigants who dress up non-speech claims in free speech garb are acting "opportunistically."[36] Owing to the importance of free speech rights to the recognition and facilitation of non-speech rights, this concern naturally arises in various contexts discussed in the book. I take the "opportunism" charge seriously, but for various reasons approach it with a degree of skepticism.

First and foremost, as Professor Schauer acknowledges, there is nothing inherently *wrong* with litigants using all of the tools at their disposal, including the Free Speech Clause, to obtain constitutional relief. Indeed, that is what we expect cause litigants and lawyers to do.

Second, as there are yet no agreed-upon "proper" uses of the Free Speech Clause, in the sense of consensus as to what purpose or purposes the provision is intended to serve, it is difficult to condemn any particular invocation as a "misuse" or misappropriation. Thus, it is difficult to label particular invocations of the Free Speech Clause or free speech rights as improper or inappropriate.

Third, insofar as critics charge that litigants are using the Free Speech Clause as a "second-best" argument, the premise depends on the relative merits of potential non-speech constitutional rights claims. Thus, judging any particular invocation to be "opportunistic" requires a careful analysis of the relative merits of different constitutional claims. In some instances, invoking the Free Speech Clause may be the only viable path to relief. In others, a free speech claim may be second-best on the merits, but nevertheless offer certain strategic benefits.

Finally, as we will see, there are potential benefits to what critics label "opportunistic" invocations of the Free Speech Clause. For example, civil rights litigants have used the Free Speech Clause to facilitate the recognition and expansion of non-speech rights such as equal protection and due process. Yet many of their invocations of the Free Speech Clause might have been labeled "opportunistic," as that term has been defined. Entrepreneurial invocations of the free speech guarantee have strengthened non-speech rights and clarified the relationship between freedom of speech and non-speech constitutional rights.

None of this means that "opportunism "critics have failed to raise serious concerns. Insofar as aggressive substitutions of free speech for non-speech rights result in textual expansionism, I have indicated that there is cause for concern. Moreover, critics worry that strategic use of the Free Speech Clause might distort free speech doctrines and rules in ways that will ultimately diminish free speech protections across the board. For example, as the domain of the Free Speech Clause expands, courts might begin to relax their ordinarily critical review of governmental restrictions or permit government to regulate speech that is currently protected under narrow categorical approaches.[37] One commentator has even warned that the trend, in regulatory challenges, of invoking freedom of speech rather than non-speech property or liberty rights may destroy the administrative state and "render self-government impossible."[38] Whether or not such dire consequences are likely to occur, we cannot rule out the possibility that some invocations of the Free Speech Clause may weaken free speech and other protections. Accordingly, although it is generally skeptical of the label, the book takes "opportunism" concerns seriously and addresses them where appropriate.

Another aspect of the Free Speech Clause's magnetism is its invocation as an analog or model for non-speech rights. Courts and commentators have proposed that we "borrow" the Free Speech Clause as a framework for non-speech rights. The basic logic of constitutional borrowing goes something like this: (1) Right X is similar to freedom of speech—in the sense that it is a "fundamental" right worthy of heightened protection, or bears some other general resemblance to freedom of speech. (2) As a result of two-plus centuries of adjudicating free speech claims, there is a well-developed doctrinal framework to draw upon. (3) Therefore, we ought to utilize the doctrines and principles developed to define free speech rights to determine the proper meaning, scope, and enforcement of Right X.

Free Speech Clause borrowing has affected both long-recognized and newly-recognized non-speech rights. One could think of the collapse of assembly, press, and petition rights into an "expressive" framework as a kind of wholesale borrowing. More specifically, as discussed in Chapter 4, proponents of Free Exercise Clause rights have advocated borrowing Free Speech Clause doctrines and principles to protect religious liberty.[39] As noted, the Supreme Court has indeed ventured down that path to some degree. Finally, Chapter 7 discusses proposals to model the Second Amendment's right to keep and bear arms on Free Speech Clause doctrines and principles.[40]

Borrowing may cause some serious complications for free speech rights, non-speech rights, and their relationships to one another. The "fit" between freedom of speech and non-speech rights may not support analogous treatment. Further, borrowers may find that when applied outside of their intended domain, free speech doctrines lead to *less* substantive protection for non-speech rights. For example, free speech doctrines may make it more difficult or even impossible to accommodate religious free exercise and may limit the right to bear arms in places or contexts where proponents believe it ought to be protected. Borrowing might also distort or diminish Free Speech Clause protections. This might occur, for example, as precedents from the Free Exercise Clause or Second Amendment contexts are applied in cases previously governed exclusively by free speech doctrines. In short, doctrinal borrowing may produce unintended—and undesirable—consequences for both non-speech and free speech rights.

Finally, in terms of complications stemming from dynamic interactions, free speech and non-speech rights sometimes conflict or experience tensions as they interact with one another. When this happens, courts generally resort to a form of constitutional balancing in which rights are "weighed" against one another.[41] Under this balancing approach, the Supreme Court has often sided with the Free Speech Clause—including in cases involving Sixth Amendment fair trial rights, privacy rights, and dignitary rights.[42] When free speech and non-speech rights directly conflict and are subject to balancing, there is often a thumb on the scale that seems to favor freedom of speech.

Most of the conflicts examined in the book are more indirect in nature, but raise similar concerns about how to balance free speech and non-speech rights. For example, freedom of speech and abortion rights have frequently been in tension with one another, particularly at or near abortion clinics where protests have sometimes threatened to interfere with access to abortion services. Chapter 7 discusses how, as firearms enter spaces from the public square to public university classrooms, the Second Amendment's right to carry firearms will come into contact and potential conflict with free speech rights and principles.

As we shall see, perhaps the most serious contemporary conflict or tension is the one between freedom of speech and equal protection rights. Some have argued that the permissive American approach to "hate speech" undermines equal protection.[43] Similarly, recognition and enforcement of Free Speech Clause-based rights not to be compelled to speak or associate sometimes conflict with anti-discrimination laws, by which the state seeks to preserve and promote equal protection.[44] In relation to the Equal Protection Clause, the Free Speech Clause is both sword and shield.[45] It facilitates speech activities and expressive associations that advance equal protection rights. However, it also protects opponents of equal treatment and social inclusion from the imposition of government orthodoxy regarding equality rights. This aspect of the free speech–equal protection relationship highlights a fundamental tension between liberty and equality.

Balancing free speech and non-speech rights is a complicated and precarious exercise. Placing too much weight on the free speech side of the scale can undermine abortion, free exercise, Second Amendment, and equal protection rights. If the Free Speech Clause is always the "winner" in a constitutional face-off with non-speech rights, those rights are by definition less secure. On the other hand, if the balance tilts too far in the direction of non-speech rights, Free Speech Clause rights might be seriously imperiled.

The bidirectional nature of the relationship complicates the balancing endeavor. Thus, if the Supreme Court were to recalibrate the balance concerning "hate speech" such that derogatory speech received less or even no protection, *proponents* of equal protection might find that their free speech rights have also been curtailed. For instance, speech derogating religious adherents and others opposed to equality rights could be treated as "hate speech."

There is no simple solution to these kinds of conflicts and tensions. However, we can better navigate them if we focus on the facilitative and mediating functions of the Free Speech Clause as it relates to non-speech constitutional rights. We need robust free speech rights—to speak, to refuse to speak, to associate, to refuse to associate—in order to advocate and mobilize for non-speech rights and to defend the democratic legitimacy of the balances that are ultimately struck. Thus, preserving both sword and shield is necessary. That does not mean the balances we have struck are perfect—only that they are a normal and necessary part of the dynamic intersection between free speech and non-speech rights.

In sum, expansionism, opportunism, borrowing, and conflicts are all byproducts of the dynamic intersection between the Free Speech Clause and non-speech rights. They highlight the complicated, and frequently complicating, intersection between these rights.

"Stereoscopic" Rights—Looking in Both Directions

Rights Dynamism works in more than one direction. As we examine the dynamic intersections between free speech and non-speech rights, it is important that we understand that these rights are "stereoscopic"—they both influence and are influenced by one another.[46]

In many instances, interactions with non-speech rights have strengthened or sharpened Free Speech Clause protections. For example, as discussed in Chapter 4, the interaction between the Equal Protection Clause and the Free Speech Clause has generated a strong viewpoint-neutrality principle that now benefits a wide variety of speakers and protects an extraordinary array of communications.

In other contexts, however, free speech/non-speech interactions have complicated or even undermined free speech protections. As we will see, doctrines relating to the distinction between speech and conduct, compulsory speech, government speech, the public forum, and the content neutrality principle have all been negatively affected to some degree by their intersections with non-speech rights.[47] The subordination of the Press Clause, Assembly Clause, and Petition Clause, as well as the borrowing of the Free Speech Clause as a model for Free Exercise Clause or Second Amendment rights, may also diminish free speech coverage and protections in unintended and unanticipated ways.

As the Free Speech Clause has come into contact with non-speech rights, it has both influenced those rights and been influenced by interactions with them. The modern Free Speech Clause is, in significant part, a product of its interactions with other constitutional rights including, but not limited to, those examined in the chapters that follow.

Free Speech/Non-speech Dynamics

In basic outline, the book begins with two chapters that are general in nature and cut across interactions between the Free Speech Clause and non-speech rights provisions. It then considers several particular free speech/non-speech rights relationships. The book concludes with a summary of lessons learned from these relationships, and a defense of a pluralistic rights system in which the Free Speech Clause plays an important, but more subdued, role that focuses on its central facilitative and mediating functions.

Chapter 1 explains the concept of Rights Dynamism, which is the process in which constitutional rights—including free speech and non-speech rights—encounter and interact with one another. It situates Rights Dynamism within current modes of constitutional analysis, and explains its relationship to constitutional interpretation.[48]

Chapter 2 examines the regulation of "rights speech"—communications about or concerning the recognition, scope, or exercise of constitutional rights.[49] It categorizes and analyzes different types of rights speech (ideological, informational, and consultative) and rights speakers (private, professional, and governmental). The chapter highlights the importance of the Free Speech Clause to healthy and robust constitutional discourse and to the exercise of non-speech rights.[50]

Chapter 3 examines the Free Speech Clause's interactions with its First Amendment cousins—the Assembly Clause, Press Clause, and Petition Clause. As noted earlier, the Supreme Court has collapsed these distinctive rights into a "Free Expression Clause. "The chapter examines the events and influences that led, in the case of each clause, to free speech expansionism. It explores the negative consequences of expansionism for both non-speech rights and freedom of speech. The chapter also considers current proposals for recovering or reviving the Assembly, Press, and Petition Clauses, but argues that we must expand the project. We need to work toward a First Amendment Pluralism that not only disaggregates the "Free Expression Clause," but also reconnects these once and still "cognate" rights.[51]

Chapter 4 addresses the relationship between the Free Speech Clause and the Free Exercise Clause. Although these provisions have a collaborative and synergistic history, beginning in the 1980s, the Free Speech Clause began to dominate their relationship. This domination has also affected, although to a lesser degree, the First Amendment's other religion clause, the Establishment Clause. In addition, the free speech/free exercise relationship has complicated Free Speech Clause doctrines, including public forum, content neutrality, and government speech. The chapter discusses these issues and proposes reinvigorating the Free Exercise Clause and reconnecting it with the Free Speech Clause, in ways that recover the mutually facilitative relationship that once existed between the two provisions. To illustrate, the chapter concludes with a consideration of the intersection between free exercise and free speech in contexts involving marriage equality and anti-discrimination laws and limits on the right to worship in public buildings.

Chapter 5 examines the complicated, and complicating, relationship between the Free Speech Clause and the Equal Protection Clause. It focuses specifically on how the Free Speech Clause performed during the race and LGBT equality movements. From these experiences, the chapter draws several general lessons concerning the utility of using the Free Speech Clause to advance equal protection rights. It also examines how these interactions influenced the interpretation and development of the modern Free Speech Clause. The chapter identifies and explains the disparate dynamics that affected these interactions between free speech and different types of equal protection claims. It closes with a discussion of the role the Free Speech Clause is likely to play in the ongoing transgender equality movement.

Chapter 6 examines the relationship between the Free Speech Clause and reproductive rights, in particular the Due Process Clause-based right to abortion. It explores early intersections between the Free Speech Clause and abortion rights, and traces the effects of later intersections as well—focusing in particular on the controversies surrounding protests and other speech activities at or near abortion clinics. These interactions have significantly affected abortion rights discourse in the United States. They have also influenced interpretations of both abortion and free speech rights. The chapter suggests ways in which we might rethink the relationship between free speech and abortion rights in ways that leverage their synergies and reduce conflicts between them.

Chapter 7 addresses the relationship between the Free Speech Clause and the Second Amendment's right to "keep and bear Arms." Relative to the other non-speech rights examined in the book, recognition of an individual right to bear arms occurred relatively recently (the Supreme Court recognized the right in 2008). As a result, the relationship between free speech and the right to bear arms is still in its early stages. So far, discussion has focused on two aspects of their intersection. Courts and scholars have considered the extent to which the nature and scope of Second Amendment rights ought to be modeled on Free Speech Clause doctrines and principles. The chapter considers the pros and (mostly) cons of "borrowing" the Free Speech Clause for this purpose. The second aspect of the developing relationship between the Free Speech Clause and the Second Amendment relates to potential conflicts between them. The chapter addresses two specific conflicts—the extent to which there is or ought to be a right to openly keep and bear arms at public protests and demonstrations, and the implications for academic inquiry of recognizing a right to carry firearms into university classrooms. The chapter considers whether and, if so, how free speech and the right to bear arms might be reconciled or harmonized in these and perhaps other contexts.

The final chapter, Chapter 8, serves two general purposes. First, it summarizes the book's findings concerning the intersections between freedom of speech and non-speech rights. It emphasizes the positive effects the Free Speech Clause has had on the recognition and development of other constitutional rights. At the same time, the chapter also acknowledges the pitfalls that attend a magnetic and constantly expanding Free Speech Clause. Second, the chapter describes and defends a concept I call "Rights Pluralism." Rights Pluralism is based on the simple premise that liberty is more secure insofar as governments are subject to multiple, independent, and substantively robust constitutional limitations. Free speech rights facilitate the recognition and enforcement of those limitations. They also mediate discourse about constitutional rights. At the same time, maintaining robust non-speech rights makes it more likely that people will be or become active participants in democratic processes that lead to constitutional change. Thus, we need to recognize, defend, and exercise *both* free speech and non-speech rights with equal vigor.[52] Perhaps most importantly, we need a Free Speech Clause that performs its antecedent and mediating functions with respect to other rights, but does not subordinate or supplant them in the process. With the hope of realizing these goals, the chapter charts a general path toward Rights Pluralism.

1

RIGHTS DYNAMISM

THIS CHAPTER PRESENTS a general approach or perspective regarding the intersection of constitutional rights, one that informs the discussion in subsequent chapters. It begins by exploring the general concept of constitutional "rights." As explained in the Introduction, constitutional rights are not just formal trumps or limits on government. They are forms of rhetoric and power. And they are relational constructs. Constitutional rights represent distinctive guarantees—the freedom of speech, or of the press, or equal protection of the laws. However, these and other rights do not exist in isolation from one another. Rather than view them as isolated blots on parchment, we ought to think of constitutional rights as actively *relational*.[1] Over extended periods of time, constitutional rights interact, associate, converse, and conflict with one another. These activities occur as part of a dynamic process of adjudication, scholarly examination, and public discourse.[2] This process affects constitutional remedies in individual cases.[3] It also influences interpretations of individual constitutional rights and, more broadly, understandings of constitutional liberty.[4]

The chapter refers to the process in which rights intersect with one another as "Rights Dynamism."[5] Professor Jack Balkin has suggested using the same label as a "general way of thinking about rights and fundamental liberties."[6] He has defined rights dynamism as "the claim that the nature, scope, and boundaries of rights, and in particular fundamental rights like speech, are continually shifting with historical, political, economic, and technological changes in the world."[7] My conception of Rights Dynamism shares the basic premise that rights are participants in, and products of, a dynamic process of change. However, Rights Dynamism is more focused than Professor Balkin's conception, in the sense that it is primarily concerned with the *relationships* between constitutional rights. As we shall see, those relationships are themselves active, contingent, and continually subject to change—owing to historical, political, and cultural influences, but also as a result of their frequent interactions.

As explained below, the process of Rights Dynamism affects a wide variety of constitutional rights. For the reasons explained in the Introduction, however, this book focuses specifically on intersections between the First Amendment's Free Speech Clause and a number of non-speech rights. Activists, litigants, scholars, officials, the media, and the public have brought freedom of speech and non-speech provisions into frequent contact with one another. The process of intersection and exchange has significantly affected the recognition, scope, and enforcement of individual rights. The meaning of many non-speech constitutional rights is indelibly linked to their interactions with the Free Speech Clause. At the same time, current understandings of the Free Speech Clause are partly the result of its interactions with non-speech rights. In other words, the interpretive dynamics of Rights Dynamism are bi-directional.

Situating Rights Dynamism

Constitutional rights and constitutional interpretation have both been subjects of wide and deep academic and judicial discourses. This chapter does not seek to provide an expansive covering theory concerning either subject. Rather, it seeks to describe and explain a process in which constitutional rights provisions come into contact with one another and influence one another's meanings. Nevertheless, since the concept of Rights Dynamism draws upon an existing literature on constitutional rights and constitutional interpretation, it makes sense to begin by broadly situating it in relation to these two subjects.

CONCEPTUALIZING RIGHTS

In a general sense, this is a book about constitutional rights. There are robust literatures on the meaning, morality, categorization, and philosophy of "rights."[8] The book does not concern itself with the deeper questions raised by this important body of work. However, for purposes of the present examination, it is important to have a sense of what constitutional rights are, how and why they interact, and how their interactions affect the interpretation and meaning of constitutional rights.

At the most basic level, constitutional rights limit governmental power and enhance individual liberty. The rights contained in the Free Speech Clause and the Second Amendment, for example, constrain governments as they regulate speech and firearms. These and other limits are explicitly written down. For example, many individual rights provisions appear in the Bill of Rights (i.e., the Free Speech Clause, Free Exercise Clause, etc.). Other constitutional rights are "un-enumerated"—in the sense that they are based on elaboration or construction of the Constitution's text (i.e., the constitutional right to abortion). This book addresses both enumerated and un-enumerated rights.

Ronald Dworkin has described rights as "trumps"—normative entitlements to be treated in certain ways, or to act in certain ways, that override other considerations.[9] In certain contexts, constitutional rights do indeed act as limited "trumps." They entitle claimants to relief from certain governmental prohibitions, requirements, or commands. Constitutional rights do not constrain governments in any absolute sense. However, where they apply, constitutional rights require that governments carefully justify exercises of granted powers. So-called "fundamental" rights, such as the freedom of speech or the free exercise of religion, require that governments sometimes demonstrate a compelling interest and narrowly tailor their regulatory means.

The conception of constitutional rights as trumps or legal constraints is narrow and formal. Constitutional rights are far more than limited constraints on governmental power. Professor Jack Balkin has conceptualized rights in much broader terms—as forms of discourse and power. As he has observed:

> Rights are a form of discourse, a way of thinking about the needs of social order and human liberty in the context of a changing world. Rights are also a source of power—first, because they are a powerful form of rhetorical appeal, and second, because the enforcement of rights recognized by the state is backed up by the power of the state. Because of this, rights and rights discourse are continually invoked by people and by groups to further their ideals, interests, and agendas: For the discourse of rights is the discourse of power, the restructuring of rights is the restructuring of power, and the securing of rights is the securing of power.[10]

This book adopts Balkin's broader conception of constitutional rights. In particular, it is important at the outset to distinguish between individual rights provisions, as represented in the Constitution's text, and their relationship to discourse and power.

The American Constitution does not contain a great many rights provisions, particularly relative to the constitutions of individual states and other advanced democracies. Many of the Constitution's rights provisions contain broad and amorphous language—for example, "freedom of speech," "the freedom of press," "free exercise of religion," etc. The fact that there are a limited number of federal constitutional rights, defined with reference to capacious language, has significantly influenced the invocation and interpretation of constitutional rights provisions.

In this system of rights, certain constitutional rights, chief among them the Free Speech Clause, have come to occupy an exalted place in the constitutional system of rights. Freedom of speech has a special relationship to both discourse and power. It facilitates discourse about rights. Freedom of speech has also been an important catalyst for the recognition and development of constitutional rights, and hence an important force in the distribution of power under the U.S. Constitution. The nature and character of constitutional rights has also encouraged litigants to aggregate and accumulate rights claims. The capacious language of certain rights provisions has invited or, in some cases, necessitated a certain degree of entrepreneurial invocation and enforcement. For example, as discussed in Chapter 4, in pursuit of constitutional relief from measures intended to restrict their public presence and activities, Jehovah's Witnesses invoked First Amendment rights of free speech, press, assembly, *and* religion. Civil rights activists, abortion proponents and opponents, gun rights advocates, and others have similarly combined, related, and mashed up free speech, equal protection, assembly, petition, and other constitutional rights. These combinations have affected the rhetoric, power, enforcement, and meaning of constitutional rights.

A few additional general points concerning the book's conception of constitutional rights are worth emphasizing at the outset. First, constitutional rights and discourse about those rights are closely connected. Americans talk a lot about constitutional rights. As Professor Balkin has noted, rights are forms of rhetoric. As discussed in Chapter 2, some critics view "rights talk" as generally self-absorbed and even harmful to American democracy. However, communications about rights, the language of rights, and the free flow of information about rights are not merely forms of rhetoric but part of a constant struggle for power. Restrictions on rights discourse diminish the trumping and rhetorical powers associated with constitutional rights. As well, limits on discourse about or concerning constitutional rights may impose limits on the actual enjoyment of those rights.

Second, constitutional rights are not static parchment barriers that were set in stone more than two centuries ago. Rather, they are part of an ongoing and dynamic struggle for power. As Professor Balkin has observed, constitutional rights are "a terrain of struggle in a world of continuous change—a site of ongoing controversies, a battleground where the shape and contours of the terrain are remade with each victory."[11] Constitutional rights, Professor Balkin has noted, are "moving targets."[12] This book examines some of their most important movements and bi-directional interactions.

Third, constitutional rights are invoked by litigants, activists, scholars, and others for a variety of purposes—rhetorical, defensive, remedial, etc. They are galvanizing constructs for civil rights movements, civic institutions, and individual litigants. Constitutional rights are also equalizers, in the sense that they can be invoked by both proponents and opponents of broader conceptions of constitutional liberty. Thus, constitutional rights are both swords and shields.

As we examine various relationships between and sometimes among rights provisions in the chapters that follow, we will see all of these rights principles and functions in action. We will see that constitutional rights, in particular freedom of speech, act as trumps, rhetorical partners, foils, symbols of power, and shapers of constitutional discourse.

INTERPRETING RIGHTS

There is also a vast academic literature on the subject of constitutional interpretation. All methodologies rely on some basic sources such as text, history, and precedent. Some pay close attention to historical or "original" understandings of the Constitution's words and phrases; others focus on ensuring that particular rights, such as those associated with the political process, are adequately safeguarded; still others look primarily to republican or libertarian principles as interpretive ideals.[13] Theorists have also focused on the identity and democratic legitimacy of those doing the interpreting—whether they are early Americans, courts, legislatures, or the people. This is not the place for a full examination of the subject of constitutional interpretation. My far more limited goal is to situate Rights Dynamism as part of a broader interpretive enterprise.

Rights Dynamism affects the interpretation of constitutional rights. As noted, constitutional rights are invoked in order to challenge distributions of power. Frequently, individual constitutional rights are invoked alongside or in proximity to other rights—as facilitators, illuminators, or sometimes as substitutes. When this occurs over time, the resulting interactions affect the interpretation of constitutional rights. Interactions between and sometimes among rights provisions do not fully determine the meanings of rights; however, they contribute, sometimes significantly, to our understandings of rights.

In its interpretive aspects, Rights Dynamism is related to some existing traditions. The first is intratextualism, which posits that constitutional meaning is a product of the connections between and among words and phrases in the Constitution.[14] A second related tradition is the common law method, which generally treats constitutional meaning as a product of case-by-case adjudications and the accumulation of precedents over time.[15] Rights Dynamism also draws upon, and shares some conceptual space with, interpretive traditions that focus on social movements, civic institutions, and other nonjudicial actors whose efforts affect or contribute to the interpretation of constitutional rights.[16]

Like intratextualism, Rights Dynamism focuses on and seeks to explain associations between and among constitutional provisions. Owing to the particular functions and powers of courts as they relate to intersecting constitutional rights, much of the action in Rights Dynamism occurs in judicial forums and results in the accumulation of precedents over time. However, like approaches that pay attention to extra-judicial actors and processes, Rights Dynamism takes account of broader historical, political, and cultural influences. Thus, although the primary focus is on the role of courts and common law adjudication, Rights Dynamism involves many other participants—including academics, political leaders, civic institutions, the press, and the public.

Further, along with other interpretive approaches, Rights Dynamism accepts the premise that it is important to understand historical connections, events, and meanings when considering the scope and substance of constitutional rights. However, like other non-originalist perspectives, Rights Dynamism also recognizes that changes in constitutional meaning are part of a dynamic, evolutionary, and fluid process that involves diverse actors and influences.

Although it shares certain ideas with and accepts some of the basic premises of other interpretive traditions, Rights Dynamism is distinct from them in important respects. Rights Dynamism is not an abstract theory or a method of constitutional interpretation. It is not a means of *resolving* constitutional ambiguities relating to the meaning of individual rights provisions. Rather, Rights Dynamism is a process lens that helps explain and illuminate those ambiguities.

Rights Dynamism is a framework for thinking about the nature, functions, and interactions between constitutional rights. It is not a set of normative principles about how those rights are best interpreted. Thus, Rights Dynamism resides much closer to the ground than high—or even low—constitutional theory. It pays particular attention to the real-world actions and forces that bring rights into contact with one another. Owing to this focus, Rights Dynamism is a messy, disorderly, and sometimes illogical process that influences, but does not wholly determine, the meanings of constitutional rights. In sum, Rights Dynamism focuses on why and how constitutional rights intersect and seeks to explain the implications of those intersections.

Finally, Rights Dynamism is more limited in scope than many interpretive approaches. It is specifically attentive to rights provisions. While Rights Dynamism may contribute to an understanding of how certain *structural* constitutional provisions relate to one another, that possibility is beyond the scope of this work. A process-sensitive approach might also help to illuminate relationships between constitutional powers and individual rights provisions. But again, for purposes of the examination in the chapters that follow, the dynamics of interest are those pertaining to the Constitution's rights provisions.

Principles and Processes

As noted earlier, one of the basic premises of the book is that constitutional rights are relational constructs. Thus, they have common historical origins and experiences. Further, as intended or at least as interpreted, rights provisions often provide overlapping substantive protections. Rights also intersect in various forums or contexts. These interactions are all part of the process of Rights Dynamism. The basic mechanics of rights interactions, as well as their interpretive implications, are discussed below. These mechanics and interpretive effects will inform the examination of free speech/non-speech rights relationships in subsequent chapters.

THE RELATIONAL NATURE OF RIGHTS

Constitutional rights are, of course, *individual* rights. This is true in the most basic sense—that is, they belong to individual persons and protect personal liberty, equality, dignity, and other interests.[17] However, constitutional rights do not exist in strict isolation from one another. To the contrary, they are connected by thick historical, precedential, doctrinal, and cultural tissues.[18] From inception to maturity, rights relate, associate, and intersect with one another. Over time, these connections significantly influence the meanings of individual rights and constitutional liberty.

Rights are relational in a variety of different respects. Constitutional rights are connected by virtue of their common origins and histories. This is one of the central insights of intratextualists—scholars who study and analyze connections between and among constitutional provisions.

Some rights, including freedom of speech and the free exercise of religion, have significant pre-ratification connections. Their relationship originated in commentary that preceded ratification of the First Amendment.[19] Thus, these rights were discussed together, and influenced one another, even prior to formal adoption. Collectively, all of the rights in the first ten amendments to the Constitution were subject to debate and adoption through the same basic processes. Ratification dynamics brought constitutional rights together, first in public debates and later in textual form. These early connections formally introduced what would later become known as the Constitution's "Bill of Rights."

Post-Civil War events significantly altered some of these connections and relationships. The adoption of the Reconstruction Amendments—the Thirteenth, Fourteenth, and Fifteenth Amendments—fundamentally altered the constitutional order. Eventually, through the process known as "incorporation" or "absorption," the Supreme Court would apply most of the rights in the Bill of Rights to states and localities as well as the federal government. The Court relied on the reference to "liberty" in the Fourteenth Amendment's Due Process Clause to literally and figuratively reconstruct the relationship between governments and rights-holders.

Reconstruction dynamics profoundly affected the meanings of individual rights, including freedom of speech. As a result of the dynamics of reconstruction and incorporation, the scope of rights expanded vertically to American states and localities. More important, both the original rights in the Bill of Rights, as well as new rights such as equal protection of the law, could now be asserted in cumulative fashion against all state actors and state actions. This placed a number of constitutional rights in close proximity to one another in adjudication, scholarly works, and public discourses. Reconstruction dynamics facilitated the aggregation of constitutional rights claims, as activists and litigants came to realize that a new and more robust menu of rights provisions was available. This was a significant milestone in the process of Rights Dynamism.

Many constitutional rights are also closely associated in terms of their substantive coverages. In many instances, they provide overlapping protections. This is the case, for example, with regard to many of the First Amendment's guarantees—freedom of speech, freedom of the press, the right to peaceable assembly and association, and the right to petition government for redress of grievances. Important questions remain concerning the "original understanding" of these coverages and the relationships the drafters understood themselves to be ratifying. However, as currently interpreted, many constitutional rights share common coverages, cores, and purposes.[20] This fact has also encouraged and facilitated their active intersection.

For example, the Fourteenth Amendment's Due Process Clause and Equal Protection Clause protect distinctive rights, but they also share a common concern with "caste" legislation and creation of a political underclass.[21] Fourth Amendment and First Amendment rights both protect a "zone of privacy" that limits governmental intrusions into certain intimate matters.[22] First Amendment free speech and free exercise of religion rights both protect a sphere of individual autonomy with regard to belief and conscience.

Of most direct concern to the present study, constitutional rights provisions have often developed and matured together—in one another's presence, and subject to one another's influence. To take a recent example, in *Obergefell v. Hodges* (2015), the Supreme Court recognized a right to marriage equality that it based upon both the Due Process Clause and Equal Protection Clause. The Court observed that these provisions are "connected in a profound way, though they set forth independent principles," and noted that the relationship between these provisions "furthers our understanding of what freedom is and must become."[23]

As Professor Laurence Tribe has observed, *Obergefell* "tightly wound the double helix of Due Process and Equal Protection into a doctrine of equal dignity."[24] This weaving together was not the product of a single case or controversy. Rather, it was the result of many decades of argument, adjudication, academic study, cultural consideration, and public debate.[25] This process of interaction is perpetual. *Obergefell* is a single decision point in an ongoing relationship in which due process and equal protection rights will continue to clarify "what freedom is and must become."[26]

The same can be said of many other rights pairings—including, as we shall see, the relationships between the Free Speech Clause and the various non-speech constitutional rights discussed in subsequent chapters. In sum, constitutional rights relate to one another in a variety of ways—historical, textual, conceptual, and practical. These relations and associations help to inform both how rights function and how they are interpreted.

THE ACTIVE INTERSECTION OF RIGHTS

So what are the actual mechanics and processes by which rights relate to one another? Although it is not possible to identify each and every way in which rights intersect and associate, we can identify the broad contours of the process of Rights Dynamism. More specific applications are discussed in the chapters that follow, which address particular rights intersections.

As discussed earlier, the formal founding and Reconstruction eras introduced and initially acquainted constitutional rights provisions. As well, and partly as a result of actions taken during these eras, constitutional rights provisions have been understood to overlap in substantive terms. Although it recognizes the importance of and includes ratification, reconstruction, and other early dynamics, Rights Dynamism is primarily concerned with more modern and contemporary events—particularly those that have occurred during the post–World War II era.

There are two principal reasons for this historical focus. First, the process of recognizing, defining, and robustly enforcing the provisions in the Bill of Rights—including the Free Speech Clause—did not begin in earnest until well after formal ratification.[27] Second, this study is primarily concerned with how *contemporary* understandings of constitutional rights have been influenced by relational processes. Modern conceptions of freedom of speech, free exercise of religion, equal protection, and other rights are informed by historical events and original understandings. However, twentieth and twenty-first century processes have been far more important to contemporary understandings of the Free Speech Clause and the non-speech rights addressed in subsequent chapters.[28]

In this respect, the real "action" of Rights Dynamism has occurred in modern invocations and discussions of rights provisions by activists, litigants, public officials, scholars, and the public. Early dynamics and interpretations of constitutional rights encouraged some of these invocations. However, the professional, strategic, social, and political activities of a multitude of participants have actually connected, combined, and mashed up the Constitution's rights provisions. Their actions were taken for a variety of reasons—to pursue specific remedies, adjudicate cases, test constitutional theories, and galvanize broad constitutional movements. Together, their activism, litigation, and discourse have produced the bulk of twentieth and twenty-first century Rights Dynamism.

Think, once again, about the relationship between the Fourteenth Amendment's Due Process Clause and Equal Protection Clause. These provisions have intersected during their formal ratification, in the course of a process of reconstruction by which they were both enforced against the states, and in a variety of contemporary contexts. In the modern era, these provisions and the rights they protect have interacted with one another in state and federal legislatures, courts, scholarly works, public debates, and of course in the lives of persons challenging various restrictions on the rights each guarantees. Over time, these varied interactions have contributed to the meaning of both clauses, as well as their relation to one another.

At the most fundamental level, constitutional rights come into contact when a governmental action potentially implicates multiple individual rights. In response, activists, litigants, and others consider and invoke multiple rights provisions. Broadly speaking, over time the rights then intersect in courts, public advocacy, policymaking, constitutional scholarship, and public discourse.

In the courts, litigants in search of an effective remedy test the boundaries, strengths, and weaknesses of different rights provisions. They often do so by invoking them cumulatively, or in the aggregate. Often this takes the form of kitchen-sink-type complaints that invoke multiple provisions. Thus, the Free Speech Clause, the Free Exercise Clause, the Due Process Clause, *and* the Equal Protection Clause will be invoked together. As discussed below and demonstrated in the chapters that follow, courts then sift through these claims, grant or deny relief, and ultimately interpret individual rights provisions. This sort of aggregate rights invocation is a common starting point for contemporary Rights Dynamism. The decision to bring multiple rights claims is generally a strategic one. Litigants invoke multiple claims in order to enhance their chances of obtaining a remedy. But the process that this initiates is much broader in scope.

As suggested earlier, this practice became much more widespread once most of the guarantees in the Bill of Rights were incorporated and applied against states and localities. At that point, litigants, activists, and social movements could rely on multiple rights provisions at once. For example, in early challenges to state social and economic regulations, litigants invoked both the Equal Protection Clause and the Due Process Clause (recently, they have also added Free Speech Clause claims to the mix).[29] As noted earlier and discussed in greater detail in Chapter 4, during the 1930s and 1940s, Jehovah's Witnesses relied on the Free Speech Clause, the Free Exercise Clause, and the Press Clause to challenge state and local laws targeting public proselytizing and other activities.

Not all of the action takes place in courtrooms. Political and constitutional movements also rely on multiple rights provisions in their public advocacy. As discussed in Chapter 5, the Civil Rights Movement deftly combined the Equal Protection Clause and the Free Speech Clause to pursue not just judicial victories but also legislative and popular support for civil rights. Civil rights activists have historically invoked free speech and press rights in order to facilitate recognition of equality, due process, and other rights. By associating free speech and equality rights, activists have been able to win a significant measure of support for both.

Similarly, recent Second Amendment advocacy has invoked the principles and doctrines of the Free Speech Clause in order to convince legislatures and policymakers to expand the right to keep and bear arms.[30] This sort of rights advocacy effectively combines rights provisions in ways that force legislators and other policymakers to more carefully consider and reckon with analogies and distinctions relating to constitutional rights. As the example shows, rights advocacy can lay the groundwork for considering—or in some cases reconsidering—how individual constitutional rights relate to one another. As explained in Chapter 7, the modern resurgence of the Second Amendment owes much to efforts to connect that provision to the Free Speech Clause. Similarly, religious adherents and religious organizations have strategically relied on the Free Speech Clause to bolster protections for religious liberties.

Public officials also invoke or discuss constitutional rights provisions in ways that bring them into contact with one another. For instance, legislators who favor robust Second Amendment rights have relied on a combination of First Amendment, privacy, and property rights arguments. Pro-choice legislators have relied on equal protection, due process, and free speech rationales. These references and invocations are also part of the process that connects and relates constitutional rights to one another.

Legal scholarship is also part of Rights Dynamism. Some constitutional law scholars have examined specific rights relationships, such as that between the Equal Protection Clause and the Due Process Clause. Others, including intratextualists, have developed general theories that focus on the connections between and among different constitutional rights provisions. Although the degree of academic influence is difficult to measure, scholarly contributions can change the nature or focus of constitutional debates and perhaps even affect the interpretation of rights provisions.[31]

For example, Samuel Warren and Louis Brandeis published a nineteenth-century law review article that substantially influenced the relationship between the right to privacy and freedom of speech.[32] Prior to and contemporaneous with the Civil Rights Movement, academic commentary emphasized the relationship between freedom of speech and racial equality.[33] And long before Justice Anthony Kennedy discussed the illuminating relationship between the Due Process Clause and the Equal Protection Clause in *Obergefell*, constitutional scholars had already identified and elaborated upon it.[34]

Finally, the general public also participates in Rights Dynamism. It does so in ways that mirror the activities of other participants. Thus, public advocates highlight connections between rights, identify alleged distinctions between or among them, and weigh in on how to resolve conflicts between constitutional rights. To take a few recent examples, Americans have participated in national discourses concerning the tensions between freedom of expression and equality, privacy and the right to bear arms, and free exercise of religion and equal protection for LGBT persons. Through its coverage of these debates, the press can also facilitate and influence public discourse about constitutional rights.

All of the foregoing dynamics were in play after state and federal governments enacted laws that limited or barred same-sex marriage. Activists, litigants, scholars, and the press engaged in a broad discourse concerning how equal protection, due process, and other constitutional rights applied to same-sex marriages. Litigants invoked multiple constitutional rights, chief among them the Due Process Clause and the Equal Protection Clause, in order to obtain constitutional remedies. Activists and the public debated how a right to marriage equality could be squared with the Free Exercise Clause and religious freedoms, a discourse that of course continues to this day. *Obergefell* concluded this phase of this process by emphasizing the importance of free speech to public discourse concerning marriage equality, and combining the Due Process Clause and Equal Protection Clause to recognize a right to same-sex marriage.

Rights Dynamism is a diverse and multifaceted process in which rights are brought into active relation with one another. The process involves rights advocacy and litigation. But it also includes public advocacy, the work of civic institutions and constitutional movements, legal scholarship, policymaking relating to individual rights, and public discourse about rights.

DYNAMIC INTERPRETATION

Over time, intersections between constitutional rights can affect the interpretation of individual rights, as well as understandings of rights relationships. As constitutional rights are invoked together, compared, contrasted, and balanced against one another, their meanings can change.

Dynamic interpretation does not *fully* establish the meaning of any particular constitutional right or rights relationship. However, it is an integral part of the interpretive and constructive process that produces changes in constitutional meaning. Thus, in addition to text, history, and precedents, in order to understand how constitutional change occurs we must also study the intersections and relations between constitutional rights.

Constitutional rights develop and mature as they are invoked, discussed, studied, and adjudicated by the various actors discussed above. As they are paired together and aggregated in court filings, scholarly accounts, and public debates, understandings of the rights and their relationships to one another change. This interpretive process typically involves frequent interactions of rights in a variety of contexts.

Dynamic interpretation never fully and finally concludes; it continues in perpetuity. As activists and parties invoke rights, courts adjudicate disputes, and citizens discuss rights, specific intersections may recur and new intersections may arise. These interactions can affirm or alter the interpretation of individual rights and their relationships. Alternatively, and more commonly, they leave things unsettled, providing litigants with future opportunities to combine, relate, or contrast different rights provisions.

Owing to the interpretive powers and functions of judges, dynamic interpretation is most visible and recognizable in the courts. It is a form or species of common law constitutional adjudication. Courts rely on ordinary inputs such as party briefs, amicus filings, and factual records as they consider individual cases and controversies concerning constitutional rights. All of the usual external influences on judicial decision-making also apply in the context of dynamic interpretation. Thus, courts adjudicating cumulative or aggregate rights claims are subject to the same kinds of social and political influences that affect how they decide other cases or controversies.

Nevertheless, dynamic interpretation is distinct from ordinary common law adjudication in certain important respects. Consider first the types of issues that arise in cases involving multiple constitutional rights. When deciding cases at the intersection of neighboring, overlapping, and sometimes conflicting rights provisions, courts must make choices regarding (1) which rights claims to validate or reject; (2) the appropriate uses or invocations of different rights provisions in relation to other provisions; (3) whether, and if so how, constitutional rights can be combined or reconciled with one another; and (4) the proper resolution of tensions and conflicts between constitutional rights.[35]

As they answer these questions, courts do not generally discuss rights in explicitly relational terms. (*Obergefell* is a notable exception.) However, even if they do not articulate their decisions in relational terms, judges are in fact engaged in a process of dynamic interpretation. When they adjudicate cumulative, aggregate, and other types of claims involving multiple constitutional rights, courts necessarily interpret the meanings of rights in relation to one another.

As for external influences, judicial receptivity to certain rights claims may be affected by changes in official or public attitudes regarding particular rights claimants or claims. Increased public recognition and support for a particular constitutional right may affect how that right is viewed not merely in isolation, but also *in relation to* other constitutional rights. At the same time, a decrease in support for a right, or sustained public conflicts regarding a particular right, may weaken its position vis-à-vis other rights.

As these considerations suggest, dynamic interpretation often involves a distinctive set of complicating factors. When activists, litigants, and courts engage with more than one rights provision at a time, the interpretive enterprise requires that they deal with different doctrinal areas associated with those rights provisions. Courts may seek to avoid, reconcile, or even ignore cross-doctrinal complications. Even if these concerns are not explicitly addressed, however, in multiple rights lawsuits judicial decisions typically cross doctrinal boundaries. This may create cross-doctrinal confusion and exacerbate existing doctrinal complexities.

Other unique concerns can arise when interpretation cuts across more than one constitutional right. For example, when courts adjudicate more than one rights claim in the same dispute, or when one constitutional right is used to facilitate another, the possibility that constitutional rights may come into conflict increases. This may result in certain rights being balanced against one another. Balancing may increase or diminish the status or effectiveness of the individual rights placed on the scale. It may also have lasting effects on their relationship.

Like other forms of common law constitutional adjudication, dynamic interpretation of individual rights is not linear—it does not progress in some sequential or orderly manner. In fact, owing in part to the involvement of more than one constitutional right, dynamic interpretation may be even more reactive, unintentional, and unpredictable than some of its common law counterparts. *Obergefell* again provides an example. By the time the Court issued its decision, the Due Process Clause and the Equal Protection Clause had interacted in judicial, scholarly, and other forums for many decades. The Court's fusion of these two provisions marked a particular culmination point in their long, meandering, and complex relationship.

Insofar as the results or products of dynamic interpretation are concerned, there are myriad possibilities. Constitutional rights may be interpreted together in ways that subordinate, complicate, restrict, illuminate, or facilitate one other.

One possible outcome, as we will see, is that interpretation truncates or short-circuits future intersections between rights. This might occur when one constitutional right is interpreted such that it supplants or subordinates another, effectively rendering one right in the relationship inert or inactive. Another possibility is that rights remain in active relation to one another, but the scope of one or both rights is affected by that right's interpretation relative to the other.[36] As the Supreme Court suggested in *Obergefell*, constitutional rights might also be interpreted such that they illuminate or clarify one another.[37] Finally, constitutional rights may also combine to form unique hybrids that are treated as more protective than their individual parts.[38]

Since dynamic interpretation cuts across two (and sometimes more) constitutional provisions, it generally also operates in more than one direction. Rights in active relationships both influence and are influenced by one another. Thus, to varying degrees, contemporary understandings and interpretations of constitutional rights are a function of their relationships to other rights.

Thus, for example, the meaning of the Equal Protection Clause is derived in part from its interactions with the Due Process Clause. The reverse is also true—the meaning of the Due Process Clause has been affected by its long-standing relationship with the Equal Protection Clause. This is generally true of the interpretive dynamic affecting rights that frequently intersect with one another.

In sum, dynamic interpretation supplements our general understanding of constitutional interpretation and changes in constitutional meaning. Along with more traditional sources such as text, history, and precedent, relational dynamics are an important source of constitutional meaning.

FREE SPEECH/NON-SPEECH DYNAMICS

The general principles and processes described above apply to a broad range of constitutional rights provisions. They apply specifically to intersections between the

Free Speech Clause and non-speech constitutional rights, which are the focus of subsequent chapters.

As I have suggested, the Free Speech Clause is the Constitution's most "social" rights provision. Its status and influence have attracted advocates, litigants, academics, and others who have sought to protect, advance, interpret, or oppose a variety of constitutional rights. Repeated invocations of the Free Speech Clause have resulted in a rich tapestry of dynamic intersections between freedom of speech and non-speech constitutional rights. As we will see, these intersections have significantly affected interpretations of non-speech rights, free speech rights, and the relationships between them. In the chapters that follow, we will examine these dynamic intersections more closely, focusing in particular on the central functions of the Free Speech Clause as they relate to the recognition, scope, and exercise of various non-speech rights.

Free speech and non-speech rights intersected in early ratification and pre-ratification debates. For example, as noted, early conceptions of freedom of the press were formed with reference to acts of religious liberty such as proselytizing and pamphleteering. Free speech and non-speech relationships were also profoundly affected by Reconstruction era and Due Process Clause incorporation dynamics. Freedom of speech was, of course, critically important to the ratification of the Fourteenth Amendment.[39] By the same token, Reconstruction and incorporation resulted in the Free Speech Clause being applied to states and localities. These processes led the Supreme Court to characterize freedom of speech as "fundamental" to ordered liberty.[40]

In the modern era, the Free Speech Clause has come into frequent and active association with non-speech constitutional rights through the general processes of Rights Dynamism described above. Thus, in both public advocacy and litigation, the Free Speech Clause has frequently been invoked in combination with an array of other constitutional rights.

For example, the modern relationship between the Free Speech Clause and its textual neighbors—the Press Clause, the Assembly Clause, and the Petition Clause—first began to take shape as litigants and activists invoked all three provisions cumulatively. During the 1930s and 1940s, Jehovah's Witnesses challenged a variety of legal restrictions on their public activities by invoking these provisions, along with the Free Exercise Clause.[41]

Similarly, during the 1950s and 1960s, civil rights activists and litigants relied on a combination of the Free Speech Clause, the Due Process Clause, and the Equal Protection Clause to challenge racial apartheid. LGBT advocates and litigants followed suit, as they pursued their own equality movement. During the 1970s and 1980s, abortion rights proponents relied on the Free Speech Clause, the Due Process

Clause, and other rights provisions in challenges to abortion-related laws and regulations. Many other speakers, in challenges to discriminatory restrictions on expressive activity, relied on both the Equal Protection Clause and the Free Speech Clause.[42]

Aggregate advocacy and cumulative claims placed the Free Speech Clause and non-speech constitutional rights in frequent and active contact with one another—in the courts, but also in public discourse about constitutional free exercise, equality, abortion, and other rights. By the end of the first third of the twentieth century, free speech and non-speech rights had begun to actively circulate and associate with one another. These intersections became more frequent over time, as advocates came to appreciate the benefits of combining free speech and non-speech rights provisions.

Opponents and resisters have also relied on the Free Speech Clause in debates about constitutional rights. During the 1980s and 1990s, abortion opponents invoked the Free Speech Clause to protect from restriction and suppression "sidewalk counseling" and other forms of dissent. Religious adherents and others who have objected to the inclusion of LGBT persons in public accommodations and private organizations have also relied on the Free Speech Clause to challenge state anti-discrimination laws. These invocations are also an important part of the dynamic intersection between the Free Speech Clause and non-speech rights such as abortion and equality.

As noted, Rights Dynamism extends beyond the processes of constitutional adjudication. Social and constitutional movements have long relied on the Free Speech Clause to facilitate their non-speech rights causes. Advocates have invoked the Free Speech Clause by analogy, as a means of pursuing equality, privacy, religious freedoms, and other constitutional rights. Religious adherents have used free speech content-neutrality principles to lobby public officials for equal access to public properties and resources. Civil rights activists have employed the Free Speech Clause as a moral battering ram in their fight against racial and other forms of apartheid. As noted, those opposed to the recognition or extension of constitutional rights have also relied on the Free Speech Clause to argue—both in courts and in the court of public opinion—for various exemptions from anti-discrimination requirements. All of these analogies, invocations, and references have forged close connections between the Free Speech Clause and non-speech constitutional rights.

Strategic decisions by constitutional movements and rights activists can significantly impact relationships between constitutional rights. For instance, starting in the 1980s, in both their general advocacy and litigation of specific cases, religious liberty advocates started to abandon the Free Exercise Clause in favor of the Free Speech Clause.[43] As discussed in Chapter 4, that decision altered the modern relationship between the Free Speech Clause and the Free Exercise Clause. Similarly, during the 1950s and 1960s, leaders of the Civil Rights Movement fundamentally changed the relationship between the Free Speech Clause and the Equal Protection Clause by relying heavily on the former—particularly in the movement's early phases—to challenge racial apartheid. Most recently, as discussed in Chapter 7, Second Amendment activists and litigants have relied on and proposed borrowing from the Free Speech Clause to define the substance of Second Amendment rights.

Constitutional scholars have also participated in this dynamic process. They have contributed detailed examinations, as well as substantive theories, regarding the relationships between the Free Speech Clause and non-speech rights including the Free Exercise Clause, the Equal Protection Clause, the Due Process Clause, and the Second Amendment.[44] This academic discourse has questioned existing relationships between freedom of speech and non-speech rights, suggested new perspectives and directions regarding these relationships, and sought to resolve conflicts between freedom of speech and non-speech rights.

Last but certainly not least, the public has participated in conversations, debates, and discourses about free speech and non-speech constitutional rights. Public officials frequently regulate, influence, and seek to participate in discourse about constitutional rights. As discussed in Chapter 2, their actions have forged important connections between freedom of speech and non-speech rights. Measures that restrict speech about Second Amendment rights, or compel speech about abortion, test the central functions of the Free Speech Clause as they relate to what Chapter 2 calls "rights speech."[45] They also affect the actual exercise of non-speech rights. Governmental funding decisions and government speech about constitutional rights can also influence the relationship between freedom of speech and non-speech rights.

In sum, with regard to historical debate, litigation, advocacy, academic commentary, and public discourse, the Free Speech Clause frequently and actively intersects with a number of non-speech rights. The general processes and principles of Rights Dynamism are implicated in these rights relationships.

As discussed earlier, Rights Dynamism affects the interpretation of constitutional rights. Dynamic interpretations do not fully establish the meanings of particular constitutional rights, or their relationships to one another. However, they are an important source of meaning. Dynamic interpretation has significantly affected the meaning of free speech and non-speech rights.

When advocates and litigants combine, compare, and contrast free speech and non-speech rights, they encourage interpreters to consider them in combination and in relative terms. Thus, when constitutional litigants aggregate or combine the Free Speech Clause with multiple non-speech rights claims in a single case, courts are called upon to consider the role or function of each clause or provision. They may also consider how freedom of speech and non-speech rights relate to one another. As discussed earlier, this is not generally done in explicit terms. However, it is a natural outcome of the interaction between free speech and non-speech rights.

In constitutional rights discourse, participants often engage with the meaning of both free speech and non-speech rights, as well as their relationship to one another. Regulating how and when speakers address topics such as abortion, equality, religion, and firearms implicates the meaning of free speech rights, but it can also affect the meaning and enforcement of non-speech rights. Further, changes in the meaning of non-speech rights can influence how free speech rights are interpreted. For example, changes to abortion doctrine that grant the state more power to persuade women not to obtain an abortion can diminish the speech rights of women and their physicians.

Not surprisingly, interpretive results in cases involving free speech and non-speech rights have varied. Sometimes these rights have been interpreted in ways that facilitate or illuminate both. This was the case, for example, during the 1930s and 1940s when Jehovah's Witnesses brought their cumulative claims. Supreme Court precedents during this era articulated some important synergies between free speech and free exercise of religion.

As noted in the Introduction, one particular concern with regard to the Free Speech Clause is its magnetism or appeal. Commentators have expressed concerns that the Free Speech Clause not be interpreted in ways that warp or overextend its meaning, diminish its core protections, or supplant other rights.[46] As we will see, such concerns have arisen with regard to a great many non-speech rights, including equal protection, abortion, and the Second Amendment right to keep and bear arms.

Over time, the Free Speech Clause has come to dominate and subordinate certain rights provisions. For a variety of reasons discussed in Chapter 3, this has occurred with regard to the Assembly Clause, the Press Clause, and the Petition Clause.[47] These provisions are now treated as *ancillary* to the Free Speech Clause. This interpretation has diminished opportunities for comparison, illumination, and potential synergies between and among the affected rights. Chapter 4 explains how something similar, but less drastic, occurred with respect to the Free Exercise Clause. In certain contexts, at least, that provision too became ancillary to the Free Speech Clause.

The unique complications of dynamic interpretation, mentioned above, have been present in the context of free speech and non-speech rights. Thus, as the Free Speech Clause and non-speech rights provisions have intersected, interpreters have grappled with the substantive aspects of more than one right. In order to limit doctrinal inconsistencies, they would ideally be familiar with the doctrines and principles relating to both rights and how they do or ought to "fit" together. However, as we will discover, this has not generally been the case.

For example, in cases involving both Free Speech Clause and Free Exercise Clause claims, interpreters should consider the status of each right, the appropriateness of relying on one right or the other in the factual context presented, and the possible effects of decisions on doctrines relating to both provisions. Sometimes, reconciling the doctrines and principles relating to free speech and non-speech rights can be particularly difficult. This complexity has produced inconsistencies and tensions in free speech and non-speech rights doctrines.

As noted earlier, dynamic interpretation is bidirectional. As it has interacted with non-speech rights, the Free Speech Clause has contributed something to their various meanings. In order to fully understand current interpretations of the Press Clause, Equal Protection Clause, or Free Exercise Clause, one must consider the influence of the Free Speech Clause on the interpretation of these rights.

At the same time, the meaning of the Free Speech Clause has itself been significantly affected by these relationships. Indeed, many current interpretations of free speech rights, doctrines, and principles can be traced to intersections between the Free Speech Clause and the Free Exercise Clause, the Equal Protection Clause, the Due Process Clause, and other constitutional provisions. As it has related to non-speech rights, the Free Speech Clause has been both a catalyst for, and an object of, significant interpretive changes.

Rights Dynamism and the dynamic interpretation it produces are perpetual. The dynamic process in which free speech and non-speech rights intersect is ongoing. None of the interpretations discussed in this book are set in stone. Indeed, as this book goes to press, scholars are working to revive and reconsider the Press Clause, Assembly Clause, and Petition Clause. They are seeking solutions for complications relating to the relationship between freedom of speech, on the one hand, and equality and religious liberty rights on the other.

Certain rights, such as the Second Amendment right to keep and bear arms, are only beginning to come into focus. As courts and commentators look to the First Amendment to interpret the Second Amendment, we can actually witness Rights Dynamism and dynamic interpretation in real time.

If history is any guide, future intersections between the Free Speech Clause and non-speech constitutional rights will be eventful and revealing. These interactions will force advocates, judges, scholars, and others to think through complicated and complicating rights relationships. And those relationships will significantly affect the meanings of both free speech and non-speech rights.

2

RIGHTS SPEECH

AS NOTED IN the Introduction, in important respects freedom of speech is antecedent to the recognition and enjoyment of other constitutional rights. One of the things that defines the Free Speech Clause's special relationship with non-speech constitutional rights is the protection it affords to communications about or concerning the recognition, scope, and enforcement of constitutional rights.[1]

"Rights speech," as I will refer to these communications, takes several different forms.[2] Some communications advocate, oppose, or render opinions concerning a constitutional right; others provide basic information about the nature or exercise of a constitutional right (i.e., how, when, or where a right can be exercised); still others are part of a consultative process concerning the exercise or enforcement of a constitutional right. Moreover, a wide range of speakers—private, professional, and governmental—convey information, ideas, and opinions concerning constitutional rights. These categories of speech and speakers form part of the broader discourse about constitutional rights.

Because this discourse connection exists to some degree with respect to all constitutional rights, and because it is so central to the relationships between free speech and non-speech rights, it is deserving of special attention. This chapter focuses on rights speech and the Free Speech Clause's important relationship to rights discourse, which are concerns that affect all of the rights discussed in later chapters.

The Dynamic Free Speech Clause. Timothy Zick.

Subsequent chapters will examine the specific relationships between freedom of speech and non-speech rights in greater depth and detail.

Rights speech, and efforts to regulate or restrict it, are important aspects of Rights Dynamism and dynamic constitutional interpretation, concepts discussed in Chapter 1. In the United States, national, state, and local governments routinely regulate, structure, and participate in debates and discussions relating to constitutional rights. When governments restrict or compel communications about or concerning constitutional rights, they initiate a dynamic that implicates both free speech and non-speech rights. Rights speech regulations are frequent and recurring points of contact between free speech and non-speech rights. As we will see, these contacts significantly affect both free speech and non-speech rights.

Rights speech implicates not only rhetorical power concerning a variety of constitutional rights, but in some cases the effective exercise of those rights. Although the nature and value of the different types of rights speech may vary, it is important to provide robust protection for private rights speech in all of its various forms. It is also necessary to constrain some forms of governmental rights speech—particularly communications that may restrict a free and open public discourse about or interfere with the exercise of constitutional rights.

It is imperative that the Free Speech Clause perform its vital function of facilitating an open discourse about constitutional rights. At the same time, the Free Speech Clause cannot do all of the work in terms of protecting rights discourse, preserving constitutional rights, and ensuring their effective exercise. I will argue that the Free Speech Clause does not itself constrain governmental rights speech; for these constraints, we must look elsewhere. More generally, free speech can facilitate the discussion and exercise of non-speech rights, but is obviously not an adequate substitute for substantive non-speech rights. Thus, while we must maintain open channels of rights discourse, we also need to devote greater attention to the substance and enforcement of the contested non-speech rights

Communicating and Regulating Speech about Rights

In the United States, rights speech and rights discourse are prevalent. So is governmental regulation of rights speech. This regulation is a critically important aspect of the dynamic intersection between free speech and non-speech rights. To get a better sense of this intersection point between free speech and non-speech rights, I begin with some preliminary information: Some illustrations of rights speech and governmental regulation of communications concerning rights; a basic typology of categories of rights speech and rights speakers; and a brief explanation of the difference between rights speech and what critics of American discourse about rights have referred to as "rights talk."

EXAMPLES AND ILLUSTRATIONS

In order to frame the consideration of rights speech, it helps to start with a simple but illustrative example—one that happens not to relate to a constitutional right discussed elsewhere in the book. The City of Norfolk, Virginia, enacted a sign code that imposed, purportedly for aesthetic and safety reasons, size and other requirements for outdoor signs. Such codes are commonplace across the United States. The sign code exempted flags or emblems (including religious ones) and works of art that did not identify or relate to specific products. Central Radio Company, Inc., which happened to be involved in an eminent domain dispute with a city agency, placed a banner on the side of its building protesting the agency's plan to take its property for public use. The banner depicted the American flag, Central Radio's logo, a red circle with a slash across the words "Eminent Domain Abuse," and a message highlighting the station's long relationship with the city and its workers.

The city determined that Central Radio's sign violated the sign code and issued a citation. Central Radio challenged the sign code on free speech grounds in federal court; a district court ruled in favor of the city, and the U.S. Court of Appeals for the Fourth Circuit affirmed.[3] Both courts concluded that the sign code was content-neutral and was justified, under what courts refer to as "intermediate scrutiny," by important aesthetic and safety concerns.[4]

Rather than getting caught up in levels or standards of scrutiny, consider instead the *type* of speech at issue in the case. Central Radio wanted to communicate a protest concerning the government's disrespect for individual property rights. More specifically, it wished to communicate a point of view about governmental abuse of the Fifth Amendment's Takings Clause, which allows government to take private property for public uses but requires that "just compensation" be paid to the owner. The Fourth Circuit opinion fails to recognize or characterize the speech in this manner, and defers substantially to the city. However, as a dissenting judge observed, "[i]n a case like this, involving political speech against the heaviest hand of government attempting to seize its citizen's land," courts must carefully consider the government's proffered justifications, their application to the facts at hand, and the possibility that enforcement is a means of suppressing a political protest.[5] As the dissenting judge stated: "[i]f a citizen cannot speak out against the king taking her land, I fear we abandon a core principle of our Constitution's First Amendment."[6]

There are a few notable things about this seemingly run-of-the-mill case. First, the speaker was engaged in rights speech, as it was attempting to communicate a perspective about or concerning the scope of a constitutional right. Second, the sign ordinance was reviewed under a deferential Free Speech Clause standard, even though it restricted a form of core political speech. Third, even the dissenting judge was not inclined, simply because the case involved rights speech, to invalidate the Norfolk code. However, the judge cited the presence of rights speech as a basis for reviewing the government's regulation with greater skepticism.

This example can be multiplied many times over. Even in a land that is otherwise teeming with free speech, restrictions on rights speech are a prevalent phenomenon across a wide range of constitutional rights (some of which are discussed in later chapters). Federal, state, and local governments all routinely regulate rights speech. Consider some additional examples, which I will refer to in the constitutional analysis of rights speech below:

Abortion

- Injunctive and statutory "buffer zones" that restrict speech at or near abortion clinics;[7]
- State-mandated disclosures requiring that physicians communicate certain factual information about abortion and the development of the fetus, and in some cases to disclose that abortion has negative health effects on the mother or will terminate a human life;[8]
- Imposition of substantial civil liability for distributing information that compares abortion providers to war criminals and advocates their trial for "crimes against humanity";[9]
- Local ordinances restricting residential picketing of an abortion provider's residence;[10]
- Laws that authorize public funding of healthcare services on the condition that recipients not advocate or even discuss abortion;[11]
- Local ordinances requiring that crisis pregnancy centers discuss the availability of abortion as a viable alternative to childbirth;[12]
- Laws or judicial orders restricting the display of aborted fetuses;[13] and
- State programs authorizing the issuance of specialty pro-life, but not pro-choice, license plates.[14]

The Right to Bear Arms

- State laws banning physicians from asking patients about firearms possession;[15]
- State laws exempting firearms records from public disclosure;[16]

- Criminal laws barring any reporter, blogger, or other person from publicly identifying an applicant for a gun permit;[17]
- Punishment of public high school and university students for communicating support for or opposition to gun rights;[18]
- Denial of official recognition to college groups advocating concealed carry and other gun rights on campus;[19]
- Laws that prohibit local authorities from using state funds for the purpose of lobbying the state legislature to enact gun control measures;[20] and
- Federal budgetary prohibitions on research relating to firearms safety or gun control.[21]

Equal Protection

- Punishment of public school students for communicating pro-LGBT or anti-LGBT viewpoints;[22]
- State bar rules that treat certain communications opposing transgender equality as a form of prohibited harassment;[23]
- Application of anti-discrimination laws in ways that require printers, T-shirt makers, and others to convey what they view as support for LGBT equality;[24] and
- State prohibitions on talk therapies that are based on the premise that homosexuality is a condition that can be "cured."[25]

These examples are illustrative.[26] They suffice to preview both what rights speech is, as well as some of the implications associated with restricting or compelling it. Note that I have adopted a definition—any communication about or concerning the recognition, scope, or exercise of constitutional rights—that is purposefully broad. As noted below, there are several different kinds of rights speech and rights speakers. Moreover, the reason for defining rights speech so broadly will become apparent as we examine more closely the implications, for both free speech and non-speech rights, of government efforts to restrict or mandate communications about or concerning constitutional rights.

There are a number of other general things to note about rights speech. First, communications qualify as such, under my definition, even if they are not sophisticated, analytical, or legalistic. The rudimentary building sign in the Norfolk case and t-shirts that display basic messages supporting, or opposing, constitutional rights are examples of rights speech. Rights speakers are not always erudite, and their audiences are not always well-informed. In short, professors and pundits do not have a monopoly on discourse about constitutional rights.

Second, rights speech is quite diverse in terms of format. Speakers convey thoughts, ideas, and beliefs about their own or others' constitutional rights in casual conversations, public meetings, op-eds, blog posts, and public protests. They do so, as noted, by way of signs and symbolic gestures. People communicate about constitutional rights in public parks, on social media, in schools and universities, and in their private associations. They discuss the exercise of constitutional rights not just with friends and acquaintances, but also with lawyers, physicians, social workers, and others who work, as discussed below, at the intersection of professional practice and constitutional rights.

Third, just like other kinds of communications, rights speech can be positive or negative in its tone or perspective. That is, rights speech includes both pro- and anti-rights communications. Like proponents of rights, those who oppose the recognition or expansion of a constitutional right can convey that opposition in a variety of ways.

Fourth, although the primary focus in terms of my analysis of rights speech is on speakers, audiences also have an interest in *receiving* communications about or concerning constitutional rights. Thus, individuals both create and consume rights speech.

Finally, as some of the examples above suggest, the *regulation* of rights speech also takes many different forms. Some regulations seek to restrict the communication of ideas or arguments pertaining to rights. Others restrict the communication of basic information about a constitutional right. However, as the examples show, rights speech is also sometimes compelled or mandated by statute, rule, or regulation. When the government mandates that a speaker communicate something about or concerning a constitutional right, it compels rights speech.

TYPES OF RIGHTS SPEECH

To further sharpen the analysis of rights speech, it is helpful to distinguish among a few different types or categories of communications. Although I will contend that all types of rights speech are worthy of First Amendment protection, categorization will highlight some important distinctions.

In terms of a basic typology, rights speech takes three forms. Some communications, such as the sign in the Norfolk case, express opinions about the recognition or scope of a constitutional right. This is *ideological* rights speech. Other communications convey basic facts pertaining to a constitutional right, such as when, where, or how a constitutional right can be exercised. This is *informational* rights speech. Still other communications go beyond basic information and pertain to the strategic, health, and other implications of claiming or exercising a constitutional right. We can call these communications, which typically occur in professional settings, *consultative* rights speech. These categories are not airtight, and there can be some overlap between them. However, they provide a rough typology of the basic forms of rights speech.

The first type, ideological rights speech, is centrally important to our constitutional system of rights. Communications that address the propriety of recognizing a constitutional right, or that convey opinions regarding the scope of a right, or that advocate for particular enforcement of a right, all address matters of undeniable public concern. That said, however, courts do not always recognize these communications as rights speech. As a result, they often fail to subject regulations of ideological rights speech to skeptical Free Speech Clause and other constitutional scrutiny.

Informational rights speech includes basic descriptions of the how, when, and where of exercising constitutional rights. It often consists of factual information relating to such exercises, the availability of resources needed for effective exercise of a right, or records pertaining to exercise of a constitutional right. This kind of rights speech provides basic, but critically important, information about constitutional rights to both individual rights-holders and the public at large.

Finally, consultative rights speech conveys information that may facilitate or, in some cases, frustrate the exercise of a constitutional right. Some informational rights speech might fit into this category—as mentioned, the categories are not meant to strictly compartmentalize. Thus, communications by licensed professionals who advise clients regarding establishing or effectuating a constitutional right, and communications intended to discourage individuals from doing so, are examples of consultative rights speech. Consultative rights speech becomes ideological rights speech when the point of the communication is not to neutrally advise, but rather to actively encourage or discourage exercise of a right.

While these forms of rights speech differ in certain respects, they are all communications about or concerning the recognition, scope, or exercise of a constitutional right. As the above examples show, governments routinely regulate across all three categories.

TYPES OF RIGHTS SPEAKERS

In addition to types of rights speech, there are also different types of rights speakers. Generally speaking, the examples above indicate that there are three different types of rights speakers—private, professional, and governmental.

Private speakers communicate the vast majority of rights speech. They engage in all three types of rights speech, but in particular ideological and informational communications. Private speakers are the primary participants in, and the principal beneficiaries of, rights discourse.

As discussed further below, some professionals communicate informational rights speech. They also engage in consultations relating to the exercise of constitutional rights. Lawyers, physicians, counselors, and other licensed professionals play important roles in terms of educating clients and patients about rights and assisting them with effectuating those rights.

Finally, governments routinely convey rights speech and participate in rights discourse. We normally think of governments as regulators of private and other communications. In many of the examples above, that is indeed the role of governments and officials—regulating speech about or concerning constitutional rights. However, governments also communicate their own viewpoints and ideas about constitutional rights. They may do this directly, for example by publicly conveying pro-equality, pro-Second Amendment, or antiabortion viewpoints. They may also influence rights speech by limiting public funding to private individuals and groups. Funds may be made available only to speakers who share the government's viewpoints about a constitutional right.

Consider a few prominent examples. De jure racial segregation and so-called "no promo homo" laws, both of which are discussed in Chapter 5, expressed viewpoints that stigmatized African-Americans and banned the "promotion" of homosexuality, respectively. These laws expressed official viewpoints or perspectives regarding race and LGBT equality. As speakers, governments can also convey messages of disapproval with regard to messages they consider to be discriminatory. For instance, in a recent decision, the Supreme Court allowed the State of Texas to deny an application for a specialty license place featuring an image of the Confederate flag—on the ground that the state, as a speaker rather than regulator of private speech, was entitled to disapprove of racist or other offensive speech.[27]

Just like all three types of rights speech, all three types of rights speakers are important to a well-functioning constitutional rights discourse. But in terms of the Free Speech Clause and the enforcement of non-speech rights, as discussed below the participation of each raises distinctive issues and concerns.

RIGHTS SPEECH VERSUS "RIGHTS TALK"

Now that we have a basic sense of what rights speech is, and who conveys it, it is necessary to draw one final distinction—between rights speech and "rights talk." Some commentators have criticized Americans' seeming obsession with constitutional rights—in particular, the *manner* in which people discuss and debate constitutional rights. Critics of "rights talk" argue that American rhetoric about rights is harmful to the nation's legal, political, and social fabrics.[28] In particular, they worry that rights talk, which they contend is often absolutist and relentlessly individualistic, ignores limits on rights claims and the need to balance individual rights and collective responsibilities.

Rights speech and rights talk share some common ground. Both concepts are concerned with public discourse about constitutional rights. Further, both are premised on the notion that it is normatively desirable to engage in discussions about constitutional rights. Finally, rights speech proponents and rights talk critics would agree that Americans talk—a lot—about their constitutional rights.

Despite these commonalities, rights speech is distinct from rights talk. Critics of rights talk take issue with *how* constitutional rights are discussed, not *whether* they ought to be discussed in the first place, or to what extent rights discourse can or should be regulated by government. The primary concern with regard to rights speech is the extent to which citizens are in fact free to debate, discuss, learn about, and exercise constitutional rights, as part of a democratic process that focuses on constraining government. In this sense, rights speech is a valuable feature of American democracy, not a bug.

Rights speech is not a form of political or social dysfunction. Rather, it is a central aspect of citizens' self-governance. Its primary concerns are whether and to what extent government ought to be constrained in the context of conversations about limits on its own powers; the manner in which constitutional rights, as powers or trumps, can or should be exercised; and the extent to which governments are permitted to intervene and communicate their own thoughts regarding constitutional rights.

How speakers choose to engage in rights speech—the content they communicate, or the specific mode of communication—relates to the tone and character of American political and constitutional discourse. Rights talk critics raise legitimate concerns about such matters. However, these are social and political problems that government cannot remedy through laws limiting speech.

Rights Speech, Free Speech, and Non-speech Rights

When governments regulate rights speech, both freedom of speech and the non-speech rights that are the subjects of discourse may be adversely affected. In order to assess these effects, we need to understand the general roles or functions the Free Speech Clause performs with regard to rights speech. We must also look in the other direction, toward the implicated non-speech rights and how they might be affected by restrictions on or mandates concerning rights speech.

FREE SPEECH CONCERNS

Rights speech is critically important to the recognition and facilitation of constitutional rights. A robust rights discourse serves all of the Free Speech Clause's principal values—self-government, the search for truth, and individual autonomy. Interference with rights speech, through various forms of regulation or compulsion, undermines these critical free speech functions and values.

One of the central functions of the Free Speech Clause as it relates to other rights is to protect a robust public rights discourse. As Akhil Amar has observed, "[t]he Constitution itself came to life in a land teeming with free speech."[29] Its provisions, including those in the Bill of Rights, are the product of a broad and robust constitutional discourse. Subsequent generations have appreciated the critical importance of free speech, particularly in terms of facilitating and supporting the recognition and exercise of other constitutional rights.

Thus, for example, Reconstruction Republicans resisted limits on freedom of speech and freedom of press precisely because they feared that governments would interfere with the recognition and exercise of equal protection rights.[30] Much later, race, LGBT, and other equality advocates relied on free speech rights to communicate and facilitate their constitutional claims. So too did proponents of other rights, including abortion, free exercise of religion, and the right to keep and bear arms. In a general sense, social and political movements all rely on the ability to communicate with the public in terms that invoke or rely upon constitutional rights.[31]

As discussed in the book's Introduction, the Free Speech Clause provides a general mediating framework in which this constitutional rights discourse occurs. Among other things, that framework demands that governments grant equal access to public fora for all speakers, prohibits censorship and suppression of speech based on its content, and generally facilitates debate on public issues that is "uninhibited, robust, and wide-open."[32] Through this framework, the Free Speech Clause has mediated public and political discourse about a wide variety of non-speech rights. It has done so, in part, by ensuring that proponents of abortion, equal protection, free exercise of religion, the right to keep and bear arms, and other constitutional rights have ample opportunities to communicate with regard to the status, scope, and exercise of these rights.[33]

Free Speech Clause protection for rights speech assists not just proponents of new rights or defenders of expansive interpretations of existing rights, but also those who resist these things or even assert conflicting rights of their own. Through freedom of speech and other expressive rights, defenders of the status quo regarding constitutional rights are empowered to resist recognition of new rights or expansion of existing non-speech rights. In other words, free speech rights enable not just offensive but also defensive forms of rights speech. By prohibiting governments from imposing an orthodoxy with regard to constitutional rights, the Free Speech Clause facilitates a full and fair discussion of these rights. In constitutional rights discourse, free speech rules and principles prevent government from silencing or compelling rights speech.

For example, the Free Speech Clause protects robust anti-equality speech—including even derogatory and hateful statements about racial, ethnic, and other groups. As discussed in Chapter 5, critics charge that protection for this form of rights speech diminishes or prevents members of minority groups from enjoying equal protection under law. However, protection for the broadest range of rights speech facilitates an open and transparent consideration of all perspectives concerning equal protection rights and principles.

As noted, free speech rights protect the right to dissent with regard to the recognition or expansion of non-speech rights. Thus, as the Supreme Court held in *Hurley v. Irish-American Gay, Lesbian and Bisexual Group of Boston*(1995),[34] the government could not force Irish-American parade organizers to include in their event a group that advocated for equal recognition and respect for gay and lesbian Irish-Americans. Similarly, in *Boy Scouts of America v. Dale* (2000), the Court held that the First Amendment barred government from forcing the Boy Scouts to accept an openly gay member whose presence was inconsistent with their own stated mission.[35] These decisions protect individuals and groups from state imposition of a form of anti-discrimination orthodoxy.

In more general terms, the Free Speech Clause supports and sustains democratic processes that lead to constitutional change. This includes the recognition of new constitutional rights, as well as new interpretations of existing constitutional rights.[36] The right to abortion recognized in *Roe v. Wade* (1973) is an example. Similarly, as discussed in Chapter 5, the race and LGBT equality movements engaged in extensive litigation campaigns challenging restrictions on public protests and the distribution of literature advocating for equal protection rights. Groups used the Free Speech Clause's mediating protections to advance their equal protection claims and agendas.

In *Obergefell v. Hodges* (2015), the Supreme Court's decision recognizing a right to marriage equality for gay and lesbian couples, the Court highlighted the importance of rights speech and rights discourse to the recognition of this right. The majority discussed the various ways in which the public and public officials had opportunities to discuss, study, debate, and litigate marriage equality prior to its decision. Justice

Anthony Kennedy described how "new dimensions of freedom become apparent to new generations, often through perspectives that begin in pleas or protests and then are considered in the political sphere and the judicial process."[37]

The Free Speech Clause also performs an important function in terms of ensuring the free flow of information—including factual information—that informs individual decision-making about rights. This facilitates individual decision-making about whether and how to pursue or exercise constitutional rights. Further, the Free Speech Clause protects individual efforts to seek out and obtain knowledge concerning constitutional rights. In this and other respects, each of the non-speech rights examined in the book depends for its full and effective enjoyment on the recognition and enforcement of free speech rights.

In light of all of these critical free speech functions relating to non-speech rights, regulation of rights speech poses a serious danger to our constitutional system of rights. Pervasive regulation of communications about or concerning constitutional rights allows governments to manage and structure discourse about those rights, again in ways that implicate both free speech and non-speech rights. Rights speech regulation may alter the nature and substance of debates about constitutional rights. It may also erect barriers to exercising those rights.

For example, as discussed below and in Chapter 6, abortion rights discourse has changed markedly over the years. Part of the change is owing to government's increased participation in that discourse, which has been sanctioned by Supreme Court decisions concerning the right to abortion.[38] In short, the Court has invited government to weigh in on the abortion right, through mandatory disclosure laws and other means. Some of these governmental interventions have altered the Free Speech Clause's mediating function, which is supposed to ensure the free and unfettered flow of information about constitutional rights. Mandatory disclosure of ideological communications about abortion rights threaten not just free speech, but also the right of abortion itself.

Some of the examples of rights speech highlighted earlier are readily identified as political speech, which is of course a core concern of the Free Speech Clause. Thus, communications about or concerning the *merits* of a constitutional right constitute speech on an obvious matter of public concern. They facilitate citizen self-governance by allowing speakers to communicate about the proper limits on governmental power.[39] The Free Speech Clause protects a vital collective interest in allowing the people to decide on the appropriate distribution of power.

As Robert Post has observed, "the First Amendment safeguards public discourse not merely because it informs government decision-making, but also because it enables a culturally heterogeneous society to forge a common democratic will."[40]

Rights speech regulations interfere with the formation of this democratic will by suppressing, dictating, altering, or manipulating speech that addresses constitutional rights. This can occur in a variety of ways—through direct regulation, limits on access to public properties, conditions on funding, restrictions on the distribution of information, and other means.

In addition to their negative implications in terms of self-governance, rights speech regulations can also interfere with the exchange of ideas and the search for truth with regard to constitutional limits on government.[41] Abortion image bans, restrictions on public access to gun permitting information, and conditional spending measures that restrict abortion speech or arms speech all prevent speakers and audiences from exchanging and accessing information that is critical to thinking about and debating constitutional rights.

Further, with regard to the truth-seeking function, rights speech regulations that *compel* speech about or concerning constitutional rights raise additional concerns. As noted, some compulsory abortion disclosures distort conversations between physicians and patients regarding the exercise of the right to abortion.[42] This concern also arises in cases where government seeks to compel pregnancy centers opposed to abortion to suggest to their patients that contraception and abortion are "viable options." These measures may also compel speakers to convey rights speech with which they do not agree.

Rights speech regulations can also interfere with the free speech autonomy of both speakers and audiences. Laws that restrict speakers' ability to choose their method of communication, ban physicians from asking patients about firearms ownership, or mandate that physicians disclose ideological information about abortion, implicate speakers' autonomy interests. These restrictions and mandates also implicate audiences' interests in receiving information about constitutional rights.[43] Some, such as mandatory abortion scripts, may use emotive appeals to manipulate target audiences.[44] This sort of structuring of rights discourse negatively affects interests in self-fulfillment and decisional autonomy.

Finally, as the Supreme Court has observed, "the First Amendment goes beyond protection of the press and the self-expression of individuals to prohibit government from limiting the stock of available information from which members of the public may draw."[45] Many rights speech regulations, including restrictions on research, advocacy, and the distribution of information about the exercise of rights, limit what speakers, journalists, and the public can learn about this important aspect of constitutional rights. Information concerning how, when, and where rights are exercised is part of constitutional rights discourse.

In sum, rights speech regulations interfere with the central mediating functions of the Free Speech Clause. They also implicate, and often offend, central Free Speech

Clause self-government, search for truth, and individual autonomy justifications. As I explain below, this does not mean that all such regulations violate the Free Speech Clause. However, thinking about them in terms of rights speech and rights discourse offers a different perspective regarding what might at first glance appear to be ordinary public order, public safety, or public records laws. The regulation of rights speech and rights discourse can be camouflaged in such measures.

NON-SPEECH RIGHTS

As indicated, the constitutional concerns relating to governmental regulation of rights speech extend beyond the Free Speech Clause. As at other intersection points between freedom of speech and non-speech rights, the effects here run in more than one direction. Regulating speech about or concerning constitutional rights does not just affect free speech rights: it also affects the recognition, status, and exercise of non-speech rights.

If governments can control the dissemination of factual information concerning equal protection, abortion, arms, and other rights, or otherwise influence discussions about those rights, they may also be able to affect the recognition, scope, and enjoyment of non-speech rights. Thus, in a very fundamental sense, the fate of non-speech rights is directly connected to the free flow and distribution of rights speech.

Pre-recognition limits on rights speech can result in proposed new rights being defeated at inception. As discussed, restrictions on post-recognition rights speech affect the ability to communicate and receive information and arguments about rights and to engage in a robust debate concerning their merits. These speech activities are critical to the granting or withholding of public support for constitutional rights. Thus, had authorities been successful in suppressing abolitionist, gay equality, pro-abortion, or pro-Second Amendment communications, the rights associated with this speech may not exist at all, or may have taken forms that we would not recognize today.

Restrictions on rights speech deprive advocates and claimants of the rhetorical power of rights. Such restrictions may also forestall or prevent reconsideration by the people, their elected representatives, and courts of decisions to grant formal recognition to a constitutional right or to expand its scope. For example, restrictions on public antiabortion speech—buffer zones, residential protest restrictions, imagery bans, and the like—impact not just free speech but also, potentially, the substance and scope of the abortion right.

Restrictions on the ability to communicate freely and openly about constitutional rights can also negatively affect their actual exercise. As discussed above, some rights speech communicates ideas and opinions about constitutional rights. Suppression of that kind of communication may impede the recognition and exercise of rights. For example, by suppressing communications about race equality, state and local restrictions on public protests during the civil rights era impeded the recognition and exercise of equal protection rights. Similarly, suppression of speech and expressive association by LGBT persons has impeded their achievement and enjoyment of equal protection under law.

Some rights speech conveys information about the consequences of exercising a constitutional right. Certain mandatory abortion disclosures ostensibly serve this purpose.[46] However, these mandates can also interfere with women's autonomy regarding the decision whether to exercise the abortion right. The Due Process Clause bars governments from coercing women not to exercise that right. But it says nothing about interference short of actual official coercion, which can also negatively impact the free exercise of the abortion right.[47] Mandating abortion speech through physician intermediaries can interfere with women's right to choose by requiring the disclosure of inaccurate, misleading, or even ideological information about abortion. Allowing or inviting the government to persuade or convince women that abortion is physically and psychologically harmful to them or another "person" may provide an effective means of restricting access to or exercise of the abortion right. Note that the same concern would arise if governments required licensed firearms dealers to convey inaccurate, misleading, or ideological information to potential purchasers of firearms. In sum, rights speech regulations are doubly dangerous—they threaten to restrict, compel, or structure communications that affect the actual exercise and enjoyment of constitutional rights.

Separate and apart from concerns about their effects on the actual exercise of constitutional rights, rights speech regulations also distort the democratic processes by which constitutional rights attain their social, political, and constitutional statuses. Maintaining open and robust discourse about constitutional rights allows citizens to decide for themselves whether to recognize a constitutional right, how much support the right merits, and how to balance a particular right's societal benefits and costs.[48] The feedback—both negative and positive—that rights speech produces can also be critically important in terms of signaling support or opposition to representatives, judges, and other officials involved with interpreting and enforcing rights.

Rights speech regulations can create a kind of de facto hierarchy of constitutional rights. Consider the very distinct ways in which legislatures have recently treated the right to abortion and the right to keep and bear arms. Officials in many states have generally treated abortion as a disfavored right, subject to an increasing array of restrictions—including mandatory disclosures and spending limits on advocacy and counseling. In contrast, state legislatures have enacted a host of measures designed to protect and facilitate the right to bear arms—including measures that deprive the public of information about firearms ownership and restrict the expenditure of public funds that might support research or advocacy relating to gun control.

Governments ought not to be permitted to impose an artificial ranking of constitutional rights through manipulation of speech about those rights. This is the prerogative of individuals, groups, and communities, who rely upon open channels of communication in order to determine which rights are to be recognized and to what degree. If there is to be a hierarchy of constitutional rights, it ought to be the product of a democratic process that is free from governmental manipulation of and interference with private speech about or concerning constitutional rights.

Private, Professional, and Governmental Rights Speech

Thus far, the chapter has expressed several general concerns regarding regulation of rights speech. It turns now to more specific free speech and non-speech concerns raised by the several examples highlighted earlier. As noted, there are three basic types of rights speech (ideological, informational, and consultative) and three categories of rights speakers (private, professional, and governmental). The discussion that follows uses the latter categorization of rights speakers to identify and analyze specific rights speech concerns.

PRIVATE RIGHTS SPEECH

As the earlier discussion showed, private speakers communicate rights speech in a variety of different ways. Communications about or concerning constitutional rights are also more pervasively regulated than generally appreciated. Not all regulations and restrictions on rights speech are unconstitutional under current Free Speech Clause doctrines. Indeed, many would likely satisfy these standards, with courts rarely even acknowledging their connection to rights discourse.

That, indeed, is precisely the problem. As the example involving the Norfolk sign code shows, courts are not sensitive to the full range of constitutional implications associated with laws that restrict rights speech. Greater sensitivity in this regard could lead to the invalidation of certain measures. But more generally, it would facilitate appropriate judicial scrutiny of official acts that regulate a form of political speech.

My purpose is not to evaluate specific restrictions based on current free speech doctrines, but rather to offer more general suggestions regarding how courts and public officials might recognize and evaluate private rights speech regulations. As the Norfolk example shows, too often judges and officials adopt a narrow perspective when reviewing rights speech regulations. Applying current free speech doctrine, judges focus on the content neutrality of regulations, rather than on the broader impact these measures can have on rights speech and rights discourse. Thus, they do not recognize the implications, for both free speech and non-speech rights, of laws and regulations that limit various forms of rights speech.

This recognition is important not because it necessarily transforms the restriction into a presumptively unconstitutional regulation of political speech, but rather because it justifies a more searching review of the free speech and non-speech implications of the regulation. Greater judicial skepticism regarding rights speech regulations can make a significant difference, both in how these measures are reviewed and in the outcomes of specific cases.

On their face, many rights speech regulations are similar to the Norfolk sign code—they appear to regulate neutrally, impact speech minimally (if at all), or operate as reasonable limits on private speech. However, as regulations of a wider and deeper constitutional conversation about rights, each such regulation allows government to alter and skew discourse about constitutional rights. Absent this recognition, free speech doctrines may appear to mediate neutrally and without any particular political or other bias. With it, however, judges can counteract doctrinal nearsightedness with regard to seemingly "ordinary" sign codes, spending conditions, restrictions on student speech, and other measures.

Recognizing the ideological and political nature of rights speech can help judges and legislatures appropriately mediate public discourse concerning constitutional rights. For example, in *McCullen v. Coakley* (2014), the Supreme Court invalidated a Massachusetts law that prohibited communication within thirty-five feet of any abortion clinic. Although the Court concluded that the law was not based on the content of speech, it nevertheless struck it down. The Court's recognition that the plaintiffs, who were sidewalk counselors, wished to exchange information and ideas about abortion—to engage in an intimate form of rights speech—plainly influenced the outcome of the case.[49]

McCullen's recognition of the importance of rights speech ought to extend more broadly to abortion protesters, who also engage in rights speech (although of a more boisterous and sometimes disruptive form). As *McCullen* suggests, judicial recognition that buffer zones, bubbles, and other restrictions on private abortion speech regulate constitutional discourse—sometimes, though not always, based on its content—would likely impact how courts review such measures.

This perspective could also affect the way courts review other regulations that affect rights speech. Some courts have upheld limits on the public display of abortion images. However, the physical, moral, and other consequences of exercising a constitutional right are an important part of discourse about that right. In that respect, abortion image bans are a particularly troubling restriction on rights speech; they are and ought to be treated as invalid content-based restrictions on political speech.

The abortion context is not the only one in which officials have suppressed ideological and informational rights speech. Thus, as noted earlier, administrators in public schools and on college campuses have treated some abortion speech, equality speech, and arms speech as inherently disruptive or inappropriate. But younger audiences should actually be *encouraged* to engage in this discourse. So long as students do so in a non-disruptive manner and the subject matter is not beyond their understanding or level of maturity, they ought to be allowed and even encouraged to participate in constitutional discourse.

Governments sometimes also use their authority to manage public resources, including taxpayer funds, in ways that restrict or compel communications about or concerning constitutional rights. Yet, again, courts rarely recognize these measures as implicating rights speech. As *McCullen* suggests, access to public properties such as streets and sidewalks is critically important to constitutional discourse. So too is access to municipal transit systems and other public spaces. In that respect, regulations banning all "political" speech from such places, which have become common, ought to be reviewed carefully. As cases suggest, these restrictions can disparately affect controversial rights speech about arms, abortion, equality, and other rights.[50] Although governments have broad authority to restrict access to these properties and to preserve them for their intended purposes, courts ought to ensure that such measures have not been adopted for the purpose of excluding specific kinds of private rights speech, and that they are otherwise reasonable regulations of speech in public venues.

Similarly, courts should also be skeptical of spending conditions that restrict or compel rights speech. Using the spending authority to suppress or dictate rights speech raises the same basic problems as does using other means of governmental power. Funding conditions relating to abortion, the right to bear arms, equality, and other constitutional rights should be reviewed carefully to ensure that governments are not improperly suppressing or dictating particular *viewpoints* about rights.[51]

Finally, courts and officials should take a more skeptical approach to measures that have the effect of concealing or suppressing information concerning the exercise of constitutional rights. Although intimate privacy rights must be preserved, basic information about the exercise of abortion, the right to bear arms, and other constitutional rights ought not to be hidden from the public. As already mentioned, bans on the display of abortion imagery suppress information relevant to the effects of exercising the abortion right. By the same token, free speech considerations ought at least to color consideration of laws that suppress empirical information about the exercise of Second Amendment rights, or restrict the use of public funds to discuss the right to bear arms or other rights with officials.

Protection of private rights speech furthers all of the principal values of the Free Speech Clause. It also helps to ensure that individuals have the broadest form of protection for non-speech rights, which depend for their effective exercise on freedom of communication, access to public venues, and the sharing of critical information about rights.

PROFESSIONAL RIGHTS SPEECH

Firearms inquiry bans, mandatory abortion disclosures, bans on "reparative" therapies, and some of the other measures identified earlier regulate communications by licensed professionals. The state sometimes relies on its power to license professionals to justify measures restricting or compelling rights speech.[52] The extent to which governments can limit professional speech is not clear. I will not try to answer that question definitively or analyze the status of professional speech generally under the Free Speech Clause. Rather, the discussion that follows will focus more specifically on the connection between a particular sub-category of professional speech—namely, professional speech about or concerning constitutional rights. In general, this speech occurs during the course of consultations and counseling relating to the exercise of constitutional rights. Some consultative rights speech conveys basic information about rights. Other communications are more ideological or normative. Whatever form they take, I will contend that they too are part of constitutional rights discourse and as such are entitled to coverage and a degree of protection under the Free Speech Clause.

Despite its different context and character, like private rights speech, professional rights speech is generally deserving of strong Free Speech Clause protections. This is owing not only to its connection to free speech values, but also to its relationship to the effective exercise of non-speech rights.

Professional Speech and the Free Speech Clause

Although I will not venture a position on the general constitutional status of professional speech, it is necessary to situate professional speech relative to the free speech guarantee. Much of what professionals do occurs through and as a result of various forms of communication or "speech." Lawyers advise clients and file briefs, doctors perform consultations and write prescriptions, and other professionals communicate with their clients in various ways.

Nevertheless, the Free Speech Clause does not broadly preclude or restrict the regulation of licensed professionals. Thus, governments are permitted to impose basic requirements relating to professional status, and to broadly regulate professional activity—including expressive activity. For example, a state requirement that lawyers or physicians be licensed to practice their professions does not implicate the Free Speech Clause.

Nor does the Free Speech Clause preclude governments from enforcing generally applicable standards of conduct or care. Thus, governments can ban the prescription of certain medications, impose civil liability and professional discipline for legal or other professional advice that causes damages, and protect clients from harmful practices. Governments can also enforce rules of evidence and procedure, impose sanctions for the filing of frivolous lawsuits, and prohibit professionals from revealing client confidences. Many, if not all, of these regulations limit communication or speech in some fashion—oral advice, written prescriptions, etc. Nevertheless, few would argue that they raise serious Free Speech Clause concerns.

Despite their broad licensing and regulatory authority, governments do not have unlimited power to regulate professional communications. The Supreme Court has been cryptic about the speech rights of professionals and their clients. In a concurring opinion that has turned out (in the absence of other guidance) to be influential, Justice Byron White suggested a distinction between public and private professional speech.[53] Under this approach, a licensed physician who gives a public speech concerning abortion or Second Amendment rights is acting as a private citizen and is protected by the Free Speech Clause. However, the same physician who provides advice about abortion or asks about firearms ownership in the context of an in-office professional consultation does not enjoy the same free speech protection—indeed, some courts have held that she enjoys no free speech protection at all.[54]

In the office consultation context, the Supreme Court has indicated that the Free Speech Clause is "implicated," but has not clarified to what degree.[55] This has left lower courts without adequate guidance with regard to a broad range of professional speech. Some lower courts have interpreted the Court's sparse comments regarding professional speech to mean that professional advice is a form of professional *conduct* not covered by the Free Speech Clause at all. Others have concluded that professional communications delivered in the office setting are entitled to some, although not to full, free speech protection. As a sign of the confusion, the Eleventh Circuit Court of Appeals considered Florida's ban on physician inquiries regarding firearms *four* separate times—three times by the same panel of judges and once before the entire court of appeals—and in doing so applied three *different* standards of review to the law.

The extent to which government may rely on its licensing power to regulate professional speech is a subject of great interest, but one subject to little concrete authority. However, whatever the scope of the government's power to regulate professional communications may be, I will argue its authority is subject to special constraints insofar as it restricts or compels professional speech about or concerning the recognition, scope, or exercise of a constitutional right.

Licensed Professionals and Constitutional Rights

Many might assume that professionals have little, if anything, to do with constitutional rights. After all, most of us see a lawyer or doctor to solve a specific problem, or to address a particular condition. But far more frequently than is generally acknowledged, professional-client consultations address or relate to the subject of constitutional rights.

This is easiest to appreciate with regard to communications between lawyers and their clients. As Kathleen Sullivan has observed, lawyers are frequently "vindicators of constitutional rights against the state."[56] Through their advice and other communications, lawyers seek to check governmental power and protect the constitutional rights of their clients. Supreme Court precedents have acknowledged the importance of lawyers' solicitation of clients with potential constitutional claims, the expressive nature of constitutional litigation, and the free speech rights of lawyers to publicly defend their clients' interests.[57]

Lawyers are natural state adversaries, and as such are frequently involved in consultations about constitutional and other rights. However, a number of other professionals perform important functions relating to their clients' constitutional rights.

For instance, physicians have long clashed with the state over the provision of medical advice to their patients regarding such things as reproductive products and services. Indeed, as discussed in Chapter 6, dissenting opinions in early Supreme Court cases regarding whether the Due Process Clause protected a constitutional right to access information about contraception were among the first to raise so-called "professional speech" concerns. In those cases, medical professionals challenged legal restrictions on the dissemination of truthful information regarding contraceptive devices and methods. The mandatory abortion disclosure laws described earlier regulate communications about or concerning abortion. Physicians have also been on the front lines in challenges to state laws prohibiting withdrawal of life-sustaining treatment and physician-assisted suicide—both of which implicate the so-called "right to die." These interactions implicate constitutional rights pertaining to end-of-life decision-making.

Other licensed professionals communicate and consult with clients in ways that impact or concern constitutional rights. Marriage counselors, family counselors, social workers, nurses, teachers, mental health counselors, and child care providers can all find themselves aligned against state licensing or other authorities on matters relating to constitutional rights. Even firearms dealers, who do not enter the same type of licensing relationship as lawyers and other professionals, could be subject to speech restrictions pertaining to Second Amendment rights.

These professionals serve a number of important functions with regard to constitutional rights. By providing factual and other information, they educate patients and clients about subjects relating to constitutional rights and facilitate their exercise. Professionals also participate in, and contribute to, the free flow of accurate information about contraception, abortion, equality, arms, and end-of-life decision-making. Thus, restrictions on professional rights speech affect more than the provision of professional advice concerning a client's personal legal, medical, or other concerns. Like private rights speech regulations, they impact discussions and personal decisions regarding the exercise of fundamental constitutional rights.

Professional Rights Speech as Free Speech

The question, however, is whether laws and regulations that restrict or mandate communications between professionals and clients about or concerning the subject of constitutional rights ought to be treated as suspect under the Free Speech Clause. Notwithstanding the fact that the speaker is a licensed professional and the audience is a client or patient, the Free Speech Clause ought to fully apply to regulations of professional rights speech. These regulations target, quite often based on content, communications that address the mechanics, propriety, and consequences of exercising a constitutional right. Like private rights speech regulations, professional rights speech regulations ought to be subject to meaningful Free Speech Clause review.

Despite the important constitutional functions performed by many licensed professionals, under the approaches adopted by Justice White and some lower courts, legislatures currently have very broad authority to restrict or structure professional rights speech. In addition to the mandatory abortion disclosure laws and bans on firearms inquiries discussed earlier, consider these examples:

- A law prohibiting licensed marriage counselors from advising their clients not to enter into interracial marriages;

- A law banning licensed family counselors from advising clients that interracial adoption may not be in the best interests of the child;
- A law barring physicians from discussing the availability of abortion, or the positive effects of procuring an abortion, with their patients;
- A law compelling physicians to inform their patients that certain pharmaceutical abortion procedures can be "reversed";
- A law requiring physicians to discuss the positive attributes of certain types of contraceptives, and to urge their patients to use them;
- A law prohibiting physicians from expressing the view that marijuana use is medically beneficial for some patients, and thus ought to be protected under state and federal law;
- A law barring lawyers from discussing the safety and legal implications of firearms possession with their clients;
- A law barring physicians from discussing end-of-life plans with their patients; and
- A law compelling physicians to present specific information to patients for the purpose of persuading them not to refuse life-sustaining nutrition and hydration (a right the Supreme Court has assumed competent adults possess).

If courts were to adopt the approach that professional advice communicated in private settings, or as part of a course of treatment, is either not covered by the Free Speech Clause because it is conduct or is entitled to something less than full protection, legislatures would presumably be free to enact all of these laws. This would be so despite the obvious fact that each of them regulates a communication between professional and client on the basis of its subject matter or viewpoint—a practice generally forbidden by the Free Speech Clause.

Moreover, the laws would be deemed valid—indeed, according to some courts would not be subject to review under the Free Speech Clause—despite the fact that each restricts or structures a conversation about or concerning a constitutional right. Note that the state could not only prohibit, but also *compel*, statements about constitutional rights, including equality, abortion, and the right to bear arms. For example, legislatures could require counselors to extol the virtues of interracial marriage, or require physicians to disseminate information that is intended to persuade women to obtain abortions. Under the broadest reading of the Supreme Court's incomplete doctrine of professional speech, these laws would at least stand a reasonable chance of surviving First Amendment challenges.

Some of the foregoing examples may seem a bit far-fetched. Then again, not long ago most might have said the same thing about a state law that imposed restrictions on the circumstances in which physicians can discuss firearms possession with their patients. Governments have turned with increased frequency to regulations of professional rights speech. Courts have thus far failed to treat these regulations as related to, much less harmful for, constitutional rights discourse.

As in other contexts, there is the concern that the Free Speech Clause not be used as a substitute for more fitting or appropriate non-speech claims. From that perspective, some might view Free Speech Clause challenges to professional speech regulations as ill-fitting or even "opportunistic" substitutes for economic liberty claims.[58]

That argument might carry some force as it concerns free speech challenges to measures such as professional entry barriers or pricing regulations. These would indeed seem to be due process challenges dressed up in free speech garb. In contrast, compulsory abortion disclosures, firearms inquiry bans, and the other examples listed above do not target any *economic* dimension of professional licensure. Rather, the laws aim squarely at the provision of critical information about rights, conversations between professional and client concerning rights, and therapies that may implicate rights.

The appropriate question in these contexts is not why free speech claims are appropriate, but why the fact of licensure permits government to compel and ban speech relating to constitutional rights. If anything, it would seem that it is the states and regulators that are acting opportunistically—to restrict or mandate political speech.

The regulation of professional equality speech, abortion speech, and arms speech affects vital communications concerning constitutional rights and may also affect the effective exercise of those rights. Consider the character and content of some mandatory abortion disclosures. South Dakota requires that abortion providers tell patients that abortion will "terminate the life of a whole, separate, unique, living human being" and that "the pregnant woman has an existing relationship with that unborn human being."[59] The doctor must also explain "all known medical risks" of abortion, including the "increased risk of suicide ideation and suicide."[60] Federal courts have upheld both the "human being" and suicide advisory scripts.[61] Other state measures, which are sometimes referred to as "speech and display" laws, require that an ultrasound be displayed to the woman and that doctors provide a detailed description of the image (including information about limbs, vital organs, position in the uterus, etc.).[62] Women can sometimes refuse to view the sonogram itself, but they must generally be informed of the sonogram results and must sign an informed consent certifying that they have received the information.

As some scholars have suggested, these and other mandatory abortion disclosure laws raise very serious free speech concerns.[63] Yet the Supreme Court and lower courts have tended to treat them as merely an aspect of informed consent. The Supreme Court and other courts ought to treat governmental efforts to structure abortion communications and discourse in this context and in these ways more skeptically.

Recognizing rights speech in these mandated communications could convince courts to reconsider the license that has been granted to governments to compel abortion speech and structure abortion discourse. It might also encourage localities to find ways other than compelling abortion speech to regulate pregnancy centers that may fail to provide full disclosure of their services to patients. Regardless of the perspective or message the government is pressing, mandating speech about or concerning abortion is dangerous to both free speech and abortion rights.

Some have expressed the concern that treating abortion disclosures and similar measures as implicating political speech might actually harm women's access to abortion. The concern is that this perspective might encourage courts to treat the abortion procedure itself as a political act rather than an aspect of women's health care.[64] But the fact is that mandatory abortion disclosures regulate the provision of factual and other information on a matter of considerable public concern. Of course, abortion consultations are primarily about receiving proper medical care. However, unlike other medical procedures, abortion services have a constitutional dimension. Thus, mandatory abortion disclosures implicate medical care, freedom of speech, *and* abortion rights.

Of course, states may legitimately compel professionals to disclose the risks of medical procedures and other treatments—including abortion. They may do so even if the purpose is to dissuade patients or clients from taking risks the state deems to be unreasonable. However, laws requiring that professionals disclose information for the purpose of persuading a patient not to exercise the abortion right, or banning communications about firearms because they might cause a patient to question the propriety of exercising Second Amendment rights, are fundamentally different. They target speech relating to constitutional rights, raising the specter that the state is using its licensure power not to control risks but to regulate discourse about rights. In short, when governments mandate or restrict professional communications about or concerning a subject relating to a constitutional right, they are not just regulating the dissemination of things such as clinical advice and medical courses of treatment—they are regulating an important aspect of constitutional discourse.

Although courts have generally failed to treat professional speech as fully protected speech, a number of scholars have argued that professional-client communications serve First Amendment self-government, search for truth, and marketplace values.[65] Commentators have focused on free speech values relating to the dissemination of expert knowledge, patients' access to information regarding courses of treatment, and respect for professional knowledge communities. However, what is so far missing from the analysis is an appreciation for the *constitutional* dimension of certain professional speech regulations.

By restricting political speech and suppressing or mandating the flow of information about rights-related subjects, professional rights speech regulations implicate core free speech concerns. These regulations also implicate non-speech rights, in the sense that they can undermine or interfere with their effective exercise. Governments can diminish or favor certain constitutional rights by restricting or mandating professional speech about or concerning those rights.

Focusing on the special category of professional rights speech highlights the untenable distinction Justice White and others have drawn between public and private professional speech. Allowing the state, through its licensing power, to regulate all speech that takes the form of "direct, personalized speech with clients," as Justice White put it,[66] risks subjecting a substantial amount of speech that relates not just to a matter of private concern but one of singular public importance.

It is certainly true that professionals are not like street corner orators, who seek to persuade or engage with broad segments of the public and, accordingly, are granted broad free speech rights. Professionals are in a relationship with the state that is structured by things such as licensure and professional standards. The state has power to regulate professionals in ways that are necessary to preserve the professional institution and protect clients from harmful interactions. However, lawyers, physicians, and other professionals are not merely professional automatons who dispense technical advice, medicines, and facts. They engage with their clients on a variety of subjects, including matters relating to constitutional rights.

Of course, physicians and patients discussing arms possession or abortion are not engaged in a seminar-like discussion of constitutional rights. However, they are engaged in discussions that touch upon, concern, and in some case affect the enjoyment of individual constitutional rights. A physician who is required to disclose not just accurate facts about abortion, but perceptions and viewpoints about it, is engaged in a (forced) ideological discourse about abortion rights. A physician banned from asking patients about firearms ownership owing, in part, to the legislature's concern that she might dissuade a patient from exercising that right is prohibited from engaging in rights discourse.

The exchange of factual information and viewpoints about the decision whether to exercise a constitutional right, the manner in which to do so, and the implications of that decision are not merely of concern to the individual client or patient. What patients learn in the examining room or professional office may affect discussions about abortion, arms, and other concerns at home, at work, or in public venues. As one commentator has noted, "professionals provide individuals with access to information that enables the latter to come to important decisions affecting their lives."[67]

In particular, they "take an active part in assisting in the vindication of existing legal and constitutional rights in courts and other government fora."[68] Even intimate, personal treatment advice can provide a basis for taking political action concerning constitutional rights. As Dean Robert Post has argued, "there is no reason why public opinion might not be formed one conversation at a time."[69]

Courts have generally elided these concerns by treating professional-client interactions relating to rights as a form of *conduct* that is not covered by the Free Speech Clause. Like the public-private distinction, however, the speech-conduct distinction ignores not just the fact that *specific communications* are often the object of regulation, but also the special constitutional functions of professionals and the free speech values associated with professional rights speech.

Under the professional conduct approach, even a lawyer's questions and legal filings in a constitutional case would ostensibly represent part of a "course of conduct" subject to state regulation. But surely the government cannot ban lawyers from interviewing their clients about certain constitutional violations, or prohibit them from bringing claims the state believes to be harmful or misguided on the merits. Nor, presumably, can the state compel lawyers to communicate specific information to clients about the special burdens of civil rights litigation, in an effort to persuade clients not to pursue such claims.

Again, in contrast to lawyers, other professionals may not be natural state adversaries. However, as discussed earlier, they are involved to a significant degree with constitutional concerns and rights. Thus, their participation in rights discourse is also deserving of free speech protection. Courts have generally failed to recognize that, as one commentator has observed, "professional speech serves to educate the citizenry, is integral to the workings of self-government, and may even itself form part of a lesson in democracy."[70] These functions are particularly associated with professional communications about or concerning constitutional rights.

Recognizing that the Free Speech Clause *applies* to professional rights speech does not mean that all regulations will fail constitutional scrutiny. Even under the most rigorous "strict" scrutiny, if the state can provide compelling reasons for mandating disclosures about abortion or restricting questions about firearms, and show that its law is narrowly tailored to address these concerns, the law will survive. However, forcing the state's ideology on professionals or patients, or protecting patients from potentially persuasive arguments about constitutional rights, are not compelling interests.

To be sure, there will be some close and difficult cases. Consider, for example, state bans on so-called reparative talk therapy for minors. Such laws appear merely to outlaw a form of therapy that is particularly harmful to minor patients. However, insofar as their purpose is to suppress expression of an old and discredited form of bigotry against gay and lesbian persons—that is, the notion that homosexuality is a curable disease—these laws implicate the Free Speech Clause. When the state uses its regulatory power to suppress a viewpoint or perspective concerning gay and lesbian equality, the Free Speech Clause requires a form of heightened scrutiny.

States have argued that reparative talk therapies are physically and psychologically harmful to minors—a contention that appears to be supported by leading psychological institutions and associations. Thus, states can plausibly and perhaps successfully argue that the purpose of the reparative therapy bans is to protect minors from harm—an undoubtedly compelling interest. The laws, which prohibit reparative therapies only for minors and otherwise permit therapists to discuss these therapies with patients, may also be narrowly tailored to further the state's interest.

Thus, governments are not flatly forbidden from regulating professional communications any time a constitutional right is implicated in the discussion. Rather, the contention is that the Free Speech Clause is implicated, and thus must be carefully addressed in such cases, owing to the possibility that the state is attempting to structure rights discourse or undermine the exercise of a constitutional right.

GOVERNMENTAL RIGHTS SPEECH

As noted earlier, governments and their officials also communicate about constitutional rights. They do so through laws and official pronouncements, as well as through the official statements of individual government actors. Laws banning same-sex marriage, protecting religious freedoms, and prohibiting government funds from being used to fund speech advocating abortion are all examples of governmental rights speech. The concept or principle of "government speech" is relatively new to Free Speech Clause doctrine, and it is still developing in and outside the courts. This final section examines the current scope and potential limits of governmental communications about or concerning constitutional rights, with a special emphasis on what, if any, function the Free Speech Clause might perform in this regard.

Government Speech and Constitutional Rights

Governments are broadly empowered to communicate with regard to policies, programs, and other matters of public concern. Through laws, policies, and other means, they adopt and communicate positions regarding the health effects of smoking, the importance of access to healthcare, and other matters relating to the public welfare. None of these communications relate to constitutional rights or typically raise any constitutional concerns.

Governments and officials also communicate with regard to a wide variety of constitutional rights. Through what has been referred to as "expressive lawmaking," governments communicate official thoughts, ideas, and beliefs about or concerning constitutional rights such as equality, privacy, religious freedom, the right to bear arms, and other rights.[71] These communications are part of the general category of "government rights speech."

We have already examined some of the basic Free Speech Clause rules for regulating private speech. For instance, content-based regulations are subject to a strict and demanding form of scrutiny, while content-neutral regulations survive if they meet a lesser standard. It is also well-established that when government subsidizes rather than regulates speech, it may exercise relatively broad control over the messages conveyed with taxpayer funds. However, it may not discriminate based on viewpoint.[72]

However, when the government conveys its own point of view—that is, acts *as a speaker*—it is not required to subsidize content and viewpoints that are inconsistent with its own. Thus, if the government provides family planning funds in order to convey a pro-life message, it is not required to fund communications that advocate or prescribe abortion. Indeed, the Supreme Court has held that when the government acts as a speaker, it is not required to comply with any of the ordinary First Amendment rules—including, most importantly, the requirement that it not discriminate based on content.[73] As speakers, governments and officials can reject private viewpoints, including those about or concerning constitutional rights, that conflict with their own or with which they disagree.[74]

The Supreme Court has not been very clear about when, or in what circumstances, the government is indeed acting as a speaker—as opposed to a regulator of private speech or a subsidizer of speech. These are obviously critical distinctions, since they establish the constitutional rules under which the government's actions are reviewed. Application of the government speech principle not only allows governments to affirmatively weigh in on constitutional issues. It also potentially allows governments to restrict private rights speech and immunize a form of official viewpoint discrimination with regard to constitutional rights. In other words, as speakers, governments can significantly affect both rights discourse and the exercise of constitutional rights.

For example, as discussed in Chapter 5, government speech about equality rights has had a profound impact on constitutional equality movements. Through racial apartheid and anti-LGBT enactments, government officials and institutions have expressed strongly negative viewpoints regarding racial and sexual orientation equality. These laws and official policies significantly affected discourse about equal protection and delayed or denied equal protection for millions of Americans. As discussed earlier, governments have communicated pro-life views through mandatory abortion disclosures and spending conditions. These expressive laws are at least partially intended to persuade women not to exercise a constitutional right.

Of course, not all governmental rights speech seeks to deter or prevent the exercise of constitutional rights. As speakers, governments and officials also communicate for the purpose of stressing the importance of access to abortion, extolling the fundamental nature of the right to bear arms, and emphasizing the need to preserve and protect the free exercise of religion. Along with private rights speech and professional rights speech, these official communications are a critically important part of our constitutional rights discourse.

Constitutional Limits on Governmental Rights Speech

One of the things that remains frustratingly unclear with regard to government speech is whether there are any constitutional limits on such communications. There are several possibilities. However, consistent with the general focus of the book, my central concern is whether the Free Speech Clause itself might limit or restrict some governmental rights speech.

The Constitution's text, Supreme Court precedents, and constitutional scholarship suggest a few potential limits on governmental rights speech. The Ninth Amendment prohibits governmental "disparage[ment]" of un-enumerated rights (rights not listed in the Bill of Rights, for example).[75] However, it is not clear that "disparagement" includes official communications that denigrate or disfavor constitutional rights. The Supreme Court has also indicated that government speech is limited by the Establishment Clause, which requires that governments remain neutral with regard to religion and not endorse particular religious sects or creeds.[76] This may limit certain governmental communications about religion or Free Exercise Clause rights. Further, as it has been interpreted by the Supreme Court, the Due Process Clause limits the extent to which government can communicate for the purpose of persuading a woman not to obtain an abortion. Although government may communicate (or fund communication of) moral and other objections to abortion, it may not *coerce* a woman or effectively deny her the right to choose.[77] Finally, with regard specifically to governmental speech about or concerning equal protection, some scholars have posited that the Fifth and Fourteenth Amendments limit governmental communications that disparage persons or convey official support for unequal treatment under law.[78]

Of more specific concern, some scholars have suggested that the Free Speech Clause may function as a partial limit on government speech.[79] For example, Professor Michael Dorf has argued that some denials of equality impose distinct *expressive* harms on individuals.[80] He contends that part of the harm in discriminatory laws and regulations inheres in the *coercion* of private speech.[81] Thus, Professor Dorf posits a law requiring that all non-heterosexuals wear a visible pink triangle in public places.[82] As he notes, the harm produced by such a law is partly expressive—it compels the wearer to self-identify as non-heterosexual and communicates an "unmistakable message of second-class citizenship."[83] However, Dorf ultimately concludes that the infirmity in such laws is only partially rooted in First Amendment compelled-speech concerns.[84] He observes that the primary harm visited upon gays and lesbians relates to the Equal Protection Clause—the imposition of second-class status owing exclusively to their non-heterosexuality.[85]

Professor Nelson Tebbe more fully embraces the Free Speech Clause as a possible limit on certain forms of governmental rights speech. Tebbe suggests that the Free Speech Clause is a direct restraint or limitation on at least some governmental communications about or concerning constitutional rights. In brief, he argues that a principle of "nonendorsement" cuts across constitutional rights.[86] The nonendorsement principle, which is based in part on Free Speech Clause concerns, prohibits government from denying full and equal citizenship to all persons.[87] Professor Tebbe contends that at least some free speech theorists would likely condemn racialized government speech on the ground that it distorts democratic discourse.[88] Under the nonendorsement principle, Tebbe observes, this kind of government speech "can constitute speakers as disregarded or disabled participants in political life."[89] Professor Tebbe claims that this affects fundamental First Amendment rights relating "to participation in the political community, including the freedom of expression."[90]

Tebbe, like Dorf, argues that equal protection is the most important constitutional limitation on anti-gay government speech. However, he also acknowledges that the "constitutional harm worked by [same-sex marriage bans] could be seen as expressive, at least in part."[91] Thus, Tebbe writes that "excluding same-sex couples from civil marriage sends an impermissible signal that their unions are not morally valued."[92] Although he ultimately grounds his nonendorsement objection to marriage bans in equal protection, Tebbe allows that "[f]ree speech could be implicated as well, insofar as members of same-sex couples are prevented from sending the message that they are married in the fullest sense or are otherwise silenced."[93] Tebbe frames the central question this way: "Under what circumstances will constitutional law refuse the community's desire to express its values in the name of healthy deliberation itself?"[94] When, in other words, can government speech be "interrupted," on the ground that it is harming democratic deliberation and freedom of expression?[95]

In these scholars' accounts, the Free Speech Clause appears to be a partial, if somewhat uncertain, substantive limit on certain types of governmental rights speech.

Under their approaches, governmental rights speech that inflicts serious harm, interferes with the exercise of constitutional rights, or harms democratic deliberation might be subject to Free Speech Clause scrutiny and limits.

Note, however, that neither Dorf nor Tebbe fully embraces the Free Speech Clause as a limitation on governmental speech about rights. Their ambivalence likely stems, in part, from the fact that governments frequently communicate with respect to and even "endorse" positions relating to constitutional rights. Thus, constraining governmental rights speech under the Free Speech Clause could broadly inhibit officials from participating in rights discourse. As other scholars have observed, governments are important participants in public discourse about matters of public concern—including constitutional rights.[96] Governments can and do perform some affirmative functions in the marketplace of ideas about rights. For example, they enhance and facilitate conversations about the moral and social underpinnings of constitutional rights, and educate citizens about the nature and scope of constitutional rights.

On this view, the state *ought* to be permitted to publicly express its views regarding contested rights such as abortion, religious liberty, equal protection, and the right to bear arms. Governmental rights speech can facilitate a more pluralistic rights discourse. What is more, some of the reasons for supporting robust governmental participation in this discourse are based on Free Speech Clause principles and values.[97] Governmental rights speech contributes to the marketplace in ideas and facilitates self-government by adding public discourse on public policy and public rights. On this view, the Free Speech Clause ought not to limit governmental rights speech, but be interpreted to affirmatively support it.

Insofar as they suggest that the Free Speech Clause itself perform a limiting function with regard to official communications concerning constitutional rights, Dorf and Tebbe may be asking the Free Speech Clause to do too much, or indeed the wrong kind of, work. Instead, limits on governmental rights speech, whether it denigrates equal protection, favors religion, or coerces women not to exercise the abortion right, ought to come from two primary sources. First, such communications may offend and violate a non-speech substantive right. The Equal Protection Clause, the Establishment Clause, and the Due Process Clause may already impose limits on governmental speech about or concerning constitutional rights. Rather than look to the Free Speech Clause as a limit, we ought to rely upon these and other non-speech rights as constraints on governmental rights speech. The first line of defense against disparaging or discouraging governmental rights speech ought to be the substantive rights the government seeks to disparage or discourage.

Second, litigants, courts, and scholars need to think more carefully about the definition and scope of the government speech principle. It is clear that we need to develop clearer standards about when and whether the government is indeed speaking, as opposed to regulating or subsidizing private speech about rights. Among other things, these distinctions are critically important to ensuring that wholesale suppression of private rights speech cannot be defended on government speech grounds. The doctrine or principle of government speech ought also to require that governmental rights speech, in particular communications that disparage individuals or discourage the exercise of rights, be clearly conveyed and closely identified with government. This clarity and transparency will allow citizens to better identify official communications about constitutional rights and hold their representatives accountable for them.

In sum, we ought to rely on substantive non-speech protections and a more limited and constrained government speech principle to address the harms inflicted by certain kinds of governmental rights speech. Official communications about constitutional rights are a legitimate and important part of constitutional rights discourse. However, the government is a uniquely powerful speaker in the marketplace. It has the capacity to communicate with the broadest audiences and access to a range of powers that can inhibit both discourse about rights and the effective exercise and enjoyment of rights. To preserve the Free Speech Clause's facilitative and mediating functions with respect to rights, we need to develop and assert substantive non-speech rights defenses to official communications and limit the principle or doctrine of government speech itself.[98]

Conclusion

Three different kinds of speakers—private, professional, and governmental—actively participate in ideological, informational, and consultative discourse about constitutional rights. Regulation of private rights speech implicates the central values and justifications of the Free Speech Clause and affects the exercise of the subject constitutional rights. Professional consultations relating to constitutional rights raise similar concerns. Finally, governmental rights speech that disparages individuals or discourages them from exercising constitutional rights implicates both free speech and non-speech concerns.

Private, professional, and governmental rights speech are all part of a broad discourse about constitutional rights. However, thus far courts have not applied the Free Speech Clause with any vigor or consistency to private and professional rights speech. Indeed, in these areas, courts often fail to recognize or identify rights speech concerns at all. Yet seemingly neutral public order, public resource, and public records laws can significantly impact constitutional rights discourse. So too with professional licensure schemes, which some courts have interpreted to grant officials near-plenary authority to regulate even professional speech that relates to or concerns constitutional rights. With regard to governmental rights speech, the Supreme Court has so far merely hinted at some constitutional limits. Insofar as the Constitution is concerned, it is not clear whether governmental rights speech is subject to any limits at all.

The Free Speech Clause must continue to perform its central function of ensuring that conversations about or concerning constitutional rights are as robust and wide open as possible. This will require that courts pay closer attention to the manner in which certain speech restrictions or mandates implicate rights discourse. Properly contextualized, regulations of private and professional rights speech ought to be subject to meaningful free speech scrutiny.

Governmental rights speech raises distinct complications. Although the Free Speech Clause is certainly relevant to the consideration of how governments communicate about constitutional rights, it asks too much of the Free Speech Clause to function as a formal limit on governmental rights speech. We ought not to discourage governments from communicating about rights. However, we ought to limit their influence in the democratic processes in which rights are discussed, interpreted, and exercised. The proper means for doing so are to enforce non-speech rights limitations and clarify the scope and substance of the government speech principle.

3

ASSEMBLY, PRESS, AND PETITION

THIS CHAPTER BEGINS the examination of specific relationships between the Free Speech Clause and non-speech constitutional guarantees. We start with three rights provisions that are close textual neighbors or cousins of the Free Speech Clause—the Assembly Clause, Press Clause, and Petition Clause. As Professor Michael McConnell has observed, despite the fact that the First Amendment contains these several distinctive rights provisions, "in recent decades, the Supreme Court has tended to collapse the various expressive freedoms of the First Amendment . . . into an undifferentiated 'freedom of expression,' or more often, simply 'freedom of speech.' "[1] Under this approach, the Free Speech Clause has subordinated and largely supplanted its close First Amendment cousins. As explained in the Introduction, this treatment partially accounts for the book's focus on the Free Speech Clause, rather than on the broader category of "expressive" rights. The fact that these four rights provisions are often treated as parts of a fictional "Free Expression Clause," or as merely ancillary to freedom of speech, is a notable manifestation of the Free Speech Clause's sweeping character.

Although assembly, press, and petition *activities* have all played pivotal roles in terms of the recognition, interpretation, and enforcement of non-speech rights—including the rights discussed in subsequent chapters—the Free Speech Clause has received the bulk of attention and corresponding credit. To be sure, there are still

The Dynamic Free Speech Clause. Timothy Zick.

references to the "right to assemble," "freedom of the press," and "petitioning" government in judicial decisions, scholarship, and public discourse. However, by and large, the "expressive rights" formulation is pervasive, and freedom of speech now stands in for the larger group of First Amendment rights. This dominance is evident even in public opinion polling. Insofar as they are able to name any First Amendment right, by a very wide margin Americans are able to identify only the freedom of speech.

The chapter primarily addresses two aspects of the phenomenon of free speech expansionism as it relates to these distinct but related rights. First, how and why did it come to pass that the Free Speech Clause subordinated *all three* of the textually distinctive rights of assembly, press, and petition? What dynamic events and influences produced the "Free Expression Clause"? Was the process the same for all of the subordinated provisions, or were the relational dynamics different? Second, the chapter considers whether it might be possible to disaggregate the "Free Expression Clause" and recombine its component rights in ways that are more synergistic and mutually facilitative. Scholars have offered specific proposals for recovering, reviving, or rediscovering the Assembly, Press, and Petition Clauses.[2] That is an important and necessary starting point. However, the chapter advances a concept of "First Amendment Pluralism" that re-connects the free speech, assembly, press, and Petition Clauses as distinct, yet cognate, rights provisions.

Early Interactions

As indicated in the Introduction, this book's primary focus with regard to free speech/non-speech rights relationships is on contemporary or modern dynamics. Specifically, the focus is on the period that begins with the "incorporation" of First Amendment and other rights against the states. Only after this occurred did these rights begin to play a more prominent role in America's constitutional democracy. However, as also suggested, early interactions can shed valuable light on the relationships between and sometimes among constitutional guarantees. Thus, we ought to pay at least some attention to the framing and Reconstruction Era dynamics that formally placed free speech and non-speech rights in proximity to one another.

FRAMING FIRST AMENDMENT RIGHTS

As First Amendment scholars have observed, the records relating to the First Amendment's ratification are sparse.[3] We have relatively little in the way of contemporaneous records concerning what those who framed and ratified the First

Amendment specifically understood the freedoms of speech, assembly, press, and petition to mean. Nor is it clear how the founders understood these rights to relate to one another. However, that is not the same as saying we have no sense at all of how these rights were generally understood, or of their relationships in these early years. Indeed, scholars continue to produce interesting findings and theories in this regard.[4]

We do know that when considering the specific language to use in the text of the First Amendment, the framers borrowed heavily from early state constitutions. Of these state constitutions, only Pennsylvania's referred to both free press and free speech rights.[5] The other state constitutions expressly provided for free press protections, but not for a separate and distinct freedom of speech. All of the state constitutions provided for petition rights, and most also made some provision for the right to assemble. Typically, assembly and petition appeared together in the text of these early state documents. Among other things, this early history suggests that had the Virginia ratifying convention used its own constitution rather than the Pennsylvania model when it proposed its plan for the Bill of Rights, the Free Speech Clause would likely not have been included.[6]

In constructing the language of the First Amendment, the framers also looked to early English practices for guidance. One possible reason for the absence of explicit free speech provisions is that at the time of the framing, assembly, press, and petition all had more venerable pedigrees than did the right to free speech. The right to petition was the oldest in the group. Rights of assembly and press were also common in early English traditions and practices. Freedom of speech was not new, at least not in the sense that British and early American citizens had not heard of, practiced, or explicitly defended the right. However, at the time the First Amendment was framed and ratified, freedom of speech may have been conceptually underdeveloped relative to assembly, press, and petition.[7] It is one of the ironies of the early history that freedom of speech, which has come to subordinate neighboring expressive rights provisions, was neither the oldest nor the most venerated of the First Amendment's rights.

Indeed, some scholars have interpreted the original materials to suggest that the Free Speech Clause was either an afterthought, or was originally thought to be subsumed under the Press Clause. As Professor David Anderson has observed: "Freedom of the press—not freedom of speech—was the primary concern of the generation that wrote the Declaration of Independence, the Constitution, and the Bill of Rights."[8] Anderson claims that freedom of speech was a late addition to the pantheon of rights, whereas freedom of the press occupied a central positon from the very beginning. Similarly, Professor Leonard Levy has claimed that freedom of speech "developed as an offshoot of freedom of the press, on the one hand, and on the other, freedom of religion—the freedom to speak openly on religious matters."[9] However, this is not a uniform interpretation of the early relationship between free speech and free press. Other scholars, examining the same materials, have concluded that it was the freedom of speech that actually birthed freedom of the press. For example, David Lange has argued that freedom of the press "evolved as an extension or amplifier of the freedom of speech."[10]

One of the things that complicates efforts to construct the early relationships between and among what would become the First Amendment's "expressive" clauses is that the framers often used "freedom of the press" and "freedom of speech" interchangeably. This has led scholars to conclude that, whichever right was prior, the two rights overlapped or may have even been coterminous with one another.[11]

Scholars continue to examine the early understanding of "expressive rights." In a recent article, Professor Jud Campbell argues that the framing generation's understanding of the relationship between free press and free speech was significantly influenced by natural rights conceptions and discourse.[12] Campbell claims that "the Speech and Press Clauses were originally rooted in a broader Founding-Era discourse about natural rights" that generally treated the provisions not as redundant but as possessing "distinct meanings."[13] Professor Campbell contends that if we want to understand these meanings, we need to study the natural rights history of the First Amendment.

Framing-era discourse also considered the freedom of speech relative to the right of assembly. The history of active assembly in the colonies and early states suggests that assembly rights may have occupied a place more central to the hearts, minds, and lived experiences of framing-era Americans.[14] However, other commentators claim that owing to the long history of the right to petition government for redress of grievances, freedom of speech may have been an offshoot of the petition right.[15]

In addition to having incomplete and conflicting accounts of how specific First Amendment dyads related to one another, we know next to nothing about why the drafting committee in the First Congress *combined* speech, assembly, press, and petition rights into a single amendment.[16] In the framing and ratification debates, these rights were often discussed together and sometimes, as in the case of freedom of speech and freedom of the press, used interchangeably. The New York ratifying convention was the first to propose a provision containing press, assembly, and petition—but not free speech—rights.[17] A separate Free Speech Clause was added later, but there is no existing record explaining why this was done. Nor is there any reported discussion of how the framers and ratifiers believed these rights provisions related to one another in form or substance.

Scholars actually differ as to whether one can answer these sorts of questions with any confidence. Professor David Anderson has suggested that we could attribute the combination of rights to Congress's recognition that the First Amendment, as proposed for ratification, was "a cluster of distinct but related rights, complementary means by which thought, belief, and expression are protected from governmental interference."[18] However, at the same time, Anderson warns against ascribing grand theories or motives to the framers and ratifiers of the First Amendment.[19]

Other scholars have posited some general connections between and among the First Amendment's speech, assembly, press, and petition provisions. Professor Akhil Amar, a leading authority on the Constitution's Bill of Rights, has offered an intratextual interpretation of the First Amendment's "expressive" rights. Amar claims that at the framing, rights of speech, assembly, press, and petition all served the central *structural* function of restraining the powers granted to the new central government.[20] Thus, both separately and in combination, these rights (along with rights relating to religious liberty) were considered to be crucial checks on the newly formed government. Majoritarian and collective rights to communicate, assemble, publish, and petition enabled ordinary citizens to resist various forms of governmental overreaching.

As an intratextualist, Professor Amar claims that the words and phrases of the First Amendment must be read in relation to one another. And he claims that once we realize that "freedom of the press," "the freedom of speech," and the other rights in the First Amendment are all informed by conceptions of popular sovereignty, it makes sense to treat them as guarantees with distinct meanings and functions but also as provisions concerned with a common cause or purpose. Professor Amar argues that as these rights were absorbed into the Bill of Rights from earlier (English and state) practices and traditions, their meanings were subtly, but critically, altered.[21] His interpretation suggests that First Amendment "expressive" rights are best understood as coordinate and cognate guarantees whose purpose was to facilitate popular sovereignty.

Framing-era events and influences indicate that the dynamics that produced speech, assembly, press, and petition rights involved English traditions, colonial practices, and natural rights discourse. However, the framing of the First Amendment raises as many questions as it answers, particularly with regard to how freedoms of speech, assembly, press, and petition were intended or understood to relate to one another.

For example, did the concept of free speech arise out of the press right, or vice versa? Did these provisions simply reflect or represent different kinds of "expressive rights," or were there important substantive distinctions among them? One thing that does seem clear, in hindsight, is that in the beginning the Free Speech Clause was not the central or subordinating provision that it would later become.[22] If there was a star during these proceedings, it was likely freedom of the press.[23] It is possible, as Professor Anderson and Professor Amar suggest, that what became the suite of rights in the First Amendment was intended to be a class of cognate and mutually reinforcing provisions. However, we must acknowledge the possibility that the framers simply had no preconceived notion of how First Amendment rights would relate to or intersect with one another, in substance or practice. As we know, these intersections have been worked out over time, as the various provisions have been invoked, exercised, adjudicated, and interpreted.

THE RECONSTRUCTED FIRST AMENDMENT

Whatever the intended original relationships between and among First Amendment rights were, it is important to consider whether post–Civil War reconstruction events and influences fundamentally altered them. Professor Amar contends that they did. He argues that Reconstruction Era dynamics altered the meanings and relationships of the First Amendment's speech, assembly, press, and petition provisions in meaningful ways.

As early as the end of the Civil War, it was evident that all of these "expressive" provisions were critically important to the process of constitutional change. Abolitionists and proponents of the Fourteenth Amendment invoked and relied upon all of them to advance their causes. Later, as free speech, assembly, press, and petition rights were absorbed through the Fourteenth Amendment's Due Process Clause and eventually made applicable against the states, their functions and meanings would change in other critical and lasting respects.

As noted earlier, Professor Akhil Amar has argued that the First Amendment's guarantees were originally intended as checks against an overreaching national government. As structural protections, the provisions primarily benefitted political majorities. However, as reconstructed, Amar argues that the Free Speech Clause and Press Clause were invoked and interpreted in ways that benefitted primarily *minority* speakers—Unionists, abolitionists, and freedmen. As Professor Amar has observed, these speakers were all "geographic, cultural, and ethnic *outsiders* who were critical of dominant social institutions and opinions."[24] Thus, as Amar observes, "[t]he new First-Fourteenth Amendment tradition is less majoritarian and more libertarian."[25]

Reconstruction and incorporation dynamics (including public debates, commentaries, judicial decisions, etc.) also altered public and private understandings of First Amendment assembly and petition rights. These were now similarly considered to be not *political* rights possessed by the privileged few (i.e., white males), but *civil* rights belonging to blacks, women, and others who were historically not considered full members of the political community.[26]

Thus, the reconstructed First Amendment—the one produced as a result of the dynamic intersection between the Fourteenth Amendment and "expressive" rights—resembled the one Americans have come to recognize. As the First Amendment's guarantees were incorporated against state and local governments, they began to take on the form of distinctive, but related, *individual* rights. These rights were enjoyed by every person, but were of particular value to minority speakers, social dissidents, and political outsiders. Abolitionists, Reconstruction Republicans, and others invoked these rights to achieve momentous constitutional and democratic changes.

Over the course of the next century, however, the Free Speech Clause would come to dominate and even supplant its First Amendment cousins. Instead of a suite of independent individual rights, the provisions of the First Amendment would collapse into a fictional "Free Expression Clause" or simply be treated as ancillary to the Free Speech Clause.

The "Free Expression Clause"

As the First Amendment's various clauses matured, the relationships between the Free Speech Clause and the Assembly Clause, Press Clause, and Petition Clause changed in drastic ways. The most notable change was that these rights generally collapsed into a "Free Expression Clause." Here is how Professor Ashutosh Bhagwat recently summarized the modern understanding of First Amendment speech, assembly, press, and petition rights:

> One noteworthy feature of the Supreme Court's modern First Amendment jurisprudence is that it is not truly a First Amendment jurisprudence at all; rather, it is a series of decisions interpreting the Religion Clauses and the Free Speech Clause. *The rest of the First Amendment—the Press, Assembly, and Petition Clauses—might as well not exist.* The Press Clause has not been addressed in over thirty years. The relevance of the Petition Clause has been limited to the peripheral issue of access to courts—and even in that sphere, a recent decision limits its independent significance. Even the nontextual right of association, which has not been entirely abandoned, has been made subservient to free speech, even though historically the right clearly derived from the Assembly Clause.[27]

As discussed in Chapter 4, Professor Bhagwat might well have added that in important respects, the Free Exercise Clause has also been subordinated to the Free Speech

Clause. In any event, few would likely dispute the accuracy of his description. We do not have a comprehensive and, perhaps more importantly, *comparative* account of how and why the Free Speech Clause came to subordinate its First Amendment cousins, and how the "Free Expression Clause" came into being.[28] This part of the chapter focuses on the dynamics that produced this seemingly contra-textual result. Understanding these dynamics will help explain how free speech expansionism occurs, and perhaps how to reverse some of its effects. It will also inform the prospects of a pluralist approach to the subject rights, which would first disaggregate and then reconnect the cognate provisions of the First Amendment.

THE INITIAL AND ENDURING ADVANTAGES OF THE FREE SPEECH CLAUSE

Before considering the clause-specific dynamics, I want to make some initial observations about the jurisprudential and intellectual advantages the Free Speech Clause has long enjoyed over its neighbors. Early judicial and scholarly accounts of the First Amendment privileged the Free Speech Clause and freedom of speech in ways that paved the way for the modern "Free Expression Clause." Modern conventions, including the manner in which courts and commentators have discussed First Amendment rights, have also contributed to the dominance of the free speech right.

It was not until the first quarter of the twentieth century that the First Amendment's "expressive" rights provisions received sustained attention from the Supreme Court and constitutional scholars. Before this, the rights were of course subjects of interest in judicial and academic quarters, as well as in public discourse more generally. However, at the dawn of the twentieth century, the First Amendment had yet to be fully "reconstructed" and incorporated. Its guarantees did not yet apply to the states, and courts and scholars had not yet advanced any convincing narrative of their respective meanings or relationships to one another. As noted earlier, the lack of ratification and other early materials elucidating the clauses undoubtedly contributed to the absence of such accounts.

At this point, the Free Speech Clause, like its neighboring First Amendment rights, was in its infancy. In some of the initial First Amendment cases to reach the Supreme Court, antiwar dissidents challenged the federal Espionage Act on First Amendment grounds. In those cases, the first group of which were decided in 1919, the Supreme Court sustained indictments based on communications that were critical of the war effort and advocated undermining it in certain respects.[29] The First Amendment claims in these cases were grounded not just in the Free Speech Clause, but sometimes in the Press Clause, the Assembly Clause, and/or the Petition Clause as well. No one right being at that time any further developed than the others, and the relative distinctions between these rights being unclear, litigants naturally invoked the panoply of First Amendment rights.

This was the Supreme Court's first opportunity to consider and develop the individual and perhaps relational particulars of the First Amendment's speech, press, assembly, and petition provisions. In addition to defining the substance of these distinct rights, the Court might have taken the opportunity to distinguish among them and even explain their relationship to one another. Instead, the Court primarily analyzed the early cases under a Free Speech Clause conception—"clear and present danger"—that focused on the content and potential consequences of a certain class or category of communication (as it would later come to be understood, words "inciting" others to unlawful action).[30]

As they debated its merits, the principal intellectual forces advocating and objecting to this standard—most notably, Justice Oliver Wendell Holmes, Jr., Justice Louis Brandeis, Professor Zechariah Chafee, and Judge Learned Hand—focused primarily on the content and effects of the speaker's *words*. To be sure, some of their intellectual forebears, including John Stuart Mill and John Milton, railed against censorship of both speaking and pamphlet printing.[31] Further, in some of the World War I cases, the speakers were engaged in what might be considered "press" activities—publishing and distributing information. This may account for why the justices sometimes referred to "free speech and press" together in some of the early cases.[32] However, although the defendants had peaceably assembled together and were also engaged in petitioning their governments for redress of grievances, these rights were essentially ignored.

Thus, it was speech—and in particular *the freedom of speech*—that occupied center stage from the very start. In his famous dissent in *Abrams v. United States*, which ushered in our modern Free Speech Clause, Justice Holmes first discussed the intent requirement under the Espionage Act and then moved on to what he described as "a more important aspect of the case. I refer to the First Amendment to the Constitution, that Congress shall make no law abridging the freedom of speech."[33] Thus, although the defendants were convicted of publishing and distributing pamphlets, activities covered by the Press Clause, Justice Holmes addressed only "the right to free speech."[34] His famous reference to the "marketplace in ideas" extolled the virtues of allowing speech and the expression of opinions, not the right to print and publish pamphlets, or to assemble with others for expressive or other purposes, or to petition government for redress of grievances.[35] Holmes's iconic dissent was fundamentally—indeed solely—concerned with the freedom of speech.

This does not mean, of course, that the Court or individual justices never cited other First Amendment clauses. In *Whitney v. California* (1927), which upheld the conviction of Anita Whitney for having served as a delegate to the 1919 organizing convention of the Communist Labor Party of California, the majority briefly considered and rejected Whitney's free speech *and assembly* claims. Justice Brandeis's concurrence, which Justice Holmes joined, referred to "free speech and assembly" no fewer than *eleven* separate times.[36] However, as is true of Holmes's dissent in *Abrams*, the passages the Brandeis concurrence are most famous for focus primarily upon the freedom of speech.[37]

The majority's framing of issues and the passages in these famous dissents plainly demonstrate the early influence—perhaps dominance is not too strong—of the Free Speech Clause and the concept of freedom of speech. Despite the fact that assembly, press, and less frequently petition rights received some honorable mentions, the Court's early decisions were then, as today, described and heralded as "free speech" precedents.[38] Indeed, the Court has itself described Justice Brandeis's *Whitney* concurrence as the "classic formulation" of the free speech right.[39] And this is how the influential dissents of Holmes and Brandeis have been, and continue to be, taught to generations of law students, future lawyers, and jurists. First Amendment casebooks generally present the Holmes and Brandeis dissents as steps on the road to the development of modern Free Speech Clause doctrine and theory, not as explications of early press, assembly, or petition rights.

These early decisions and their focus on free speech spawned an academic discipline devoted specifically to the Free Speech Clause and, to a lesser extent, "expressive" rights. Influential early theorists, including Alexander Meiklejohn, focused principally on the justifications for protecting the freedom of speech.[40] Meiklejohn's operative metaphor was the town hall meeting, a gathering that often involves peaceable assemblies that debate petitions for government redress and action. Nevertheless, Meiklejohn focused on the importance of free speech to voter education and effective exercise of the franchise.

Other prominent theorists similarly focused on the Free Speech Clause, freedom of speech, or "expressive" rights. Thomas Emerson's influential treatise, *The System of Freedom of Expression* (1971), devoted attention to speech, assembly, press, and petition, but it was primarily concerned with free speech—its exercise, justifications, and relationship to democratic governance.[41] Emerson was an early adopter of the phrase "freedom of expression," which collapses or aggregates speech, assembly, press, and petition rights into a conception primarily concerned with freedom of communication. Like Meiklejohn's seminal work, Emerson's theoretical contributions were principally concerned with describing, explaining, and justifying the freedom of speech.

During this formative period, nothing approaching this kind or degree of energy was devoted to explicating assembly, press, or petition rights. From the start, then, the Free Speech Clause and the freedom of speech exerted special influence on judicial, scholarly, and public attitudes and understandings of the First Amendment. Early treatments cast a considerable free speech shadow over rights to assembly, press, and petition. As we will see, owing to other events, this shading would later become a virtual eclipse.

Why might early jurists and thinkers have gravitated toward the Free Speech Clause and the concept of free speech? As discussed earlier, the adoption and ratification materials offered little guidance concerning the substance of, much less the relationship between and among, the First Amendment's clauses. Both before and after the Reconstruction Era, "freedom of speech" was an effective rallying cry for dissident and minority speakers. Courts and scholars, being generally free to choose where to focus their energies, continued to devote special attention to the Free Speech Clause in the World War I and postwar periods. Further, activists, litigants, judges, and scholars likely all viewed the Free Speech Clause and freedom of speech as rhetorically and otherwise useful rubrics for resisting governmental oppression and protecting dissident voices and ideologies. Thus, as we will later see, the Free Speech Clause offered a basis for the Court to rule in favor of Jehovah's Witnesses without granting them "special" free exercise rights, to facilitate civil rights and race equality through the recognition and enforcement of basic speech rights possessed by all, and to protect the institutional press without granting it any special rights. In sum, as one scholar has observed, "free speech arrived on the national stage when and how it did because the *idea* of free speech provided a malleable and culturally resonant solution to the most pressing concerns of the era."[42]

Finally, at the outset, we ought also to take note of certain conventions regarding invocation and discussion of First Amendment rights, particularly although not exclusively in the courts. First, from the beginning and continuing today, the Supreme Court rarely invokes these rights with reference to formal clauses—the Free Speech Clause, Assembly Clause, Press Clause, etc. More typically, the Court writes in general terms about "freedom of speech," "the right of assembly," "freedom of the press," and "the right to petition"—or simply "the First Amendment." One reason this book uses the more formal clause designations is to emphasize that they are in fact separate and distinct *textual* provisions, with presumptively independent meaning and significance.

Second, the Court's textual approach is indicative of a certain nonchalance or even carelessness when it comes to First Amendment rights. The Court has often been reluctant or unwilling to spell out in explicit terms which of the First Amendment's guarantees is actually doing the work in its decisions. This was true in the World War I cases, where "free speech and press" were sometimes invoked. Stated bluntly, the Court has often seemed to be fudging matters by refusing to explicitly distinguish between or among the First Amendment rights it is enforcing or interpreting. For their part, scholars have often followed suit, lumping the First Amendment's "expressive" guarantees together or exhibiting a similarly cavalier attitude about which clause or clauses are being discussed or constructed.[43]

Before considering in more specific terms the dynamics that resulted in the subordination of the Assembly Clause, Press Clause, and Petition Clause, we ought to appreciate the critical head start the Free Speech Clause and freedom of speech received. Although assembly, press, and petition rights have been, and continue to be, critically important to American constitutional democracy, for much of our history there has been a disproportionate focus on the Free Speech Clause, freedom of speech, and "expressive" rights. As noted, there is some irony in this, particularly when one considers the rather humble and arguably subordinate position the Free Speech Clause occupied at the framing of the Bill of Rights.

THE ASSEMBLY CLAUSE

As discussed, many early state constitutions expressly protected the right of peaceable assembly. In modern First Amendment jurisprudence, the Assembly Clause has only occasionally received significant attention. As noted earlier, the right was repeatedly invoked, alongside the freedom of speech, in Justice Brandeis's concurrence in *Whitney v. California* (1927).

Thereafter, the assembly right did remain in the national and international spotlights to some extent. The right of assembly, again in conjunction with the freedom of speech, also provided critical aid to the Civil Rights Movement. However, after the civil rights era, the Assembly Clause and the right of assembly largely faded from First Amendment jurisprudence, scholarly works, and public discourse. Litigants turned increasingly to the Free Speech Clause, even in cases involving collective activities that fit more comfortably within the history and language of the Assembly Clause. Ultimately, the assembly right was transformed—first into the right of "association," and later into the right of "expressive association." This transformation, which was complete by the 1980s, subordinated the right of peaceable assembly to the Free Speech Clause and situated it within the "Free Expression Clause."

The dynamics that brought about the transformation from assembly to association, and the Assembly Clause's eventual collapse into the Free Expression Clause, occurred over the course of several decades. They involved many different influences and institutions, including of course the Supreme Court. Professor John Inazu, a leading authority on the Assembly Clause, has published a comprehensive account of the clause's history and contemporary meaning.[44] My account of the dynamics between the Free Speech Clause and the Assembly Clause draws liberally from Inazu's study.

As Professor Inazu and others have observed, the Assembly Clause's initial entanglement with neighboring rights did not involve the Free Speech Clause but rather the Petition Clause. The First Amendment protects "the right of the people peaceably to assemble, and to petition the government for a redress of grievances." One interpretation of this language is that it creates a narrow right to assemble, for the specific purpose of presenting petitions to government. By the end of the nineteenth century, the Supreme Court had indicated support for this interpretation.[45] Some scholars also adopted this narrow interpretation of the Assembly Clause.[46] Of course, if the Assembly Clause was indeed tethered to the Petition Clause in this way, its scope would be drastically limited—not only because it would be limited to petitioning activity but also, as we will see, owing to the narrowing of the Petition Clause itself.

Professor Inazu persuasively argues that this interpretation of the Assembly Clause is erroneous. It ignores critical drafting details and, more importantly, a historical record that clearly demonstrates that the framers and ratifiers of the First Amendment understood the right to peaceably assemble in far broader terms.[47] In these respects, the Supreme Court's treatment of the Assembly Clause is an example of the cavalier manner in which the discrete clauses of the First Amendment have been lumped together or aggregated in ways that limit their meaning and enforcement.

As it happens, the Court's narrow interpretation of the Assembly Clause did not entirely suppress the recognition and exercise of assembly rights.[48] Indeed, as Professor Inazu demonstrates, throughout the nineteenth and twentieth centuries, the right of assembly was frequently invoked and considered in American legal and political discourse. Religious organizations, abolitionists, suffragists, and union workers all explicitly relied on the right of assembly. Further, twentieth century Supreme Court decisions did not invariably follow the crabbed interpretation that merged the assembly and petition guarantees. Again, Justice Brandeis's famous *Whitney* concurrence relied extensively on both free speech *and* assembly.[49]

At the 1939 New York World's Fair, the right of assembly was feted as one of the Constitution's celebrated "Four Freedoms" (along with religion, speech, and press). Two years later, in his State of the Union address, President Roosevelt omitted assembly from his remarks addressing the "four essential human freedoms." However, as Inazu explains, the right of peaceable assembly continued to play a significant role in American politics and culture.[50]

Alas, the Assembly Clause managed to escape the textual snare of the Petition Clause only to be swallowed up by the Free Speech Clause. As Professor Inazu observes, by the end of the 1960s, "the right of assembly in law and politics was largely confined to protests and demonstrations."[51] And even in those contexts, Supreme Court decisions were being grounded in a developing free speech framework rather than a distinct doctrine of peaceable assembly. In other words, by the middle of the twentieth century, assemblies were formally protected not in their own right, but rather as a means of facilitating certain kinds of speech or expression. As Inazu observes, by the early 1980s, "the Court swept the remnants of assembly within the ambit of free speech law."[52]

In *Liberty's Refuge: The Forgotten Freedom of Assembly* (2012), Professor Inazu examines a variety of dynamics that led to the Assembly Clause's subordination to the Free Speech Clause. He explains how a new and un-enumerated constitutional right of *association* gradually replaced the right to assemble. Inazu also demonstrates that this right of association came to be based not on the Assembly Clause, but on the Free Speech Clause. The discussion that follows focuses on the principal highlights of this dynamic process.

As Professor Inazu explains, the Assembly Clause became a right of "expressive association" through a complex process that entailed, first, judicial recognition of a right of "association" and, second, a gradual linking of that right to Free Speech Clause principles.[53] This connection was forged over the course of two eras or periods, which Inazu refers to as the "national security era" (1940s–1960s) and the "equality era" (1960s–1980s).[54] In each of these eras, political, jurisprudential, and theoretical factors shaped the right of association and ultimately merged it into the Free Speech Clause.

During the 1930s, the Supreme Court "incorporated" or applied the Free Speech Clause and the Assembly Clause to the states. At that critical point, the Court described the right of assembly as a "right *cognate to* those of free speech and free press and . . . equally fundamental."[55] In *NAACP v. Alabama* (1958), the decision that first recognized an independent "right of association," the Court grounded the new right in *both* the freedom of speech and the right of assembly.[56] Although it was based in part on assembly principles and precedents, the right of association extended only to collective action "for the advancement of beliefs and ideas."[57] Thus, the association right seemed to be centrally based on free speech principles.[58]

Contemporaneous press accounts of the decision demonstrate a degree of confusion regarding the newly recognized right.[59] In subsequent cases, the Court offered little clarification. It continued to link "association" with both freedom of speech and the right of peaceable assembly.[60] Some First Amendment scholars defined the right of association in terms of assembly, while others linked it to the Free Speech Clause and/or the Press Clause.[61] As Professor Inazu observes, owing in part to this uncertainty, the right of association was "more likely to be shaped by the intellectual context in which it emerged than by 'traditional constitutional doctrines.' "[62]

As the rights of association or expressive association were being debated in the courts and law reviews, pluralist political theories were gaining popularity. As Professor Inazu explains, these theories, which focused on achieving balance and harmony within American democracy, fostered a concept of association that emphasized stability and homogeneity in groups.[63] Lawyers and judges, including Supreme Court justices, were educated within and hence presumably influenced by this intellectual framework. Thus, over time, a right of association developed in which groups such as the NAACP, which supported democratic values such as equality, were protected but groups such as the Communist Party, which espoused views antithetical to democratic values, were not.[64] This forged a critical link between a group's expressive content and its enjoyment of collective "associational" rights.

During what Inazu calls the "civil rights era," the Free Speech Clause crept further into the picture. As Professor Inazu explains, the continuation of this dynamic process during what he calls the "equality era" also had political, jurisprudential, and theoretical dimensions.

Politically, the primary issue was whether associational rights could justify various forms of private discrimination against African Americans.[65] This political clash produced precedents in which the Court was obliged to explain the limits of constitutional exclusion. In doing so, it sometimes focused on the *expressive* harm—or lack of it—to groups wishing to exclude African Americans from commercial, social, and educational institutions.

For example, in *Runyon v. McCrary* (1976), the Court construed the Civil Rights Act of 1866 to prohibit racial discrimination in private, commercially operated, nonsectarian schools.[66] Part of the Court's reasoning was that the compelled inclusion of African-American students would not affect the schools' teaching or otherwise affect its ability to communicate ideas and beliefs.[67] These, of course, are classic free speech concerns. Meanwhile, in the seemingly very distant area of reproductive rights, some justices had articulated a new (and similarly un-enumerated) "right to privacy." Under this right, associations were treated as forms or means of expression. Here, too, protection for association was considered valuable mostly or solely to the extent that it facilitated *expressive* freedoms.[68]

As Inazu explains, during the 1970s, Rawlsian liberalism, which was based on premises of stability, consensus, and public reason, led to the development of a right of association "conditioned by equality, self-respect, and other liberal values."[69] According to this iteration of the right of association, illiberal groups did not have full associational autonomy. Thus, their right to exclude was subject to certain limits. And again, those limits were primarily defined in expressive terms.

In *Roberts v. United States Jaycees* (1984), for example, the Supreme Court divided the right of association into "intimate" (privacy-based) association and expressive (free-speech-based) association.[70] It held that Minnesota's anti-discrimination law, which compelled the Jaycees to accept women as full voting members, did not violate the Jaycees' right of "expressive association" because the compelled inclusion would not "impede the organization's ability to engage in . . . protected activities or to *disseminate its preferred views*."[71] After *Roberts*, non-intimate groups that were unable to demonstrate they were "expressive" simply failed to qualify for protection under the First Amendment right of association. In other words, with regard to the right of association, *Roberts* and other precedents defined a free speech criterion—expressiveness—as a condition of coverage.

The Supreme Court also made some other doctrinal moves that would seal the fate of the Assembly Clause and render it ancillary to the Free Speech Clause. *Roberts* applied a standard of review, based on "compelling state interests unrelated to the suppression of ideas," that closely tracked the strict scrutiny standard applicable to content-based speech restrictions.[72] In a subsequent case, the Court clarified that a group wishing to maintain a right of association claim must demonstrate that it was "organized for specific expressive purposes" and that it "will not be able to advocate its desired viewpoints nearly as effectively if it cannot confine its membership."[73]

Evidence of the full extent of free speech subordination has come in more recent cases. Thus, in *Christian Legal Society v. Martinez* (2010), the Court "merged" the free speech and association claims of a Christian group that challenged a public law school's requirement that it take "all comers"—including those who did not share its religiously-based commitments—in order to obtain certain school benefits.[74] The Court declined to separately analyze the group's "expressive association" claim, concluding that it was essentially duplicative of its free speech claim.

An important part of the dynamic that is missing from Professor Inazu's account relates to the advantages the Free Speech Clause enjoyed as a result of judicial precedents and scholarly conventions elevating the early status of the freedom of speech. Inazu's account shows how the development of a right of association, and a right to privacy, eventually produced a right of "expressive association." But why make "voice" or expression so central to the new right? After all, it seems obvious that not all assemblies or associations exist for the purpose of conveying messages or viewpoints.[75] For example, many social clubs do not seek to convey discernible "viewpoints" or "messages" to the public. The right of "peaceable assembly" might just as well be considered a freestanding right to assemble for *any* lawful purpose, without regard to communication or expression.

The Free Speech Clause's early jurisprudential and intellectual advantages made the turn to expression more likely. The Free Speech Clause was textually capacious enough to serve as a kind of umbrella guarantee for assembly rights. Beginning with the World War I cases and proceeding through the Hughes Court era of the 1930s and 1940s, the Supreme Court consistently manifested a preference for free speech principles and doctrinal frameworks. Even before the national security and equality eras Inazu identifies, the Free Speech Clause had become a constitutional, political, and social superstar—first among putative equals in the realm of First Amendment rights.

By the 1980s, when the Supreme Court recognized a right of "expressive association," the Free Speech Clause had already been used to provide expansive protection for minority and dissident *speakers* for decades. It was not much of a stretch to apply the same principles to minority and dissident *groups*. Moreover, by this time Free Speech Clause doctrines, standards of review, and principles had significantly matured, particularly relative to other "expressive" rights—including the assembly right, which had for a time been tied to the Petition Clause and thereafter was only intermittently invoked. It likely seemed a logical next step to apply free speech principles and rights to collective activities.

In the speech-saturated political and cultural eras that birthed the right of association, focusing on voice and official viewpoint suppression made considerable jurisprudential sense. The expressive association idea afforded collective protections that essentially mirrored those enjoyed by individuals under the Free Speech Clause. The concept of "expressive association" recognized the value in collective action, but limited the scope of the right to protection for group voices and viewpoints. The new right relied on existing free speech principles such as speaker autonomy, viewpoint neutrality, and public forum doctrine. These building blocks were readily at hand. In short, owing in part to its early advantages and subsequent maturation, the Free Speech Clause provided a familiar framework for other First Amendment rights.

As Professor Inazu's account shows, the dynamics through which the Free Speech Clause effectively supplanted the Assembly Clause were varied and complex. They involved an initial entanglement with the Petition Clause, a transformation of assembly into association, and finally an effective surrender to the Free Speech Clause in the form of a right to "expressive association."

THE PRESS CLAUSE

The story of the Press Clause's intersection with the Free Speech Clause shares some similarities with the Assembly Clause narrative. The Supreme Court has not based a decision solely on the Press Clause in more than three decades.[76] Like the Assembly Clause, the Court has generally interpreted the Press Clause as ancillary to the Free Speech Clause and as one of the collection of First Amendment "expressive" rights.

It has stated on many occasions that the Press Clause grants the so-called "institutional" press—reporters, the media, etc.—no greater rights than those enjoyed by other speakers under the Free Speech Clause.[77]

This is a long and rather hard fall from grace. As discussed earlier, during the framing and ratification periods, the Press Clause was arguably deemed the most important among the First Amendment's "expressive" guarantees.[78] All state constitutions provided for a free press right, while only one contained a distinct free speech provision. The subject of prior restraints and licensure of printing presses was a central focus of discourse surrounding the Press Clause. Nevertheless, despite this early treatment and the obvious importance of a free press to American democracy, the Press Clause has all but disappeared from judicial decisions. That does not mean, of course, that the institutional press is unable to function or that it does not benefit from laws and customs that facilitate its activities. However, as one commentator observed, "as a matter of positive law, the Press Clause actually plays a rather minor role in protecting the freedom of the press."[79]

The dynamics that led to the Press Clause's subordination to the Free Speech Clause and general "expressive" principles spanned decades. As discussed earlier, during the World War I era, litigants challenging the Espionage Act and other laws restricting political dissent frequently invoked both the Press Clause and Free Speech Clause (and sometimes the Assembly Clause as well). Although free press and free speech rights would sometimes be mentioned together in published decisions, the Supreme Court did not attempt to distinguish between them in the World War I cases or in other early engagements with the First Amendment. The Court did not develop any freestanding Press Clause jurisprudence, choosing instead to follow the guidance offered by the Free Speech Clause.

As discussed further in Chapter 4, this pattern would continue during subsequent phases of the First Amendment's development. Thus, during the 1930s and 1940s, Jehovah's Witnesses invoked the Free Speech Clause, the Press Clause, the Assembly Clause, *and* the Free Exercise Clause in a legal campaign against state and local restrictions on public proselytizing. However, as we will see, the Hughes Court did not articulate distinctive coverages or doctrines relating to any of these rights. As it had in the World War I cases, the Court preferred to articulate holdings and rationales in Free Speech Clause terms.

Prominent First Amendment commentators may have played an important role in stunting the initial growth and development of the Press Clause. Blackstone wrote in his famous *Commentaries* that freedom of the press was limited to "laying no previous restraints upon publication, and not in freedom from censure for criminal matter when published."[80] Dean Leonard Levy's influential work agreed that the early history supported a narrow interpretation of the Press Clause, one that was limited to prohibiting licensing and other "prior restraints" on publication.[81] At the beginning of the twentieth century, the Supreme Court expressed support for this narrow interpretation.[82]

The Court never formally adopted Blackstone's interpretation of the press guarantee. One reason for this might be that some mid-twentieth-century scholarship challenged his and others' narrow interpretation. For example, Professor Zechariah Chafee suggested that the press guarantee provided at least some degree of protection to already published materials.[83] However, even Chafee's bottom line conclusion, which was shared by other scholars of the era, was that whatever its scope, the Press Clause was essentially interchangeable with the Free Speech Clause—as Chafee put it, the clauses "appear virtually to coincide as legal concepts."[84] Chafee's interpretation relied, in part, on the work of earlier commentators, who had reached essentially the same conclusion.[85]

Of course, as Dean Levy and others were quick to point out, the American people were free to adopt other interpretations of these provisions. After all, the First Amendment's framers and ratifiers did not have occasion to consider the constitutional status of a structured "press" or media enterprise such as existed by the mid-twentieth century. Nor, it appears, did they consider the relationship between free speech and free press. Outside the courts, then, it was possible to develop a social and cultural interpretation of the Press Clause that treated it as granting special status or rights to the institution or members of the press. However, the combination of Supreme Court decisions and Press Clause scholarship created a high bar to formally interpreting the press guarantee as a freestanding, broadly protective provision separate and apart from the Free Speech Clause.

As David Anderson has observed, the Press Clause did enjoy a "heyday" in the Supreme Court during the period from 1930s to the 1960s.[86] As noted earlier in the discussion of the Assembly Clause, it was during this period that President Roosevelt publicly touted freedom of the press as an essential constitutional freedom. As well, during the post–World War II era, the United States advocated the adoption of press freedoms in international charters and institutions.[87] Relatedly, during this same period, some Supreme Court decisions involving press claims, notably challenges to taxes imposed on the press, relied explicitly on the Press Clause.[88] In some later cases involving direct regulations of newspapers and other media entities, the Court similarly relied on the Press Clause without mentioning the Free Speech Clause or freedom of speech.[89] The Press Clause was most likely to be explicitly and separately relied upon when government taxed press institutions or directly regulated them.

However, even during the Press Clause's so-called "heyday," the Court did not develop any doctrines or principles specific to the Press Clause itself. It did not seem to matter whether the operative clause was the free speech or free press provision, since either seemingly would have sufficed as a ground for invalidating the laws under review. As evidence confirming this thesis, after it collapsed the free press and free speech rights in the mid-1970s, the Court retroactively *reinterpreted* these "Press Clause" cases as resting on free speech principles.[90]

Moreover, even during the Press Clause's "heyday," the Supreme Court began to collapse the Free Speech Clause and Press Clause, for example by referring to "free speech and free press" rights or sometimes simply to "freedom of expression."[91] In *New York Times v. Sullivan* (1964), the Court's iconic decision altering state civil libel rules to ensure breathing space for robust criticism of government, free speech and free press were invoked together and interchangeably.[92] In the mid-1970s, the Court handed down its last decision based exclusively on the Press Clause. Since then, it has either read the Free Speech Clause broadly enough to cover "press" claims or, when that has not been possible, it has rejected such claims.[93]

Despite their treatment as interchangeable provisions, subordinating the Press Clause to the Free Speech Clause in this manner was consequential. Freedom of speech generally requires that governments remain neutral with regard to the identity of the speakers it regulates and the content of their speech. This means that claims of "special" rights—of access to governmental proceedings for the institutional press or media, for example—might offend the free speech neutrality principle. Media representatives were themselves somewhat divided with regard to seeking any "special" rights or privileges under the Press Clause. A power to regulate the press, or license it in some way, posed grave dangers for institutions engaged in gathering and reporting news about government.[94] Still, some such claims were ultimately presented to the Court, which rejected them and relied instead on the Free Speech Clause.

Why merge the Press Clause with the Free Speech Clause and freedom of "expression" more generally? As noted, the United States had long touted the virtues of a free press, and even encouraged other nations and the international community to adopt free press provisions of their own. Domestically, the collapse of free press into free speech and "expressive" rights came at a time when, politically and culturally speaking, the institutional press was enjoying something of a "heyday" or revival. As the Court was merging the Press Clause and Free Speech Clause, the institutional press was revealing Watergate crimes and publishing exposés on the Vietnam conflict. Newsgathering and investigative journalism were then hailed as a necessary check on corrupt government, and reporters were popular figures in American culture.[95]

We do not have a comprehensive account of the dynamics that caused the free speech turn with respect to press rights. However, in broad terms, it appears that jurisprudential, intellectual, and cultural influences led to treating the press right as part of the freedom of speech or the more general collection of "expressive" rights.

I have already pointed to some the historical and intellectual barriers to treating the Press Clause as a freestanding and distinct guarantee. As with the other "expressive" clauses, we ought not to discount the built-in advantages of the Free Speech Clause. By 1975, when the Supreme Court's free press jurisprudence finally seemed to be ripening, free speech doctrines were already in place and well-developed.[96] By this time, the coverage of the Free Speech Clause had expanded such that it covered most, if not all, conceivable press activities. These included the central functions of gathering information and disseminating it to broad public audiences.[97] As was the case with regard to the Assembly Clause, the Free Speech Clause offered a handy and ready-made framework for protecting press rights. Indeed, the Court may have learned that lesson in part as a result of its interaction with the right of peaceable assembly.

To be sure, claimants and commentators were pressing courts to recognize some press rights that were separate and apart from freedom of speech. Invoking the Press Clause, press and media organizations sought special access to government institutions, proceedings, and records. At the same time, commentators such as Jerome Barron, who were concerned about the unequal distribution of media access and power in the United States, were advocating that government impose equal access rights on "the press."[98] These cases and arguments provided opportunities to consider the special meaning of the Press Clause.

However, when it finally took up the central question of whether the Press Clause protected rights distinct from the Free Speech Clause, the Court turned first to some of the First Amendment scholarship discussed earlier. Chief Justice Burger, writing for the Court in an important early case, relied heavily on the work of Professor David Lange.[99] Lange conceded that the framing materials did not provide a clear answer to the question, but argued nevertheless that "the freedom of the press evolved as an extension or amplifier of the freedom of speech."[100] Along with other scholars, he claimed that the two clauses were essentially interchangeable.[101] The scholarly accounts provided authority for interpreting the Press Clause as an extension of the Free Speech Clause. They also allowed the Court to dispose of the nettlesome special-access and compelled-access questions by rejecting the contention that the Press Clause had anything to say about them on its own terms.

To be sure, the Court was undoubtedly concerned about the difficulties inherent in categorizing or defining something called "the press" for purposes of assigning constitutional rights.[102] Does this cover institutional media, individual reporters, pamphleteers, or all of the above? There was also the fact that historical materials suggested not an institutional interpretation, but rather one that included even the lonely pamphleteer as constituting "the press." In addition, there was a tension between defining a special category of "press" and the presumption against governmental licensure of the press.

Still, not everyone was convinced that the Press Clause was essentially interchangeable with the Free Speech Clause. Justice Potter Stewart argued that the Free Speech Clause protected an individual right of expression, while the Press Clause protected the *institutional* rights of a "Fourth Estate."[103] Stewart's view also found some favor in constitutional scholarship. For example, Melville Nimmer defended an interpretation of the Press Clause that was quite similar to Justice Stewart's.[104] Nimmer was convinced that the Press Clause and Free Speech Clause could be separated, and that they served related but distinctive functions. However, the "Fourth Estate" and Nimmer interpretations never garnered the support of a majority of the Court.

The Free Speech Clause and "expressive rights" formulations may also have been attractive in a broader intellectual and historical sense. Although Watergate and the conduct of the Vietnam War highlighted the value of investigative journalism, many important "press" cases were decided during a cultural and political era that emphasized individual expressiveness and institutional skepticism.[105] These intellectual currents were at odds with recognition of a collective or structural right for an "elite" institutional press, but were consistent with a focus on "expressive" rights that belonged to all. In this sense, too, the Free Speech Clause was a better "fit" with conceptions of individualism and institutional skepticism.[106]

Further, free speech rights and "expressive" freedoms had served important functions during the civil rights era of the 1950s and 1960s. As discussed in Chapter 5, civil rights advocates had successfully relied on free speech and other "expressive" rights to create breathing space for political dissent and organization. Although rights of press and assembly were also critical to the success of the Civil Rights Movement, freedom of speech was the most prominent right in judicial decisions of this era. Thus, the Court's treatment of the Press Clause during the mid-1970s was following a familiar constitutional script.

Whether one views it as the path of least resistance or as defensible on the merits, the Supreme Court ultimately adopted the free speech or "expressive rights" interpretation of the Press Clause. However, this does not mean that the press right simply disappeared, as the Assembly Clause appeared to do circa 1980. Although the Court refused to recognize "special" press rights, its published decisions continued to extoll the values of a free and independent press.[107] Even though the Court was not willing to recognize freestanding press rights, many legislatures enacted laws shielding the institutional press from campaign finance laws, taxes, and other regulatory requirements. Members of the institutional press also enjoyed special access and other privileges. After the Court refused in *Branzburg v. Hayes* (1972)[108] to recognize even a qualified press privilege for reporters' confidential sources, many states enacted statutory shield laws.[109]

The judicial and academic treatment of the Press Clause as ancillary to the Free Speech Clause arguably jibes with how Americans view the status of the press freedom and the press itself. To the extent they recognize and can identify First Amendment rights at all (a recent survey indicates only about one in four Americans can name a single First Amendment guarantee, and half of respondents recall freedom of speech), Americans are likely to lump the speech and press guarantees together.[110] For a variety of reasons, they are also less likely to trust or revere journalists and the press than Americans were in the 1970s.[111] Like the Court, the public still retains a high level of goodwill toward the intrinsic values associated with a free and independent press. But also like the Court, citizens seem to separate those values from the recognition of special or formal rights on behalf of the institutional press or media.

These are the principal dynamics that led the Supreme Court to adopt the view that the Press Clause is merely "complementary to and a natural extension of Speech Clause liberty."[112] Insofar as the Press Clause remains constitutionally enforceable, it is generally as a component of what the Court has referred to as "freedom of expression."[113] However, the relationship between the Press Clause and the Free Speech Clause remains a subject of robust judicial and academic debate. In the Court's blockbuster campaign finance decision, *Citizens United v. FEC* (2010), two justices—the late Antonin Scalia and John Paul Stevens—debated whether the Press Clause has force independent of the Free Speech Clause.[114] Further, as discussed below, some First Amendment scholars have advocated reviving the Press Clause. Some have offered constitutional definitions of "the press" and argued on behalf of granting press members substantive rights separate and apart from those covered by the Free Speech Clause.[115] As these debates and arguments show, the dynamic intersection between the Press Clause and the Free Speech Clause are perpetual and ongoing. It remains to be seen whether these dynamics will ultimately remove the Press Clause from the long shadow of the Free Speech Clause.

THE PETITION CLAUSE

Like its cousins, the right to petition government for the redress of grievances also has a venerable historical pedigree. Nearly all state constitutions adopted between 1776 and 1780 contained a "petition" provision.[116] James Madison's proposed bill of rights contained a Petition Clause that was textually separate from its free speech, assembly, and press provisions.[117]

However, despite its historical pedigree and early status, the Petition Clause, like the Assembly Clause and Press Clause, has now been "collapsed into the right of free speech and expression."[118] As we have with regard to assembly and press, we will consider the principal dynamic forces that have brought about petition's subordination to freedom of speech.

As discussed earlier, some nineteenth-century Supreme Court precedents mistakenly linked the rights of assembly and petition. The people enjoyed a right to assemble, the Supreme Court suggested, only for the limited purpose of presenting petitions. The Assembly Clause managed to recover its footing, at least for a time. By contrast, at least as a jurisprudential matter, the Petition Clause never really thrived on its own terms. In the nineteenth century, the Supreme Court sometimes recognized the independent importance of the right to petition (although it was still mentioned along with assembly).[119] Further, in some early twentieth-century cases, the right to petition was cited along with other "expressive" rights. Later, the right to petition would make some other cameo appearances in Supreme Court opinions.[120]

However, by the mid-1980s, Supreme Court precedents focused primarily on the connections between the Petition Clause and other First Amendment rights—particularly the Free Speech Clause. The Court explained in one case that "[t]he right to petition is cut from the same cloth as the other guarantees of [the First Amendment], and is an assurance of a particular freedom of expression."[121] The Court also stated that the Petition Clause and the Free Speech Clause are "subject to the same constitutional analysis."[122] In its most recent consideration of the relationship between the Petition Clause and the Free Speech Clause, the Court observed: "It is not necessary to say that the two Clauses are identical in their mandate or their purpose and effect to acknowledge that the rights of speech and petition share substantial common ground."[123]

Thus, by the mid-1980s, just as it had earlier swallowed up the Assembly Clause and Press Clause, the Free Speech Clause had subordinated the Petition Clause too. Petitioning, like associating and publishing information, was considered a means or form of expression covered by the free speech guarantee. Unlike the Assembly Clause, the Petition Clause was never afforded any kind of independent significance. And in contrast to the Press Clause, the Petition Clause never enjoyed a "heyday" in the Supreme Court.

The Petition Clause has received far less attention from constitutional scholars than the Assembly Clause and Press Clause. Seeking to remedy this oversight, Professor Ronald Krotoszynski has published *Reclaiming the Petition Clause* (2012), in which he provides a comprehensive consideration of the ancient and modern right to petition. Professor Krotoszynski presents both a detailed history and comparative account of petitioning. His book offers some important insights into the special dynamics that led to the Free Speech Clause's subordination of the Petition Clause.

As Professor Krotoszynski observes, petitioning, in the original sense of presenting grievance papers to the U.S. Congress and expecting a formal response, began to fall out of fashion as early as the 1830s. This does not mean that Americans ceased petitioning their governments. Indeed, in terms of public participation, Krotoszynski identifies the period 1844–1919 as the "golden age" of petitioning in the United States.[124] However, during that period, the *form* of petitioning changed markedly. Rather than present specific grievances directly to legislatures, advocates began to organize and present *mass* public petitions. Mass petitions concerning subjects such as women's suffrage and the rights of Native Americans were a hybrid form of speech, assembly, and petition activities. As the practice developed, petitioning became a means of amplifying voices and communicating public sentiment on a broad scale. This made petition more akin to a rally or demonstration and less like the traditional written request for a legislative response.

As I emphasized in the Introduction, a constitutional right is a form of both rhetorical and actual power. By altering its basic form, the people themselves actually changed the meaning of the right to petition. Over time, petitioning evolved into a form of rhetorical expression—one not directed to legislators and officials, as in the classic case, but directed to the public at large in search of a response from the masses. As Professor Krotoszynski observes: "Petitioning morphed from a parliamentary practice into a form of mass participatory politics."[125]

Unlike assembly and press, this transformation had less to do with broad intellectual currents or shifting jurisprudential fault lines regarding the right to petition than with the public's own instrumental use of the right. Over time, as it became a form of dialogue, communication, or messaging, petitioning more and more resembled "speech." In this form, the right to petition fit comfortably within the expanding coverage of the Free Speech Clause and its doctrinal framework which included protection for protests, demonstrations, and other forms of public contention.[126] Once again, the Free Speech Clause presented itself as an effective substitute for a neighboring First Amendment right.

Scholars never generated a body of work to counteract or challenge the idea that petition was simply another form of expression. Indeed, outside the context of issues relating to access to courts, very few scholars paid much attention to the Petition Clause. Professor Krotoszynski's book, which seeks to revive the Petition Clause, swims against a generational tide of politics and jurisprudence that has rendered the Petition Clause "the First Amendment's poor relation."[127]

By the time the Supreme Court was asked to review formal and independent petition claims in the modern era, public practice and academic consensus had essentially positioned the Petition Clause as an historical relic. People did not submit formal petitions anymore, and to the extent citizens wanted to engage in mass petitioning, the Free Speech Clause already offered adequate coverage. Thus, judicial decisions concerning the right to petition largely reflected the change in form that had occurred during the "golden age." Like the assembly and press rights, the petition right was supplanted by the Free Speech Clause.

Expressive Dynamics

The dynamics that subordinated the assembly, press, and petition rights to the Free Speech Clause shared some common elements. All were affected by the jurisprudential and intellectual advantages enjoyed by the Free Speech Clause and the freedom of speech. The lack of clear historical or original meaning with regard to any of the "expressive" clauses created an obstacle to treating these rights as substantively distinct and independently enforceable. The Supreme Court's penchant for eliding the possible differences in coverage, its seemingly cavalier attitude toward the text of the First Amendment, and its preference for free speech doctrines and principles, also contributed to the aggregation of the generic "expression" right.

However, there were important differences in the dynamic intersection between the Free Speech Clause and its three neighbors. The Assembly Clause was first mistakenly appended to the Petition Clause, an interpretive error the Court never officially corrected. The morphing of assembly into association, and then into expressive association, occurred despite efforts to popularize the assembly right in political discourse and its continued exercise by the people in various movements and private groups. As Professor Inazu observes, political and intellectual influences played a significant role in the transformation of the assembly right into one of voice or expressive association.

The Press Clause experienced some unique judicial dynamics. Free press and free speech had long been used interchangeably, including during the framing era. The Supreme Court continued this trend, essentially from the moment it encountered the free speech and press rights together in the World War I cases. Despite its "heyday" in the courts and critical historical moments such as Watergate and the Vietnam War, the Press Clause never broke free of the magnetic pull of the Free Speech Clause. Pragmatic concerns, including the difficulty of defining "the press" and difficulties relating to assigning such an entity special rights, also posed a significant deterrent in terms of disaggregating free press and free speech rights. Ultimately, the Court's treatment of the Press Clause tracked the public's apparent sense of the value of a free press. The Court, like the public at large, acknowledged the values inherent in having a free and independent press, but balked at recognizing any special rights for such an elite institution. Thus, the press right was subsumed into the free speech right not primarily based upon intellectual or political forces (legislatures were, after all, willing to enact press protections), but based upon the seemingly intractable practical difficulties with allowing the press right to stand on its own bottom.

Finally, the Petition Clause's relationship with the Free Speech Clause was driven in part by the judicial and intellectual dynamics that affected the assembly and press rights. But it was primarily the people's own use and adaptation of the petition right that sealed its fate. The morphing of petition during its "golden age," from the presentation of individual grievances to a form of mass politics, created a close and irresistible resemblance between petition and speech. Thus, modern-day petitioning closely resembled some of the essential forms and functions of the free speech right—to engage in mass politics and public contention, through demonstrations and protest against government, for the purpose of presenting grievances.

These dynamics show that interactions between the Free Speech Clause and non-speech neighboring rights share some commonalities but also exhibit important differences. The differences, in particular, are relevant to any project whose purpose it is to reconsider, recover, or rescue these particular rights from the vortex of the Free Speech Clause. Understanding these dynamics also informs the prospects for reconsidering the "Free Expression Clause" more generally, including the chances that its elements can be reconstituted as cognate and mutually reinforcing rights provisions.

Reconsidering the "Free Expression Clause"

The Free Speech Clause has had a profound effect on its First Amendment non-speech neighbors. It has largely supplanted the Assembly Clause, Press Clause, and Petition Clause. Free speech doctrines, principles, and theories now govern claims under these seemingly distinctive provisions. The nature of this relationship has also significantly affected the Free Speech Clause. As it has absorbed the activities of association, newsgathering and distribution, and presenting grievances to government officials, the Free Speech Clause has expanded in terms of coverage, function, and status. Further, it comes as little surprise that when asked about First Amendment rights, Americans recall the Free Speech Clause more readily than any of its cognate cousins. The "Free Expression Clause" is the generic product of Free Speech Clause expansionism. The question is whether this generic clause can be disaggregated, and then recombined to produce a pluralistic First Amendment consisting of cognate and mutually facilitative rights.

As discussed, "freedom of expression" has long been part of the constitutional lexicon. The expansion of the Free Speech Clause into areas of press, assembly/association, and petition has undeniably secured valuable coverage and protection for a wide variety of expressive activities. However, stretching the Free Speech Clause and freedom of speech to cover everything contemplated by three other seemingly independent provisions has placed considerable stress on Free Speech Clause's text, doctrines, and principles. Activities that appear, both textually and conceptually, to be covered by the press, assembly, or petition provisions have been shoehorned into a single provision covering "the freedom of speech." Free speech doctrines relating to things such as symbolic conduct, content-neutrality, and the public forum may not address, or may awkwardly cover, the core harms of restrictions on assembly, press, or petition activities.[128] Further, as discussed below, treating everything relating to communication as a free speech concern can also confuse or complicate free speech doctrines.[129]

These concerns are separate and apart from the obvious textual problems associated with collapsing four different rights into one singular "expressive" guarantee. The words of the Constitution matter. Whether the question relates to the meaning of what constitutes a "search" under the Fourth Amendment, or the scope of Congress's power under the commerce clause to regulate "commerce" that takes place "among the states," interpreters seek to give effect to the words of the Constitution. The "Free Expression Clause" treats the Assembly Clause, Press Clause, and Petition Clause as constitutional redundancies. This violates a fundamental canon of constitutional interpretation.[130]

Two things need to happen if the individual rights in the First Amendment are to be given appropriate recognition and meaningful independent enforcement. The first is that the "Free Expression Clause" must be disaggregated, such that each individual clause is recognized as independently meaningful and not merely part of an undifferentiated mass of "expression." The second is that, once properly disaggregated, these rights need to be reconnected to one another as "cognate" and complementary provisions.

DISAGGREGATING THE "FREE EXPRESSION CLAUSE"

Recent scholarship has advocated for the recovery or reclaiming of the Assembly Clause, Press Clause, and Petition Clause.[131] Groups, particularly dissenting and marginalized associations, are under sustained pressure to conform to equality and other legal principles. Owing to attacks by elected officials as well as cultural and economic pressures, the notion of a free and independent press has never seemed more vulnerable. And the peoples' access to elected representatives has increasingly been limited in ways that create political strife and alienation.

Thus, Professor Inazu argues that we must "look past association and recover assembly."[132] As he explains, a recovered Assembly Clause, one rooted in the long tradition of organizing and joining, would offer more robust protections for a diversity of expressive and non-expressive groups—dissenting, political, *and* expressive. To accomplish these ends, Inazu argues, we need a freestanding right of assembly—one unencumbered by the Free Speech Clause's message-based framework.[133] Inazu proposes a distinct conception of the assembly right, and defends it on textual, theoretical, and pragmatic grounds.

Professor Sonja West and other scholars have similarly objected to the Press Clause's treatment as a constitutional redundancy.[134] West argues that the Press Clause protects the unique *non-speech* functions of checking government and gathering and conveying information to the public about newsworthy matters.[135] Professor Randall Bezanson similarly contends that the press "should be understood as more than a technology, more than just another voice."[136]

These scholars differ with regard to how exactly the Press Clause ought to be revived or recovered, and the extent to which this is possible. Professor West argues that the Supreme Court was simply wrong to give up on defining an institutional press that merits special or distinctive treatment.[137] Professor Bezanson similarly believes "the press" refers to a distinctive (although not necessarily an institutional) form, but is skeptical of claims for special newsgathering or other rights for the press.[138]

To be sure, scholars contending for an institutional definition of the press are swimming upstream, against a current of scholarship and jurisprudence that is skeptical of the notion that "the press" can or should be defined in this manner.[139] But those skeptical of transformative interpretive change need look no further than the recent revival of the Second Amendment, which was on life support for most of American history until the Supreme Court breathed new life into it. Recent scholarship on the Press Clause is part of the dynamic process by which the relationships between and among constitutional rights can change over time. As new pressures and challenges to a free and independent press materialize, scholars and courts may begin to reconsider the extent to which the Press Clause ought to be deemed coterminous with the Free Speech Clause.

Finally, Ronald Krotoszynski contends that we ought to "reclaim" the Petition Clause.[140] Krotoszynski proposes that the modern right to petition be defined in such a way that it protects "some sort of access to the government and its officers, coupled with a presumption against punishment for those who seek to exercise this right of access."[141] Professor Krotoszynski does not contend that the Petition Clause is wholly unrelated to the Free Speech Clause. Thus, he recognizes that petitioning activity is often "conjoined with the exercise of other forms of expressive freedom, including speech, assembly, and association."[142] However, he proposes a separate doctrine or jurisprudence for the Petition Clause, one that defines "petition" broadly, provides for a presumption of access to government officials for certain kinds of petition activity, and protects petitioners from being punished for criticizing government.[143] Krotoszynski does not propose that we return the right of petition to its original form. Rather, leveraging the dynamics that transformed petition into a form of mass politics, he proposes a special set of rules to govern modern retail and mass petition activities.

Disaggregation through recovery or revival would produce some significant benefits. For instance, Professor Inazu's conception of the reinvigorated assembly right would protect a broader range of noncommercial, non-expressive groups than the right of "expressive association." It would also draw attention to the pre-expressive aspects of assembly, including activities relating to group formation, which have received diminished First Amendment protection in cases such as *Christian Legal Society v. Martinez*. Inazu's recovered assembly right may also clarify or bring more appropriate balance to the intersection between anti-discrimination laws and the rights of groups to determine their own makeup and membership.

With regard to press rights, a revival of efforts to define the press and extend special access and other newsgathering rights to it would place the rights of a free and independent press on more solid constitutional footing. As discussed, currently the press enjoys only the generic free speech rights that other newsgatherers and speakers have. Even placing the issue of independent constitutional status on the table serves to remind various constituencies—the courts, government officials, and the public—that there is a separate Press Clause in the First Amendment.[144] Reconsidering press rights could lead to more robust rights for newsgathering and, what may be just as critical today, constitutional immunities from governmental demands for information. As Professor Bezanson observes, formally recognizing such rights would not necessarily require that courts adopt a narrow, corporate, *institutional* conception of "the press."[145]

Disaggregation of free press and free speech rights can also lead to analytical clarity. This is so *even if* one accepts the view that the press freedom extends to anyone who publishes information to the general public.[146] For example, Professor Michael McConnell argues that the Supreme Court's much-discussed (and, in some quarters, much maligned) decision in *Citizens United v. FEC* (2010) was wrongly decided under the Free Speech Clause. He argues that the decision, which invalidated a provision of federal election law that banned corporations and labor unions from spending their own funds to broadcast viewpoints about candidates, directly implicated the Press Clause and ought to have been decided on that basis.[147] Deciding the case on Press Clause grounds, McConnell contends, would have (1) obviated the need to decide whether corporations are entitled to First Amendment rights; (2) clarified the Court's analytical approach, under the First Amendment, to campaign contributions and expenditures; and (3) rendered unnecessary the adoption of a rule that treats all speaker-based distinctions as constitutionally suspect.[148] In short, deciding *Citizens United* as a Press Clause case rather than a Free Speech Clause case would have had the dual virtues of reviving the former and avoiding further analytical complications relating to the latter. Reviving the Press Clause does not have to entail recognizing special rights. As McConnell demonstrates, disaggregating free press and free speech can produce analytical clarity and other non-institutional benefits.

Finally, as Professor Krotoszynski argues in his book, developing a separate petition doctrine could facilitate citizen access to government officials in ways current Free Speech Clause doctrine cannot or will not accomplish. Thus, under current doctrine governments can effectively silence some speakers by displacing them. A petition right that focuses on access to officials may provide a substantive right of access not covered under the Free Speech Clause. More generally, Krotoszynski contends that a reclaimed petition right would provide broader protection, in a variety of contexts, for what he calls "petitioning speech."[149] Some of this coverage would arise under the Petition Clause itself, while other aspects would arise from a combination of independent but mutually reinforcing petition, speech, and assembly rights.

FIRST AMENDMENT PLURALISM

Professor Krotoszynski's observation regarding the potential combination of First Amendment rights raises the prospect of reconnecting independent speech, assembly, press and petition rights as "cognate" or mutually reinforcing provisions.[150] Thus, the first step is to revive or recover versions of the Assembly Clause, Press Clause, and Petition Clause that are not subordinate to the Free Speech Clause. The next step is to reconstitute these rights as facets of a pluralistic First Amendment that treats them as discrete, but synergistically related, provisions.

Interpreting speech, assembly, press, and petition freedoms as cognate provisions better reflects the text and contemporary exercise of First Amendment rights than does the generic "expressive rights" interpretation. The First Amendment does not codify "expressive" rights, but rather separate rights provisions with presumptively distinctive coverages and functions. Constitutional and political movements have relied on the combination of *all* of the First Amendment's rights, not just the Free Speech Clause. As Professor Krotoszynski suggests, most forms of public contention involve not merely speech, but also separate elements of assembly and petition as well. Further, as Professor Inazu has demonstrated, many groups form for reasons other than communicating ideas and viewpoints to the public.

With regard to speech, assembly, press, and petition, Professor Ashutosh Bhagwat argues that "these rights usually operate in combination with one another, and are much more effective in combination as well."[151] He observes:

> Speech is the lifeblood of associations, because the formation and activities of associations require speech. Group petitioning is fundamentally linked to assembly, since before the advent of mass, electronic communication, assemblies were the only means to create such petitions. Speech is greatly enhanced by association and assembly, because speech on behalf of large groups of citizens is far more likely to influence others (including public officials) than that of individuals acting alone.[152]

Professor Bhagwat articulates the central premise of what I refer to as "First Amendment Pluralism"—that speech, assembly, press, and petition rights are independent, cognate, and mutually facilitative. As discussed in Chapter 8, First Amendment Pluralism is part of a broader conception of "Rights Pluralism," which focuses on the dual necessity of maintaining conceptual and enforcement space between constitutional rights while also leveraging their valuable synergies.

A pluralistic First Amendment, like a pluralistic system of constitutional rights more generally, is not merely a theoretical conception. First Amendment Pluralism would require that governments defend their actions against separate and independently enforceable free speech, assembly, press, *and* petition claims. First Amendment Pluralism would also strengthen and fortify both free speech and neighboring non-speech rights, in the manners suggested by Professor Bhagwat.

The framers and adopters of the First Amendment understood that constitutional liberty requires a multitude of checks, balances, and rights. We can no more entrust that liberty to a single check—that is, separation of powers, federalism, bicameralism—than we can make it dependent on one or even a few rights provisions. To ensure effective democratic participation, protection of minority groups and viewpoints, access to governmental decision-makers, and other democratic ends, each of the First Amendment's rights provisions must be independently recognized and enforced. Once they are effectively disaggregated, we can pursue and develop their cognate capacities.

As discussed, the Supreme Court's approach has been to collapse speech, assembly, press, and petition rights into a single conception of "expressive" rights. Some prominent free speech theorists, including Alexander Meiklejohn, Robert Post, and Cass Sunstein, have also focused their energies on "expressive" rights and the Free Speech Clause. Leading theoretical accounts thus have generally elided assembly, press, and petition rights, even though they are every bit as critical to self-governance and the search for truth as the free speech guarantee.[153]

More recently, scholars have started to correct this course. For example, Professor Bhagwat argues that it is not enough to rescue or recover the First Amendment's subordinated clauses. We must also, he contends, recognize that freedoms of speech, assembly, press, and petition serve collective *democratic* purposes and functions.[154] Bhagwat posits that separately and in combination, these First Amendment rights suggest a concept of citizenship that emphasizes active participation in democratic processes. From this perspective, in order to engage effectively in activities such as political debate, protest, and voting, citizens need to be able to invoke and exercise independent and mutually reinforcing speech, assembly, press, and petition rights.

Professor Inazu has also advanced a version or conception of First Amendment Pluralism. He focuses on a somewhat different combination of rights—speech, assembly, press, and *free exercise of religion*.[155] As Inazu observes, the Supreme Court has occasionally recognized that these rights are connected to one another. For instance, the Court has recognized that the rights all merit a "preferred" constitutional status. Inazu argues that this combination of rights once protected "a pluralistic civil society that tolerated genuine disagreement and shielded private groups from the imposition of majoritarian norms."[156] In part owing to the dominance of the Free Speech Clause, Inazu contends, First Amendment rights no longer operate as *complementary* checks on the imposition of majority norms.[157] Professor Inazu is particularly concerned about the effects that Free Speech Clause expansionism has had on religious groups, which frequently adopt positions contrary to majority norms, but his pluralistic conception, like Bhagwat's, also has broader implications.

As these scholars have observed, we need to understand that no matter how much ground the Free Speech Clause can cover, facilitating citizens' participation in democratic processes and protecting them from governmental overreach will require the recognition and enforcement of the full complement of First Amendment rights. Thus, non-expressive assemblies, non-speech press functions, and the peoples' need to reach increasingly distant and inaccessible public officials all necessitate a more pluralist version of the First Amendment.

As Professor Inazu observes with regard to First Amendment dynamics, "[t]here is no nefarious force behind the loss of [First Amendment Pluralism]—it developed through a series of reactions and counter-reactions to cases, statutes, and social movements."[158] As a result of the dynamic processes of change and interpretation discussed earlier, we are left with a leading Free Speech Clause and a supporting cast of neighboring First Amendment rights.

One of the things Rights Dynamism demonstrates is that this understanding is not final or set in stone. Scholars have made significant contributions in terms of challenging the subordination of assembly, press, and petition rights. They have presented facts, histories, and theories that, if accepted, could lead to the recovery or revival of these rights. Their work is part of the perpetual process in which rights intersect, and through which they are constantly interpreted and reinterpreted. What remains to be seen is whether the combination of legal, intellectual, political, and social forces can alter current interpretations of First Amendment rights and, as importantly, their relation to one another.

4

RELIGION

THE RELATIONSHIP BETWEEN the First Amendment's Free Speech and Free Exercise Clauses shares many attributes with others discussed in the book. These provisions have intersected with one another from the very beginning—indeed, in conceptual terms, since prior to their formal ratification. Both rights were described, in early Supreme Court precedents, as "preferred" and "fundamental." During a significant portion of their relationship, the Free Speech Clause and the Free Exercise Clause mutually facilitated and illuminated one another. They have generally functioned as distinct, but overlapping, protections for freedom of conscience, belief, and certain types of communication.[1]

However, like other relationships involving the Free Speech Clause, this one too has been complicated and complicating. Over time, the relationship between the Free Speech and Free Exercise Clauses has changed dramatically. During the 1930s, the Supreme Court began to demonstrate an analytical preference for deciding cases on free speech grounds—even when free exercise rights were also implicated. In later decades, in certain contexts, that preference ripened into a form of Free Speech Clause expansionism.[2] Adding to the complexities, in this instance not just two, but three, constitutional clauses dynamically intersected. The interpretation of the First Amendment's *other* religion clause—the Establishment Clause—has also been affected by the relations between the Free Speech Clause and Free Exercise Clause.[3]

Finally, and in keeping with the "stereoscopic" character of free speech/non-speech rights relationships, the intersections have affected the interpretation of Free Speech Clause doctrines and principles.

This chapter explores the dynamic relationship between the Free Speech Clause and the Free Exercise Clause. It explains how and why, in certain contexts, the Free Speech Clause has subordinated the Free Exercise Clause. It discusses the harms associated with that subordination, which in certain respects are similar to those discussed in Chapter 3's examination of the Assembly, Press, and Petition Clauses. The chapter also examines the prospects for reuniting the free speech and free exercise guarantees as cognate and synergistic provisions. The challenges in this regard are discussed in connection with two contemporary conflicts involving the interaction of the clauses: legal restrictions on public worship and the application of anti-discrimination laws to religious adherents who refuse to provide services in connection with same-sex weddings.

Introduction and Early Associations

The framers and ratifiers of the First Amendment drafted and adopted distinctive protections for freedom of speech and the free exercise of religion. As noted in Chapter 3, the congressional debate and ratification records relating to the First Amendment are sparse. Among other things, the framers did not make explicit—either in their deliberations or in the text of the Constitution—what the specific relationship between freedom of speech and the free exercise of religion was or ought to be.

As Professor Ashutosh Bhagwat has observed, the Religion Clauses—the Free Exercise Clause and the Establishment Clause—and the remainder of the rights in the First Amendment (freedoms of speech, press, assembly, and petition) have "distinct historical roots."[4] When he sent his original proposals to Congress, James Madison did not connect the Religion Clauses with what would later become other First Amendment rights, including the Free Speech Clause. Instead, he listed them separately, indicating that their protections were considered to be distinct. Moreover, the Free Speech Clause, Assembly Clause, Press Clause, and Petition Clause were all combined into a single amendment relatively early in the ratification process. The Free Exercise Clause and the Establishment Clause were added much later, again as a separate proposed amendment.

Of course, this drafting history does not establish that the Free Speech Clause and the Religion Clauses had nothing at all to do with one another. Indeed, even before the First Amendment's ratification, "expressive" and religious liberties were already closely connected in the minds of early Americans.[5] As Michael McConnell has observed, colonial religious adherents relied on speech and press activities to distribute tracts to the public.[6] Other scholars have posited that the long history of free speech and free exercise rights shows that religious rights were actually antecedent, at least in some respects, to free speech rights.[7]

As noted, the Constitution does not make these connective tissues explicit. However, the early history provides some evidence that the Free Speech Clause and the Free Exercise Clause were meant to offer distinct but overlapping protections for "expressive" and religious rights—generally speaking, liberties relating to conscience and communication.[8] Indeed, as discussed below, during certain periods of American history and jurisprudence that is essentially how free speech and free exercise rights have related to one another. Like others discussed in the book, however, the relationship between the Free Speech Clause and the Free Exercise Clause has been worked out over an extended period of time.

That process began, in earnest, during the 1930s and 1940s. During this period, Jehovah's Witnesses brought a raft of constitutional challenges to restrictions on proselytizing, soliciting, and other public activities, which were often aimed directly at suppressing their religious practices.[9] At this time, the United States was becoming more pluralistic in terms of religious beliefs and practices. Manifestations of religious pluralism were sometimes met with official suppression and private violence. Thus, Jehovah's Witnesses were frequently targeted by public officials, law enforcement, and violent mobs for attempting to communicate or practice their religious beliefs in public places.[10]

In response, the Witnesses did something fateful in terms of the development of the free speech-free exercise relationship. Although their principal complaint was that their religious freedoms were being targeted for suppression, a claim that would seem to reside squarely in the domain of the Free Exercise Clause, the Witnesses brought a number of different constitutional rights claims. In lawsuits as well as public discourse defending their activities, they invoked the Free Speech Clause, Assembly Clause, Press Clause, *and* Free Exercise Clause.[11] As we will see, the Witnesses' innovative strategy of bringing these aggregate constitutional claims had a significant impact on the development of First Amendment rights.

The Witnesses' rights claims offered the Supreme Court another early opportunity to consider both the independent substance of First Amendment rights and their relationship to one another (the first being the World War I cases, discussed in Chapter 3). Not much is known about the internal workings or deliberations of the Hughes Court, which decided the Jehovah's Witnesses cases.[12] As discussed in more detail below, the Court's understanding of the relationship between freedom of speech and the free exercise of religion appears to have evolved over time in response to a variety of influences. However, based on its published opinions, we do know that one of the first things the Hughes Court did was to declare that freedom of speech, freedom of the press, and the free exercise of religion were all "fundamental" rights that belonged to a "preferred" class of liberties.[13] Thus, as early as the 1940s, First Amendment rights that may have originated separately were joined together in terms of their preferred status.

The Hughes Court also connected the Free Speech Clause and Free Exercise Clause in other respects. As discussed below, in some cases the Court highlighted the synergistic connections between and among First Amendment rights. For example, the Court described the First Amendment's various clauses as guarantees that "have unity in the charter's prime place because they have unity in their human sources and functioning."[14] With regard to the Free Speech Clause and Free Exercise Clause, the Court sometimes addressed overlapping principles and coverage. For instance, *Cantwell v. Connecticut* (1940)[15] invalidated—on *both* free speech and free exercise grounds—a permit scheme that targeted religious solicitation. The Court observed:

> In the realm of religious faith, and in that of political belief, sharp differences arise. In both fields the tenets of one man may seem the rankest error to his neighbor. To persuade others to his own point of view, the pleader, as we know, at times, resorts to exaggeration, to vilification of men who have been, or are, prominent in church or state, and even to false statement. But the people of this nation have ordained that in the light of history, that, in spite of the probability of excesses and abuses, these liberties are, in the long view, essential to enlightened opinion and right conduct on the part of the citizens of a democracy.[16]

In this passage as well as others, the Hughes Court interpreted free speech and free exercise as distinct, but overlapping, *democratic* guarantees. Thus, a truly free people required the protections of both, in order to resist imposition of governmental orthodoxies in the realm of both politics and religion.

Whatever the Founders may have intended with regard to the relationships between and among First Amendment rights, from an early point in their formal relationship freedom of speech and the free exercise of religion were treated as two of the central pillars of a pluralistic First Amendment and a pluralistic framework of constitutional rights. From the 1930s onward, these provisions have been frequently invoked, adjudicated, and discussed together.

During roughly this same early time period, this conception of fundamentally connected rights was voiced in public discourse. As Professor John Inazu has observed in his work on the Assembly Clause, freedoms of speech, press, assembly, and religion were celebrated at the 1939 New York World's Fair.[17] They were also heralded in newspaper opinion pieces around the country, and by President Franklin Roosevelt, who described them as "the pillars which sustain the temple of liberty under law."[18] Similar characterizations of First Amendment rights were conveyed and relied upon in some lower-profile discourse. This suggested an early public understanding that freedoms of speech, assembly, press, and religion functioned synergistically in ways that secured constitutional and personal liberties.[19]

Thus, by the early 1940s, the Free Speech Clause and the Free Exercise Clause (along with other First Amendment rights) were linked together in judicial and public discourses. The Hughes Court recognized that these "fundamental" and "preferred" rights worked in tandem to secure personal liberty. Public officials and the public at large had also begun to recognize and appreciate the synergies of these First Amendment rights.

From Preferentialism to Subordination

Although the Hughes Court, public officials, and the public at large were beginning to recognize the basic connections between the Free Speech Clause and Free Exercise Clause, the actual enforcement of these rights began to take a different direction. In its First Amendment decisions, the Hughes Court often cited or acknowledged several First Amendment rights at once. However, it generally exhibited a strong preference for articulating its rulings in rationales and doctrines associated with the Free Speech Clause.[20] Over time, this preference for free speech or "expressive" rationales would ripen into an approach in which the Free Exercise Clause would be partially subordinated to the Free Speech Clause. By the 1980s, even in cases where the Free Exercise Clause presented an independent and viable basis for relief, claimants and courts would abandon it in favor of the Free Speech Clause.

FREE SPEECH CLAUSE PREFERENTIALISM

Although the Jehovah's Witnesses invoked multiple First Amendment clauses, the Hughes Court did not treat them all equally. Indeed, although the Court characterized the Free Exercise Clause as being among the Constitution's "fundamental" and "preferred" rights, it rarely analyzed free exercise claims independently of other First Amendment claims.

A common disposition was to hold that the challenged statute or ordinance violated freedoms of speech, press, *and* free exercise of religion—without in any way differentiating among the clauses. In this respect, the Hughes Court approached the First Amendment's clauses much as the Court had in the World War I cases.

In general, the Hughes Court gave little or no separate consideration to the Free Exercise Clause.[21] In terms of case dispositions, the clause did not seem to carry independent significance. Rather, the Free Exercise Clause claim prevailed only insofar as it was paired with the Free Speech Clause or, in some instances, another First Amendment right. As explained below, this approach did not preclude the Hughes Court from articulating some early free exercise and anti-establishment principles. However, in general, this was an indirect consequence of the Court's articulation of Free Speech Clause rationales.[22]

Consider, for example, perhaps the Court's most famous decision of this era, *West Virginia State Board of Education v. Barnette* (1943).[23] *Barnette* involved a challenge by the Witnesses to a state mandate that public school children salute the flag each school day. In their Supreme Court briefs, the Witnesses focused primarily on the Free Exercise Clause. They argued that the flag salute mandate violated creedal commands that they not worship false civil authorities. However, the Supreme Court decided *Barnette* primarily as a Free Speech Clause case involving a right not to be compelled to communicate official orthodoxy with respect to the U.S. flag.[24] Although *Barnette* underscored the importance of freedom of speech, press, religion, and assembly, the decision was principally grounded in free speech autonomy and anti-orthodoxy principles.

What explains the Court's strong preference for the Free Speech Clause in *Barnette* and other decisions? After all, by the early 1940s, neither the Free Speech Clause nor the Free Exercise Clause had established much of a jurisprudential foothold. The two provisions had only recently been "incorporated" against the states, and the Court was only beginning to examine their scope and application. Moreover, the Witnesses had hardly abandoned the Free Exercise Clause; in fact, as noted, in cases such as *Barnette* they made that clause the principal focus of their argument. In the vast majority of cases, the Witnesses' central claim was that a religious minority was being singled out for the purpose of suppressing religious practices or compelling acts that violated religious principles.

A number of factors likely led to the Court's preference for the Free Speech Clause. As discussed in Chapter 3, the World War I First Amendment decisions had exhibited a strong preference for analyzing claims in terms of the free speech guarantee. In the Witness cases, the Hughes Court followed suit.

The political context in which the Witness cases arose may also have influenced the nature of the Court's analysis. Professor Steven Feldman has argued that the transformation of American democracy during the 1920s and 1930s, from a republican to a more pluralistic system, helps explain the Court's affinity for the Free Speech Clause.[25] According to Professor Feldman, the justices may have perceived the Witnesses' religious liberty claims as being in some tension with emerging

American democratic ideals.[26] Thus, he suggested, mostly Protestant jurists may have viewed the Witnesses as "outsiders" pursuing *special* religious rights, rather than broad-based democratic values such as those at the core of freedom of speech and press.[27] As Professor Feldman explained:

> One reason, then, that the Protestant-controlled Supreme Court favored free expression over religious freedom during the 1930s and 1940s was that the religious freedom claims were more likely than the free expression claims to intensify the salience of the Justices' separation of the claimants as outsiders.[28]

Professor Feldman's explanation suggests that both external and internal dynamics affected the early relationship between the Free Speech Clause and the Free Exercise Clause. According to this account, external political changes affected the perception of the Witnesses' claims. Internal judicial biases reflected these political changes, and pushed the Court in the direction of the Free Speech Clause and away from the Free Exercise Clause. While the Court formally recognized the "fundamental" and "preferred" status of the Free Exercise Clause, it articulated its reasons for ruling in the Witnesses' favor in Free Speech Clause terms.

Although these political and personal factors may have contributed to Free Speech Clause preferentialism, other factors likely enhanced the relative attractiveness of the Free Speech Clause. Consider, for instance, the text of the clauses. The activities authorities were actively suppressing—communicating and assembling in public, distributing religious literature, and soliciting memberships and donations—closely resembled "speech," "press," and "assembly." In that basic respect, the Witnesses' grievances may have seemed like the natural province of the Free Speech Clause and other "expressive" liberties. These were already considered "public" rights, whereas religious exercise was still largely the province of private organizations and churches.

Consistent with this narrative, by the 1930s, the public streets had already been the focus of pitched free speech battles involving labor agitators, political dissenters, and others.[29] In that respect, the Jehovah's Witnesses' claims likely represented natural extensions of the fundamental issue raised by some early conflicts—namely, whether government had the authority to suppress "expressive" activities on public streets.

Further, in terms of its own agenda, the Hughes Court may have been more interested in addressing the general matter of speakers' access to public streets than it was in explicating specific religious rights in those places. Thus, internal Court agenda-setting may have influenced the move toward the Free Speech Clause.

Cross-doctrinal considerations may also have pushed the Court in the direction of the Free Speech Clause. As noted, the Free Speech Clause and the Free Exercise

Clause were both in their jurisprudential infancies when the Witnesses brought their constitutional challenges. However, a few substantive differences had already emerged.

When the first Witnesses' claims arrived at the Court, the Free Exercise Clause had been interpreted narrowly—primarily, if not exclusively, as a protection for religious *beliefs* rather than religious *acts*.[30] Thus, it was unclear to what extent the free exercise guarantee extended beyond protecting individual rights of conscience and belief. By contrast, even at this early stage, the Court had begun to extend Free Speech Clause and other "expressive" rights to public speeches and assemblies. Moreover, the Court had interpreted the Free Speech Clause to cover some "symbolic conduct"—that is, actions that have an expressive component.[31] And the Court had interpreted the Free Speech Clause to cover caustic criticism and other offensive speech.[32]

In sum, free speech doctrine was developing in a manner that supported decisions striking down bans on public proselytizing and other forms of expressive contention. A variety of factors—the strategic decisions of religious claimants to aggregate claims, the specific nature and substance of these claims, the identity of the claimants, external social and political changes, internal judicial attitudes and agendas, and doctrinal developments—were all part of a broad dynamic context that influenced the Supreme Court's early turn toward the Free Speech Clause.

FREE EXERCISE CLAUSE SUBORDINATION

As discussed in Chapter 3, by the late 1960s, the Free Speech Clause had assumed a dominant position relative to other First Amendment rights. Freedom of speech, assembly, press, and petition were being collapsed into a generic "Free Expression Clause" or treated as "ancillary" to the Free Speech Clause. By the 1980s, the Assembly Clause, Press Clause, and Petition Clause had all been subordinated to the Free Speech Clause. During the 1980s, the Free Exercise Clause would suffer a similar fate, at least in certain contexts. Proponents of religious freedom strategically abandoned the Free Exercise Clause in favor of the Free Speech Clause—even in cases where the former afforded a viable path to vindicating religious liberty.

The process that led from free speech preferentialism to free exercise subordination was itself complex and multifaceted. Social, doctrinal, and political factors all influenced this process, as did a variety of institutional, judicial, and political actors.

As mentioned earlier, during the 1930s and 1940s, freedom of speech and free exercise of religion were touted by President Roosevelt and others as indispensable constitutional freedoms. In the Hughes Court era, these rights were actually described as "cognate" provisions.[33] As time passed, however, the notion of "cognate" rights faded from published opinions and constitutional discourse. Academic treatments and law school courses segregated freedom of speech and the Religion Clauses.[34] This was likely owing in part to the fact that in the courts, free speech and free exercise doctrines were developing on separate tracks. As discussed in Chapter 3, by the middle of the twentieth century, most of the intellectual energy relating to the First Amendment was devoted to fleshing out the boundaries of the expanding Free Speech Clause.

Despite this general approach, social and political events once again would bring freedom of speech and free exercise into contact with one another. During the 1970s and 1980s, concerns regarding the constitutional separation of church and state led some localities to adopt policies that singled out religious adherents for exclusion from certain public properties and facilities. In response, bible study groups and other religious organizations challenged their exclusions from public schools and other facilities made available, after hours, to a wide variety of secular groups.

As had civil rights activists before them, religious liberty advocates turned to the courts to assert their rights of access to public places. As Professor Steven Brown has documented, beginning in the 1980s, religious adherents started to look toward the courts more frequently and systematically than they had in the past.[35] Religious advocacy organizations pushed back against what members perceived to be a hostility to religion in public life. In this environment, "New Christian Right" organizations began to fund and focus on litigating constitutional claims on behalf of religious adherents who had been excluded from public places, or who had otherwise suffered allegedly discriminatory treatment.[36]

Like the Jehovah's Witnesses, New Christian Right organizations sometimes combined Free Speech Clause and Free Exercise Clause claims. However, litigants often abandoned the Free Exercise Clause altogether. Professor Brown describes this important shift in strategy: "Perhaps surprisingly, New Christian Right lawyers neither boldly renounce the Supreme Court's Establishment Clause rulings of the past nor offer any new interpretation of the Free Exercise Clause to protect religious expression. Instead, they turn to the Free Speech Clause of the First Amendment."[37] Religious liberty advocates publicly declared their intention to use the Free Speech Clause to challenge discriminatory access policies across the nation.[38]

Some basic background concerning Free Exercise Clause doctrine helps to put this strategic shift into perspective. Prior to 1990, religious adherents whose actions or exercises were incidentally affected by laws and regulations could bring suit under the Free Exercise Clause. Their claims were reviewed under a "strict scrutiny" standard, which ostensibly meant that courts would review government actions skeptically and demand both compelling reasons for the burden imposed and that government tailor laws and regulations closely to the harm they were seeking to prevent.[39]

This approach gradually fell out of favor, in part because the Court had difficulty consistently applying the purportedly strict standard.[40] In 1990, the Supreme Court decided *Employment Division v. Smith* (1990).[41] *Smith* dramatically changed the free exercise landscape. It held that neutral and generally applicable laws and regulations that incidentally burden religious exercise were essentially outside the coverage of the Free Exercise Clause. *Smith* thus substantially diminished the protections afforded to religious adherents under the Free Exercise Clause.[42] In particular, the decision held that religious adherents were not entitled to constitutionally mandated exemptions from neutral and generally applicable civil and criminal laws. As later cases made clear, however, *Smith* left standing the rule that *purposeful* discrimination against religion or religious exercise was still reviewable under a demanding strict scrutiny standard and was presumptively unconstitutional.[43]

As the pre-*Smith* equal access cases reached the Supreme Court in the 1980s, the Court signaled that it was receptive to Free Speech Clause claims. In fact, in several cases, the Court relied *exclusively* on the Free Speech Clause—in most instances without so much as even mentioning the Free Exercise Clause. The Court adopted this approach even though *Smith* had not yet been decided, and even though purposeful discrimination against religious adherents was presumptively unconstitutional under the Free Exercise Clause.

Thus, in *Widmar v. Vincent* (1981), the Court upheld the Free Speech Clause claim of a registered student group that had been denied access to a state university's facilities for the purpose of engaging in "religious worship and religious discussion."[44] The Court concluded that religious worship and discussion were "forms of speech and association protected by the First Amendment."[45] *Widmar* did not even mention the Free Exercise Clause. It rested solely on free speech doctrines relating to access to "public forums" and the free speech principle of content neutrality. As the Court concluded: "In order to justify discriminatory exclusion from a public forum based on the religious content of a group's intended speech, the University must therefore satisfy the standard of review appropriate to content-based exclusions."[46]

Later equal access cases would similarly rely exclusively on the Free Speech Clause. Indeed, during the post-*Smith* era, the Rehnquist Court transformed the Hughes Court's *preference* for rationalizing decisions in free speech terms into a framework that rested *solely* on the Free Speech Clause. Under this approach, the Free Exercise Clause played no role—even, again, where the central claim involved *explicit discrimination against religious adherents*.[47]

Smith made it far more difficult to prevail under the Free Exercise Clause—particularly in cases where the government's actions only incidentally affected religious practices. Yet as the equal access cases show, as long as a decade prior to *Smith*, religious adherents had already turned toward the Free Speech Clause. Further, in post-*Smith* cases, claimants likewise eschewed the Free Exercise Clause even when the government's policy expressly discriminated against religious adherents.[48] Thus, although *Smith* itself did not preclude all reliance on the Free Exercise Clause, religious adherents and Supreme Court decisions focused exclusively on the Free Speech Clause.

There were likely several reasons for this strategic turn toward the Free Speech Clause. First, proponents of free exercise rights may have learned something valuable from the Hughes Court decisions. The preference for Free Speech Clause explanations and holdings highlighted the moral force of the Free Speech Clause and the relative attractiveness, in terms of both judicial and public support, of grounding public access claims on freedom of speech grounds. Like the Hughes Court the Rehnquist Court seemed to realize that free speech rights were attractive owing to the fact that they were general, not special, freedoms.

Second, religious liberty activists had closely studied the strategies and experiences of civil rights claimants. One of the lessons they likely internalized was that the Free Speech Clause was a powerful mechanism for facilitating the recognition of and protection for non-speech rights.

Third, relying on the Free Speech Clause appeared to avoid or sidestep possible Establishment Clause complications associated with providing public benefits to religious adherents and religious groups. As discussed further below, the Establishment Clause had been interpreted to bar government from providing not only direct funds but also some indirect benefits to churches and religious organizations. As Jay Sekulow, one of the principal architects of the free speech strategy, observed in an interview conducted in 1995: "[T]he free speech strategy has proven effective with judges across the ideological spectrum against opponents who rely on the First Amendment's clause against the establishment of religion."[49]

Fourth, cross-doctrinal developments may have influenced the shift to free speech claims. As noted, the Supreme Court was not able to consistently apply the pre-*Smith* free exercise doctrine. In many cases, this meant that although the Court applied a heightened scrutiny standard, religious adherents lost their free exercise claims.[50] As well, Supreme Court decisions striking down school prayer and certain public religious displays suggested that at least certain religious speech was either not going to be covered by the Free Exercise Clause and/or might be barred by the Establishment Clause.[51]

By contrast, in the decades between the Hughes Court's decisions and the Rehnquist Court's reconsideration of the free speech/free exercise relationship in the equal access cases, the Free Speech Clause's coverage and protection had expanded significantly. By the 1980s, the Court had already developed the core of its public forum doctrine, which extended free speech protections to public properties other than public streets and parks.[52] Further, as discussed in Chapter 5, in part owing to the Civil Rights Movement's invocation of equality rights and aided by an outpouring of academic commentary, the Court had elaborated strong content-neutrality rules under the Free Speech Clause.[53] Under free speech doctrine, laws and regulations that discriminated based on the content of speech—including religious subject matters and viewpoints—were subject to strict scrutiny and presumptively invalid.[54]

Moreover, by the 1980s, the Free Speech Clause had become capacious enough to cover not just religious discussions, but many religious practices and associations as well. Under Free Speech Clause doctrine, actions intended to convey a message to some audience that is in turn likely to understand it are considered covered "speech," and restrictions on such communicative acts are generally subject to a standard of intermediate scrutiny.[55] Under this free speech framework, religious activities, perhaps including prayers, rituals, and even worship services were all plausible candidates for Free Speech Clause coverage. Doctrinally, then, the Free Speech Clause was an attractive substitute for the less certain Free Exercise Clause.

Smith, as noted, considerably weakened Free Exercise Clause coverage and protection.[56] Although, as noted, post-*Smith* decisions clarified that explicit forms of discrimination against religion could still be challenged under the Free Exercise Clause, the scope of constitutional free exercise rights appeared to be much narrower in scope and far less certain in application than Free Speech Clause counterparts.[57]

Finally, as had likely occurred on the Hughes Court, the Rehnquist Court's internal dynamics may have influenced the Free Speech Clause turn. Reliance on the Free Speech Clause may have generally comported with the Court's agenda regarding both free speech and religious rights. Under the free speech approach, the Court could plausibly claim to be protecting both. Reliance on the Free Speech Clause responded to religious adherents' concerns that *Smith* exhibited a hostility to religion or religious freedom. Granting religious speakers access to public facilities on the basis of the Free Speech Clause facilitated religious participation in public programs and public life.

In sum, a variety of influences, events, and institutional actors influenced the movement from Hughes Court Free Speech Clause preferentialism to Rehnquist Court Free Exercise Clause subordination. During the equal access era of the 1980s and 1990s, new disputes about religion in public places—this time public auditoriums rather than public streets—reunited the Free Speech Clause and Free Exercise Clause. Strategic litigation choices, cross-doctrinal developments, the enhanced coverage and status of the Free Speech Clause, and the Supreme Court's own internal dynamics turned a preference for free speech into a more general subordination of free exercise rights.

The equal access free speech decisions did not signal the demise of the Free Exercise Clause, which remained important in other contexts. However, they marked a new phase in the relationship between the Free Speech Clause and Free Exercise Clause. Rather than view these rights as "cognate" and synergistic guarantees, some began to wonder whether the Free Exercise Clause had become "redundant."[58]

Interpretive Dynamics

The turn from Free Speech Clause preferentialism to partial Free Exercise Clause subordination produced some notable interpretive effects with regard to both clauses. Meanwhile, a third provision, the Establishment Clause, was brought into the interpretive mix. Modern interpretations of all three provisions are partially rooted in their dynamic interactions over time.

FREE EXERCISE AND ESTABLISHMENT

As explained earlier, although the Jehovah's Witnesses combined free exercise and free expression claims, the Hughes Court generally preferred to articulate its decisions in Free Speech Clause terms. However, preferentialism did not completely blind the Court to the complementary nature of these two "cognate" rights.

To the contrary, one reading of the Hughes Court decisions is that they used the Free Speech Clause to articulate the broad contours of the Free Exercise Clause and, to a lesser extent, the Establishment Clause. Later, in the equal access cases, the Free Speech Clause was relied on to facilitate religious free exercise. In the process of granting access to public facilities on Free Speech Clause grounds, the Rehnquist Court altered Establishment Clause baselines respecting the provision of public benefits to religious adherents. This interpretive move facilitated greater access by religious adherents to public resources. In some instances, it arguably supported providing public funds directly to religious actors and institutions.

Despite the free speech tenor of the Hughes Court decisions, modern Religion Clauses jurisprudence is partially rooted there. For example, the Court applied free speech principles to conclude that religious adherents had a right to access the streets on equal terms with others, and for the express purpose of engaging in religious activities.[59] The Court also shielded religious proselytizing and recruiting from a variety of repressive state and local laws.[60] Further, it barred government from discriminating against or targeting religion or religious activities, invalidated prior restraints on religious exercise, and struck down tax schemes that effectively suppressed religious practices.[61]

The broader framework of modern Free Exercise Clause doctrines can also be discerned in the early Hughes Court decisions. When it held that religious adherents were entitled to access public streets under the Free Speech Clause, the Court also recognized that religious adherents were entitled to enjoy certain public resources.[62] Applying general Free Speech Clause principles, the Hughes Court also held that religious adherents were not generally entitled to exemptions from neutral and generally applicable laws such as content-neutral permit requirements.[63] This position actually anticipated the *Smith* decision, which would not come down for several decades.

At the same time, the Hughes Court held that government was prohibited from discriminating against religion or singling it out for special burdens.[64] This too remains a central aspect of Free Exercise Clause protection. In cases such as *Barnette*, the Court emphasized that the Free Exercise Clause protects freedom of belief and conscience, and prohibits government from compelling action that violates individual religious tenets. In addition, again primarily relying on free speech principles, the Hughes Court held that governments were prohibited from imposing unconstitutional conditions—that is, forcing one to choose between practicing a chosen religion and receiving government resources—on religious adherents.[65] Finally, the Court established that government officials were not empowered to determine whether a religious belief was sincere, or whether an activity in some sense "counted" as religious in its nature or purpose.[66] Again, these holdings represent central premises of modern Religion Clauses doctrine.

In this respect, although the Free Speech Clause was the explicit protagonist in decisions, the Hughes Court still approached free speech, assembly, press, and free exercise rights as "cognate" and complementary. In the course of articulating the basic free speech rights of religious adherents, the Court simultaneously set forth basic principles of religious liberty. Those principles would be more completely fleshed out in the decades to come, and are in some cases still a work in progress. However, notwithstanding its clear preference for free speech justifications, we should not overlook the contributions of the Hughes Court to modern-day understandings of free exercise rights.

By contrast, the Rehnquist Court equal access cases arguably diminished free exercise rights. Religious adherents clearly benefitted from the free speech strategy, at least in the sense that they were able to challenge discriminatory exclusions from public facilities. However, invocation and application of Free Speech Clause public forum and content-neutrality rules contributed little to the advancement of free exercise rights. Indeed, under these precedents, religious *adherents* were generally treated as religious *speakers* who sought equal (content-neutral) treatment from government officials. Claimants explicitly argued, and the Rehnquist Court held, that the exercise of religion in these cases was a form of "speech" protected by the Free Speech Clause.

As a result, in cases such as *Widmar*, the Court did not dwell on the fact that religious practices had been targeted for exclusion from public properties. Rather, those practices were treated as religious communications, which were the province of the Free Speech Clause. Unlike the Hughes Court, the Rehnquist Court did not mention religious freedom or connect it to the expressive liberty recognized by its precedents. The equal access decisions were articulated, reported, and subsequently have been studied as free speech precedents.

The Supreme Court subordinated free exercise to free speech in other respects. As it narrowed free exercise rights in *Smith*, the Court recognized what it called "hybrid" rights claims.[67] This judicial invention appears to save some free exercise claims, but only if they are appended to some other fundamental right—such as, the Court noted, a claim that freedom of speech had been violated. Thus, a claimant armed with a naked free exercise claim receives no relief, whereas one that pleads a free speech violation might have a cognizable claim. Even assuming, as many judges and scholars doubt, that we are to take this concept seriously,[68] in "hybrid" free speech/free exercise claims, the Free Speech Clause is doing all the work.

As noted, in the equal access cases there were actually three intersecting provisions. In addition to free speech and free exercise, the Rehnquist Court's decisions also implicated, and in some important respects complicated, understandings of the First Amendment's Establishment Clause. In particular, the Court muddied the waters somewhat concerning the *baselines* used to determine when public funding of religion violates the Establishment Clause.

Those principles and baselines are notoriously complicated.[69] But in simple terms, under modern Establishment Clause doctrine, governments may include religious adherents as beneficiaries of public resources made available to all on equal and nonsectarian terms.[70] However, the Establishment Clause imposes limits on official support for religion, including the granting of *direct* forms of financial aid to religious actors and institutions.[71]

As noted, the Hughes Court granted religious adherents early and significant access to a specific public resource—the public streets. The right it recognized was a narrow but important one—to equality of treatment in terms of access to these public forums. However, when the Rehnquist Court turned to the Free Speech Clause's "public forum" doctrine to mediate access by religious adherents to public buildings, it adopted a much broader interpretation of permissible governmental subsidies for religion.[72] Under the Court's equal access free speech precedents, if *all* government programs that are open to a diversity of speakers and views constitute public forums, and if access to public forums is the sort of *incidental* benefit to religion the

Establishment Clause permits, then it appears to follow that *any* form of subsidy that can be characterized as a "public forum" must be made available to religious as well as secular claimants.[73]

This, in fact, was the Supreme Court's reasoning in cases such as *Rosenberger v. Rector and Visitors of the University of Virginia* (1995),[74] which invalidated the exclusion of a religious student publication from a university's student activities fund. The exclusion of religious perspectives from the program, said the Court, discriminated against religious editorial viewpoints and thus violated Free Speech Clause rules relating to regulation of speech in a so-called "limited" public forum (essentially, a public property open to only certain classes of speakers).[75] According to the Court, the activities fund was a "metaphysical" forum, and religious publications could not be excluded based on their religious viewpoints. The Court also concluded that indirectly providing university funds to an expressly religious publication would not violate the Establishment Clause.[76] It reasoned that the student activities funding policy was neutral with regard to religious sects, any religious speech would not be attributed to the university, and no funds would flow directly to the religious organizations themselves.[77] The Court concluded that any benefit to religion from "neutral" access to the university's public forum would not constitute an establishment of religion.[78]

In his dissent, Justice David Souter argued that the Court had, for the first time, "approve[d] funding of core religious activities by an arm of the State."[79] He claimed that the provision of student activities funds to a religious publication violated the rule that "direct aid to religion is impermissible."[80] Justice Souter also contended that the equal access precedents, which allowed access to speakers for traditional expressive activities in public fora, could not be stretched to cover things such as the provision of printing funds to religious publications.[81] The public forum cases, Justice Souter argued, "cannot be lifted to a higher plane of generalization without admitting that new economic benefits are being extended directly to religion in clear violation of the principle barring direct aid."[82]

Rosenberger strongly suggested that under the free speech framework adopted by the Court in the equal access cases, public forum doctrine had effectively become a new Establishment Clause baseline. Then, in *Capitol Square Review and Advisory Board v. Pinette* (1995),[83] the Court held that the Ku Klux Klan could erect a Latin cross in a public plaza next to the Ohio capitol building. Four justices concluded that communication of private religious speech *cannot* violate the Establishment Clause where it is (1) "purely private," and (2) "occurs in a traditional or designated public forum, publicly announced and open to all on equal terms."[84] Notably, the plurality refused even to apply the Establishment Clause's "endorsement" test, which asks whether a reasonable observer would perceive the unattended cross as governmental support for or favoritism toward religion.[85]

Thus, the Rehnquist Court's application of the Free Speech Clause in religious access cases has influenced modern Establishment Clause baselines. Extending the logic of the equal access precedents, *Rosenberger* used public forum principles to set the boundaries of public aid under the Establishment Clause. In *Pinette*, the Court was just one vote shy of recognizing a kind of "public forum exception" to the Establishment Clause's long-standing endorsement test.[86]

This movement of the Establishment Clause's goalposts, as it were, may have indirectly influenced the Supreme Court's most recent decision on aid to religious institutions. In *Trinity Lutheran Church v. Comer* (2017),[87] the Court held that Missouri could not prohibit churches and other religious organizations from directly receiving public funds to be used for repairs to religious properties.[88] Although the Court did not invoke the public forum doctrine or the equal access cases, the decision is a natural extension of those precedents. The logical progression is that just as they are entitled to equal access to the public forum under the Free Speech Clause, religious adherents are entitled under the Free Exercise Clause to equal access to other public resources—even if this means that churches are sometimes the direct recipients of taxpayer funds.

In sum, during the Rehnquist Court era, the intersection between the Free Speech Clause and the First Amendment's Religion Clauses resulted in both the partial subordination of the Free Exercise Clause and the importation of public forum doctrine into Establishment Clause jurisprudence. In the equal access cases, the Free Exercise Clause largely disappeared. In public resource cases, the Establishment Clause was connected to Free Speech Clause public forum principles that may have broadened the scope of permissible public aid to religion.

In a more general sense, the dominance of the Free Speech Clause altered the relationship between freedom of speech and free exercise of religion and the interplay among the First Amendment's Free Speech Clause, Free Exercise Clause, and Establishment Clause. Over time, a presumption (at least in cases involving state funding of religion) that anti-establishment concerns trump free exercise and free speech principles has been transformed into a presumption that the Free Speech Clause controls or at least significantly determines the outcomes in such cases. This transformation has resulted in some important protections for religious adherents, who were among other things able to gain equal access to government buildings and public funds. However, as argued below, Free Speech Clause doctrines are not always directly responsive to religious liberty concerns. In fact, in the long run, they may be less beneficial to religious adherents than many appear to assume.

FREE SPEECH AS FREE EXERCISE

So far, the focus has been on the Religion Clauses. However, when rights guarantees interact with one another, dynamic forces operate in more than one direction. The relationship between the Free Speech Clause and the Free Exercise Clause has also left some indelible marks on the former.

Indeed, interactions between freedom of speech and free exercise of religion during the Hughes Court era significantly influenced the early development of the free speech right.[89] As it adjudicated the rights of Jehovah's Witnesses to access public streets for the purpose of speaking and proselytizing, the Hughes Court articulated many of the basic principles of what would later become modern Free Speech Clause doctrine. Indeed, it is only a slight exaggeration to say that one could teach nearly *all* of these fundamental principles simply by studying the Hughes Court decisions.

Challenges to suppressive laws and regulations targeting religious speakers and religious practices encouraged the Court to recognize and elaborate basic Free Speech Clause rights. Prior to the Witnesses cases, the Court had generally adopted the view that public streets and parks were under the exclusive and plenary control of the governments that held title to them.[90] However, beginning in the 1930s, the Court began to recognize that "public forum" properties such as public streets and public parks had "immemorially" been open to the public for the purpose of communicating and assembling. These properties, the Court reasoned, were held in trust by government for the benefit of all speakers.[91]

Through challenges to restrictions on the ability to distribute literature and otherwise engage with audiences in the public streets, the Witnesses forged the first significant breathing space for public debate and information distribution in public places.[92] In rulings striking down solicitation bans, discriminatory license taxes, prior restraints, and permit schemes, the Hughes Court emphasized that *all* speakers, including religious ones, had a right to access public streets and parks.[93] These minimal and equal access principles would later form the basis for the modern public forum doctrine.

In the Witnesses decisions, the Hughes Court also made clear that state and local governments could regulate the time, place, and manner of expression and attend to other public order concerns.[94] However, it struck down facially discriminatory laws, permit schemes that were based upon the unbridled discretion of public officials, and discriminatory taxes and penalties.[95] The Court also indicated that some speech is not covered, as a categorical matter, by the First Amendment's Free Speech Clause—thus anticipating the modern "categorical balancing" approach to free speech coverage.[96] The Hughes Court also held that officials could not suppress speech merely because it offended public audiences.[97]

In fact, with regard to freedom of speech, there was much more in these early precedents. Among other things, the Hughes Court decisions (1) held that speech restrictions based on the content of speech, or the identity of the speaker, were presumptively unconstitutional;[98] (2) recognized a First Amendment right of willing audiences to *receive* information;[99] (3) held that audiences who were captive in their homes had the right to decide whether to receive unwanted expression;[100] (4) recognized that even false statements of fact could add value to public debate;[101] (5) rejected governmental efforts to characterize speech as "commercial," and thus outside the First Amendment's coverage, on the ground that the publisher might receive some remuneration for her materials;[102] and (6) held that the Free Speech Clause protects a right not to speak or be compelled to communicate.[103] Again, all of these concepts and principles are now central aspects of modern First Amendment doctrine.

Perhaps just as important, the discriminatory treatment and explicit exclusion of religious speakers encouraged the Court to think about the reasons or justifications for protecting free speech rights. Decades before the Warren Court made its storied turn, during the 1960s, toward liberal protection for free speech rights, the Hughes Court drew connections between public religious speech and concepts such as the marketplace of ideas and democratic self-government.[104] The Court also recognized the autonomy interests of religious speakers, and the importance to individual self-fulfillment of communicating religious ideas.[105]

The Rehnquist Court equal access decisions, as well as later applications of the public forum doctrine in religious speech cases, retained and in some instances further elaborated the core concept of the public forum, the requirement of content-neutrality, and other basic Free Speech Clause principles. However, in some respects, the strategic turn toward the Free Speech Clause discussed earlier resulted in doctrinal complexity and confusion. This was true, in particular, with regard to the public forum doctrine, the definition of "speech," and the principle of viewpoint neutrality.

With regard to the public forum, cases involving religious speech and speakers expanded the concept in meaningful respects. For instance, in religious speech cases the Court recognized "metaphysical" forums and elaborated on the concept of the "limited public forum"—a public place that is open to only some speakers or subject matters.[106] However, these developments raised some questions about the generalizability of the Court's holdings. Thus, recognizing a "metaphysical" forum in *Rosenberger*, in the form of the student funding program, allowed the Court to decide the case favorably on Free Speech Clause grounds. As Professor Abner Greene has observed, the Supreme Court has invalidated restrictions in limited public forums on the ground that they are viewpoint-based *only* in religious speech cases.[107] Thus, although the Court added "metaphysical" and "limited" public fora to Free Speech Clause doctrine, it is not clear to what extent these things benefit a broad class of speakers, or if they apply only to a narrow class of religious speakers.

To be sure, religious adherents have not always benefitted from the application of public forum and other free speech principles. As mentioned, *Christian Legal Society v. Martinez* (2010) upheld a state law school's requirement that the Christian Legal Society (CLS) accept "all comers" as members.[108] The Court concluded that the organization's associational rights effectively "merged" with its Free Speech Clause rights, and rejected CLS's free speech claim on public forum doctrine grounds.[109] As commentators have observed, in *Martinez*, the Free Speech Clause displaced not just free exercise rights but associational rights as well.[110]

In other religious speech cases, by contrast, the Supreme Court has determined that public forum principles are inapplicable or out of place. This has been so even in traditional public fora such as public parks.[111] For example, in *Pleasant Grove City, Utah v. Summum*, the Court held that although town officials had accepted a Ten Commandments monument for display in a public park, they were not obligated under the Free Speech Clause to accept another religious monument offered by a different religion. The Court held that the government communicated through the monuments it accepted (including, presumably, the Ten Commandments statue), and that when they engaged in communication rather than regulation officials were not required to comply with Free Speech Clause doctrines concerning regulation of speech in the public forum.[112] Thus, in *Summum*, public forum doctrine and content neutrality rules were both submerged, seemingly to avoid Free Speech Clause and Establishment Clause concerns associated with the display of a religious symbol.[113]

During the Rehnquist Court equal access era, some complications also arose relating to the definition of "speech" and the application of Free Speech Clause viewpoint-neutrality rules. Commentators have criticized the Court's categorical treatment of *all* forms of religious activity—solicitation, proselytizing, prayer, teaching, and perhaps even worship—as "speech."[114] Some have also taken issue with the Court's insistence that the exclusion of religion or religious speech is always, and necessarily, a form of *viewpoint* discrimination.[115] This approach to religious speech seems to elevate it above even political content, which can be excluded from certain types of public fora.[116] Treating all religious speech as viewpoint-related also suggests that the government may not be able to exclude any forms of religious communication, including worship, from public programs.[117]

Of course, there is nothing inherently wrong with religious adherents invoking the Free Speech Clause to gain equal access to public properties. As I have maintained elsewhere in the book, labeling free speech claims "opportunistic" or inappropriate is a tricky proposition. Among other things, there is no agreed-upon "appropriate" set of invocations. What is more, in contexts like this, the label fails to account for the fact that the Free Speech Clause is a critical facilitator of non-speech rights. This includes religious rights.

However, claimants and courts may have pushed aside the Free Exercise Clause without thinking through all of the implications for freedom of speech. As indicated, the strategic turn to the Free Speech Clause has affected public forum, coverage, and content neutrality standards. Arguments and decisions seem to have manipulated the public forum doctrine in ways that muddy its parameters in other cases. Further, rather than treat religious speech as perhaps a distinctive category, the Court has suggested that worship itself is "speech," and that religion is a non-excludable viewpoint. These pronouncements will not be confined to the category of religious speech, which has not been treated as special in any sense. They will affect forum, definitional, and neutrality concerns in other free speech contexts.

In sum, the intersection of the Free Speech Clause and the Religion Clauses has produced multi-directional doctrinal and other complications. In order to make space for the exercise of religious rights in public places, courts have sometimes bent and stretched free speech doctrines and concepts in ways that are likely to complicate their application in other contexts.

First Amendment Pluralism

Over time and for a number of different reasons, the Free Speech Clause has come to dominate the conversation even when what is centrally at stake is religious liberty. As I have argued, this has marginalized the Free Exercise Clause, complicated the interpretation of the Establishment Clause, and sowed confusion regarding Free Speech Clause coverages and doctrines. At this point, the Free Speech Clause and Free Exercise Clause are no longer viewed as complementary and cognate provisions. The provisions no longer seem to reinforce and illuminate one another. Instead, an "undifferentiated free speech framework" now applies across the board to religious communications, activities, and associations.[118]

As I argued in Chapter 3, however, relationships between and among First Amendment rights (indeed, among constitutional rights more generally) are not set in stone. The dynamics that affect them are perpetually changing. We can and, I argue, ought to return to a framework in which freedom of speech and freedom of religion function as distinctive but mutually reinforcing rights. That project must include efforts to ensure that invocations of the Free Speech Clause do not render the Free Exercise Clause redundant or superfluous. More broadly, as I argued in Chapter 3, we need to recover and enforce a First Amendment Pluralism that treats *all* of the First Amendment's clauses as distinctive but mutually reinforcing.

THE HARMS OF FREE SPEECH SUBORDINATION

Although they have distinctive ratification histories, the Free Speech Clause and Free Exercise Clause share deep conceptual roots. Freedom of speech (and press) can be traced, in part, to pre-ratification religious pamphleteering and proselytizing. During the first third of the twentieth century, the two clauses were regarded by the Supreme Court, government officials, and the public as part of a class of "fundamental," "preferred," and "cognate" rights. Together, the Free Speech Clause and Free Exercise Clause have offered significant protection against discriminatory laws, compelled orthodoxy, and public exclusion. Although in early cases the Supreme Court preferred the terms and rationales of free speech, the relationship between freedom of speech and free exercise was often synergistic and mutually reinforcing.

Recognition and enforcement of free speech, press, and assembly rights created the first public breathing space for the free exercise of religion. In turn, recognition of free exercise rights helped to create a strong foundation for what would become core "expressive" rights—speech, assembly, press, and petition. As the Supreme Court observed in *Barnette*, the compulsory flag salute case: "One's right to life, liberty, and property, to free speech, a free press, freedom of worship, and other fundamental rights may not be submitted to vote; they depend on the outcome of no elections."[119]

This early relationship between "cognate" provisions has turned into one dominated by free speech doctrines, principles, and concerns. On one hand, the current free speech-free exercise relationship, though certainly not ideal, has produced significant benefits for religious adherents. Invocations of the Free Speech Clause and other "expressive" provisions have resulted in equal access to public properties and programs. Freedom of speech has prohibited government from suppressing and discriminating against religious communications, as well as some sectarian practices. Further, in contrast to the Free Exercise Clause as interpreted in *Smith*, the Free Speech Clause can lead to invalidation of laws that only *incidentally* burden religious exercise.[120] Thus, it offers a broader domain of coverage and protection for religious communications and practices.[121] From this perspective, religious adherents, like other civil rights claimants, have successfully leveraged the protections of the Free Speech Clause to secure religious rights.

However, in this context, the Free Speech Clause has done more than facilitate religious rights. In some respects, Free Exercise Clause rights are now treated as *ancillary* to Free Speech Clause rights. The result is similar to the conception (discussed in Chapter 3) of "expressive association," which treats assemblies as covered by the First Amendment, but only insofar as they involve speech or communication.[122] If religion is, or in some broad sense becomes, just a form of "speech," then does the Free Exercise Clause become surplusage? Stated differently, if everything a religious adherent does—praying, proselytizing, worshipping, etc.—is covered and protected by the Free Speech Clause, then what distinctive purpose does the Free Exercise Clause actually serve?

The problem, then, is not the potential for some "opportunistic" leveraging of the Free Speech Clause, but rather a form of textual "expansionism" by which the Free Exercise Clause collapses into the Free Speech Clause.[123] As we saw in Chapter 3 with regard to the Press Clause, Assembly Clause, and Petition Clause, Free Speech Clause expansionism obscures what is distinctive about non-speech rights. It also places considerable pressure on free speech doctrines to do the work of independent but "cognate" rights provisions.

For example, in terms of facilitating free exercise, the Free Speech Clause's public forum and content-neutrality doctrines have been useful tools. However, these standards do not come close to capturing the essence of the harm to religion and religious adherents from certain kinds of governmental discrimination.[124] As one commentator has observed, "destroying a religion is much more than stifling a response. It often involves the destruction of a community and a way of life."[125]

Indeed, religious adherents may well find that the Free Speech Clause provides less coverage than the Free Exercise Clause does. The Free Speech Clause framework *standardizes* religion and religious speakers. It treats these things like everything and everyone else in the public forum. Religious speakers can speak and act, but only under the same terms as other speakers and actors. For example, their speech and symbolic actions cannot be suppressed or discriminated against. But these free speech neutrality rules are based on the supposition that there is nothing special or distinctive about religious communications or creedal activities. The Free Speech Clause is not concerned with the religious character of the communication—indeed, under neutrality principles, it cannot be so concerned.

Owing to this fact, reliance on the Free Speech Clause may lead to some disappointing results. In fact, it may result in religious adherents receiving *less* protection than they would even under a post-*Smith* Free Exercise Clause. For example, precedents that treat religion as a *viewpoint* may help religious adherents gain access to public properties today, but may make it more difficult or even impossible in future cases to obtain accommodations for religious practices.[126] Indeed, under the Free Speech Clause, it is possible that *any* singling out of religion—including in federal and state laws that seek to provide relief from burdens on sincerely held religious beliefs—might violate Free Speech Clause content-neutrality rules by preferring religious communications to others.[127] For similar reasons, public forum and other free speech doctrines may provide religious adherents with less protection against governmental funding conditions than the Religion Clauses.[128]

Finally, the Free Speech Clause framework offers no protection at all to religious acts and practices that cannot plausibly be characterized as "expressive."[129] To be sure, a great many religious acts can be characterized as speech. But not all can, and those excluded would receive no coverage or consideration under the Free Speech Clause.

Religious adherents are not the only ones who stand to lose under Free Speech Clause expansionism. Communities concerned about maintaining a basic degree of separation between church and state may find that an expansionist Free Speech Clause undermines anti-establishment principles. In particular, expansionism could bind the hands of public officials who have convincing secular reasons for wanting to exclude religion or some religious practices from certain public programs and public fora.

The Supreme Court has recognized that officials are permitted some leeway in terms of excluding religion from public programs.[130] Strict application of free speech doctrines and principles may threaten what the Court has referred to as the "play in the joints" between the Free Exercise Clause and Establishment Clause. The idea is that while officials *may* include religion in public programs consistent with the Establishment Clause, the Free Exercise Clause does not *require* that they do so. However, the logical implication of the Free Speech Clause argument, which was relied upon in *Rosenberger*, is that because it constitutes a point of view or perspective religion *cannot* be excluded from anything that can be characterized as a "public forum." Since the public forum concept is flexible enough to cover a wide variety of programs, including "metaphysical" ones, government may lose its flexibility to exclude religion from certain public programs.

The Free Speech Clause has produced some short-term benefits for religious adherents. However, in the long term, it does not place their religious liberties on a secure footing, and may harm political communities by depriving them of some means of maintaining separation between church and state. For these and other reasons, it is imperative that the Free Exercise Clause not be wholly supplanted by the Free Speech Clause.

FREE SPEECH AND FREE EXERCISE AS "COGNATE" RIGHTS

As Professor John Inazu has observed, relying heavily on a "rudderless public forum doctrine and a malleable concept of viewpoint neutrality," courts have ceased cultivating the relationships between and among free speech, free exercise, and other First Amendment rights.[131] Inazu argues that reorienting analysis in ways that take a more pluralistic perspective would specifically benefit religious groups by allowing them "to pursue their own visions of the good" and "stand in opposition to majoritarian norms."[132] More broadly, a pluralistic approach would encourage the development of the kind of political and social pluralism that the Free Speech Clause alone simply cannot produce. In essence, Professor Inazu advocates engaging with the First Amendment in ways that recognize and enforce *all* of its guarantees.[133] Chapter 3 advocated a similar "First Amendment Pluralism" with respect to free speech, assembly, press, and petition.

As noted earlier, the Free Speech Clause and Free Exercise Clause were once considered "cognate" or complementary rights. Although it generally preferred to speak in free speech (and sometimes free press) terms, the Hughes Court understood that the First Amendment's rights provisions are synergistic and mutually illuminating. However, since the 1980s, the notion of complementarity has generally been missing in judicial and scholarly accounts of the free speech and free exercise guarantees.

In the case of the Free Speech Clause and Free Exercise Clause, a condition precedent for a return to "cognate" status is that free exercise regain its stature as a fundamental right. This does not necessarily require that *Smith* be reversed, although that would obviously elevate and reinvigorate the Free Exercise Clause. Even without *Smith*'s demise, steps can be taken to reinvigorate the Free Exercise Clause and encourage its synergistic interaction with the Free Speech Clause and other First Amendment rights.

Litigants can reclaim the Free Exercise Clause by invoking it, in the many instances where *Smith* still allows this to occur. The Free Exercise Clause was abandoned prematurely, in some cases even prior to *Smith*. Litigants can revive it, in part, by developing cases and arguments centering on the principle of *religious* discrimination—instead of, or in certain contexts in addition to, expressive discrimination. For example, the Supreme Court's recent decision in *Trinity Lutheran*, which invalidated the exclusion of religious recipients from a public works program, was based solely on the Free Exercise Clause. The Court did not look to the public forum doctrine or other free speech concepts to invalidate the exclusion. More generally, scholars can continue to develop arguments and theories that revive a substantively robust Free Exercise Clause, again even within the parameters of *Smith*.[134]

At a minimum, reviving the Free Exercise Clause in this sense would force courts to re-engage with it as an independent guarantee. Revival might discourage the approach, represented in cases such as *CLS v. Martinez*, to "merge" free exercise, assembly, and other claims with Free Speech Clause claims.[135] As I argued in Chapter 3, a government forced to defend its actions against a number of independent constitutional claims will be more constrained than one that must only satisfy Free Speech Clause doctrines and principles.

If successful, revival of the Free Exercise Clause may produce opportunities for synergistic interactions between free exercise and free speech rights. Here I am referring not to the so-called "hybrid" claims nominally recognized in *Smith*. As

I indicated earlier, the "hybrid" free exercise-free speech claim is itself an example of Free Speech Clause dominance.

Rather, combining the Free Exercise Clause and Free Speech Clause would entail a return to the Hughes Court's conceptual approach to "cognate" free speech, free exercise, and other rights. A pluralistic analysis entails careful articulation of the distinctions and connections between and sometimes among constitutional rights provisions. In the case of the Free Exercise Clause and Free Speech Clause, this means conducting a thoughtful assessment of the extent to which both religious and communicative values are implicated by a particular law or policy.[136]

Barnette, the compulsory flag salute case, offers an instructive example. Although the decision is generally cited for the principle that governments cannot "compel speech," a careful reading of *Barnette* reveals that the Court relied on *both* free speech and free exercise values. The Court discussed both the religious and expressive bases for the students' objections, examined the nature of sectarian and secular symbolism, mentioned the significance of "creeds" and ceremonies, and explained why the compulsion of "belief" was ultimately prohibited. To be sure, there is more "free speech" than "free exercise" in *Barnette*, but that is likely owing to the Court's desire to establish a broad anti-orthodoxy principle. In any event, the Court generally avoided the "precedential walls" associated with reliance on isolated constitutional rights provisions.[137]

The iconic *Barnette* decision suggests a potential way forward in terms of how we debate and adjudicate intersecting free exercise and free speech claims. It points toward a more holistic and cumulative consideration of distinct free speech and free exercise values and principles. The approach would rely on a conception of overlapping, synergistic, and mutually illuminating rights. Imitating *Barnette* would not clear up all of the doctrinal confusions and complexities that currently affect the intersection of free speech and free exercise rights. However, it could lead to more transparent assessments of the constitutional interests implicated in certain cases.[138] It might also result in narrower judicial holdings, as courts place less pressure on individual clauses, including the Free Speech Clause.[139] The final part of the chapter illustrates this approach, using two contemporary controversies at the intersection of free exercise and free speech.

WORSHIP AND WEDDINGS

Free exercise and free speech continue to interact in some high-profile conflicts. In one context, the equal access decisions discussed earlier have raised the question whether the Free Speech Clause requires that religious *worship* be included in public forums such as public school buildings.[140] The Free Speech Clause has also been invoked by wedding photographers, bakers, and a host of other religious merchants who claim that application of anti-discrimination laws compels them to communicate a message of approval for same-sex couples' unions that conflicts with their religious beliefs.[141]

Framing the exclusion of worship services from public buildings as a Free Speech Clause concern is problematic for a number of reasons. The coverage question is quite complicated. The Supreme Court has said that worship *can be* expressive.[142] Indeed, at first glance, worship services would appear to consist of a combination of pure speech and symbolic actions. On the other hand, worship services are a distinctive kind of *religious activity*. In recent cases, government has typically excluded only worship, while religious study, prayers, and other forms of religious speech have not been excluded. But how are courts to distinguish "worship" from other religious activities? Does the attempt to do so implicate the sort of entanglement with religion the Establishment Clause forbids?

Adding to this complexity, in the equal access context the fact that something is expressive is not dispositive. Rather, as discussed earlier, under the public forum doctrine the critical question is whether an exclusion of worship constitutes an invidious form of *viewpoint* discrimination. However, determining whether worship communicates a specific viewpoint is a difficult task. Again, how does a judge or official decide that question without engaging in forbidden theological or ecclesiastical inquiries?[143]

Worship combines elements of speech, assembly, and free exercise of religion. Thus, in assessing its exclusion, litigants and courts ought to take all three of these constitutional components into account. Again, this cumulative approach would engage transparently with all of the affected rights, and also consider whether, in combination, they provide a basis for relief.

As noted, under many current worship exclusions, the expressive components of the activity—prayer, the singing of hymns, etc.—are not excluded from the public forum. Nor are discussions about religion, theology, or other substantive concerns. Rather, a particular form of communal gathering is targeted by worship exclusions. The group seeks to practice its religious faith in a public setting that is already available for related activities. Thus, what is actually being excluded is a special kind of gathering, one that occurs for the purpose of *exercising religion* in a manner that is both conventional and centrally important to adherents.

In this context, as in others involving free exercise rights, the Free Speech Clause's public forum and viewpoint neutrality doctrines are not irrelevant. However, they do not address the core claim or the most important consequence of official exclusion. In fact, they might misdirect the constitutional inquiry—away from the consequences of targeting a particular form of religious free exercise, and in the direction of whether religious "viewpoints" have been singled out for exclusion.

Given the results in the free speech "equal access" cases, the inclination to rely on the Free Speech Clause is understandable. However, the worship exclusion cases are only partially about opening up breathing space for religious discourse in the public square. More centrally, they concern the right to gather in public places for purposes that combine speech, assembly, and free exercise elements.

A pluralistic assessment would take each of these constitutional elements into account. If the government is purposefully discriminating against or targeting religious practices for special burdens, then the central question is whether it can justify those burdens under the Free Exercise Clause and the Establishment Clause. While the exclusion of worship happens to affect some expressive conduct, it does so only incidentally and as a result of the character of worship itself. In other words, the question is not whether worship is "speech" or whether it constitutes a "viewpoint," but rather whether the targeted exclusion of religious gatherings and activities violates the plural rights of the First Amendment.

Thus framed, such claims do not simply restate *Smith*'s "hybrid" claim in reverse, relying on a primary free exercise claim and a subordinate free speech claim. The Free Exercise Clause would itself constitute an independent basis for decision. The recognition of free speech and assembly harms would not save an otherwise invalid free exercise claim. However, they would provide a more holistic accounting of the constitutional harms that result when religious worship is subject to explicit exclusion.

Despite their success with free speech claims in the equal access context, religious adherents are not necessarily worse off under this sort of pluralistic analysis. Indeed, in certain respects, they would be better situated to contest worship exclusions. For one thing, all of the potential constitutional harms would be accounted for, and all constitutional aspects of worship—speech, assembly, and free exercise—would be addressed. Moreover, in terms of the freedom to practice religion, the Free Exercise Clause forbids government from targeting religion and religious practices for exclusion or punishment absent compelling reasons. The Establishment Clause forbids government from endorsing or establishing religion, and also from evincing hostility toward it. Whether excluding or including worship would violate the Establishment Clause is a critical question litigants and courts must address.[144] Under current neutral access Establishment Clause doctrine, it may be that including worship in a general program of access would not constitute an unconstitutional endorsement of religion.[145] But that is something that needs to be assessed, rather than merely assumed.

As noted, one benefit from proceeding in this pluralistic manner is that it clarifies what is at stake in terms of constitutional rights. Another is that it requires litigants and courts to consider the *relationships* between and among the Free Speech Clause, Assembly Clause, Free Exercise Clause, and Establishment Clause. Combining rights provisions could create more compelling access claims than are available under clause-bound approaches. Even if it does not create stronger claims, this approach would provide a clearer sense of the relationship between freedom of speech and free exercise of religion. Placing the free speech and free exercise claims side by side and analyzing them together shows that there are important differences between excluding *discourse* about religion or religious viewpoints and excluding the actual *practice* of religion.

Further, combination analysis would clarify the Establishment Clause implications of worship exclusions. Under the free speech public forum analysis, the central question (assuming the policy is viewpoint neutral) is whether excluding worship is "reasonable" owing to concerns that *include* the possibility that inclusion will endorse religion. The reasonableness inquiry focuses primarily on whether exclusion will serve the primary functions of the public property in question. By contrast, the Establishment Clause may impose a more serious limitation for worship in public buildings than the Free Speech Clause analysis suggests. The question under the Establishment Clause is not whether exclusion is "reasonable" in light of the forum, but whether inclusion of worship *transforms* the forum into something akin to a public church and thus results in an official endorsement of religion. Again, placing the various clauses in contact with one another clarifies and redirects the analysis in ways that highlight the central constitutional principles and values at stake.

Conflicts that have arisen at the intersection of same-sex marriage and anti-discrimination laws are raising similar difficulties and concerns. Religious adherents who object to being compelled to take photographs, arrange flowers, or bake cakes for same-sex couples have relied on both free exercise and free speech rights as grounds for exemption from anti-discrimination laws that ban unequal treatment of gay and lesbian persons.

In some recent cases, religious adherents have relied more heavily on the Free Speech Clause to resist these laws. However, as in the case of worship exclusions, the central objection to engaging in many of these activities is not narrowly communicative, but religious. Thus, the merchants claim that application of state anti-discrimination laws actually compel them to *participate* in a religious ceremony. That compulsion makes them complicit, as the merchants see it, in a sinful activity. Thus, what they are being forced to "express" through the act of engaging in commerce is the *legitimacy* of same-sex marriage. Understood this way, the compulsion relates most centrally to religious orthodoxy.

To be sure, the free speech right is still implicated in these cases. Compulsion of specific words or messages would violate *Barnette*'s anti-orthodoxy principle. This sort of compulsion affects not just words, but also beliefs regarding the political issue of equal protection. It also implicates rights of conscience, which are protected under both the free exercise and free speech provisions.

So far, courts have not been very hospitable to the free speech argument.[146] Part of the reason for this could be that the Free Speech Clause does not go to the heart of the claim—that being forced to provide services compels merchants to actively participate in a ceremony they view as sinful. The cake-baker, photographer, and hair stylist are not being compelled to utter words of approval, or not merely to do so. Their compulsion is of a different character, one that the Free Speech Clause by itself cannot remedy.

If what is being compelled in the context of weddings is a form of *active participation* in a ritual or ceremony with deep religious significance, neither rights provision alone provides a sufficient remedy. As in *Barnette*, the combination of communicative and ritual compulsion constitutes the harm. The Free Speech Clause ensures autonomy with regard to religious speech, including statements and symbolic acts. The Free Exercise Clause protects conscientious objectors from participating in what they sincerely believe to be sinful activity. And as *Barnette* observed, the compulsion of *belief* connects the two clauses.[147] As Justice Jackson famously wrote: "If there is any fixed star in our constitutional constellation, it is that no official, high or petty, can prescribe what shall be orthodox in *politics*, nationalism, *religion*, or other matters of opinion or force citizens to confess *by word or act* their faith therein."[148]

As the passage from *Barnette* instructs, in the wedding context, we need not ignore the Free Speech Clause altogether. However, it ought to be contextualized such that its significance is accurately reflected. In cases involving the actual compulsion of written or spoken words, the Free Speech Clause is the principal limitation. But in cases challenging the compulsion of religious rituals or ceremonies, the Free Exercise Clause is the primary rights provision.

In many cases, merchants in the post-marriage equality cases are seeking a religious accommodation to state anti-discrimination laws, one that frees them of the compulsion to participate in actions they view as facilitating sin.[149] They do not seek the accommodation so that they may freely express their views with regard to same-sex marriage; the anti-discrimination laws do not target expression and, in any event, that particular right is protected by the Free Speech Clause. Rather, the accommodation they seek would allow religious merchants to engage in an act—refusing service—that they believe is compelled by their faith.

In both the worship and wedding examples, the commanding presence of the Free Speech Clause tends to obscure more than illuminate matters. In these conflicts, freedom of speech and free exercise of religion are both implicated. With respect to worship, exclusion does affect a means of expression. More important, it singles out for exclusion a central religious practice. With respect to weddings, compelling certain commercial activity may affect merchants' creative and expressive autonomy in some narrow class of cases. However, the central claim is that it mandates a form of participation in religious rituals. The question is whether compelled photography, baking, hair dressing, and makeup artistry facilitates a sinful act.

In general, a pluralistic analysis would address all rights separately *and* explicitly consider how they relate to one another. It would more transparently articulate the distinct, but often complementary, constitutional values protected under different rights provisions. The ultimately goal is to achieve a full and honest accounting of the scope of government's authority as it relates to religious practices that happen also to be expressive. Whether religious worship can be conducted in public forums or religious objectors are entitled to narrow or broad accommodations relating to commerce with same-sex couples depends on a pluralistic accounting of the First Amendment rights implicated by worship exclusions and anti-discrimination laws.

5

EQUAL PROTECTION

CHAPTERS 3 AND 4 examined why and how the Free Speech Clause came to dominate or subordinate certain First Amendment rights provisions. The relationship between the Free Speech Clause and the Equal Protection Clause[1] is of a different character. Here, the Free Speech Clause has not dominated or subordinated the non-speech rights provision. Rather, it has functioned as a critical facilitator of constitutional equality and a generally effective mediator of discourse about equal protection rights.[2] Although the Free Speech Clause and Equal Protection Clause are currently enforced under separate constitutional doctrines, they remain indelibly linked. Indeed, it is impossible to fully understand either the Free Speech Clause or the Equal Protection Clause without understanding their relationship to one another.

The relationship between these constitutional rights has not always or in all respects been facilitative and synergistic. Over time, equality advocates discovered some serious limits to their free speech strategies. At some critical moments, courts interpreted the Free Speech Clause in ways that limited or denied coverage for certain forms of equality expression. By contrast, the Free Speech Clause's robust protection for hate speech and the recognition of negative free speech rights—the right not to communicate and the right not to associate—have complicated governmental efforts to pursue equal protection rights for all persons.

The Dynamic Free Speech Clause. Timothy Zick.

We obviously cannot analyze, in a single chapter, all aspects and events concerning the relationship between freedom of speech and equal protection. Scholars have addressed constitutional equality movements in historical, political, and cultural detail. Instead, this chapter focuses on the *relationship* between the Free Speech Clause and the Equal Protection Clause. It focuses specifically on the manner in which the race and LGBT equality movements have affected that relationship.[3] Although *all* equality movements have relied on free speech, racial and sexual orientation equality rights have a unique relationship with freedom of speech. These movements faced unique forms of censorship. In response, they developed some of the most sophisticated free speech strategies.

The intersection between the Free Speech Clause and the Equal Protection Clause generates several general lessons, in particular for equality advocates. The chapter uses those lessons to organize its consideration of the free speech-equality relationship. It closes with an application of those lessons to the ongoing transgender equality movement.

Early Connections

From the very beginning of their formal relationship, freedom of speech has facilitated the recognition and enforcement of equal protection. This aspect of the relational dynamic actually preceded ratification of the Fourteenth Amendment's Equal Protection Clause.

The Free Speech Clause, along with freedom of the press and freedom of assembly, performed an important facilitative function during the process that led to the ratification of the Reconstruction Amendments. Reconstruction Republicans were acutely aware of the importance of protecting the right to debate and defend equal protection rights for the newly freed slaves. During debates concerning what would eventually become the Fourteenth Amendment, they frequently invoked the First Amendment's Free Speech Clause and Press Clause to resist official efforts to suppress abolitionist speech.[4]

Thus, freedom of speech was a critical mechanism for defending and ultimately achieving the adoption of constitutional equality rights. In this fundamental sense, the Equal Protection Clause is itself a product of the freedom of speech.

The bond between the Free Speech Clause and the Equal Protection Clause was strengthened further during the 1930s, when the Supreme Court held that the former constrained not just Congress but also the states.[5] The process of "incorporating" the Free Speech Clause (which the Court accomplished using the Fourteenth Amendment's Due Process Clause) considerably expanded the reach and domain of the Free Speech Clause. Indeed, the most significant precedents and doctrines in the free speech-equal protection area were the result of challenges to state and local laws.

After incorporation, equal protection advocates and movements began to rely more heavily on the Free Speech Clause. Ultimately, incorporation enabled civil rights activists to resist state and local efforts to silence their movement. Race equality advocates would not be the only ones to turn to the Free Speech Clause to resist governmental discrimination and censorship. As they invoked free speech to obtain constitutional equality, advocates would simultaneously build out the Free Speech Clause.

Lessons from Equality Advocacy

LESSON 1: FREE SPEECH RIGHTS ARE MOST CRITICAL DURING THE EARLIEST STAGES OF CONSTITUTIONAL EQUALITY MOVEMENTS, WHEN ADVOCATES SEEK TO ESTABLISH A RIGHT OF "EXPRESSIVE EQUALITY."

As the Reconstruction example shows, obtaining recognition for basic free speech and other First Amendment rights has been critical to the advancement of constitutional equality. Individuals and activists have used the Free Speech Clause as a gateway or bridge to substantive Equal Protection Clause protections. In particular, they have leveraged "expressive equality"—the right to communicate on equal terms with others—to gain recognition for racial and sexual identity, mobilize politically, and generally advance constitutional equality rights. The NAACP developed and executed a sophisticated strategy to use the Free Speech Clause to secure rights under the Equal Protection Clause. More recently, LGBT advocates have used the Free Speech Clause to facilitate the recognition of their constitutional equality rights.[6] Expressive equality has been an important gateway right.

In the United States, no group has faced more resistance, official and private, to recognition of their equal protection rights than African Americans. From emancipation, through Jim Crow, and throughout the civil rights era, federal and state officials imposed a system of racial apartheid that denied basic civil and constitutional rights—including First Amendment rights—to African Americans. Legal restrictions often targeted free speech and other "expressive" rights, with the idea that silencing the movement would lead to its failure.

In response to these limits, activists invoked a variety of constitutional provisions to challenge and eliminate the vestiges of slavery, including the Fourteenth Amendment's Due Process Clause and Equal Protection Clause. However, the star of this era was the First Amendment—in particular, the Free Speech Clause.[7]

During the 1950s and 1960s, civil rights activists and litigants relied heavily on the Free Speech Clause to establish their rights to be present in public places and to communicate with regard to equal protection rights. In federal courts, the NAACP, which spearheaded a national strategy for civil rights litigation, engaged in an intensive campaign that focused first on securing recognition and enforcement of basic First Amendment rights.[8] The NAACP challenged, on Free Speech Clause grounds, a variety of state laws and practices: limits on access to public properties for the purpose of engaging in peaceful protests; laws restricting the solicitation of clients for civil rights litigation; arrests of peaceful protesters pursuant to "public order" laws such as breach of peace and disorderly conduct; state libel laws; efforts to compel disclosure of civil rights organizations' membership lists; and racial segregation at private lunch counters.[9]

Many of these early lawsuits were aimed at securing basic free speech and other First Amendment rights. However, they served another purpose as well, one that was highly symbolic but critically important. The NAACP used the Free Speech Clause to obtain the first equality rights for African-Americans. Judicial recognition of "expressive equality"—the ability to speak, associate, and publish information on equal terms with others—was both a victory for free speech rights and a gateway to substantive equal protection rights.[10]

The NAACP's free speech campaign did not merely establish that governments were barred from suppressing what Chapter 2 referred to as "rights speech"—communications about or concerning equal protection rights. Rather, it secured recognition of a right to *equal treatment under law* with regard to communicating, protesting, and publishing information. In this respect, free speech rights were the first formal rights to equal treatment African-Americans enjoyed in the United States. Indeed, for a long period of time, these were the *only* equality rights African-Americans enjoyed.

The NAACP free speech strategy combined the Free Speech Clause and the Equal Protection Clause in ways that furthered rights under both provisions. Freedom of speech was a necessary antecedent to substantive equal protection. As discussed below, the civil rights era precedents were also critically important to the expansion of the modern Free Speech Clause.

Of course, the NAACP's strategy was not solely focused on securing judicial precedents. As discussed further below, successful Free Speech Clause litigation allowed activists and advocacy groups to mobilize politically on behalf of equal protection rights.[11] In this sense, as well, freedom of speech was an important early bridge to race and LGBT equal protection rights.

<u>LESSON 2</u>: FREE SPEECH RIGHTS ARE CUMULATIVE AND ITERATIVE. CONSTITUTIONAL EQUALITY MOVEMENTS BUILD UPON THE FREE SPEECH CLAIMS, STRATEGIES, AND PRECEDENTS OF THEIR PREDECESSORS, AND INNOVATE BY ENGAGING IN UNIQUE EXPRESSIVE ACTIVITIES AND BRINGING NOVEL FREE SPEECH CLAIMS.

In similar ways and largely to similar effect, LGBT equality advocates relied heavily on the Free Speech Clause in the earliest stages of their movement. As Professor Carlos Ball has observed, the Free Speech Clause played a crucial role "in creating the political, social, and legal conditions that have permitted sexuality-based identities and communities to form and thrive while allowing the LGBT movement to achieve many of its objectives."[12]

Achievement of these objectives was partly the result of the LGBT equality movement's imitation of the NAACP free speech strategy. In the initial phases of their movement, LGBT activists turned frequently and with significant success to the Free Speech Clause. To be sure, they also relied on other constitutional provisions, including the Due Process Clause and the Equal Protection Clause. However, the Free Speech Clause was a central part of the equality campaign from the start.

Like race equality advocates before them, LGBT activists understood that obtaining free speech rights was a necessary precondition for seeking substantive constitutional equality rights down the road. As Professor Ball has succinctly described this perspective, "free speech came first and equality came second."[13]

Thus, like the race equality movement, the LGBT equality movement focused first on establishing "expressive equality" rights. These included rights to publicly identify as gay or lesbian; to meet and organize as gay and lesbian persons; and to publish information about the lives and concerns of gay and lesbian persons.[14] As was the case during the Civil Rights Movement, LGBT free speech rights were recognized long before due process, "privacy," or equal protection rights had gained any traction in the courts and other venues. Indeed, again for a period of several decades, free speech rights were the *only* recognized LGBT constitutional equality rights.[15]

LGBT activists invoked the Free Speech Clause to challenge a wide variety of official acts of censorship and repression. At first, even basic free speech rights to publish information or gather for political purposes were not secure. In conflicts concerning basic public protest rights and rights of association, LGBT equality advocates successfully invoked the civil rights era free speech precedents from the 1950s and 1960s. These precedents were critically important to the recognition of LGBT expressive equality rights. In this respect, new equality advocates invoked the accumulated free speech precedents of a prior movement to advance their agenda.

LGBT equality advocates did not rely exclusively on civil rights era free speech precedents. They also innovated and expanded the free speech strategy. Civil rights era protesters had relied on various forms of expressive self-help, including sit-ins, peaceful demonstrations, and public protests. During the early phases of their own movement, LGBT activists engaged in some similar activities. But they also opposed various kinds of sex censorship in unique ways—for example, through cross-dressing, gay pride parades, and other forms of expression unique to their movement. In response to legal and social measures designed to keep them fully closeted, LGBT advocates used the Free Speech Clause to escape that fate.

As Professor Ball has observed, the Free Speech Clause and LGBT equality have been "inextricably linked since the early days of the LGBT movement in the United States."[16] One important link was the strategy, evident at the outset of each movement, of seeking and obtaining "expressive equality" rights. Once secured, each movement used these rights in ways suited to their distinct circumstances. LGBT equality advocates both piggy-backed on civil rights era free speech gains, and riffed on them in ways unique to their movement.

LESSON 3: THE FREE SPEECH CLAUSE PERFORMS CRITICAL MEDIATING AND LEGITIMATING FUNCTIONS WITH REGARD TO THE RECOGNITION AND ENFORCEMENT OF CONSTITUTIONAL EQUALITY RIGHTS.

The first stage of the civil rights and LGBT equality movements involved securing recognition for basic free speech rights. The second stage, generally speaking, involved exercising and leveraging those rights in ways that advanced substantive equal protection and other constitutional rights.

The Free Speech Clause provided a crucial mediating framework for this purpose. In the free speech mediation stage, both proponents and opponents of the recognition and expansion of equal protection rights invoked free speech rights and engaged in free speech activities. Free Speech Clause precedents, doctrines, and principles provided a common set of ground rules for arbitrating public discourse concerning constitutional equality rights.

Constitutional movements communicate messages by various means, toward the ultimate goal of changing or defending the existing constitutional order. As Robert Post and Reva Siegel have observed, "the First Amendment ensures that all Americans can express their beliefs about the Constitution."[17] The Free Speech Clause facilitates this constitutional discourse by providing a process framework for constitutional change. As discussed in Chapter 2, free speech ensures that there are fair and open democratic channels for constitutional rights discourse. Over the long term, the Free Speech Clause's mediating framework also lends political legitimacy to the outcome of debates—including disputes concerning the recognition, scope, and enforcement of constitutional rights.

The ability to communicate ideas, concerns, and principles relating to equal protection rights has been vitally important to constitutional equality movements and to American democracy in the broader sense.[18] It was during the civil rights era that the Supreme Court announced, in *New York Times Co. v. Sullivan* (1964), that the "central meaning" of the Free Speech Clause is that debate regarding matters of public concern should be "robust, uninhibited, and wide open."[19] More specific ground rules for mediating constitutional equality debates were added during this period. These included the requirement that governments exhibit neutrality with regard to the content of speech, provide equal access to public properties for the purpose of expression, and allow citizens to assemble and organize in the pursuit of equality rights. As discussed further below, civil rights era free speech precedents also established that speakers had a constitutional right to speak and associate *anonymously*.[20]

These ground rules made possible a wide-open and robust discourse concerning racial equality. The story of how civil rights advocates exercised their free speech and other First Amendment rights in pursuit of constitutional equality has been well-told by legal historians and other commentators.[21] As these accounts show, activists utilized expressive equality rights to participate in marches and public protests, distribute publications, and organize activities that significantly advanced the civil rights agenda. As the movement garnered media and public attention, protests and other expressive activities transformed local instances of racial injustice into a national conversation about segregation and racial equality.[22] In this way, civil rights activists relied on the free speech framework to significantly expand the geographic reach and appeal of their movement. Images of public contention produced public and, eventually, official support for the race equality movement.

As *New York Times v. Sullivan* indicated, a critically important aspect of Free Speech Clause mediation is that it allowed civil rights activists to communicate sharp criticisms of governments and official policies with regard to racial segregation. It also assisted them in mounting attacks on de jure and de facto forms of race discrimination in a variety of different places—in the streets, in proximity to state legislatures, in national and local publications, and in the courts.

By creating breathing space for public discourse about race, the Free Speech Clause helped to mediate a national conversation that continues today. Exercise of free speech rights has allowed race equality advocates to make moral, political, and legal arguments in support of full and equal citizenship. At the same time, as discussed further below, the Free Speech Clause's neutrality principle has also allowed opponents of racial equality claims to publicly communicate their own dissenting ideas and viewpoints.

Perhaps most importantly, the combination of "expressive equality" rights and free speech mediation facilitated political mobilization on behalf of racial equality. This was critically important to legislative enactments such as the Civil Rights Act of 1964 and the Voting Rights Act of 1965. Thus, free speech mediation protected out-of-doors expressive activities and indoor adjudication, lobbying, and other forms of political expression.

To be sure, the NAACP's free speech litigation did not directly cause this landmark legislation. However, the groundwork for these political acts took place in meeting halls, public streets, and lunch counters across the nation.[23] Free speech mediation empowered civil rights claimants, facilitated political organization, and nationalized the discourse concerning constitutional equality. Over the long term, the Civil Rights Movement effectively leveraged Free Speech Clause mediation to gain constitutional and legal equality for African-Americans.

The same Free Speech Clause mediating principles that facilitated the Civil Rights Movement have also been critically important to public discourse about sexual orientation and LGBT equality. In the United States, "uninhibited, robust, and wide-open" discourse concerning matters of human sexuality has, to put things mildly, not been the norm. However, free speech mediation created critical breathing space for discourse about human sexuality and sexual orientation.

Indeed, Professor Dale Carpenter has written that "[t]he First Amendment created gay America."[24] Expressive equality secured basic rights concerning public visibility and association. More generally, free speech mediation rules prohibited governmental suppression of sex-themed expression based on its content. As discussed below, this mediating principle was not always faithfully enforced with regard to gay and lesbian expression. However, over the long term, many LGBT persons would use the mediating principles of the Free Speech Clause to escape the apartheid of the closet.[25]

As Professor William Eskridge has observed, the Free Speech Clause was "profoundly radical—facilitating the formation of a gay *nomos*, a community of sex-positive and gender-bending idealists, and requiring sex-negative America to give gays a hearing."[26] During most of the twentieth century, governmental authorities criminalized and suppressed gay and lesbian literature and erotica on the ground that it was deviant and dangerous.[27] However, by the early 1980s, advocates had successfully invoked the Free Speech Clause to obtain protection for most forms of gay and lesbian erotica.[28]

Over time, Free Speech Clause mediation rules, most importantly the content-neutrality principle, facilitated more open (if not uninhibited) public discussion concerning sexuality and sexual orientation. The fact that gay men and lesbians had rights to communicate and associate anonymously, owing again to civil rights free speech precedents, helped contribute to more candid and robust national discourse about LGBT concerns and rights.

Owing to free speech mediation, the American public was better able to access information about the nature of sexual orientation, gay and lesbian culture, and the specific equality claims made by LGBT persons. As LGBT information and individuals began to escape the closet, there was an increase in the public and private flow of information about once-taboo subjects. The influence of free speech mediation was even reflected in American culture and entertainment, as television shows and other cultural beacons began—haltingly and stereotypically at first—to include gay and lesbian characters and scenarios.

As was the case during the civil rights era, LGBT free speech litigation was a necessary precondition for broad-based political mobilization. As Professor Eskridge has observed, by 1969 LGBT persons had attained basic free speech and other First Amendment rights. This, he notes, was the year the famous Stonewall riot triggered mass political mobilization by gay men and lesbians.[29] In the ensuing decades, LGBT activists would vigorously exercise free speech and other First Amendment rights to protest discrimination on the basis of sexual orientation and to lobby for equality rights.

As Professor Ball observes, these cultural and political transformations were only possible owing to the successes of the LGBT movement's free speech strategy. As during the civil rights era, this strategy was much broader than securing vital judicial precedents. It included the robust exercise of free speech rights *outside* the nation's courtrooms—for example, in political discourse about anti-sodomy laws, AIDS, and marriage equality.[30] LGBT activists, at both the "elite" and grassroots levels, participated in marches, protests, lobbying, information campaigns, and retail politics as part of a campaign to alter cultural, moral, and legal understandings of sexual minorities.

As one would surmise, many of the conversations and debates regarding the equal treatment or cultural acceptance of LGBT persons have been tense and emotionally charged. Nevertheless, Free Speech Clause mediation has generally required both that different perspectives be heard and that the debate be open and transparent. When opponents of marriage equality insisted, in *Doe v. Reed* (2010), that they had a Free Speech Clause right to keep their signatures on anti-marriage-equality referendum petitions private, the Supreme Court rejected the claim. Although the Court did not question the mediating rule of anonymity, it concluded that absent evidence that the signatories would be harassed or harmed by disclosure, the Free Speech Clause did not shield their names. *Doe* insisted on a measure of transparency in debates concerning the scope of marriage equality rights. It required what Justice Scalia described, in his concurring opinion, as "civic courage" in public discourse.[31]

Free speech mediation has contributed to some monumental changes in terms of LGBT constitutional equality rights. Most recently, in *Obergefell v. Hodges* (2015), which recognized a right to marriage equality, the Supreme Court emphasized the important function that freedom of speech had played in producing its decision. The Court noted the various opportunities the public and public officials had to discuss, study, debate, and litigate marriage equality prior to its decision. Justice Anthony

Kennedy specifically described how "new dimensions of freedom become apparent to new generations, often through perspectives that begin in pleas or protests and then are considered in the political sphere and the judicial process."[32] The dissenters argued that public discourse concerning gay and lesbian equality should have been allowed to continue. In their view, the Court had short-circuited an ongoing public discourse about marriage and equality rights.[33] But despite their differences, the majority and dissenting justices found common ground in the principle that freedom of speech plays a critical mediating function with regard to public discourse about constitutional rights.

In sum, just as civil rights activists had before them, LGBT activists exercised the "expressive equality" rights they had obtained and leveraged free speech mediation principles to engage in equality discourse and mobilize politically. Free speech mediation helped create the social, political, and legal climate that produced significant gains in terms of LGBT constitutional equality.

LESSON 4: AS A FACILITATOR OF CONSTITUTIONAL EQUALITY RIGHTS, THE FREE SPEECH CLAUSE HAS SIGNIFICANT LIMITATIONS AND DRAWBACKS—INCLUDING UNCERTAIN COVERAGE FOR IDENTITY SPEECH, STRONG PROTECTIONS FOR HATE SPEECH, RECOGNITION OF NEGATIVE AND EXCLUSIONARY FREE SPEECH RIGHTS, AND A GOVERNMENT SPEECH PRINCIPLE THAT IS NOT SUBJECT TO FREE SPEECH MEDIATION RULES.

Aspects of the Free Speech Clause's mediating framework, which generally functions as a means of ensuring robust and open equality discourse, have made it more difficult for some individuals to obtain full equality rights. Identity speech has not been fully protected. Content-neutrality rules protect not only advocacy on behalf of equal rights, but also dissent and various forms of resistance to such rights. Under current free speech standards, this protection extends to "hate speech" that denigrates individuals based on race, sexual orientation, and other characteristics. Further, during the LGBT equality movement, in particular, the Free Speech Clause was successfully invoked in ways that undermined state efforts to promote equality. Finally, as discussed in Chapter 2, as interpreted, the Free Speech Clause recognizes a government speech principle that is not subject to mediation rules. This principle enables, but does not limit, government anti-equality speech.

Identity Speech

Although it facilitated equal protection claims and ultimately played a significant role in terms of the recognition of constitutional equality rights, the Free Speech

Clause did not always deliver for equality advocates. Despite the fact that judges generally found free speech claims persuasive or even compelling, the Free Speech Clause did not protect race or LGBT equality advocates from some harmful forms of state repression and abuse. These failures were not devastating to constitutional equality movements; but they were stark reminders that the free speech strategy had limits.

As noted, race and LGBT equality advocates successfully invoked the Free Speech Clause in cases involving rights to protest in public, distribute information about their movements, and assemble for the purpose of advancing their causes. As Professor Harry Kalven, Jr. observed, an important part of the civil rights free speech strategy was to highlight the unique harms of segregation by challenging limits on African-Americans' *presence* in certain public and private places. According to Kalven, the NAACP wanted to "make the Supreme Court confront the Negro's constitutional claims and grievances and give the Negro his constitutional due."[34]

In terms of establishing or enhancing the visibility of African-Americans, this strategy had limits. Free speech rights did not always protect the expression of racial identity, either in the form of symbolic acts of defiance or with respect to the confrontational presence Kalven mentioned. Most notably, free speech challenges to the arrests of civil rights activists who participated in lunch counter sit-ins were unsuccessful. Professor Kalven described the sit-ins as a form of "self-help as a speech activity."[35] But at the Supreme Court, most of the justices did not think the sit-in arrests implicated the Free Speech Clause at all.[36] Nor, in some later cases, were civil rights litigants able to convince the Court that the Free Speech Clause protected a right of access to symbolic venues such as jails.[37]

Although they were important, these setbacks did not demonstrate a broad failing of the civil rights free speech strategy. As one would expect in a movement that spanned decades and challenged a system as deeply ingrained as racial apartheid, there were Free Speech Clause defeats. Taking the longer view, although the Free Speech Clause failed to protect racial presence and identity in the sit-in and some other cases, these failures may have influenced the Court's interpretation of the Free Speech Clause as it related to other forms of racial self-expression. Thus, although they did not prevail on their free speech arguments in the sit-in cases, civil rights activists were able to successfully challenge, on free speech grounds, a breach of peace conviction based on a silent protest of racial segregation in a public library reading room.[38] Thus, presence and "identity speech" claims did not always or invariably fail.

For closeted individuals, self-expression and identity speech are critically important means of challenging governmental discrimination and censorship. To a greater degree and to more serious effect than race equality advocates, LGBT persons experienced setbacks in this respect.

Despite existing civil rights free speech precedents, during the 1950s and 1960s, governments at all levels continued to harass and discriminate against gay men and lesbians.[39] The federal government's purge of gay men in its employ, during the so-called "Lavender Scare" of the 1950s, was one aspect of a coordinated campaign of official harassment and censorship of sexual identity.[40] Merely *identifying* as gay or lesbian, or being suspected of these identities, was grounds for termination.

Moreover, although publishers of gay and lesbian magazines were generally spared prosecution under federal obscenity laws, Supreme Court decisions concerning gay and lesbian pornography and other sexually themed materials conveyed what Professor Eskridge has described as "an orthodoxy of compulsory heterosexuality" that validated "discriminatory treatment of homosexual speech."[41] Thus, during the critical early stages of the LGBT equality movement, the Free Speech Clause did not protect and facilitate all forms of sexual identity speech.

Interpretations of the Free Speech Clause by federal courts, including the Supreme Court, left some troubling gaps in coverage. These interpretations would eventually change, as courts applied free speech neutrality principles in ways that treated homosexual and heterosexual perspectives in sex-themed materials in a similar manner.[42] Nevertheless, as Professor Eskridge's work has shown, the Supreme Court and the lower courts took their time in reaching this decision point.

LGBT employees and others discovered that courts would not embrace coverage for all forms of sexual orientation identity speech. Many gay men and lesbians were fired from their jobs, or discharged from branches of the U.S. armed forces, simply for communicating their sexual orientation. These adverse actions were related to a new approach to homosexuality and sexual orientation. Governments and public officials treated homosexuality as a disease, and enacted a raft of what Professor Eskridge has called "no promo homo" measures.[43] Under this approach, although gay men and lesbians were generally free to communicate their sexual orientation at public events and in public venues, laws and regulations treated coming out in workplaces, schools, military branches, and other contexts as grounds for dismissal.

Professor Eskridge has described the free speech challenges to employment and military dismissals "as a test of the first amendment itself."[44] Insofar as sexual radicals were treated differently from political and other radicals in terms of their free speech rights, he contended, the Free Speech Clause failed a critical test.

And fail it did, in the vast majority of cases. Thus, in the area of public employment, public employees could not generally convince courts that they had a free speech right to divulge or communicate their sexual orientation.[45] Similarly, the free speech claims of gay and lesbian military personnel discharged under the "Don't Ask, Don't Tell" regulations were rejected in the federal courts of appeal.[46] In general, the courts concluded that the military's policy regulated conduct, not speech, and that statements by gay and lesbian service members regarding their sexual orientation could validly be used against them.

Thus, just as in the lunch counter sit-in cases of the 1960s, gay men and lesbians could not convince the courts that their identity speech was covered by the Free Speech Clause. Although the damage to the race equality movement was marginal, by contrast these rulings were far more significant defeats for LGBT equality. "No promo homo" policies like "Don't Ask, Don't Tell" allowed government to continue closeting gay men and lesbians in places of employment and other critical contexts. In a broader sense, as Professor Eskridge's observation suggests, the Free Speech Clause seemed to fail a critical test concerning protection for sexual dissent. Despite the long tradition of coverage for dissident expression of various kinds, the courts drew the line at gay and lesbian self-identification. They did not view this speech as a form of protected political dissent.

Of course, to characterize these results as a failure of the Free Speech Clause assumes that the clause was properly invoked in the first place. Professor Fred Schauer has raised doubts in this regard. Schauer has described the free speech challenges to the military's policy as an example of free speech "opportunism."[47] As discussed in the Introduction, the basic critique is that non-speech constitutional claims are being "dressed up" as free speech challenges in a strategic gambit to appeal to courts' affinity for free speech arguments. Other scholars have raised concerns that free speech "opportunism" could lead to free speech "expansionism"—the subordination of other clauses or areas of law.[48]

Professor Schauer has contended that the essential harm of "Don't Ask, Don't Tell" was not inhibition of speech, but rather denial of equal treatment to gay and lesbian military personnel. He also argued that the free speech claims were "doctrinally dubious," in part because the Supreme Court had already held that government was allowed to use a person's speech as evidence of a crime.[49] Indeed, he claimed that the free speech arguments were even *more* dubious than other constitutional claims plaintiffs did not bother to assert—including arguments that the regulations violated the Free Exercise Clause or the Fifth Amendment right against self-incrimination.[50] Schauer contended that gay and lesbian plaintiffs recast their equality and other claims in free speech terms, in a strategic ploy to convince judges and the public that the military's policy was morally unsound.[51] Thus, he described the Free Speech Clause attack on "Don't Ask, Don't Tell" as a "second-best fallback position" chosen to "give sympathetic judges a doctrinal handle and possibly to persuade members of the public as well as the judiciary of the rightness of the claim."[52]

As I indicated in the Introduction and have argued elsewhere, I am generally skeptical of the "opportunism" label—particularly insofar as it has pejorative connotations.[53] For one thing, as Professor Schauer has conceded, there is currently no agreed-upon method of distinguishing pure or proper invocations of the Free Speech Clause from impure or inappropriate ones. Moreover, as Schauer has also admitted, in the context of cause lawyering and adjudication, "opportunistic" is another word for effective. After all, the point of litigating is to win your client's case. As the NAACP's litigation strategy showed, it makes sense to use all of the constitutional tools at hand—and as we have seen, the Free Speech Clause has generally been a very effective tool.

As well, at the time the "Don't Ask, Don't Tell" claims were brought, despite the precedents Schauer referred to, Free Speech Clause claims were more viable than claims under the Free Exercise Clause, the Fifth Amendment protection against self-incrimination, and the Equal Protection Clause. Indeed, as Professor Eskridge and Professor David Cole have demonstrated, the free speech claims fit squarely into the First Amendment's tradition of protection for expressive conduct and political dissent.[54] Moreover, in relative terms, one could argue that litigants challenging "no promo homo" laws had no real choice but to invoke the Free Speech Clause. With the exception of "expressive equality," the Constitution did not generally affect the apartheid of the closet. Finally, although it may be the case, as Professor Schauer contended, that plaintiffs' claims implicated equal protection harms, in this as in other contexts we have examined, free speech and constitutional equality were closely connected.

Professor Schauer is ultimately concerned that invoking the Free Speech Clause opportunistically could negatively affect its "core" coverage for political expression. But even if that were a legitimate concern in other contexts, the "Don't Ask, Don't Tell" cases did not implicate it. Although the courts did not recognize it as such, the identity speech in those cases was, in fact, *political* speech.[55] Further, Professor Schauer argued that if invocations of the Free Speech Clause are based on goals "external to the First Amendment rather than as a consequence of the purposes the First Amendment was designed to serve, we may as a nation find ourselves with a cultural understanding of the First Amendment that diverges substantially from what a less misused First Amendment would have produced."[56] But again, this criticism also fails in the "Don't Ask, Don't Tell" context—particularly once the civil rights identity claims are properly understood as serving, rather than undermining, core Free Speech Clause values such as self-government and the search for truth.

There remains the concern that these challenges, if successful, might have resulted in the expansion of the Free Speech Clause into new territory previously occupied by the Equal Protection Clause or some other constitutional guarantee. In the civil rights context, at least, free speech "expansionism" has not been a problem. Since at least the civil rights era, freedom of speech and equal protection have lived in relative harmony with one another. As discussed, litigants have turned to the Free Speech Clause to secure basic expressive rights ("expressive equality") and to mediate debates about constitutional equality. In matters relating to substantive equality, however, they have ultimately looked to the Equal Protection Clause. In other words, despite its active use during the civil rights and LGBT equality campaigns, the Free Speech Clause has not threatened to subordinate the Equal Protection Clause. This fact is reflected in current constitutional doctrines. Discrimination based on expressive content is policed under the Free Speech Clause, whereas discrimination based on race and other suspect characteristics is the clear domain of the Equal Protection Clause.

Like civil rights advocates before them, LGBT equality advocates did not overreach when they invoked the Free Speech Clause to challenge restrictions on identity speech. In the short term, courts did not recognize the political character of identity speech. However, as Professor Schauer acknowledges, the long-term strategy of associating constitutional equality movements with the Free Speech Clause likely generated public, academic, and official support for those movements.[57] Although individual free speech claims were not always successful, the hearing that the Free Speech Clause demanded for African-Americans and LGBT persons ultimately resulted in recognition of the expressiveness of racial and sexual orientation identity.

As we have seen, in some civil rights era cases, the Supreme Court ultimately treated presence as a form of symbolic expression. With regard to LGBT identity claims, this recognition was evident in later cases, including *Obergefell*, the Court's marriage equality decision. Thus, in holding that there is a constitutional right to marriage equality, the Court observed that the Constitution protects "a liberty that includes certain specific rights that allow persons, within a lawful realm, *to define and express their identity*."[58] This recognition has not assured full equality rights; for instance, federal employment discrimination law still contains no protection against discharge based on sexual orientation. However, the expressiveness of LGBT identity has been recognized as an aspect of constitutional liberty.

In sum, at least in the short term, the failure of "identity speech" claims during both the civil rights and LGBT equality movements was an important limitation in terms of the speech clause strategy. However, by pressing these identity claims, litigants encouraged the Court and the general public to view identity as an important form of expression. Over the long term, using the Free Speech Clause to forge this connection may have advanced the cause of constitutional equality for both movements.

Hate Speech

Through its mediating principle of content neutrality, the Free Speech Clause protects the speech rights of those who advocate as well as those who oppose constitutional and other forms of equality. The same rights that racial and sexual minorities have relied upon to obtain equality rights have been invoked by opponents of those rights. In the United States, content neutrality rules have been interpreted as protecting even hateful and derogatory communications that deny the equal status and dignity of racial and other minorities.

As discussed earlier, mediated equality discourse has been essential to assuring the democratic legitimacy of constitutional change with respect to constitutional equality. However, serious tensions or conflicts arise when individuals communicate hateful and derogatory viewpoints or beliefs regarding racial and other minorities. This has been a vexing point of intersection between the Free Speech Clause and Equal Protection Clause. Protecting hateful and derogatory speech diminishes the prospects of some individuals for achieving constitutional and other forms of equality. However, prohibiting such communications deprives others of the ability to communicate dissent and to resist official efforts to mandate orthodoxy, including with regard to equality rights.

Unlike other nations, including other Western democracies, the United States has generally resolved this tension in favor of free speech rights. The Supreme Court has deviated from this principle only once, in the 1950s—and its decision, which upheld a state "group libel" law as applied to racist propaganda, is generally viewed as having been significantly undermined (if not overruled sub silentio) by subsequent precedents.[59] The general mediating rule, which the Court has affirmed in recent cases, is that governments may not suppress or restrict racist, homophobic, or other forms of hateful speech based on their subject matter or point of view.[60]

This approach opens the door to the most virulent forms of racist speech and gay-bashing. It permits members of the Ku Klux Klan to burn crosses in public ceremonies and espouse the racial inferiority of African-Americans. It allows members of the Westboro Baptist Church to display a banner reading "God Hates Fags" near a military funeral.[61] Some commentators find this intolerable. They have argued that this interpretation of the Free Speech Clause violates the equality rights of the targets of hateful and derogatory speech.[62] They urge the United States to join the community of nations in allowing government to prohibit hateful and derogatory speech.[63]

Here, as in other contexts, courts and commentators are essentially balancing rights—in this instance, equal protection and free speech. Protecting speech that denigrates or undermines personal equality allows speakers to inflict psychological and other personal harms on minorities. It also makes it more difficult to achieve broader equal protection goals, including full acceptance and inclusion of racial and sexual minorities. However, as I observed in Chapter 2, insistence on governmental neutrality with regard to speech that concerns (even remotely) constitutional rights, serves compelling interests of its own. Without denying its serious harmful effects, even hateful rights speech contributes something to an open discourse about individual equality. Even if it does not contribute much of substance, the constitutional calculus is that virulent forms of hate speech must be protected in order to prevent government from imposing anti-racist or pro-LGBT orthodoxies. As suggested earlier, insisting on governmental neutrality with regard to racial segregation or marriage equality lends a degree of democratic legitimacy to the resolution of those conflicts.

Again, this is not to deny the harm in hate speech, including the significant constraints it has placed on efforts to achieve constitutional equality for oppressed minorities. However, at this critical intersection between equal protection and free speech, the mediating principle of neutrality is essential to ensuring that equality rights are not achieved through official censorship and suppression. In this context, as in others, the Free Speech Clause ultimately mediates and facilitates equality rights by assuring that they are the product of neutral processes open to all points of view.

The Negative and Exclusionary Dimensions of Free Speech

Governmental efforts to foster or promote equality have been hampered or limited by a free speech mediation rule that is closely related to the content-neutrality principle. The rule prohibits government from compelling speech. The Free Speech Clause has been interpreted to bar governments from compelling speakers to communicate state-sanctioned thoughts, beliefs, or ideas.[64]

Faced with state and local anti-discrimination laws that prohibit discrimination based on race or sexual orientation in "public accommodations" (essentially, businesses or other organizations that invite and serve the general public), organizations opposed to the inclusion of African-Americans and LGBT persons have asserted Free Speech Clause rights to exclude them on the ground that their mandatory inclusion compels speech and expressive association (a right discussed in Chapter 3). In this respect, the Free Speech Clause is being used not as a sword to advance equal protection claims, but as a shield to defend against different forms of compelled support for equality.

For reasons discussed later, the compelled speech mediating rule did not have any appreciable effect on the race equality movement. However, it significantly impacted governmental efforts to pursue LGBT equality. In challenges to anti-discrimination laws, groups opposed to LGBT participation in public events and inclusion as organizational members invoked the Free Speech Clause and the right of "expressive association." In *Hurley v. Irish-American Gay, Lesbian, and Bisexual Group of Boston* (1995), the Supreme Court upheld a claim, brought by Irish-American parade organizers in Boston, that forcing them to allow an LGBT group to march in their parade violated the Free Speech Clause.[65] And in *Boy Scouts of America v. Dale* (2000), the Court held that the application of anti-discrimination laws to the Boy Scouts of America, which would have compelled the group to accept openly gay individuals as Scout members and leaders, violated the right of "expressive association."[66]

These decisions relied on expressive and associational autonomy principles to allow groups to exclude LGBT persons from public accommodations and noncommercial private organizations. They confirmed the central lesson of the hate speech cases, namely that governments cannot compel an official orthodoxy with regard to LGBT equality. As the Court observed in the Boy Scouts case, "[t]he First Amendment protects expression, be it of the popular variety or not."[67]

Hurley and *Dale* complicated governmental efforts to recognize and facilitate the equality rights of LGBT persons. However, these precedents also barred the government from imposing pro-LGBT equality messages on speakers or interfering with the expressive activities of associations. They applied basic free speech mediation principles that require equality rights and equal status to be achieved through autonomous discourse rather than official compulsion or forced association.

The Court did not always apply these rules consistently. For instance, in *Christian Legal Society v. Martinez* (2010), a Christian student group unsuccessfully challenged a public law school's decision to deny official recognition to the group unless it accepted gay and lesbian members. Hastings Law School adopted an "all comers" policy under which student groups seeking official recognition from the school were required to accept as members any interested student—regardless of whether that student accepted the group's viewpoints or policies.[68] The Christian Legal Society (CLS) required that its members sign a "Statement of Faith" and agree to live their lives in accordance with the group's creedal principles, which prohibited sex outside of marriage and "unrepentant homosexual conduct."[69]

CLS challenged the law school's policy on the ground that by forcing the group to admit gay men and lesbians as members, it violated the right of "expressive association" recognized in *Dale*. The Court declined even to address this claim on the merits. Instead, it held that where the government conditions speech in a "limited public forum," the Free Speech Clause requires only that the condition be viewpoint neutral and reasonable. The Court concluded that the "all comers" policy was both neutral as to viewpoint and reasonable: "Hastings, caught in the crossfire between a group's desire to exclude and students' demand for equal access, may reasonably draw a line in the sand permitting *all* organizations to express what they wish but *no* group to discriminate in membership."[70]

CLS indicates that at least where the government offers private groups the carrot of funding, rather than wields the stick of regulation, it may insist on inclusion of LGBT members. The decision does not allow governments to enforce inclusionary polices where private resources are used to organize and support associations. Nevertheless, *CLS* raises concerns about the subordination of the right of association to free speech mediating principles governing access to public forums. As discussed in Chapter 3, the right of association has already been subject to subordination in the sense that it only covers "expressive" forms of association. The Court's determination that CLS's associational claim "merged" with and was governed by its free speech claim raises further concerns about the tendency of the Free Speech Clause to supplant other constitutional rights.

LGBT equality advocates have experienced their own setbacks in terms of invoking the exclusionary principle to challenge governmental policies they perceive as discriminatory. In *Rumsfeld v. Forum for Academic and Individual Rights, Inc.* (2006) (*FAIR*), a group of law schools invoked this principle, and the corresponding right of expressive association, in a challenge to a federal law that conditioned the receipt of funds on granting equal access to campus facilities to military recruiters. The law schools objected that the funding condition compelled them to speak in support of the "Don't Ask, Don't Tell" regulations, which were then in effect and which they opposed, and burdened their expressive rights by forcing them to associate with military recruiters. The Supreme Court unanimously rejected these claims.[71] The Court concluded that the mere presence of military recruiters on law school campuses did not compel speech or compel the law schools to associate with military recruiters. The decision indicated that there were some limits to the Free Speech Clause's exclusionary dimension, which *Hurley* and *Dale* had relied upon to invalidate the application of anti-discrimination laws.

In the context of the LGBT equality movement, this line of cases was a significant reminder that the Free Speech Clause imposed limits on forced inclusion and compulsion of equal treatment. *Hurley* and *Dale* recognized free speech rights to exclude. This preserved cultural and social space for dissenting groups and organizations to resist government orthodoxy concerning equality. But protecting that space limited the government's ability to pursue equal rights for LGBT persons. *CLS*, which came relatively late in the LGBT equality movement, limited the right of exclusion to some extent (and, as noted, subordinated associational rights). *FAIR* denied an exclusionary claim intended to advance LGBT equality rights, and indicated that the Free Speech Clause's exclusionary dimension was limited to genuine instances of compelled speech and mandated association.

As significant as they were to the advocates and to the movement, these decisions were the beginning, rather than the end, of the dynamic intersection between free speech and LGBT equality in this context. As Professor Ball has emphasized, other forms of expression and activism supplemented these litigation efforts.[72] *Dale* was not the last word regarding the Boy Scouts' exclusionary policies. Public and political backlash to these policies was sustained and ultimately effective. The Boy Scouts reconsidered and eventually repealed its national policy excluding openly gay members. Similarly, political pressure eventually resulted in congressional repeal of the military's "Don't Ask, Don't Tell" regulations. Hastings Law School won its lawsuit defending the "all comers" policy. However, colleges and universities continue to debate the merits of such policies. In all of these respects, free speech mediation has allowed activists and opponents to respond to the recognition of free speech exclusionary rights.

Government Speech and Equality

A final complicating limitation of the Free Speech Clause as it relates to equal protection involves the principle of government speech. As noted in Chapter 2, governments weigh in on constitutional rights in a variety of ways. The Free Speech Clause does not limit these communications. Thus, when they speak on matters relating to equality, governments are free to espouse pro-equality or anti-equality speech.[73] Because the ordinary mediating principles do not apply, a government communicating about equal protection need not comply with content-neutrality rules. When it speaks, government can reject or suppress private messages that it disfavors.

As it pertains to equal protection concerns, the government speech principle empowers governments to engage in derogatory and equality-denying communications. De jure segregation laws and "no promo homo" policies are two categories of governmental anti-equality speech. These laws deprived African-Americans and LGBT persons of substantive equality rights. However, as discussed in Chapter 2, these official communications also produced significant expressive harms. Some scholars have suggested that the Free Speech Clause might limit some discriminatory governmental communications.[74] However, these laws have never been challenged or invalidated on general free speech grounds.

The absence of free speech limits on government equality communications reflects the Free Speech Clause's traditional function as a mediator of private equality discourse. As suggested in Chapter 2, we should not expect the Free Speech Clause to do the work of limiting governmental equality speech. Rather, challengers ought to focus on developing equal protection arguments challenging hateful and derogatory government speech and cabining the government speech principle.[75]

There is a potential mediating role the Free Speech Clause can play in this context. As commentators have suggested, governments can be a positive force in terms of equal protection discourse.[76] They can use their speech powers, in non-compulsory ways, to persuade citizens to support equal treatment under law. We can see some evidence of this persuasive effect in equal protection jurisprudence. Courts can be effective equality communicators. As a result of political and constitutional discourses concerning race equality, the truth of *Brown v. Board of Education*'s central conclusion—that racial segregation *communicates* the inferiority of African-Americans—has been revealed. As well, all of the Supreme Court's LGBT equality precedents have recognized that the challenged laws *stigmatized* homosexuals, *declared* them unequal, and *communicated* animus toward them.[77] These cases communicate some of the expressive harms associated with denials of equal protection.

LESSON 5: THE RELATIONSHIP BETWEEN THE FREE SPEECH CLAUSE AND THE EQUAL PROTECTION CLAUSE IS BI-DIRECTIONAL; INTERACTIONS BETWEEN THE CLAUSES HAVE LEFT INDELIBLE MARKS ON BOTH.

As the book has emphasized, the relationship between freedom of speech and non-speech rights is bi-directional. As free speech and non-speech rights have intersected over long periods of time, both have been profoundly affected. This has certainly been true with regard to the relationship between free speech and equal protection. We have examined how freedom of speech has affected race and LGBT constitutional equality rights. At the same time, equal protection advocacy has transformed the Free Speech Clause in some vital respects. Indeed, current understandings of free speech doctrines, principles, and values owe much to the influence of the Equal Protection Clause.

Neutrality and Other Core Free Speech Principles

The frequent intersection between freedom of speech and equal protection rights has led to the recognition and development of several core Free Speech Clause principles. As the two clauses interacted with one another in adjudication and rights discourse, the meaning of the Free Speech Clause changed in some fundamental respects.

Perhaps the most significant and enduring influence relates to the Free Speech Clause's content-neutrality principle. During the 1950s and 1960s, the Supreme Court's frequent consideration of equal protection claims made an important impression on the justices. Over time, as the Court reviewed laws under the Free Speech Clause, it began to interpret it as prohibiting governmental discrimination against speakers, messages, and viewpoints.[78] During the civil rights era, the Court began to recognize content neutrality as a central limitation on government regulation of speech. In essence, the Court borrowed Equal Protection Clause antidiscrimination rules to interpret the modern Free Speech Clause.[79]

In early cases, the Court viewed claims that the government had discriminated against speakers primarily as raising equal protection concerns.[80] Later, as it developed and applied free speech content-neutrality rules, the Court reviewed freedom of speech and equal protection claims on separate, but related, tracks. Governmental discrimination served as the joist connecting the two doctrinal areas. Each provision was interpreted to protect an individual right to equal treatment under law—in the broader sense, under the Equal Protection Clause, and with more specific regard to rights to communicate, under the Free Speech Clause.

Content neutrality was not the only central Free Speech Clause principle revealed as a result of the dynamic intersection with equal protection. As discussed earlier, civil rights advocacy relied to a significant extent on free speech claims. Thus, in *New York Times Co. v. Sullivan* (1964), the Supreme Court examined the extent to which newspapers reporting on civil rights violations could be held civilly liable under what were then very strict state law libel rules. Those rules, which were often used to intimidate the press and speakers, were a serious impediment to the progress of race equality. *Sullivan* refashioned the state's libel laws to comport with what it said was the central command of the Free Speech Clause—that debate on public issues should be "uninhibited, robust, and wide-open."[81]

As discussed earlier, this became one of the most important mediating principles of the Free Speech Clause. And that mediating principle has, in turn, significantly influenced the development of free speech rights. Among other things, it has shaped doctrines in the areas of defamation, advocacy of unlawful action, protection for offensive and hateful speech, and access to public properties for expressive purposes.

The Court's involvement with free speech claims during the civil rights era also contributed to the articulation and development of some of the central values or justifications for freedom of speech. This includes the idea that freedom of speech is important to self-government.[82] Writing contemporaneously with the Civil Rights Movement, Professor Kalven predicted that "we may come to see the Negro as winning back for us the freedoms the Communists seemed to have lost for us."[83] Kalven was referring to a period during the 1950s, when Communists and other radicals routinely lost free speech challenges to laws suppressing speech that criticized the draft or U.S. war effort.[84] One of the rights the civil rights protesters "won back" was the invaluable freedom to criticize government.

Subsequent movements, including the LGBT equality movement, cemented this legacy and confirmed the central meaning of the First Amendment. The LGBT equality movement effectively kept the Free Speech Clause and Equal Protection Clause in conversation with one another. LGBT equality advocates did not need to "win back" free speech rights that had been lost by their predecessors. Rather, they were able to rely upon and fortify dissenters' rights bequeathed by the Civil Rights Movement. That is not to say that the LGBT equality movement did not add to the scope and substance of the Free Speech Clause. To the contrary, it demonstrated that protection for "uninhibited, robust, and wide-open" discourse could extend to at least some forms of sexual dissent.

Thus, at both conceptual and theoretical levels, equal protection activism deeply influenced the meaning and scope of the Free Speech Clause. That activism encouraged the adoption of a content-neutrality principle, revealed the "central meaning" of the Free Speech Clause, and left a mark on a variety of free speech doctrines that have been critical to speakers and dissenters of all types.

Public Forums and Public Protests

In somewhat more specific terms, equal protection advocacy strengthened some key free speech doctrines. Two are particularly noteworthy. As a result of the equal protection-free speech interface, speakers gained stronger rights of access to public properties. This access was critically important to the recognition and development of related public protest rights.

During the 1950s and 1960s, civil rights protesters invoked the Free Speech Clause to gain access to public streets and other places. In this endeavor, race equality advocates were not starting from scratch.[85] As discussed in Chapter 4, the free speech campaign of Jehovah's Witnesses had resulted in some minimal access to public venues for speech and other First Amendment activities.[86] The NAACP's litigation campaign strengthened and ultimately expanded these public access rights. It significantly contributed to the "public forum" doctrine, which governs speech rights in public streets, parks, and other venues.[87]

By gaining access to public forums, civil rights activists created vitally important breathing space for political protests and other forms of public contention.[88] For the first time, the American public got a glimpse of the power and significance of First Amendment public protest rights.[89] Although the streets had been used for expressive purposes before, the civil rights era ushered in a new era of public speech and contention. This experience enabled subsequent movements, causes, and dissenters to lay special claim to public streets and other places.

Thus, along with *Sullivan*'s "central meaning," the civil rights era public forum precedents produced a more expansive free speech guarantee. The courts recognized a special easement that entitled speakers to access public streets, parks, and other places for the purpose of communicating grievances and aspirations to the public and to public officials.

Anonymity, Association, and Autonomy

Equal protection advocacy led to the recognition of some other free speech rights. Rights to associate and communicate with others anonymously are products of the Civil Rights Movement. As explained in Chapter 3, so is the First Amendment right of "expressive association," which includes the right not to associate.

During the civil rights era, private and official forms of intimidation threatened to inhibit or suppress civil rights activism. In *NAACP v. Alabama* (1968), the Supreme Court recognized a right to associate with others, which included the right to engage in collective action anonymously.[90] Two years later, the Court held that the distributor of a flyer concerning race equality and civil rights had a free speech right to communicate anonymously.[91] First Amendment anonymity rights have broadly facilitated the communication of controversial ideas and beliefs—including, today, in cyberspace.[92]

The LGBT equality movement confirmed the importance of anonymous speech rights. It has generally left these rights as it found them, with one possible exception. In *Doe v. Reed* (2010), a case discussed earlier, the Supreme Court held that a state law requirement that petition signatures collected by anti-marriage equality referendum proponents be treated as public records did not violate the Free Speech Clause.[93] The Court held that in the context of public lawmaking, the state's interests in detecting and preventing fraud outweighed the free speech right to engage in anonymous speech.

Although it rejected the petition-signers' free speech claim, *Doe* did not significantly undermine the right to communicate anonymously. The Court did not question the existence of the right to engage in anonymous speech. Nor did it embrace absolute transparency, even in the context of referenda and other popular lawmaking processes. Rather, *Doe* applied election law precedents relating to disclosure, which allow petition signers who are subject to real threats of reprisal to invoke a First Amendment right to anonymity.

NAACP v. Alabama also recognized, for the first time, a right to associate with others for expressive purposes.[94] This new right recognized the value in collective expression. It extended First Amendment protections beyond the individual to groups, organizations, and institutions. The Supreme Court had denied the associational claims of communists and other radical groups. But its concern that Alabama and other states were suppressing the equality advocacy of the NAACP and other civil rights groups led the Court to recognize a right to associate for expressive purposes.

First Amendment associational rights have facilitated social and political activities by a wide variety of groups, including political parties, civic institutions, and religious groups.[95] In the crucial early stages of the LGBT equality movement, advocates relied on these associational rights to challenge crackdowns on gay and lesbian bars and the exclusion of gay and lesbian student groups from public university campuses.

The recognition of a right *not to associate* during the later stages of the LGBT equality movement has also been critically important to speakers and expressive organizations. The earlier discussion focused on the manner in which some invocations of this right posed obstacles to the state's pursuit of equality rights. However, from the perspective of private groups, the right not to associate protects important expressive autonomy and internal governance rights. To be sure, the Court's treatment of this First Amendment right raises many questions. Indeed, some have been quite critical of the Court's conceptualization and application of the "expressive association" right.[96] For example, Professor Andrew Koppelman has observed that the Supreme Court's decisions can plausibly be read to support either or both of the following propositions: "All antidiscrimination laws are unconstitutional in all their applications," or "citizens are allowed to disobey laws whenever obedience would be perceived as endorsing some message."[97]

The Court's earlier cases, which involved exclusion of individuals based on race and gender, were decided under what appeared to be a straightforward balancing approach weighing expressive association rights against equal protection concerns.[98] The Court's approach in LGBT exclusion cases has been far more deferential to organizational concerns and seemingly less committed to the enforcement of anti-discrimination laws.[99] The doctrine of expressive association undoubtedly requires further clarification. However, that does not wholly undermine the importance or utility of the right itself, to a wide variety of associations and organizations.

Finally, equal protection advocacy has influenced free speech autonomy rights in other critical respects. Most significantly, it has contributed to our understanding of the right not to be compelled to communicate.[100]

During the civil rights era, free speech conflicts centered primarily on official efforts to stifle or suppress expression and advocacy on behalf of racial equality. Thus, First Amendment attention tended to focus on rights *to* speak, assemble, and criticize government. By contrast, as discussed earlier, during certain phases of the LGBT equality movement attention shifted to First Amendment rights *not to* speak.[101] As they did with the right not to associate, opponents of LGBT inclusion invoked the right not to speak as a means of challenging the application of anti-discrimination laws.[102] As discussed earlier, so did proponents of LGBT equality, who resisted what they viewed as commands to adopt and articulate anti-LGBT messages such as "Don't Ask, Don't Tell."

In *Hurley*, the Supreme Court held that application of anti-discrimination laws to force parade organizers to accept an LGBT contingent violated a right to speaker autonomy. Later, in *FAIR*, the Court unanimously rejected the claim that conditioning federal funds on granting equal access to military recruiters violated the law schools' right not to be compelled to speak or associate.[103] The Court's confirmation of the right not to be compelled to speak is an important reminder of the importance of free speech autonomy and the First Amendment's ban on compelled orthodoxy. *FAIR* is also an important reminder, that these protections are limited to genuine instances of compulsion.

In important respects, the contemporary system of American free speech would be unrecognizable absent the intersection between free speech and equality occasioned by constitutional equality movements. The Civil Rights Movement produced a number of landmark rulings that shaped the First Amendment's central doctrinal and normative principles, in ways that continue to affect the scope and meaning of free speech rights. It secured recognition for rights to criticize government in the strongest terms, to access public streets and parks for expressive purposes, to associate with others for expressive purposes, to engage in anonymous speech and association, and to resist government-imposed orthodoxy with regard to political and other concerns. With the exception of a couple of notable complications, the LGBT equality movement largely affirmed and strengthened these rights.

LESSON 6: FREE SPEECH CLAUSE DYNAMICS VARY DEPENDING ON THE NATURE OF THE EQUAL PROTECTION CLAIM.

As we have seen, during the civil rights and LGBT equality movements, common dynamics affected the interactions between the Equal Protection Clause and Free Speech Clause. However, there were also some important distinctions in these dynamics. Free Speech Clause interactions differed in some respects, depending on the nature of the equality claims being pursued.

General Orientations

As we have seen, there are a number of commonalities in terms of how the Free Speech Clause has interacted with constitutional race and sexual orientation equality claims. But constitutional equality movements arise in response to distinctive concerns. They use and involve different forms of expressive resistance. The civil rights and LGBT equality movements arose in starkly different historical, social, and political contexts. So naturally, we would expect some variation in terms of the interactions between the Free Speech Clause and these distinctive equality movements.

One notable distinction was the general orientation of the equal protection and free speech provisions. During the Civil Rights Movement, this relationship was generally synergistic and mutually illuminating. Contrast this orientation with the decidedly more complicated relationship between freedom of speech and equality concerns relating to sexual orientation.

In part, this difference could be traceable to the discipline and centralization of the race equality movement, in particular its free speech strategy. What Professor Kalven has referred to as the NAACP's "assault on the Constitution" was a masterful civil rights litigation campaign.[104] In particular, the NAACP used the Free Speech Clause to brilliant effect—aggregating public assemblies, protests, and sit-ins to advance equality claims. This was a first-of-its-kind, centralized, and disciplined free speech advocacy agenda.

As discussed, the LGBT equality movement also relied on free speech and other First Amendment rights to advance equal protection. Particularly in its early phases, the movement relied on litigation tactics and activism that piggybacked on the experiences of the Civil Rights Movement. However, as scholars have shown, on the whole the free speech claims of this era were only "relatively successful."[105] As discussed, free speech protection for some sexually explicit speech was denied. Further, employment dismissals and "Don't Ask, Don't Tell" free speech challenges regularly failed in the courts. As discussed, the Free Speech Clause was effectively interposed in ways that diminished or undermined LGBT inclusion and equality.

There are several possible explanations for this distinct and more negative orientation between free speech and equal protection. There was indeed a coordinated effort to use the Free Speech Clause to advance LGBT equality. But it was difficult, if not impossible, to imitate the NAACP's "strategic assault" in challenges to this distinctive form of apartheid. The formal and informal closeting of gays and lesbians, as well as the repressive sex culture in the United States, posed unique barriers to the Free Speech Clause strategy.

LGBT litigants had relatively little difficulty obtaining basic rights to protest and communicate in public forums. However, gay literature and pornography, self-identification in employment and other contexts, and gender-bending expression posed some new challenges for free speech theory and interpretation. Hard-wired cultural and institutional norms, in addition to free speech doctrines that were not suited to assimilate all forms of LGBT expression, resulted in a free speech litigation track record that was less successful than the NAACP's.

Equality Rights

We have asked in this chapter both what the Free Speech Clause can do *for* equal protection claims and what equal protection advocacy and rights can do *to* free speech rights. To understand the different experiences of the race and LGBT equality movements with regard to their free speech advocacy, we must also look in the direction of the Equal Protection Clause.

As they invoked the Free Speech Clause, race and LGBT advocates came to court armed with significantly different *equality* backgrounds and rights. During the 1960s, the Supreme Court generally greeted First Amendment claims by civil rights litigants warmly. When they started their free speech campaign, civil rights activists did so armed with the Court's ruling, in *Brown v. Board of Education* (1954), that unequal treatment at the hands of government violated the Equal Protection Clause.[106] Continued resistance to *Brown*, particularly in the southern United States, likely influenced the Warren Court's perception of civil rights free speech claims. As the Civil Rights Movement progressed, its Free Speech Clause claims also received increased public support.

No similar judicial commitment to gay and lesbian equality existed during *any* phase of the LGBT movement. There was nothing like *Brown* to provide a constitutional tailwind for the Free Speech Clause claims of LGBT equality advocates. Indeed, it was not until the mid-1990s, in *Romer v. Evans* (1996), that the Supreme Court held that states were prohibited from *literally* denying gay men and lesbians equal protection of the law.[107] However, *Romer* did not treat sexual orientation, like race, as a "suspect" and therefore presumptively invalid trait. In fact, no Supreme Court case to date has made this move. *Romer* barred governments from treating gays and lesbians as a pariah class for purposes of the Equal Protection Clause. But the decision went no further. And, in any event, it came much too late to buoy LGBT free speech advocacy during the 1980s and early 1990s. Nor did *Romer* add any real support to LGBT claimants' challenges to the exclusionary policies of the Boy Scouts and other organizations. Unlike race-based exclusions, LGBT exclusions were not considered to be suspect.

In sum, in contrast to the Civil Rights Movement, the LGBT equality movement lacked substantive Fourteenth Amendment support for its First Amendment agenda. Without this support, LGBT activists were still able to obtain basic "expressive equality" rights, but otherwise found that the Free Speech Clause offered no relief from "no promo homo" and other discriminatory policies.

Expressive Exclusion

As discussed earlier, one critically important distinction between the race and LGBT equality movements was the emergence and frequent invocation of Free Speech Clause-based exclusionary rights. The Supreme Court's recognition and enforcement of such rights during the 1990s represented a break from prior precedents involving race- and sex-based discrimination.[108] Why didn't we see these claims as frequently during the Civil Rights Movement? And why were they at least somewhat successful during the LGBT equality movement?

During the 1950s and 1960s, proponents and defenders of racial segregation did not typically look to the Free Speech Clause as a source of exclusionary power. In one nearly-forgotten case, five drive-in restaurants and a sandwich shop that refused to serve African-Americans invoked the *Free Exercise Clause* as a defense to paying attorneys' fees under the Civil Rights Act of 1964.[109] In a footnote, the Supreme Court essentially adopted the opinion of a lower court judge that the claim was "patently frivolous."[110]

Whether Free Speech Clause defenses would have received a better reception at the Court is unknown. Segregationists did not typically invoke the Free Speech Clause for this purpose. One possible reason might have been that they really had little need to do so. Prior to the passage of the Civil Rights Act of 1964, a few states had enacted laws that prohibited racial and other forms of discrimination in public accommodations. However, even these laws were not energetically enforced against private property owners—including public accommodations open to the public. The Supreme Court did not recognize Congress's power to enforce similar federal laws until 1964.[111] Moreover, segregationists could resist access claims under constitutional principles of state action, which permitted free speech and other challenges only to *official* forms of government action. Governments also could, and often did, privatize properties in order to avoid desegregation orders.[112] Private owners could rely on property rights and trespass laws. Finally, private self-help, including the use of intimidation and violence, limited the force of state and federal anti-discrimination laws.

Even if segregation's proponents and defenders had needed or wanted to raise Free Speech Clause compelled speech or expressive association claims, these arguments would have been strategically and doctrinally problematic. As discussed earlier, the Supreme Court did not formally recognize the First Amendment right of association until the 1950s.[113] And when it did so, the Court justified the right as a means of *resisting* racial oppression and inequality. It would have been incongruous, to say the least, for the Court to simultaneously recognize a negative and exclusionary right of association that would have lent significant constitutional support to the continued racial segregation *NAACP v. Alabama* and other cases sought to rebuke.

By contrast, those who resisted gay and lesbian inclusion did so in the very different context of a proliferation of broadly interpreted public accommodation and anti-discrimination laws. State action and property rights arguments were not viable defenses to these laws. However, by the 1990s, rights against compelled speech and association had developed respectable pedigrees.[114] These developments in Free

Speech Clause doctrine aided the exclusionary theory asserted in *Hurley*, *Dale*, and other cases.

As noted, on the Equal Protection Clause side of the ledger, those challenging anti-discrimination mandates during the LGBT equality movement did not have to argue around any *Brown*-like precedent recognizing the substantive equality rights of gay men and lesbians. The Supreme Court had developed a tiered scrutiny framework for Fourteenth Amendment equal protection claims, in which racial discrimination was highly suspect but other classifications received weaker—in some cases, far weaker—degrees of judicial scrutiny.[115] Under that framework, as observed earlier, the Court has never designated sexual orientation a suspect trait. Applying "rational basis" scrutiny, which requires only that the governmental regulation is rationally related to a legitimate end, more or less assured that expressive rights would outweigh any equality interests.

Again, one of the most important distinctions between the race and LGBT equality experiences, in terms of their interactions with the Free Speech Clause, was the relative strength of Equal Protection Clause rights during the same period. Broader conceptions of substantive equality affected the efficacy of civil rights free speech claims. In sum, while free speech rights can move equality claims forward or hold them back, Fourteenth Amendment rights can likewise facilitate or impede free speech advocacy.

Synergy and Illumination—Transgender Equality

The six lessons examined in this chapter reveal a dynamic, complex, and perpetually changing relationship between free speech and equal protection. At its best, this relationship is synergistic and mutually illuminating: free speech and equality work in tandem to advance constitutional liberty, and clarify each other's contribution to that important end.

We can use an ongoing equality movement to emphasize the chapter's lessons and to highlight the possibilities for synergy and mutual illumination. The chapter has generally assumed that transgender equality can be considered as part of a broader LGBT movement. In many ways, this is a fair characterization. However, the experiences of gay men, lesbians, transgender persons, and others is hardly monolithic. For instance, while other equality activists may benefit from *Obergefell*'s recognition of a marriage equality right, a movement focused more narrowly on the rights of transgender persons might well prioritize other issues. Consider, for example, the conflict over state laws that would require individuals to use the restroom associated with the gender assigned to them at birth.[116] These laws raise free speech and equal protection concerns that bear some resemblance to discrimination based on sexual orientation, but raise their own distinctive legal and constitutional concerns.

Assuming transgender persons are pursuing distinctive constitutional and other equality claims, what do the lessons of the chapter suggest about their movement? How might we expect or hope the relationship between free speech and equal protection will play out in this context?

Expressive equality is important to all equality movements. However, in contrast to prior equality advocates, transgender persons will not have to devote significant litigation and other resources to obtaining basic Free Speech Clause rights. Those rights are firmly established, in large part owing to the efforts of prior movements.

Indeed, transgender equality activists have already been vigorously exercising expressive equality rights in political and cultural spaces. Free speech rights have facilitated public discourse about the nature and characteristics of gender. They have also enabled political mobilization toward the end of securing transgender equality rights. In a relatively short period of time, transgender persons have used Free Speech Clause mediation to produce a significant degree of social and political recognition. They have also leveraged mediation rules to establish, again in relatively short order, a degree of cultural identity and visibility.[117]

This visibility, coupled with past judicial experience with identity speech, should limit one complication that negatively affected prior equality advocates. As discussed, in the past, courts were slow to recognize that presence and identity can be expressive. As transgender activists challenge official efforts to enforce gender norms, and seek recognition for the right to self-identify as male, female, or other, they are in a stronger position to prevail. As noted earlier, the Supreme Court has explicitly acknowledged a connection between sexual identity and expression. In this regard, *Obergefell's* opening lines bear emphasis: The Constitution protects "a liberty that includes certain specific rights that allow persons, within a lawful realm, *to define and express their identity*."[118]

Still, there will likely be efforts to rely on the Free Speech Clause as a means of excluding transgender persons from certain events, programs, or private organizations. Opponents of transgender inclusion can rely on cases such as *Hurley* and *Dale*, which recognized dissenters' rights not to speak or associate. As discussed earlier, the scope of this free speech exclusionary dimension needs to be clarified. *CLS v. Martinez* suggests that courts need to think more carefully about the effect of "all comers" policies on associational rights, particularly as those rights relate to deeply held organizational commitments. At the same time, cases like *FAIR* show that not *all* official efforts to ensure minority access violate First Amendment expressive rights. There should be enough play in the joints between the Free Speech Clause and the

Equal Protection Clause to allow officials to pursue important equality interests despite incidental effects on freedom of speech and expressive association. In other words, *Dale* cannot mean that all anti-discrimination laws that protect transgender rights are unconstitutional.

As they seek to advance the transgender equality agenda, advocates should devote energy and resources to developing equal protection arguments and rights. As prior movements show, just as free speech can facilitate equality rights, so too can the Equal Protection Clause support free speech claims. Recognition of a person's transgender status as a "suspect" or "quasi-suspect" characteristic for purposes of the Equal Protection Clause would strengthen free speech claims and also likely weaken expressive exclusion rights.

As has been true during prior equality movements, the actual exercise of free speech rights will likely be as or more important to the recognition of transgender equality than specific free speech victories. As suggested, these activities will occur in the political branches as well as in social and cultural venues, where people will debate and determine the scope of transgender equality rights. This aspect of the movement will be assisted by the free speech mediation rules discussed earlier.

Since their first official encounters, during the Reconstruction Era, the Free Speech Clause and Equal Protection Clause have exhibited synergistic tendencies. Unlike the relationships examined in Chapters 3 and 4, this one has never been dominated by the Free Speech Clause. Rather, racial, sexual, and other minorities have relied on the Free Speech Clause to facilitate the early recognition of "expressive equality" rights and to mediate public conversations about the nature and necessity of equal protection. The Free Speech Clause does not guarantee any particular substantive results with respect to the obtainment of constitutional equality. It does not, indeed cannot, mandate public support and acceptance of sexual or other minorities.

As Professor Toni Massaro has observed: "As an all-encompassing metaphor or a complete theory of constitutional rights for gays, lesbians, and bisexuals, [freedom of expression] falls short."[119] This is at once obvious and profound. As I have argued in previous chapters, free speech works most effectively in tandem with other rights—as part of a plural system of cognate provisions, with overlapping but mutually facilitative coverages. The most important advancements in terms of constitutional equality have resulted from the aggregation and accumulation of free speech, equal protection, and due process claims. This synergy helped to produce the constitutional, political, and social changes that led to *Brown*, the Civil Rights Act of 1964, and to the Supreme Court's decision in *Obergefell.*

Like prior equality advocates, transgender and other future equality claimants will not seek to *supplant* the Equal Protection Clause with the Free Speech Clause. Instead, if they use it wisely, they will invoke and leverage the Free Speech Clause's protections to create the conditions for recognition of substantive equality rights. Relying on the "central meaning" of the Free Speech Clause announced in *New York Times v. Sullivan*, they will engage in "uninhibited, robust, and wide open" discourse about their equality claims. In this fashion, freedom of speech and equality will be further and mutually illuminated.

6

ABORTION

AS PART OF its general consideration of "rights speech," Chapter 2 considered the extent to which governments regulate communications about or concerning abortion. This chapter takes a closer and deeper look at the relationship between the First Amendment's Free Speech Clause and the constitutional right to abortion. Like the other relationships we have examined, the relationship between the Free Speech Clause and the constitutional right to abortion, which is based in the Fourteenth Amendment's Due Process Clause, is both complicated and complicating. Freedom of speech was critical to the recognition and subsequent exercise of abortion rights. However, as interpreted, the Free Speech Clause has sometimes served as an impediment to the recognition and effective exercise of abortion rights. Interpretations of the Free Speech Clause have impacted abortion rights, sometimes in negative ways. At the same time, significant changes to abortion rights have influenced important Free Speech Clause doctrines and principles.

The first part of the chapter examines the social, political, and jurisprudential ties that bind the Free Speech Clause and Due Process Clause reproductive rights together. The chapter then considers the more complicated and complicating aspects of the relationship, including the bi-directional influence of these rights and tensions that have developed between them. The chapter concludes by suggesting that we recalibrate the relationship between the Free Speech Clause and abortion

The Dynamic Free Speech Clause. Timothy Zick.

rights. We ought to reduce the power governments have to control information and discourse concerning abortion. This requires rethinking some free speech doctrines that permit governments to use speech to structure and manipulate abortion discourse. At the same time, we need to devote more energy and attention to developing the "undue burden" standard, which currently governs the scope of abortion rights under the Due Process Clause and prohibits governments from placing substantial obstacles in the path of women seeking abortions.[1] Again, we ought to pay closer attention to the informational obstacles being placed in this path.

Free Speech as Abortion Rights Catalyst

As it has for many constitutional rights, freedom of speech (along with assembly, press, and petition rights) has facilitated the recognition, expansion, and exercise of abortion rights. In terms of constitutional doctrine, reproductive rights, including the right to abortion, can be partly traced to Free Speech Clause principles and protections. In a broader sense, the Free Speech Clause's protections for advocacy, rights discourse, and the free flow of information facilitated the recognition and exercise of abortion rights.

THE FIRST AMENDMENT ROOTS OF THE RIGHT TO ABORTION

Relative to other rights we have examined, the constitutional right to procure an abortion is a relatively modern conception. There were no founding or Reconstruction Era interactions between freedom of speech and the abortion right. As initially recognized in *Roe v. Wade* (1973), the right to abortion was characterized as a "privacy" right rooted in the Due Process Clause of the Fourteenth Amendment.[2] However, *Roe*'s roots were not solely planted in the Due Process Clause. As with so many constitutional rights, the path to recognition involved the Free Speech Clause.

The recognition of reproductive and procreative rights has been a product, in part, of First Amendment-based informational and autonomy principles. The abortion right recognized in *Roe* was an extension of individual rights to access and use contraceptives. Those rights were based on the right to communicate and receive information about contraceptive devices. In *Griswold v. Connecticut* (1965), the Supreme Court invalidated a Connecticut law that made it a crime to procure, or assist another in procuring, contraceptive devices or services.[3] The law applied to both married and unmarried couples. Physicians who prescribed contraceptive devices to their married patients challenged the law on constitutional grounds. Their principal argument was that the law violated the "liberty" to choose whether to become pregnant, which they claimed was protected by, among other provisions, the Fourteenth Amendment's Due Process Clause.

A central aspect of the physicians' argument was that the Connecticut law violated a "right to privacy" with respect to reproductive choice. However, the physicians did not rely solely on the Due Process Clause's protection of "liberty." Instead, they argued that a right to privacy with regard to intimate concerns was rooted in a number of constitutional provisions—including the First Amendment's Free Speech Clause. Indeed, the physicians' Supreme Court brief relied heavily on the connection between freedom of speech, thought, and association and the right to make decisions concerning whether to conceive a child.

In *Griswold*, the Supreme Court invalidated the Connecticut law. However, the justices could not agree on a single rationale for their ruling. Some concluded that there was a Due Process Clause-based right to procure and use contraceptives. Others located the right, in part, in the Ninth Amendment, which they argued protected rights not specifically enumerated in the Constitution.[4] Justice William O. Douglas, who authored an opinion for the Court, located the "right to privacy" in the Free Speech Clause and other constitutional rights provisions, which he observed had "penumbras, formed by emanations that help give them life and substance."[5] Specifically, in recognizing a right to privacy with regard to contraceptive information and use, Justice Douglas relied heavily on the First Amendment's protections for thought, information flow, assembly, and association.[6]

In subsequent cases involving privacy rights, including *Roe v. Wade*, the Supreme Court relied more explicitly on the Due Process Clause. However, the First Amendment continued to provide important background principles for these rights. *Roe* itself, although based primarily on the Due Process Clause, was premised on the notion that, at least in the first trimester of a pregnancy, communications between patient and physician were an aspect of the abortion right. *Planned Parenthood of Southeastern Pennsylvania v. Casey* (1992), which affirmed the central holding of *Roe* that a woman has a right to choose to terminate a pregnancy, also relied on *Griswold* and First Amendment precedents recognizing free speech and expressive association rights.[7]

As we will see, *Casey* is also based, in part, on speech principles that allow governments to structure physician-patient communications in certain ways and more generally to communicate official positions regarding abortion rights. Other Supreme Court "privacy" precedents have similarly emphasized the close connection between freedom of speech and fundamental rights.[8] In sum, free speech and other First Amendment rights have influenced the recognition and scope of constitutional privacy rights, including the right to abortion.

ABORTION RIGHTS DISCOURSE

As the book's Introduction observed, constitutional rights are a form of rhetoric and part of a contested discourse. As in the case of other constitutional rights, the ability of abortion proponents and opponents to exercise free speech rights has greatly influenced the recognition and development of abortion rights.

Through content neutrality, public forum, and other rules, the Free Speech Clause mediated a long and sometimes contentious abortion discourse in the United States. Prior to *Roe v. Wade*, the Free Speech Clause facilitated state and local debates about the availability and effects of abortion. Protesters, advocates for women's rights, and opponents of abortion publicly debated whether and to what extent abortion should be recognized as a constitutional right. In these debates, the Free Speech Clause ensured that speakers had access to public properties for the purpose of expressing their views on abortion, required that governments remain neutral with regard to the content of abortion speech, and protected rights to communicate and receive information concerning abortion. In sum, the Free Speech Clause allowed activists, litigants, and organizations to frame, debate, and adjudicate the constitutional and moral legitimacy of the abortion right. *Roe* was a product of this discourse.[9]

Of particular importance, freedom of speech allowed social movements and countermovements to develop and communicate positions concerning abortion. As Professor Reva Siegel has observed, social movements that seek constitutional change must ultimately persuade the public that their causes are associated with accepted public values.[10] Constitutional change movements, including the pro- and anti-abortion movements, can effectively participate in abortion rights discourse *only* insofar as free speech and other First Amendment rights are protected. The freedom to speak, publish, and protest, and to gather with others for these purposes, has allowed abortion proponents to frame and communicate their viewpoints concerning abortion rights. It has performed the very same functions for countermovements that have resisted and sought to overturn the abortion right.

During the 1960s, abortion activists used speeches, demonstrations, public testimonies, publications, and lawsuits to persuade political officials, courts, and the public that the medical model of abortion, which focused on the rights of physicians and women's safety, did not properly account for important equality, dignity, and liberty values associated with the right not to conceive or bear a child.[11] These speeches and demonstrations would reframe public debate over abortion. As Professor Siegel has observed, among other things these activities "expressed women's social standing, their authority to govern their own lives."[12]

Expressive activities also helped frame abortion rights as *constitutional* rights—indeed, part of a more comprehensive "Bill of Rights for Women."[13] Public advocacy led to some legislative reform and eventually to *Roe*, which embraced the idea that ultimately it was women—not physicians, parents, husbands, or others—who possessed a constitutional and fundamental right to choose whether to terminate a pregnancy within the limits set by *Roe*.[14]

Rights protected under the Free Speech Clause have also aided the antiabortion or "pro-life" movement. In their expressive activities, antiabortion activists have invoked public values relating to, among other things, the rights of the unborn, the sanctity of life, theology, and morality. They have relied on public speeches, anti-*Roe* demonstrations, and the distribution of information about the negative effects of abortion on fetuses, women, and society at large.

As discussed in Chapter 2 and further below, antiabortion speakers have relied on different kinds of expressive street politics—including sidewalk counseling, targeted picketing of abortion providers' residences, and public protests near health-care facilities that provide abortion services—to convey their messages. One of the more remarkable stories of the pre- and especially post-*Roe* abortion debate is the extent to which conservative and religious speakers turned to freedom of speech to oppose abortion rights and to challenge restrictions on their ability to dissent with regard to those rights.

As a result of all of this Free Speech Clause-mediated expressive activity, abortion discourse changed markedly over the years.[15] As noted, abortion rights activists have been successful in terms of convincing officials and the public that the right to terminate a pregnancy is a fundamental right that must be respected at least prior to fetal viability. On the other hand, antiabortion-rights advocacy has made significant inroads on the abortion right as recognized in *Roe*. In particular, it has emphasized the state's own interest in protecting potential life as well as the health and safety aspects of abortion procedures. Recently, opponents' messaging has changed to include the argument that abortion physically and psychologically harms women.[16]

The Free Speech Clause has provided the basic and essential framework for this abortion rights discourse. Public debate has occurred through a variety of means and in a range of forums, including news publications, academic articles, public speeches, demonstrations, lobbying, and litigation. *Roe, Casey*, and other Supreme Court decisions about abortion rights are important decision points; they have both reflected and affected what has become a national abortion rights discourse.

ACCESS TO INFORMATION

For Free Speech Clause mediation to be effective, speakers must be able to communicate and audiences must be able to receive information about abortion. In the United States, state and federal laws have sometimes restricted access to basic information regarding contraceptive devices and abortion services. The Free Speech Clause played a critical role in terms of removing these information barriers. This has been critically important to the exercise of reproductive rights.

As explained in Chapter 2, both the recognition and effective exercise of constitutional rights depend upon the freedom to communicate and receive information about those rights. What that chapter referred to as "informational rights speech" comes in many forms. At a minimum, it includes information about when, where, and how an individual can exercise a constitutional right.

Roe recognized a constitutional right to abortion. However, unlike *Griswold*, which specifically addressed restrictions on giving advice pertaining to contraception, *Roe* did not review restrictions on access to information about abortion services. At the time *Roe* was decided, some federal and state laws criminalized the distribution of information about abortion. These laws could be traced back to the late nineteenth century, when federal laws strictly regulated the distribution of information considered "obscene" or "immoral."[17] Victorian-inspired laws and regulations prohibited the use of the mails to distribute information about contraceptive devices and abortion services. Moreover, under federal and state laws, it was a crime to procure or assist in procuring an abortion. Thus, for a significant period of time in American history, communications about the basic mechanics of abortion—that is, where and how a woman could actually procure one—were subject to criminal penalties.

Griswold suggested that such laws were unconstitutional. *Roe* recognized a constitutional right to procure an abortion, which assumed some consultation with physicians. Thus, speech advocating or assisting the procurement of abortion was presumably no longer speech in furtherance of a crime. However, neither of these precedents established that all reproductive speech, even informational rights speech, was protected by the Free Speech Clause. Indeed, advertisements—flyers, pamphlets, and other materials—proposing the sale of contraceptives or the procurement of abortion services did not appear to be covered speech. The Supreme Court had long treated advertisements for goods and services—"commercial speech," as it would later come to be known—as beyond the coverage of the Free Speech Clause.[18] This would change in the mid-1970s, when the Supreme Court held that commercial speech was deserving of some protection.[19]

That change came partly as a result of a case involving abortion speech. *Bigelow v. Virginia* (1975) reviewed a prohibition on advertisements for abortion services.[20] Virginia law made it a crime to sell or circulate any publication that encouraged or prompted the procuring of an abortion. A newspaper, the *Virginia Weekly*, published an advertisement for abortion services, and circulated it on the nearby campus of the University of Virginia. The advertisement informed readers that abortion was legal in New York. It also offered to make arrangements for the procurement of an abortion, and to assure proper placement at accredited hospitals for that purpose. The publisher was tried and convicted for violating the Virginia law. While the case was on appeal, the Supreme Court handed down its decision in *Roe v. Wade*. Notwithstanding *Roe*, the Virginia Supreme Court affirmed the publisher's conviction.

The Supreme Court reversed. The Court held that the mere fact that speech took the form of an advertisement for services did not strip it of all Free Speech Clause protection. As it explained, the advertisement in question obviously pertained to a matter of great public concern:

> Viewed in its entirety, the advertisement conveyed information of potential interest and value to a diverse audience—not only to readers possibly in need of the services offered, but also to those with a general curiosity about, or genuine interest in, the subject matter or the law of another State and its development, and to readers seeking reform in Virginia. The mere existence of the Women's Pavilion in New York City, with the possibility of its being typical of other organizations there, and the availability of the services offered, were not unnewsworthy. Also, the activity advertised pertained to constitutional interests. [citing, inter alia, *Roe v. Wade* (1973)]. Thus, in this case, appellant's First Amendment interests coincided with the constitutional interests of the general public.[21]

Thus, in addition to pertaining to a matter of general public concern, the pamphlet was an example of what Chapter 2 calls "rights speech"—a communication about the recognition and exercise of a constitutional right. As *Bigelow* suggests, before and after *Roe*, advertisers and providers of abortion services sought to inform the public about the availability of abortion services and the means of procuring an abortion. As the *Bigelow* Court was undoubtedly aware, had it ruled against the newspaper, the state would have been free to restrict or perhaps even deny access to abortion services by suppressing information about their procurement.

Bigelow was an important abortion rights decision. The Court concluded that the Free Speech Clause protected against state efforts to deny women information about the Due Process Clause right recognized in *Roe*. As we will see, state efforts to restrict the flow of information about abortion are a troubling aspect of the intersection between free speech and the right to abortion. *Bigelow* is an early decision recognizing the need to ensure the free flow of informational rights speech. Subsequent decisions did not always follow this early lead.

Abortion-Limiting Speech and Limits on Abortion Speech

The Free Speech Clause has been at the center of a variety of disputes and conflicts concerning access to, and discourse about, abortion. Indeed, for a number of reasons, some of them relating to changes in the interpretation and scope of abortion rights, free speech doctrines and principles have sometimes dominated the constitutional conversation about abortion. Governments and private actors have relied on abortion-limiting policies and private communications to reduce or prevent access to abortion. Legislatures and courts (through injunctive measures) have mandated or restricted speech in ways that influence and structure conversations about abortion rights. These actions have severely tested the mediating function of the Free Speech Clause, which has been pressed into service to protect both free speech and abortion rights. As we will see, the Free Speech Clause has a mixed record in this regard. It has been asked to perform some functions that the Due Process Clause once performed.

MANDATORY ABORTION DISCLOSURES

Having access to basic information about or concerning abortion services is critically important to the exercise of the abortion right. As discussed earlier, *Bigelow* invalidated the suppression of informational abortion speech on free speech grounds. However, under post-*Roe* interpretations of the abortion right, governments have wide latitude to structure abortion conversations and consultations in ways intended to persuade women not to exercise their right to obtain an abortion.[22]

Shortly after *Roe v. Wade* recognized a constitutional right to terminate a pregnancy, the Supreme Court clarified that state and federal governments were not required to fund or otherwise support access to abortion services.[23] The Court held that governments were entitled to make a "value judgment," through the allocation of funds or other means, that childbirth was preferable to abortion.[24]

In *Planned Parenthood of Southeastern Pennsylvania v. Casey* (1992), the Supreme Court went even further. It concluded that governments are allowed to give effect to official positions on abortion by seeking to persuade women not to exercise their constitutional right to abortion. The Court held that this was permissible so long as governments did not unduly burden the abortion right by coercing women not to exercise it.[25]

In a later case involving a ban on late-term abortions, the Court, relying on *Casey*, emphasized that the government was entitled to express "respect for the dignity of human life" and to "use its *voice* and its regulatory authority to show its profound respect for the life within the woman."[26] *Casey* had retained the abortion right. However, the decision significantly recalibrated the private and public interests relating to abortion. In particular, through a progression of post-*Roe* decisions, the Court allowed governments more leeway to communicate their preference for life.

This invited the enactment of laws and regulations aimed at influencing women's decisionmaking with regard to abortion. One popular measure has been to mandate that physicians provide women with certain information when they meet to consult about the procedure. In pre-*Casey* decisions, the Court had invalidated such provisions on Due Process Clause grounds, concluding that they were not intended to assist women in their decision-making but rather to deter them from exercising the right to abortion.[27] *Casey* overruled these decisions. It upheld Pennsylvania's mandatory abortion disclosure law, which required that physicians disclose to patients seeking an abortion the nature of the procedure, the health risks of the abortion and of childbirth, and the probable gestational age of the unborn child.[28]

After rejecting the due process challenge to the disclosure provision, the Court addressed the physicians' alternative argument that the Free Speech Clause prohibited compulsory abortion disclosures:

> All that is left of petitioners' argument is an asserted First Amendment right of a physician not to provide information about the risks of abortion, and childbirth, in a manner mandated by the State. To be sure, the physician's First Amendment rights not to speak are implicated . . . , but only as part of the practice of medicine, subject to reasonable licensing and regulation by the State . . . We see no constitutional infirmity in the requirement that the physician provide the information mandated by the State here.[29]

In addition to failing to clearly set forth any free speech standard for such measures, the Court's perfunctory treatment elided the fact that much more than ordinary "informed consent" was at stake. With regard to the pregnant woman's decision whether to bear a child, *Casey* held that the government was permitted to (1) take steps "to ensure that this choice is thoughtful and informed," (2) "enact rules and regulations designed to encourage her to know that there are *philosophic and social* arguments of great weight that can be brought to bear in favor of continuing the pregnancy to full term," and (3) enact a "*reasonable framework* for a woman to make a decision that has such profound and lasting meaning."[30] As one commentator observed, *Casey* sanctioned a framework in which the government could "structure the woman's decision-making process" and "open up the expressive channels of speech to the pregnant woman while she is engaged in deliberation about her choice."[31] In essence, the Court was "granting leeway to the government to voice its own opposition to abortion."[32]

Mandatory abortion disclosures are manifestations of dynamic changes in the law of abortion and free speech. As noted, under the Due Process Clause, the Supreme Court granted governments significant authority to communicate their antiabortion views, so long as measures did not constitute an "undue burden" on the right to abortion. Under the Court's reasoning, mandatory abortion disclosure provisions, such as the one Pennsylvania enacted, did not cross the line from persuasion to coercion. With regard to the Free Speech Clause, *Casey* suggested that as licensed professionals, physicians had very limited (if any) rights under the Free Speech Clause. As I noted in Chapter 2, that conclusion is not supported by the Court's free speech precedents. Nevertheless, insofar as licensed physicians enjoy limited or perhaps no free speech rights in the context of patient consultations regarding abortion, they are unable to challenge mandatory disclosure laws on the ground that they compel speech.

Whereas *Bigelow* recognized the importance of the free flow of information about abortion services, *Casey* ushered in a framework in which governments could compel physicians to disclose, and women to receive, informational abortion speech. *Roe*'s implicit reliance on the virtues of a free exchange of information between physician and patient, at least in the early terms of a pregnancy, was replaced with a structured discourse in which official communications made their way into abortion consultations. This intervention takes place at one of the most critical points in the woman's decision-making process—her consultation with an abortion provider.

Since *Casey*, legislatures have enacted a variety of measures that structure conversations in this way.[33] Some of these measures go well beyond mandating the disclosure of basic factual information regarding the abortion procedure—that is, the kind of "informed consent" information one might receive in connection with other medical procedures.[34] States have tested the boundaries of their power to structure abortion consultations by mandating increasingly specific "scripts" detailing the abortion procedure and mandating ideological statements such as "abortion terminates a living being."[35]

At this point, mandatory abortion disclosure laws are generally permitted under the Due Process Clause "undue burden" standard, and are not generally prohibited under the Free Speech Clause's compelled speech doctrine. These interpretations of constitutional rights permit governments to structure consultations in ways that pressure women not to exercise the right to abortion.

ABORTION SPEECH GAG ORDERS

As a function of their power to distribute taxpayer funds, governments have also been allowed to prohibit physicians from even mentioning abortion as a viable medical option to women seeking care at funded facilities. In *Rust v. Sullivan* (1991),[36] the Supreme Court held that the federal government could prohibit physicians working at federally-funded family planning projects from engaging in abortion "counseling" or "advocacy" while using program funds.[37] Federal regulations required that if asked about abortion services, physicians at funded projects should respond that the facility "did not consider abortion an appropriate method of family planning."[38]

In *Rust,* physicians and patients argued that the federal funding restrictions amounted to viewpoint discrimination in violation of the Free Speech Clause.[39] They claimed that the restrictions allowed all methods of family planning to be discussed, with the sole exception of abortion. The Court rejected the Free Speech Clause argument. It reasoned that when the government distributes taxpayer funds, it is permitted to limit "activities"—including, apparently, the communication of information about those activities—to the scope of the funded project.[40] In a subsequent case, the Court reinterpreted *Rust* to hold that when the government *speaks* about abortion, it is entitled to assure that its own message is "neither garbled nor distorted by the grantee."[41] Thus, in a project created to fund pregnancy and other prenatal healthcare services, the government is allowed to prohibit the expenditure of funds for abortion services *and* to ban abortion speech that might lead to the provision of such services.[42]

Abortion funding gag rules are the flip side of the mandatory abortion disclosures discussed above. They *suppress* communications about abortion in ways that can significantly deter exercise of the abortion right—particularly for poor and marginalized women who depend on publicly funded clinics for abortion services. As did *Casey,* the decision in *Rust* signaled a restructuring of the relationship between abortion rights and freedom of speech.

For women who use public clinics affected by the restrictions on abortion speech, this may be their only opportunity to receive unbiased medical advice. Yet here, too, the Free Speech Clause has been of no use to physicians or the women consulting them. The Supreme Court has granted government broad authority to determine which speech it will fund—even if that means communications about abortion are censored in the process and some women will not receive vital information concerning abortion.

PRIVATE SPEECH THAT RESTRICTS ACCESS TO ABORTION

As noted earlier, the Free Speech Clause protects the communications of both proponents and opponents of abortion. In some contexts, antiabortion speech has threatened to limit access to abortion services. Some means of communicating antiabortion messages—in particular, sidewalk counseling, public protests near healthcare facilities, and threatening communications—can impede physical access to abortion facilities and services. In this context, the Free Speech Clause has been interpreted to limit the impact of antiabortion speech on physical access to abortion services.

Abortion proponents used the Free Speech Clause to facilitate recognition of a Due Process Clause right to privacy, engage in abortion advocacy, and procure coverage and protection for commercial advertisements pertaining to abortion rights. In the decades following *Roe*, antiabortion activists and organizations secured and defended mandatory disclosure requirements and strict funding conditions affecting abortion speech.

Antiabortion protesters also invoked the Free Speech Clause to defend the right to engage in various kinds of "street politics" at or near abortion clinics.[43] Chapter 2 argued, in general, that the Free Speech Clause ought to be interpreted to protect abortion speech in this context—whether that speech communicates pro- or antiabortion messages. However, the Free Speech Clause does not provide license to speakers to interfere with the exercise of constitutional rights, including the right to abortion.

During the 1980s and 1990s, the areas near abortion clinics were often volatile and even violent places.[44] Sidewalk counselors (individuals who seek through one-on-one counseling to persuade women not to have an abortion) and protesters used the public spaces near healthcare facilities, where women sought abortion services, to convey their messages. Counselors sought to persuade women not to procure abortions. Protesters conveyed moral and other forms of opposition to abortion.

Some of the antiabortion activists' expressive activities raised concerns regarding women's physical access to abortion services. They also implicated the personal safety of the women who visited the clinics and those in their employ. For instance, abortion opponents sometimes blocked access to healthcare facilities and harassed women and abortion clinic staff members in order to prevent abortions from occurring.

At the urging of abortion rights advocates, and in response to access and safety concerns, courts and legislatures imposed a variety of injunctive and statutory limits on free speech activities near clinics providing abortion services.[45] Antiabortion activists invoked the Free Speech Clause to challenge these measures. The lawsuits ushered in a contentious phase in the relationship between the Free Speech Clause and the right to abortion. Abortion opponents wanted *Roe* overturned—for many, that was, and remains, the ultimate goal. Failing that, they wanted to take their message to places where it might have the most immediate and meaningful impact.

The Court's decisions made clear that means of communicating that had the effect of physically blocking ingress to or egress from healthcare facilities were not covered by the Free Speech Clause. Neither, of course, were violent acts or threatening communications. However, under longstanding free speech principles, non-violent counseling, protests, and other forms of private abortion speech were protected.

In its abortion clinic protest cases, the Supreme Court generally upheld injunctive provisions aimed at ensuring meaningful access to healthcare facilities. It did not permit anti-abortion speech to be used to limit basic access to abortion services. The Court engaged in a form of rough balancing, under which counselors and protesters were allowed to engage in free speech activities so long as they did not prevent access to abortion clinics and services. In this way, the Court used the principles of the Free Speech Clause to prevent abortion opponents from placing obstacles in the path of women seeking abortions—the same function served by the Due Process Clause as applied to governmental burdens on abortion.

Not everyone has been pleased with this balance. Abortion opponents have complained that the Court's balancing sometimes jeopardized the ability to convey antiabortion speech. Pro-choice advocates have contended that the Court's abortion clinic free speech cases leave women vulnerable to street harassment and other modes of communication that operate as effective barriers to obtaining abortion services. In terms of abortion-limiting speech, the Court's decisions make clear that at a minimum, the Free Speech Clause cannot be relied upon by private speakers to effectively nullify access to abortion rights.

SIDEWALK COUNSELING

One particular method of communicating antiabortion speech raises some difficult free speech questions. Sidewalk counseling, which involves face-to-face conversations with women who present at abortion clinics, is a method of communicating antiabortion speech that many women find uncomfortable and off-putting. Since it relies on face-to-face communication, sidewalk counseling can give rise to concerns about physical access and harassment. States and localities generally resolved this issue by limiting the locations where speakers could interact with clinic patients. They created buffer zones around the clinics, in which speech activities are limited or banned. They also created protective bubbles around clinic patients, into which counselors could not enter without consent.

These regulations eventually made their way to the Supreme Court. In *Hill v. Colorado* (2000), the Supreme Court upheld a Colorado law that banned speakers within one hundred feet from the entrance of a health care facility from coming within eight feet of a person, without their consent, for the "purpose of passing a leaflet or handbill to, displaying a sign to, or engaging in oral protest, education, or counseling with such other person."[46]

Given the buffer zone around the facilities, the Colorado law was not plausibly aimed at securing physical access. Rather, its purpose seemed to be to protect unwilling women from encountering anti-abortion sidewalk counselors as they approached the health care facilities. The Court concluded that the law was content-neutral (because it banned *all* protest, education, and counseling) and tailored to address important interests in health and safety. More specifically, the Court held that the Colorado law served to protect a "privacy interest in avoiding unwanted communication."[47] Interests in protecting captive audiences had previously been recognized only within the home. In the abortion context, however, the Court extended the privacy interest to public streets and places near health care facilities providing abortion services.

Hill has been roundly criticized, by commentators from across the political spectrum as well as some of the justices on the Court.[48] The criticisms are twofold. First, critics have challenged the Court's conclusion that the Colorado law is content-based. Second, they have objected to the recognition of a "privacy" right or interest in avoiding offensive and unwanted speech in what have traditionally been considered forums for expression—including public sidewalks and streets.

In a more recent case involving limits on sidewalk counseling, the Court seemed partially responsive to these criticisms. In *McCullen v. Coakley* (2014), the Supreme Court invalidated a Massachusetts law that created a thirty-foot buffer zone around all abortion clinics in the state.[49] The majority treated the law as content-neutral, but invalidated it on the ground that it was not tailored to address access and public order concerns. Although *McCullen* did not overrule *Hill*, it sided with sidewalk counselors who argued that they could not meaningfully and effectively engage with women seeking access to abortion services from outside the buffer zones. In stark contrast to prior cases, which had lumped all antiabortion speech into the category of "protest," the Court went out of its way to observe that the sidewalk counselors were different:

> Some of the individuals who stand outside Massachusetts abortion clinics are fairly described as protestors, who express their moral or religious opposition to abortion through signs and chants or, in some cases, more aggressive methods such as face-to-face confrontation. Petitioners take a different tack. They attempt to engage women approaching the clinics in what they call "sidewalk counseling," which involves offering information about alternatives to abortion and help pursuing those options.

* * * *

> Petitioners are not protestors. They seek not merely to express their opposition to abortion, but to inform women of various alternatives and to provide help in pursuing them. Petitioners believe that they can accomplish this objective only through personal, caring, consensual conversations.[50]

As the passages make clear, the Court was defending the practice of sidewalk counseling against the charge that it was a form of disorderly harassment and intimidation. Unlike protesters, the Court reasoned, sidewalk counselors are not engaged in aggressive forms of anti-abortion speech. Although it did not explicitly overrule *Hill,* the Court rejected state efforts to protect women on public sidewalks and streets from the communication of (one assumes mostly) unwanted appeals by sidewalk counselors. Instead, it seemed to suggest that sidewalk counseling was a particularly valuable form of public antiabortion speech.

McCullen is merely the latest in a long line of Supreme Court precedents seeking to balance women's right to obtain an abortion and speakers' right to communicate opposition to abortion, at or near health care and abortion facilities. Although abortion clinics are not the free speech culture war battlefields they once were, *McCullen* demonstrates that they remain an important part of the dynamic between free speech and abortion rights. The Court has upheld some limits on abortion speech, particularly relating to protesters' disruptive activities. *McCullen* suggests that limits on the speech of sidewalk counselors are to be treated skeptically under the First Amendment.

RESIDENTIAL PICKETING

Abortion clinics are obviously not the only places where anti-abortion speakers have sought to convey their messages. Some have sought to picket or protest near the residences of abortion providers. One arguable aim of this kind of expressive activity is to deter abortion providers from rendering their services. Thus, we may view this as a form of potentially abortion-limiting speech. However, like sidewalk counselors, residential picketers are also engaged in communicating anti-abortion viewpoints. Thus, measures limiting this practice may also restrict abortion speech.

Of course, residential picketing is not something only abortion opponents do. Other speakers sometimes seek out the objects of their protest messages where they live—both because this is where the intended audience resides and because targeting the residence may be highly symbolic. Abortion protesters also target residences for both of these reasons.

In *Frisby v. Schultz* (1988), the Supreme Court addressed a local ordinance that banned "focused picketing"—as the Court described it, the act of maintaining a continuous presence outside a person's residence.[51] The Court upheld the ordinance as a content-neutral means of furthering interests in preserving residential privacy and tranquility. *Frisby* interpreted the Free Speech Clause to prohibit what the Court seemed to consider a particularly aggressive or offensive form of antiabortion protest. However, the Court was careful to observe that its decision did not authorize local governments to prohibit the use of residential sidewalks generally, including for the purpose of conducting antiabortion protests and demonstrations. Thus, picketers were permitted to march on the public sidewalks and communicate the same message they would otherwise have focused on the abortion provider's residence.

Frisby's concern for residential privacy is not surprising. Unlike the interest in privacy relied upon in *Hill*, privacy interests in the home are well-established. Antiabortion speakers have no right to force unwanted speech on abortion providers while they are in their homes, rendering them essentially captive to messages piped in from the streets and sidewalks. On the other hand, the Court was clearly concerned that localities not be allowed to ban *all* residential protests.

Here, again, the Free Speech Clause was invoked to mediate a conflict at the intersection of abortion and free speech rights. The balance it struck likely pleased neither speakers nor abortion providers. The speakers were deprived of an effective and highly symbolic means of communicating their opposition to abortion. The abortion provider, no doubt relieved not to be held captive to focused picketing, may nevertheless perceive residential antiabortion protests, which are clearly animated by his presence in the neighborhood, as a form of intimidation and harassment.

THREATS TO ABORTION PROVIDERS

One form of abortion-limiting speech that crosses a constitutional line consists of communications that threaten abortion providers with serious bodily injury or death. Speakers who communicate such threats can be held liable under state stalking and harassment laws. They can also be subject to significant fines under the federal Freedom of Access to Clinic Entrances Act (FACE).[52] As its name suggests, FACE is primarily concerned with preserving physical access to healthcare facilities. However, the Act also prohibits the intentional communication of threats against abortion service providers. These communications can restrict access to clinics through a form of intimidation.[53]

In a controversial decision, the full Ninth Circuit Court of Appeals upheld a substantial civil verdict against an antiabortion group under FACE's threat provision.[54] The group had circulated posters and other materials alleging that specific abortion providers were "guilty of crimes against humanity." They also operated a website—the "Nuremberg Files"—on which they posted the names, addresses, and other information regarding abortion providers, as well as information concerning whether the providers had been killed or wounded.[55]

A sharply divided appeals court held that the Free Speech Clause did not protect implied threats communicated to or about specific abortion providers by means of the group's posters and website.[56] Although the speakers made no explicit threat against any individual physician, the court's majority concluded that under the circumstances—which included murders of abortion providers after comparable materials had been distributed by another group—even an *implicit* threat of violence could support liability.[57]

Several dissenting judges claimed that the majority had interpreted and applied FACE in a manner that suppressed political speech relating to abortion rights.[58] According to the dissenters, in the absence of any actual or intended threat, the antiabortion speech was fully protected by the First Amendment.[59] They warned that upholding the verdict would chill abortion-related and other forms of political advocacy.[60]

Like many of the other examples we have considered, the "Nuremberg Files" case raises difficult questions relating to the intersection between free speech and abortion rights. One the one hand, speakers cannot be allowed to intimidate abortion providers through communications that threaten death or serious bodily harm. These kinds of communications threaten access to abortion. On the other hand, speakers have free speech rights to communicate opposition to abortion in even vile and deeply offensive ways. As we have seen throughout this discussion, allowing speakers to resort to forms of speech that suppress access to abortion threatens the exercise of abortion rights. However, limiting speech in an effort to preserve access to abortion may constrict political speech about abortion rights.

Time and again, the Free Speech Clause has been drawn into this conundrum, to arbitrate between abortion and free speech rights. The manner in which free speech principles and precedents have mediated at this intersection has significantly affected both discourse about and access to abortion. As we will now see, as it has performed these tasks, the Free Speech Clause has itself been affected in various respects.

Abortion and/or Free Speech Precedents?

Like the other relationships examined in the book, the interactions between the Free Speech Clause and the right to abortion are bi-directional. We have examined how the invocation and enforcement of free speech rights have impacted the recognition, enjoyment, and enforcement of abortion rights. In this respect, although generally characterized as free speech controversies, the various policies and decisions discussed above were about abortion rights. However, in important respects, these controversies affected the interpretation and understanding of freedom of speech. Free Speech Clause coverage for commercial advertisements, judicial review of speech injunctions, the content neutrality principle, the speech rights of licensed professionals, and the government's authority to restrict speech as subsidizer or speaker were all affected by the communication of abortion-limiting speech and measures restricting abortion speech. Beyond these doctrinal effects, the cases revealed an important dynamic shift in abortion advocacy. During the 1980s and 1990s, conservative Christians and others in the "pro-life" movement, who had generally opposed liberal interpretations of constitutional rights, became frequent advocates for expansive free speech rights. Their attitudinal and strategic turn toward the Free Speech Clause meant that the culture war over abortion rights would often be litigated in free speech terms.

COVERAGE FOR COMMERCIAL SPEECH

As discussed earlier, for a long period in American constitutional history, commercial advertising was not treated as "speech" covered by the Free Speech Clause. This changed during the 1970s, when the Supreme Court reversed course and held that commercial speech was entitled to some (although not full) coverage. Efforts to suppress information about abortion were critical to this expansion in free speech coverage.

Constitutional law scholars and casebook editors tend to give pride of place in this regard to *Virginia State Board of Pharmacy v. Virginia Citizens Council, Inc.* (1976), which invalidated a Virginia law limiting consumer access to drug pricing information.[61] In fact, however, the Court first made this move in *Bigelow v. Virginia* (1975), which was decided a year earlier. Prior to *Bigelow*, the Court had recognized that the mere presence of a commercial motive or payment for advertising did not remove speech from coverage.[62] However, the Court had not yet held that speech proposing a commercial transaction was covered by the Free Speech Clause.

As discussed earlier, *Bigelow* was an abortion speech case. The advertisements at issue pertained primarily to the procurement of abortion services—how, when, and where to procure a legal abortion. They also suggested that states beyond Virginia had taken a different and more expansive approach to abortion rights. The Court might have treated the advertisement as one outside the coverage of the Free Speech Clause. It seemed to make a real difference to the Court that the advertisement in

Bigelow was not about an ordinary product or service. Although it proposed a commercial transaction, the advertisement related to a matter of critical public concern. Its content was important to free speech values such as self-government and the search for truth. Indeed, the Court observed that "the activity advertised pertained to constitutional rights."[63] A year later, in *Virginia Pharmacy*, the Court concluded for the same reasons that *all* truthful and non-misleading commercial advertising was entitled to some protection under the Free Speech Clause.

Recognition of the abortion right was important to the result in *Bigelow. Roe v. Wade* was decided as *Bigelow* was making its way through the federal courts. The distributors of the advertisement were able to leverage *Roe* to secure protection for informational and ideological abortion speech. They understood that in order to make the newly recognized abortion right meaningful, women would need access to information about how legal abortions could be procured.

Bigelow marked the first time commercial speakers were able to successfully link advertisements for services to free speech values. The precedent started or pushed the Court down a path that would in very short order bring "commercial speech" out of the First Amendment shadows. Subsequent decisions did not afford commercial speech precisely the same degree of protection as other covered communications.[64] In Chapter 2, I argued that advertisements pertaining to constitutional rights ought to be considered a form of rights speech granted *full* coverage and protection. Thus far, the Court has not taken that approach. However, the fact that it afforded *any* protection at all to commercial advertisements was a momentous development in terms of Free Speech Clause jurisprudence.

INJUNCTIONS, CONTENT NEUTRALITY, AND PUBLIC PRIVACY

The intersection between free speech and abortion rights in the abortion clinic context, which represented a major fault line, also had some interpretive consequences for free speech rights. Three of the most important effects relate to judicial review of speech injunctions, the principle of content neutrality, and the seeming recognition of a right to avoid unwanted speech in public places.

Speech-Focused Injunctions

On two occasions, the Supreme Court reviewed judicial injunctions restricting the speech of antiabortion protesters and sidewalk counselors.[65] One question facing the Court was which standard of review to apply to such injunctions. On the one hand, speech injunctions appear to restrict communications based on content, which ordinarily triggers a demanding or "strict" level of judicial scrutiny. On the other hand, injunctions target speech and speech activities for content-neutral reasons—for example, because the speakers have engaged in past misconduct such as blocking physical access to abortion clinics or harassing clinic employees.

The Court settled on a degree of "intermediate" scrutiny for speech injunctions.[66] This drew a fierce dissent from Justice Antonin Scalia, who claimed that the Court in adopting this standard had departed from settled Free Speech Clause doctrine. Justice Scalia observed that the abortion clinic injunctions had been sought by "persons and organizations with a business or social interest in suppressing" the view of "a single-issue advocacy group."[67] In his view, then, the injunctions directly targeted antiabortion speech and should have been reviewed—and invalidated—under the strictest standard of First Amendment scrutiny.

As he often did in abortion speech cases, Justice Scalia attributed the Court's purported departure from settled law to the fact that "the context here is abortion."[68] He asserted that in the abortion context, the Court applied speech-restrictive rules to restrict antiabortion advocacy. He claimed that the Court's abortion speech precedents constituted a "powerful loaded weapon lying about" for others to invoke in efforts to stifle viewpoints with which they disagreed.[69]

As Professor Daniel Farber has observed, at the time the Supreme Court decided the clinic injunction cases, it had not definitively established a standard of review for speech injunctions.[70] Thus, Justice Scalia's claim that the Court had departed from past practice in order to uphold restrictions on antiabortion speech seems to overstate things. However, if the law was indeed unsettled or unclear, the Court in the abortion clinic injunction cases made a move to settle and clarify it. It adopted a standard of review that governs speech injunctions not only in abortion cases, but in other contexts as well.

As Justice Scalia concluded in one of the abortion speech injunction cases: "What we have decided seems to be, and will be reported by the media as, an abortion case. But it will go down in the lawbooks, it will be cited, as a free-speech injunction case–and the damage its novel principles produce will be considerable."[71] Whether or not this dire prediction will come true, Justice Scalia's fundamental point was accurate and, as we will see, generalizable: the abortion skirmishes discussed earlier affected not just abortion politics and abortion rights, but free speech standards and rights as well.

Counseling and Content Neutrality

One of the central commands of the Free Speech Clause is that officials must generally remain neutral with regard to private speakers' viewpoints.[72] The Supreme Court's abortion clinic speech cases did not always faithfully apply this rule. They complicated the content neutrality analysis, by failing to consistently apply it.

As mentioned earlier, the Colorado law upheld in *Hill v. Colorado* (2000) prohibited only certain unwanted approaches by speakers—in particular, those that entailed "counseling" or "advocacy."[73] In addition to Justice Scalia, who again argued that the Court was bending or breaking the free speech rules in order to suppress antiabortion speech, scholars from across the political spectrum also condemned the Court's analysis.[74] The language of the law, not to mention the history leading up to its passage, demonstrated that the legislature was targeting the speech of sidewalk counselors.

Here, too, Justice Scalia argued that the presence of the abortion right was distorting free speech doctrine. He had "no doubt that this regulation would be deemed content-based *in an instant* if the case before us involved antiwar protesters, or union members seeking to 'educate' the public about the reasons for their strike."[75] He described *Hill* as yet another precedent in the Court's "relentlessly proabortion jurisprudence" and repeated his charge that "the [free speech] jurisprudence of this Court has a way of changing when abortion is involved."[76] Justice Scalia closed his dissent in *Hill* with this criticism:

> What is before us . . . is a speech regulation directed against the opponents of abortion, and it therefore enjoys the benefit of the "ad hoc nullification machine" that the Court has set in motion to push aside whatever doctrines of constitutional law stand in the way of that highly favored practice. Having deprived abortion opponents of the political right to persuade the electorate that abortion should be restricted by law, the Court today continues and expands its assault upon their individual right to persuade women contemplating abortion that what they are doing is wrong.[77]

Advocates urged the Court to overrule *Hill's* content neutrality holding in *McCullen v. Coakley* (2015), which invalidated a Massachusetts law that established a thirty-five-foot buffer zone around all facilities in the state where abortions were performed.[78] Despite the fact that the law applied only to speakers at or near abortion clinics and permitted some clinic employees to speak inside the buffer zone, the Court once again treated the law as content-neutral. In a departure from many precedents reviewing content neutral laws, the Court invalidated the law on the ground that it was not narrowly tailored to serve the state's interests in maintaining access and public order.

Once again, Justice Scalia argued in dissent that it "blinks reality to say, as the majority does, that a blanket prohibition on the use of streets and sidewalks where speech on only one politically controversial topic is likely to occur—and where the speech can most effectively be communicated—is not content-based."[79] He concluded: "The obvious purpose of the Massachusetts Reproductive Health Care Facilities Act is to 'protect' prospective clients of abortion clinics from having to hear abortion-opposing speech on public streets and sidewalks."[80]

Like the injunction holdings, the Court's applications of the content-neutrality rule in cases such as *Hill* and *McCullen* are not confined to the abortion speech context. These are free speech precedents, and as such can be relied upon by legislatures and officials defending non-abortion speech regulations. *Hill* intimated to lower courts that they were free to disregard not only the context of enactment, but even the text of a law targeting only particular facilities or modes of expression closely associated with particular speakers. Given the importance of the content discrimination determination in free speech cases—it sets the standard of review, which is often dispositive—*Hill* is a significant Free Speech Clause decision. *McCullen* ensured that, at least for now, this aspect of *Hill* remains good law.

Abortion Speech and Public Privacy

Under the Free Speech Clause, audiences do not generally have a right to privacy in public places and governments do not have a valid interest in protecting audiences from offensive speech conveyed in public forums.[81] As *Frisby* shows, individual privacy rights and interests can be relied upon to prevent speakers from forcing communications on persons captive within their homes.[82] However, in the public streets and on the public sidewalks, the constitutional calculus is quite different. In those places, there is no right to be protected from unwanted communications.

Once again, the abortion clinic speech cases suggested a different rule. While stopping short of recognizing a privacy right in public places, *Hill* credited the state's argument that it had an important interest in protecting women from unwanted protest and sidewalk counseling near abortion clinics. As Justice Scalia observed, however, there is no "right to be free of unwelcome speech on the public streets while seeking entrance to or exit from abortion clinics."[83] If there is such a right, it is difficult to see why it would not apply also to labor picketing and other modes of speech that public audiences might also deem unwelcome or offensive.[84] Like the other rules we have examined, a free speech-limiting right to public privacy can either be confined to abortion speech, which would demonstrate its discriminatory nature, or be applied to a range of public expression, thus imperiling far more than antiabortion speech.

McCullen may indicate that in an appropriate case, the Court is poised to reject this aspect of *Hill*.[85] However, the fact that it did not do so means that the right to, or interest in, protection from unwanted speech applies on our public streets and sidewalks (and in other places as well). Although the Court struck down the buffer zone law, Justice Scalia characterized the decision as one that "carries forward this Court's practice of giving abortion-rights advocates a pass when it comes to suppressing the free-speech rights of their opponents."[86] "There is," he wrote, "an entirely separate, abridged edition of the First Amendment applicable to speech against abortion."[87]

Justice Scalia has been criticized for overstating the implications of the Court's abortion clinic free speech cases, and for being moved by his own antiabortion biases (both personal and doctrinal—he made no secret that in his view *Roe* was invalid and ought to be overturned). In this respect Justice Scalia was hardly alone.[88] Nevertheless, the justice raised an important point about the intersection of abortion and free speech rights. The Court's abortion clinic free speech decisions were often reported on as part of the culture wars over abortion rights in the United States. Indeed, they were part of that skirmish. But they ultimately produced some significant *free speech* rulings. As Justice Scalia urged, we ought not to lose sight of this bidirectional effect.

PROFESSIONAL SPEECH

The intersection between the right to abortion and the Free Speech Clause also raised some significant issues relating to the speech rights of licensed professionals. As explained in Chapter 2, these issues cut across several constitutional rights. However, owing to the special role of physicians in the exercise of abortion rights, the free speech rights of licensed professionals has been a particular point of concern in the abortion context.

As discussed earlier, *Casey* confirmed that a woman has a right to choose to end her pregnancy. However, *Casey* also held that the state has an interest *throughout* the pregnancy in the fetus's potential life. As we have seen, this interest empowers the state to weigh in on the abortion decision. Under the "undue burden" standard applied under the Due Process Clause, so long as the measures they adopt are not coercive, the state may seek to persuade women not to exercise the abortion right.

State legislatures have enacted laws that require physicians to communicate basic facts about the fetus, abortion, and childbirth to women who attend abortion consultations. As noted earlier, some have gone beyond compelling basic facts and information and have sought to compel detailed scripts and ideological objections to abortion. Proponents of these measures defend them as part of informed consent, and view them as an appropriate means by which the state expresses its respect for life. Opponents see them as a commandeering of private speakers and as inherently coercive measures designed not to inform women but to overcome their free will and autonomy.

The central free speech issue raised by mandatory abortion disclosures is whether physicians and other healthcare providers, who are licensed by the state pursuant to specific professional standards, have a Free Speech Clause right not to be compelled to communicate as the state commands. Mandatory disclosure laws raise the question whether state licensure extinguishes or severely limits the free speech rights of professionals. As discussed in Chapter 2, that is a rather complicated question.[89]

In the abortion cases, the Supreme Court had an opportunity to clarify this unsettled aspect of the Free Speech Clause. In summarily concluding that the Pennsylvania mandatory disclosure provision "implicated," but did not violate, the Free Speech Clause, *Casey* suggested a permissive approach to professional speech regulations. As noted in Chapter 2, if this approach governs, the speech rights of stockbrokers, lawyers, therapists, and a host of other professionals licensed by the state may be subject to detailed and even ideological mandates and restrictions.[90]

Like the other abortion-related decisions under consideration, what the Court has said concerning the constitutionality of mandatory disclosures affects not only abortion rights but important free speech rights—in this case of licensed professionals and their clients—as well. *Casey* is not likely to be the Court's last word on the free speech rights of professionals. However, what little the case said about the matter has already significantly influenced the development of professional speech jurisprudence.

GOVERNMENT AS SUBSIDIZER AND SPEAKER

The abortion-free speech interface has influenced two other important aspects of free speech doctrine. The first relates to the government's authority to regulate private speech when it funds expression. The second concerns the government's effect on private speech and speakers when it functions as a speaker or communicator.

As discussed earlier, *Rust v. Sullivan* upheld a federal spending condition that imposed an abortion "gag rule" on healthcare providers receiving federal healthcare funds. The Supreme Court concluded that when the government makes funds available to further interests in childbirth and childcare, it is not required to fund consultations or advocacy concerning abortion. Although *Rust* suggests that there may be some limits to the extent to which the state may interfere with the physician-patient relationship, its essential holding is that physicians at funded facilities have no Free Speech Clause rights to engage in abortion speech.

Rust affects the ability of physicians to communicate, and poor women to receive, information about abortion services. Like *Casey*'s validation of mandatory disclosure laws, *Rust* allows governments to structure conversations about abortion in ways that may distort physicians' advice and deprive women of information critical to autonomous decisionmaking concerning abortion. Of course, these precedents apply outside the abortion context as well. They establish broad governmental power to condition funding on speech and information flow restrictions—including outright prohibitions on certain communications.

The Supreme Court has interpreted *Rust* as a decision recognizing the government's own power to communicate.[91] That power is even more consequential, particularly as it pertains to *private* speech. Under the government speech principle, government speakers are not required to comply with the Free Speech Clause's content neutrality rules.[92] Thus, when it acts as a speaker or communicator, the government can openly discriminate based on viewpoint.

In sum, like other "abortion" decisions, *Rust* significantly affects the exercise of free speech rights. Funding recipients and private speakers seeking access to government funds and programs have fewer, less robust, and in some cases *no* free speech rights at all.

THE FREE SPEECH TURN

As these various issues and doctrines show, late twentieth century conflicts over abortion rights were often fought on free speech grounds. Changing interpretations of the Due Process Clause as it related to abortion rights partially explain this shift in focus. However, deeper cultural and movement-based dynamics were also at play.

As discussed in Chapter 4, during the 1980s and 1990s, advocates for religious rights made a strategic turn away from the Free Exercise Clause and toward the Free Speech Clause. In cases challenging exclusionary policies that barred religious groups from using public buildings or participating in public programs, litigants in many instances relied exclusively on free speech doctrines and principles. The strategic turn was designed to take advantage of content neutrality, public forum, and other free speech mediating principles. And it was quite successful; the Supreme Court invalidated several programs that excluded prayer and other religious expression.

Around the same time, abortion opponents made a similar strategic turn. As the cases discussed show, they looked to the Free Speech Clause to challenge injunctions and laws that excluded them from public forums near abortion clinics, residences, and other symbolic places. In this area, too, conservative speakers embraced a liberal interpretation of free speech rights that included the right to express unpopular dissent and even offensive ideas. Thus, advocates and groups that had previously objected to constitutional liberalism—including with respect to the abortion right—embraced it in their drive to create breathing space for antiabortion speech.

This was an important legal shift. But it was also a dynamic cultural change in the relationship between abortion and free speech. It brought the Free Speech Clause to the fore of the abortion culture wars.

Antiabortion advocates did not always embrace a liberal interpretation of free speech rights. They also realized that controlling speech about abortion was a means of affecting exercise of the abortion right. Thus, they turned to measures such as mandatory disclosures and gag rules to limit discourse about abortion and to diminish resort to the abortion procedure. This agenda also had the effect of placing the Free Speech Clause front and center, as abortion providers turned to compelled speech and public forum mediating rules to challenge restrictions on abortion speech.

Reassessing the Abortion-Free Speech Relationship

The relationship between abortion and free speech was once synergistic. Free speech principles, values, and precedents contributed to the recognition and exercise of reproductive and abortion rights. However, the relationship has been strained considerably by two related influences. The first is the expansion of the governmental agenda, particularly after *Casey*, to influence abortion decisionmaking through speech regulation. This has included regulation of both antiabortion and proabortion speech. The second is the weakening of the Due Process Clause, which once limited some governmental efforts to influence abortion decisionmaking through speech regulation and more generally protected a fundamental right to abortion. Reassessing the relationship between abortion rights and freedom of speech requires addressing both of these influences, toward the goal of reconnecting with their synergistic past.

SPEECH RESTRICTIONS AND/AS ABORTION REGULATIONS

As we have witnessed in previous chapters, constitutional rights relationships often experience significant shifts and transformations over time. As we have seen, the Free Speech Clause was instrumental in terms of the initial recognition of the abortion right and the later mediation of abortion rights discourse in the United States. Eventually, in *Roe* and then more explicitly in *Casey*, the Supreme Court grounded the abortion right in the Fourteenth Amendment's Due Process Clause and adopted the "undue burden" standard to govern abortion regulations.

This was an important moment in the relationship between the abortion right and the Free Speech Clause. It did not sever the connection, but rather altered its future dynamics. As part of the transformation of the abortion right, the government was invited to structure consultations and conversations between women and their physicians in ways that communicated its own preferences and viewpoints concerning abortion.[93] More generally, since it had become clear that the core abortion right recognized in *Roe* was to be retained as an aspect of "liberty" under the Due Process Clause, speakers and states seeking to limit abortion rights began to look for ways to influence access to and attitudes about abortion.

The transformation inevitably pushed the constitutional debate in the direction of the Free Speech Clause. Protesters assembled at or near abortion clinics, on sidewalks outside the residences of abortion providers, and in other public places to attempt to influence public attitudes and individual decisionmaking with regard to abortion. Online speakers targeted abortion providers in potentially threatening publications. Federal, state, and local authorities responded with restrictions on antiabortion expression and advocacy. Meanwhile, legislatures turned to mandatory disclosures, spending conditions, and other measures targeting speech as a means of influencing abortion decisionmaking.

All of this activity placed extraordinary pressure on the mediating principles and functions of the Free Speech Clause. Abortion speech conflicts raised questions about access to public forums for expressive purposes, the application of content neutrality rules, and compelled speech. They also raised complex issues relating to professional speech rights, funding conditions affecting speech, and the government's own speech concerning abortion. Although, as we have seen, all of these conflicts also concerned access to and decisionmaking about abortion, the Due Process Clause played no role in their resolution—even though, prior to *Casey*, it had been invoked to invalidate measures such as mandatory abortion disclosures.

One of the central themes of this free speech turn was the frequency with which governments turned to speech regulations to influence abortion discourse and decisionmaking. Controlling or limiting speech became a means of regulating abortion. Governments scarcely sought to hide their biases in this regard. They enacted and enforced abortion speech regulations that suppressed or compelled abortion communications—as determined, in many cases, by their support for or opposition to abortion.

As we have seen, in the hands of justices affected by their own biases concerning the underlying abortion right, Free Speech Clause mediating principles were not always up to the task of policing such regulations.[94] Thus, content neutrality principles seemed to be misapplied in *Hill* and *Rust*, speakers' access to public forums was limited by a previously unheard-of "right to be let alone" on the public streets and sidewalks, and the prohibition on compelled speech was disregarded in *Casey*.

These and other precedents speak to the perils of allowing government to affect abortion access and discourse by compelling or limiting speech. As I argued in

Chapter 2, governments often fail to appreciate or actively ignore the impact speech regulations can have on constitutional rights. For their part, courts often fail to recognize a "rights speech" regulation when they see one. This has contributed to governments seeking to manipulate or regulate constitutional rights through enactment of speech mandates and restrictions. The phenomenon is bipartisan. Legislatures are using speech mandates and other regulations to both limit and expand effective access to abortion services.

On the limiting access side, consider North Carolina's "Woman's Right to Know Act," which was enacted in 2011.[95] The law required that prior to performing an abortion, physicians had to perform an ultrasound, display the sonogram, and describe the fetus to women seeking abortions. The physician was required to display the sonogram so that the woman could see it, and describe the fetus in detail, "includ[ing] the presence, location, and dimensions of the unborn child within the uterus and the number of unborn children depicted," as well as "the presence of external members and internal organs, if present and viewable."[96] The physician also had to offer to allow the woman to hear the fetal heart tone. Under the law, a physician was required to display and describe the image during the ultrasound, *even if the woman actively "averted her eyes" and "refused to hear."* These procedures were added to the state's general informed consent provisions, which already required that physicians explain the abortion procedure and attendant risks to women. Physicians who violated the law could be held liable for damages and have their medical licenses suspended.

On the expanding access side, municipalities have required that crisis pregnancy centers, which provide pro-life counseling to pregnant women, communicate clearly and prominently (in advertisements and other materials) that abortion services are available elsewhere and that patients should consult a qualified medical professional to discuss all of their options.[97] Local governments contend that these mandatory disclosures combat misleading advertising by the pregnancy centers. The centers, whose principal mission is to persuade women to choose childbirth over abortion, contend that the mandated disclosures violate the Free Speech Clause on the ground that they compel speech with which the centers disagree—namely, that abortion is a viable option for women faced with an unwanted pregnancy.

Both kinds of enactments raise serious problems with manipulating speech and information to regulate abortion access. In the name of informed consent, the North Carolina law went far beyond any need to regulate the medical profession and threatened women seeking abortions with serious psychological harms. Meanwhile, crisis pregnancy centers have been compelled, through sometimes detailed and onerous requirements, to communicate abortion information to patients even though abortion clinics are not required to inform *their* patients of the availability of access to adoption and other non-abortive options.

As I argued in Chapter 2, both types of laws regulate rights speech, and both in my view merit heightened free speech scrutiny. However, the fundamental problem with these sorts of laws is that the state has increasingly turned to speech mandates and regulations to influence abortion access and decisionmaking. And as the free speech jurisprudence in this area has demonstrated, courts are generally ill-equipped to enforce the sort of content neutrality and other mediating principles required to ensure that speech is not manipulated to serve these ends.

The Free Speech Clause is no longer being used to facilitate the recognition of a fundamental right through neutral mediating principles. It is being used to assess governmental efforts to manipulate the preservation or elimination of a recognized right to abortion. Unless and until courts recognize these measures for what they are, the Free Speech Clause will continue to perform this function unevenly at best.

REVIVING THE DUE PROCESS CLAUSE

When it comes to the abortion right, the Free Speech Clause continues to play a critical role in terms of creating space for public debate and discourse about the legitimacy and limits of the abortion right. However, as we have seen, abortion rights are not the province of the Free Speech Clause. Their scope and enforcement are rooted in the Due Process Clause's protection of individual liberty.

It is highly unlikely that the Supreme Court will return to pre-*Casey* interpretations of the Due Process Clause, some of which would provide a non-speech basis for invalidating mandatory abortion disclosures and perhaps other speech-related measures. What we might more modestly hope for is that courts (and officials) will take due process liberty concerns into account when they assess speech-restrictive measures relating to abortion rights. This is not to suggest that the Free Speech Clause be pushed aside, but rather that there be some consideration of the due process implications of measures mandating or restricting abortion expression.

Consider again North Carolina's "Woman's Right to Know Act," which was discussed earlier. Breaking from sister circuits, which have upheld similar disclosure mandates, the Fourth Circuit Court of Appeals invalidated the North Carolina law.[98] The court described it as a "quintessential compelled speech" measure that forced physicians to convey the state's ideological viewpoint regarding abortion.[99] It concluded that the law "interferes with the *physician's* right to free speech beyond the extent permitted for reasonable regulation of the medical profession, while simultaneously threatening harm to the patient's psychological health, interfering with the *physician's* professional judgment, and compromising the doctor-patient relationship."[100]

Notice what is almost entirely missing from the court's constitutional analysis. First, since the challenge is brought under the Free Speech Clause, there is no mention of the "undue burden" standard. Although *Casey* permitted states to mandate the disclosure of factual information, the North Carolina law goes much further. Litigants can and should press Due Process Clause claims in such cases; this is particularly important owing to the Court's apparently limited conception of professional speech rights. Second, the decision focuses primarily on the free speech rights of *physicians*, their professional judgment, and the doctor-patient relationship. While adverse effects on the *woman's* psychological health are mentioned in passing, other harms associated with the coercive law are not considered. Third, the court's free speech analysis does not mention the woman's autonomy right to make the abortion decision free from coercive state measures.

The central question, it would seem, is whether the North Carolina law imposes an "undue burden" on the woman's right to choose by effectively coercing her not to exercise it. But under the Free Speech Clause analysis, issues of coercion and choice are not treated as germane. The primary concern, again, centers on the free speech rights of physicians and the effect on the professional relationship.

This is the physician-centered perspective that early advocates for a right to abortion had railed so strongly against. Although when properly enforced the Free Speech Clause can help ensure that information relating to reproductive rights flows freely, it is the Due Process Clause that protects women from the kind of physical and psychological coercion imposed by the North Carolina law.

We need to channel greater intellectual and other resources into the enforcement and interpretation of the Due Process Clause. That need has only become more acute in the face of recent state efforts to burden abortion rights. Speech regulations are only part of the agenda. State legislatures are also restricting when, where, and how abortions can be lawfully performed. They are imposing burdensome requirements, such as admitting privileges measures and surgical center regulations, which may leave women in certain states without access to licensed abortion providers.[101] The Supreme Court and lower courts have indicated that the "undue burden" standard imposes meaningful limits on states' power to restrict access to abortion.[102]

As is true in other contexts, the Free Speech Clause is no substitute for independent and robust due process, equal protection, free exercise, and other non-speech rights. Indeed, one of the themes that cuts across the rights relationships examined in the book is that the Free Speech Clause is a necessary, but ultimately insufficient, vehicle for the advancement and exercise of non-speech constitutional rights.

The starting point and central framework for considering abortion rights has shifted too far in the direction of the Free Speech Clause. Free Speech Clause advocacy is distracting both proponents and opponents of abortion from what is truly at stake. If they want to preserve the right to choose, abortion defenders will need to look beyond the Free Speech Clause. They will need to alter the focus and terms of debate, from the *right to speak* (or not speak) to the *right to choose*.

In the cases discussed in this chapter, it is noteworthy that the Due Process Clause and the right to abortion were never mentioned—even though, as all were surely aware, the right to abortion was implicated in all of them. With the exception of Justice Scalia, who wrote in dissent, the justices seemed to go out of their way to avoid any consideration of *Roe, Casey*, and the abortion right. However, implicitly or subconsciously, *Roe* seems to have provided a background principle or baseline for the justices' free speech decisions.

Abortion access concerns may have led the Court's majority to, as Justice Scalia charged, stack the deck against antiabortion protesters—by subjecting speech injunctions to lower-level scrutiny, applying the content-neutrality rule in ways that saved restrictions on antiabortion counseling, and recognizing a public right to privacy. On the flip side, some of the justices' negative views concerning *Roe* and abortion rights may have led them to dismiss free speech challenges to mandatory abortion disclosures and conditional funding measures.

Even if we cannot achieve a significant turn in the dynamic relationship between abortion and free speech rights, this time back toward the Due Process Clause, we can and should at least hope for a greater level of transparency in judicial decisions and legislative debates concerning abortion speech restrictions. Recognizing that abortion speech restrictions are not just about speech rights would be an important first step toward a more transparent and comprehensive consideration of the constitutional interests involved.

7

ARMS

THIS CHAPTER CONSIDERS a final relationship—that between the Free Speech Clause and the Second Amendment's right to "keep and bear Arms."[1] As in other instances examined in the book, the connections between these two rights run very deep. In legal writings and commentaries, the Second Amendment has often been associated with or analogized to the Free Speech Clause. Free speech enabled activists, civic organizations, and scholars to advocate on behalf of the recognition of an individual right to keep and bear arms. In *District of Columbia v. Heller* (2008), which recognized this right, the Court invoked free speech precedents, doctrines, and analogies both to support recognition of an individual right to bear arms and to suggest its scope.[2] Finally, both before and after *Heller*, courts and scholars have looked to the Free Speech Clause to construe the Second Amendment.

The chapter argues that notwithstanding its positive influence on the recognition of Second Amendment rights, the Free Speech Clause should not serve as a doctrinal model for constructing the right to keep and bear arms. Borrowing of this nature will likely diminish or confuse *both* rights, which pertain to very different activities, serve distinct purposes, and raise disparate regulatory concerns. The Second Amendment needs space to develop on its own, according to the interests and values it serves. That does not mean that the First Amendment and Second Amendment will have nothing to do with one another going forward. Free speech and firearms will continue to intersect. Those intersection will continue to illuminate the meaning and scope of both clauses, and affect their relationship to one another. In this regard, the chapter examines two current intersections—the presence of firearms at public protests, and the carrying of concealed weapons in university classrooms.

Text, Analogy, and Principle

The primary focus of this chapter, and the book in general, is the contemporary interactions between constitutional rights provisions. However, a brief look at the earliest interactions between the Free Speech Clause and the Second Amendment highlights some significant and lasting connections.

As ratified, the texts of the two clauses obviously appear next to one another. The ordering itself is not constitutionally significant. The first two amendments did not originally appear side by side. It may be more significant that the First Amendment and Second Amendment share some language in common. Both provisions refer to rights belonging to "the people"—to peaceably assemble, in the case of the First Amendment, and to keep and bear arms, in the case of the Second Amendment. Both provisions also use strong language of prohibition, stating that governments "shall" not infringe First Amendment and Second Amendment rights.

As discussed in Chapter 3, the ratification records with regard to the First Amendment are quite sparse. In the case of the Second Amendment, such records are virtually nonexistent. As a consequence, we do not know precisely how the framers believed these two rights related to one another, if at all.

However, other evidence suggests that the two provisions were considered to be analogous. Indeed, as Professor Eugene Volokh has noted, "[a]nalogies between the First Amendment and the Second (and comparable state constitutional protections) are over 200 years old."[3] These early analogies were not solely to freedom of speech; freedom of the press was also invoked as a comparable right, as was the right to peaceably assemble. However, they do establish that free speech and firearms were frequently compared to one another.

Eighteenth and early nineteenth century courts and commentators reasoned, for example, that the right to publish was limited in a manner similar to the right to keep firearms.[4] In his widely read *Commentaries on the Laws of England*, Sir William Blackstone placed free speech and the right to keep and bear arms in the same general class of rights—personal rights fundamental to a free people.[5] Thus, from a very early point in American constitutional history, First Amendment and Second Amendment rights were connected to one another in constitutional discourse.

To be sure, some of these remarks took the form of offhand references or superficial analogies. However, they are some evidence that in the minds of early jurists and commentators, the two provisions were related to one another in some respects. As we will see, free speech and firearms analogies played an important role in *Heller*'s eventual recognition of the individual right to keep and bear arms, and in post-*Heller* debates regarding the scope and substance of the Second Amendment.

Some have argued that more than simple analogies connect the First Amendment and Second Amendment. Professor Akhil Amar argues that the framers of these two amendments likely viewed them both as *structural* protections against the newly formed national government.[6] Amar contends that at the framing of the Bill of Rights, these two provisions were intended to serve similar federalism and democracy-facilitating functions. Specifically, they constrained the newly created national government by making explicit that it could neither deprive speakers of their words nor militiamen of their arms. Thus, Congress was forbidden by the First Amendment to (or lacked the power to) abridge the freedom of speech or press. The Second Amendment proclaimed that a right to keep and bear arms, which belonged to a citizen "militia" drawn from local communities, "shall not be infringed."

As Professor Amar also argues, Reconstruction dynamics transformed the Constitution's first two amendments.[7] The post–Civil War First Amendment, which would eventually apply to the states as well as to Congress, began to take the form of the strong *individual* right we recognize today—the one that broadly and robustly protects dissident speakers, publishers, and organizations from government suppression. Meanwhile, Amar claims, the post-Reconstruction Second Amendment, unmoored from its structural roots and federalism concerns, was transformed into something more akin to the First Amendment's personal protections for speech, press, assembly, and petition.

Amar's account is one of the few to try to explain the early connective tissues of the First Amendment and Second Amendment. Through framing and Reconstruction era dynamics, the two rights provisions functioned initially as structural protections and later as something more akin to the individual rights provisions we know today.

Freedom of Speech and the Individual Right to Bear Arms

As was the case with other constitutional rights we have examined, the Free Speech Clause has facilitated and mediated a robust public discourse regarding Second Amendment rights. *Heller* is the product of decades of agitation, litigation, lobbying, discourse, scholarship, and legislative debate concerning Second Amendment rights. All of these activities, it bears repeating, were protected by the First Amendment.

Civic organizations, litigators, scholars, and courts have all participated in a dynamic process which ultimately resulted in formal recognition for an individual right to keep and bear arms. The road from formal ratification to the recognition of an individual right to bear arms was a long one. For most of the nation's history, there was a scholarly and judicial consensus that the Second Amendment guaranteed only a collective, militia-based right to bear arms.[8]

Professor David Cole has narrated how the National Rifle Association (NRA) and other civil society organizations worked state-by-state to alter this collectivist interpretation.[9] In an effort to gain support for an individual right to keep and bear arms, these organizations and their members lobbied, wrote letters, distributed pamphlets and other information to the public, and participated in state and local politics. Professor Cole largely credits these efforts with bringing about the change in Second Amendment interpretation that produced *Heller*. He argues that the Constitution, and federal constitutional litigation in particular, had relatively little to do with it.

Professor Cole demonstrates that civil society organizations played a central role in the Second Amendment movement that led to the *Heller* decision. They were important players in the dynamic process that would ultimately lead to formal judicial recognition of an individual right to keep and bear arms. Of course, as noted, freedom of speech and other First Amendment rights facilitated the activities of these organizations. In this sense, at least, the Constitution had a lot to do with interpretive change. Just as public discourse helped bring about the Supreme Court's recognition of a right to marriage equality in *Obergefell* (Chapter 5), free speech activities were necessary catalysts for *Heller*.

The First Amendment was less visible during the lead up to *Heller* than it had been in prior constitutional movements. Unlike race and LGBT equality advocates, Second Amendment proponents were not forced to litigate their basic free speech rights before exercising them. Rights to communicate about the constitutional right to keep and bear arms, to publish information about that right, and to organize for the purpose of expressing support for it were all clearly protected by the First Amendment. Despite its lack of visibility, the Free Speech Clause was critical to the success of the Second Amendment movement.

Professor Cole also downplays the importance of federal court litigation in the Second Amendment movement. Since the nineteenth century, and most recently in 1939, the Supreme Court had seemingly rejected the view that the Second Amendment protects an individual right to bear arms.[10] As they were bound by the Court's pronouncements, lower federal courts did not have latitude to rule to the contrary. Nevertheless, litigants continued to bring cases in which they claimed governments had violated an individual right to keep and bear arms akin to freedom of speech and other "fundamental" rights.

These claims and analogies were uniformly rejected.[11] As one federal appeals court explained:

> It is abundantly clear both from the discussions of this amendment contemporaneous with its proposal and adoption and those of learned writers since that this amendment, unlike those providing for protection of free speech and freedom of religion, was not adopted with individual rights in mind, but as a protection for the States in the maintenance of their militia organizations against possible encroachments by the federal power.[12]

Although the claims failed, they kept the issue before the courts and linked free speech and firearms rights in judicial discourse. As in other cases, although free speech claims failed in the short term, over the long term associating the right to keep and bear arms with free speech paid dividends. In the meantime, as Professor Cole shows, civil society organizations and other advocates worked on a state-by-state basis to gain support for an individual rights interpretation of the Second Amendment. Their advocacy relied, in part, on the free speech analogy.

The dynamic process that brought about changes in the interpretation of the Second Amendment also included a robust scholarly re-examination of the right to keep and bear arms. As mentioned, for two centuries the prevailing view was that the Second Amendment protected a collective, militia-based right rather than an individual or personal right. Starting in the 1970s, scholars began to publish articles in law reviews in which they articulated and defended an individualist interpretation of the Second Amendment.[13] Confirming Professor Cole's observation about the important role of civil society organizations, the NRA was actively involved in supporting these efforts.[14]

The individual rights interpretation of the Second Amendment gained greater academic credibility when leading *liberal* constitutional scholars began defending it. In 1989, Sanford Levinson, a prominent law professor at the University of Texas, published an essay in which he suggested that courts and scholars had misread the Second Amendment as a collective right.[15] Notably, Professor Levinson's argument relied in part on an analogy between the right to engage in *political speech* and the right to keep and bear arms.[16]

In the early 1990s, Yale constitutional law professor Akhil Amar published two articles (which would later form the basis for the intratextual work discussed earlier) in which he embraced a right of "the people" to bear arms for insurrectionist purposes.[17] Amar, too, argued that freedom of speech and other First Amendment rights helped illuminate the substance of Second Amendment rights. For example, he observed: "[T]o see the Amendment as primarily concerned with an individual right to hunt, or protect one's home, is like viewing the heart of the speech and assembly clauses as the right of persons to meet to play bridge, or to have sex."[18]

A 1994 essay by Professor William Van Alstyne, another prominent constitutional scholar, sought to connect and reconcile the Constitution's first two formal amendments. Like Professor Amar, Professor Van Alstyne found partial support for an individual rights interpretation of the Second Amendment in judicial and scholarly interpretations of the First Amendment's Free Speech Clause.[19] Finally, in 1999, Laurence Tribe, perhaps the most prominent liberal constitutional law professor of his time, wrote in his popular constitutional law treatise that he supported an individualist interpretation of the right to keep and bear arms.[20]

For most of American history, the notion that the Second Amendment protects a personal or individual right to keep and bear arms was considered an off-the-wall proposition. The First Amendment, and the Free Speech Clause in particular, helped to change that view in two general ways.

First, through protected expressive activities, civil society organizations, litigants, activists, and scholars were able to engage in a robust discourse about the nature and substance of Second Amendment rights. As some scholars have pointed out, Second Amendment rights discourse, particularly in recent years, has sometimes been dysfunctional and unproductive.[21] But it is the *fact* of this discourse, rather than its tone, that matters most in terms of initial recognition of a constitutional right. Protection for expressive activities contributed to a robust constitutional discourse in which individual and collectivist interpretations of the Second Amendment were freely debated.

Second, as we have seen, the Free Speech Clause served a critical analogic function. Scholars, litigants, courts, and commentators compared and contrasted the manner in which First Amendment and Second Amendment rights were interpreted and enforced. Some of these arguments took the form of simple analogy—that is, two rights sharing similar language and belonging to "the people" ought to be interpreted in a similar manner. Others, such as Professor Amar's, were more sophisticated intratextual arguments that examined textual, structural, and historical connections between the two provisions. These efforts ultimately put pressure on advocates of a collectivist interpretation of the Second Amendment to explain and justify the disparity in treatment relative to the Free Speech Clause.

Borrowing the Free Speech Clause

The Free Speech Clause played an important role in generating support for an individual rights interpretation of the Second Amendment. As courts and scholars have turned from recognition of the right to keep and bear arms to questions of its substance and scope, the Free Speech Clause has performed an even more prominent role. Courts, scholars, and advocates have sought to borrow free speech doctrines and principles to flesh out the Second Amendment's individual right to keep and bear arms. As I contend below, Free Speech Clause borrowing may end up having serious and largely negative interpretive consequences for *both* the right to keep and bear arms and the freedom of speech.

HELLER AND THE FREE SPEECH CLAUSE

In *District of Columbia v. Heller* (2008), the challengers to the District of Columbia's restrictive gun law, which banned the possession of handguns even in the home, made passing references in their briefs to the First Amendment. In its decision, the Supreme Court relied significantly on free speech principles, precedents, and doctrines. The Court invoked the First Amendment when addressing the status, scope, and manner of reviewing Second Amendment rights. In subsequent judicial decisions and Second Amendment scholarship, the Court's references to the Free Speech Clause encouraged proposals to explicitly rely on free speech standards to interpret the right to keep and bear arms.

Heller's invocation of the First Amendment and the Free Speech Clause connected free speech and the right to bear arms in three respects. First, Justice Scalia, writing for the Court, sought to burnish the Second Amendment's status by comparing it to the First Amendment. Both provisions, he asserted, codified preexisting rights; and both were the product of a long dormancy followed by renewed judicial and public engagement.[22] This comparison was intended to place the Second Amendment in the same orbit as the more established First Amendment.

Second, the Court invoked the Free Speech Clause analogy in addressing the Second Amendment's scope. For example, it noted that just as the Free Speech Clause's protection extends to modern forms of speech (such as Internet communications), so too must the Second Amendment's scope extend beyond the types of arms available at the founding.[23] At the same time, the Court observed that the Second Amendment, like the First Amendment, does not protect *all* exercises of the right in question.[24] Just as there are limits on free speech coverage, there must also be some limits on the coverage of the right to keep and bear arms. Thus, just as speakers are not entitled to communicate whatever they wish, keepers and bearers of firearms are not entitled to purchase and carry whatever weapons they like.

Finally, in terms of methodology, the Court rejected calls by Justice Stephen Breyer and others for an "interest-balancing" approach to Second Amendment rights—that is, a weighing of the individual's right to keep and bear arms against the state's interests in regulating such activities. Once again, the majority opinion invoked the Free Speech Clause: "The First Amendment contains the freedom of speech guarantee that the people ratified, which included exceptions for obscenity, libel, and disclosure of state secrets, but not for the expression of extremely unpopular and wrong-headed views. The Second Amendment is no different."[25] In addition, the Court expressly rejected any form of "rationality" review for Second Amendment regulations, arguing that this form of low-level judicial review has never been applied in the free speech context.[26]

Together, the Court's various invocations of the First Amendment's text, history, and principles emphasized the close connections between free speech and firearms rights. As we have seen in prior chapters, litigants have frequently sought to leverage the Free Speech Clause to burnish "new" non-speech constitutional rights or defend extensions of existing rights. The *Heller* Court was engaged in a similar exercise—using comparisons to the Free Speech Clause to legitimize the Second Amendment and inform its future enforcement.

FREE SPEECH STANDARDS, SUBSTANCE, AND THEORY

Previous chapters have examined how and why Rights Dynamism sometimes leads to the Free Speech Clause subordinating and sometimes even supplanting non-speech constitutional rights. Rights that have suffered this fate include the Assembly Clause, Press Clause, and Petition Clause (Chapter 3). To a lesser degree, the Free Speech Clause has subordinated or obscured the Free Exercise Clause (Chapter 4) and the Due Process Clause right to abortion (Chapter 6).

A related concern has arisen at the intersection between the Free Speech Clause and the Second Amendment. As we have seen, analogies between these clauses have been in circulation since before the framing of the Bill of Rights. Free speech analogies turned out to be important to the recognition of an individual right to keep and bear arms in *Heller*. However, courts and scholars have moved beyond simple analogies. They have proposed a form of constitutional borrowing or modeling in which Free Speech Clause standards, principles, and values are used to define the meaning of the Second Amendment. This sort of borrowing does not entail supplanting the Second Amendment by replacing it with the Free Speech Clause. Instead, borrowing proposes to explicitly fashion the Second Amendment in the image of the Free Speech Clause.

Free speech borrowing has a certain degree of surface appeal. For example, as *Heller* suggests, just as under Free Speech Clause doctrine certain categories of speech are not covered (obscenity, for example), so too might we interpret the Second Amendment as not covering certain categories of arms or particular manners of keeping and bearing them. This is a classic form of reasoning-by-analogy, quite familiar to constitutional law and legal analysis more generally. However, borrowing is a more specific and consequential endeavor. It purports to rely on the Free Speech Clause to determine the standards, doctrines, and values by which specific exercises of Second Amendment rights will be adjudicated. Borrowing would go a long way toward defining the future Second Amendment.

Heller's references to the First Amendment have encouraged lower courts to embrace constitutional borrowing in this sense.[27] Some courts have suggested that judicial standards of review for Second Amendment rights ought to specifically track First Amendment free speech standards. This would entail applying "strict" judicial scrutiny to some regulations (such as bans on handgun possession in the home), while reviewing other regulations under a less demanding "intermediate" scrutiny standard applied to many speech regulations.[28] Scholars have likewise proposed that Free Speech Clause standards serve as a framework for reviewing Second Amendment regulations.[29] Not all courts or scholars suggest a rigid application of free speech standards in Second Amendment cases.[30] However, many are looking squarely in the direction of the Free Speech Clause as they seek standards of review for Second Amendment regulations.[31]

Courts and scholars have also looked to the Free Speech Clause to determine the *scope* of Second Amendment rights. Borrowing in this sense can lead to some very narrow interpretations of Second Amendment rights. For example, Professor Darrell Miller has argued that firearms should be treated like obscenity has been treated under the Free Speech Clause—that is, protected only insofar as keeping and bearing occurs within the home.[32] This "homebound" interpretation drew a sharp rebuke from Professor Eugene Volokh, who argued that we ought not to analogize "a core category of private arms to one of the least protected and marginal categories of speech (obscenity)."[33]

Free speech borrowing has also been proposed in an effort to defend more expansive interpretations of the Second Amendment. Thus, scholars have invoked Free Speech Clause doctrines to defend interpretations of the Second Amendment that would extend its protections to noncitizens and prohibit the government from compelling citizens to keep and bear arms (just as they are prohibited from compelling speech).[34] Some have also proposed limits on firearms licensing that draw upon First Amendment doctrines relating to prior restraints and government licensure.[35] The Free Speech Clause has been broadly interpreted to cover and protect an extraordinary array of communications and expressive activities. Some believe that borrowing its doctrines and methods will lead to expansive interpretations of the Second Amendment.

On close inspection, however, there are serious flaws with this sort of analogic borrowing. Professor Greg Magarian has identified several of them. In general terms,

Magarian observes that the distinction between speech and action, the complexity and nuance of "speech" as a concept, and the unitary focus on "speech" in the Free Speech Clause (devoid as it is of collectivist language) all differentiate the Free Speech Clause from the Second Amendment.[36] He also identifies important normative distinctions between these rights. Among these, he contends, is the fact that speech is generally viewed as a "constructive and desirable activity that advances personal fulfillment and social welfare," whereas many view the keeping and bearing of firearms as "at best an instrumental activity."[37]

Professor Magarian also questions whether Free Speech Clause interpretive methods provide a useful or proper model for Second Amendment rights. Whereas *Heller* is based primarily on originalist methods and understandings, in the free speech context historical interpretations play virtually no role at all. Further, Magarian contends that *Heller*'s simplistic borrowing of free speech categoricalism—the notion that there is a non-exhaustive list of categorical exclusions from the right to keep and bear arms—is not likely to hold up very well under a free-speech-like analysis.[38] Application of Free Speech Clause standards of review depends primarily upon whether the regulation at issue is based on "subject matter" or "viewpoint" or on some factor unrelated to these things. However, as Professor Magarian notes, no similar conception or principle distinguishes gun regulations for Second Amendment purposes.[39] Thus, mechanically speaking, free speech borrowing is a poor tool for constructing Second Amendment doctrine.

Nor would the Free Speech Clause's categorical coverage exclusions (i.e., obscenity, fighting words, malicious libel, child pornography, etc.) be useful in construing the scope of the Second Amendment. For example, obscenity doctrine is the product of legal, cultural, and moral considerations that do not apply in the case of Second Amendment rights.[40] Similarly, the Free Speech Clause's presumption that prior restraints on speech are unconstitutional has no force when it comes to gun regulations. As Professor Magarian observes, the historical record regarding licensing of firearms is quite different from that concerning licensure of speech and press.[41] As importantly, he writes: "Speech and guns cause different sorts of harms. That critical difference justifies, indeed compels, distinct sorts of procedural restrictions on government regulation."[42]

Borrowing also poses some potential theoretical difficulties. As noted earlier, Professor Amar identified a shared concern with self-government that may have animated adoption of what would become the Constitution's first two amendments. Other scholars have also suggested that there is some overlap between free speech justifications and Second Amendment values.[43]

However, this overlap or resemblance may not lead where these scholars suggest—to an individual rights justification for the Second Amendment. Drawing on theoretical debates regarding the Free Speech Clause, Professor Magarian asserts that the Second Amendment, even as interpreted by the Court in *Heller*, must serve some *collectivist* purpose.[44] As discussed further below, Magarian identifies a conceptual concern that freedom of speech and the Second Amendment share—namely, enabling dynamic political change.[45] That shared value is the key, according to Professor Magarian, to understanding that borrowing Free Speech Clause justifications to inform Second Amendment values leads to the conclusion that *Heller* rests on faulty premises relating to "individual" versus "collective" rights.

In early years, the process of relating the First Amendment and Second Amendment relied on very simple analogies. But as modern courts and scholars have grappled with the nature and scope of Second Amendment rights, they have turned more directly to the Free Speech Clause. Unlike analogic reasoning, borrowing has led to specific proposals to model the Second Amendment on free speech doctrines and principles. In addition to the "fit" concerns discussed above, there are good reasons to think that free speech borrowing will benefit neither firearms nor free speech rights.

WHY BORROWING IS BAD FOR BOTH AMENDMENTS

In the absence of authoritative Second Amendment precedents other than *Heller*, which itself trades on general Free Speech Clause analogies, litigants, lower courts, and scholars have relied on free speech doctrines to construct Second Amendment rights. From the perspective of both firearms and free speech advocates, borrowing is a perilous gambit.

What would a Second Amendment modeled on the Free Speech Clause actually look like? *Heller* suggests a strong categorical individual right, based primarily on originalist understandings. The majority explicitly rejects interest balancing—weighing burdens on constitutional rights against the government's interests in regulating the activity of keeping and bearing arms.[46] It thus appears to adopt a rule-based and categorical approach that would yield very broad Second Amendment coverage.

However, a Second Amendment modeled in the image of the Free Speech Clause would likely be far more anemic than *Heller* indicates. For one thing, as Professor Miller observes, a categorical approach could lead to a strictly home-bound interpretation of the Second Amendment. Even assuming that interpretation is not adopted, Second Amendment rights developed in the image of a categorical Free Speech Clause would likely be far narrower than *Heller* suggests.

As scholars have argued, *Heller*'s purported categorical approach leaves Second Amendment law even murkier than free speech doctrine, which relies only partly on categorical standards.[47] Because *Heller* is so unclear about the core values the Second Amendment protects (other than self-defense) and the justifications for some of its apparent carve outs (felons, sensitive places, etc.), courts will inevitably end up doing what they have long done in the free speech context—balancing interests.[48] Thus, our experience suggests that a Second Amendment jurisprudence developed in the image of the Free Speech Clause will likely incorporate a significant degree of the interest balancing *Heller* foreswears.[49]

Professor Mark Tushnet argues that borrowing free speech doctrines to resolve Second Amendment issues will ultimately lead to interest balancing and hence a far less rigidly pro-arms Second Amendment.[50] As Tushnet observes, the Free Speech Clause has been interpreted with reference to a combination of (1) defining the categories of covered speech, (2) developing variable standards of review for different classes of speech, and (3) directly balancing the impairment of speech against the government's interests in regulation. Under any of these three approaches, Second Amendment rights would be constructed through some form of interest balancing. Under some of them, particularly (3), the scope of Second Amendment rights would likely be much narrower than *Heller* suggests. As Professor Tushnet observes, although complete bans on handgun possession in the home (and perhaps some broad bans on carrying firearms in public) would violate the Second Amendment, under a free speech approach most regulations would probably survive judicial scrutiny.[51]

In this respect, Second Amendment advocates, who are invoking the Free Speech Clause in a bid to expand Second Amendment rights, will likely not be as pleased with the results as they suppose. Moreover, owing to the stark differences between the two clauses in terms of subject matter, regulatory interests, and justifications, any Second Amendment doctrine based explicitly on the Free Speech Clause is likely to be even murkier than the free speech doctrines it seeks to emulate.

There is also the possibility that free speech borrowing will undermine the theoretical foundation for an individual right to keep and bear firearms. As noted earlier, Professor Magarian argues that free speech borrowing must confront a serious *theoretical* conundrum. Free speech justifications have run the gamut from collectivist concerns such as self-government to purely individualistic concerns relating to speaker "autonomy."[52] Professor Magarian argues that the preamble to the Second Amendment, which refers to "a well-regulated militia" and "the security of a free state," compels the conclusion that the Second Amendment's individual right to bear arms must serve at least some *collective* purpose.

The problem is that the Free Speech Clause, as interpreted, offers an alternative and preferred method of securing a free state and deposing despotic governments—open and robust political debate, up to and including advocacy of the violent overthrow of government.[53] As Magarian suggests, violent insurrection through the use of firearms "short-circuits political debate in order to impose on the polity the insurrectionists' justification for violence."[54] However, even acknowledging a collectivist purpose for the Second Amendment would undermine the right that *Heller* recognizes. In other words, firearms advocates may find that borrowing free speech justifications to support Second Amendment rights undermines the very notion that there is an *individual* right to bear arms.

In practical and theoretical terms, borrowing the Free Speech Clause to build out the Second Amendment right to keep and bear arms is problematic for the Second Amendment. Of course, opponents of broad Second Amendment rights will cheer this narrowing influence. However, judged from the perspective of those advocating on behalf of Second Amendment rights, borrowing imperils the right to keep and bear arms. The Free Speech Clause covers a distinctive and unique concern ("speech"), is plagued by its own methodological and doctrinal incoherence, and serves collectivist purposes that do not map well onto the Second Amendment—and may even be inconsistent with *Heller*'s interpretation. These and other tensions and complications suggest that it would be better to develop the right to keep and bear arms according to its own purposes and values rather than rely explicitly on the Free Speech Clause.

As I have emphasized throughout the book, the effects of rights intersections are generally bidirectional. Most of the attention in the courts and scholarly literature has focused on how the Free Speech Clause might inform the scope and enforcement of Second Amendment rights. However, as litigants, courts, and scholars continue to press free speech borrowing in Second Amendment contexts, there could also be significant downsides for free speech rights.

For example, the development and application of Second Amendment standards of review might lead some courts to draw free speech analogies resulting in similar applications in the free speech context. Depending on how Second Amendment standards of review actually develop, more lenient standards applied to certain firearms regulations could be applied to free speech regulations as well. The deference authorities may have to regulate certain arms or manners of carrying arms could seep into free speech analysis.

There could be more specific bidirectional complications. *Heller* suggests that regulations of public exercises of Second Amendment rights might be subject to a lesser degree of scrutiny than those affecting in-home exercises. Applying that logic to free speech regulations would mark a significant departure from current doctrine, which extends broad protection to public expression.

Similarly, judicial decisions upholding firearms licensing regulations might result in changes in how judges approach speech licensure. Right now, licensure is viewed with great skepticism under the Free Speech Clause and the Press Clause; prior restraints are presumptively unconstitutional. It is not likely that courts would reverse course entirely with regard to this issue. However, insofar as firearms and free speech are deemed to be entitled to the same basic protections, more lenient review of firearms licensure could cut into the Free Speech Clause's longstanding skepticism concerning prior restraints.

Some categorical free speech standards might also be affected by this intersection. Thus, were people to exercise or threaten to exercise Second Amendment armed insurrectionism, courts might be pressured to reconsider Free Speech Clause categorical standards relating to incitement, true threats, and perhaps other speech categories that are currently narrowly defined.[55] This too could lead to watered down coverage under the Free Speech Clause.

Other existing free speech standards are also incompatible with aspects of *Heller* and possible future extensions of its reasoning. For instance, under free speech content neutrality rules, discrimination based on speaker status is generally suspect. Insofar as it allows for such discrimination, for example in the case of felons or other classes of individuals categorically denied firearms, the Second Amendment is inconsistent with this approach. If these rights are going to be treated the same under First Amendment and Second Amendment standards, free speech status discrimination rules might be affected.

These are merely some examples. As we have seen when examining other rights relationships, the degree of influence rights have on one another depends on the frequency, nature, and character of their interactions. The doctrinal dynamics that will impact free speech and firearms rights are only just beginning. If the history of other rights relationships is any guide, we should expect some bidirectional effects.

Armed Protests and Classroom Carry

So far, we have focused on doctrinal and theoretical connections between free speech and firearms rights. This is just one aspect of the dynamic process that will influence the relationship between these rights. Free speech and firearms are currently interacting in even more tangible settings, including public protests and college classrooms. These intersections are also part of the relational dynamic between the two rights. Both contexts raise important questions about whether freedom of speech and the right to keep and bear arms are inherently incompatible. With regard to compatibility, the primary concern in the context of protests and classrooms will not be what the Free Speech Clause has to say about the right to keep and bear arms, but rather whether Second Amendment rights will be interpreted in ways that limit the tensions between free speech and firearms. America's long experience with free speech rights can, however, help to contextualize the exercise of Second Amendment rights in these and other public venues.

ARMING PUBLIC PROTESTS

My consideration of the intersection between free speech and firearms at public protests and similar events takes the law as it currently exists. Despite having many opportunities to do so, the Supreme Court has not yet addressed whether there is a Second Amendment right to carry firearms in public.[56] Nevertheless, nearly every state now authorizes some form of a right to openly carry firearms in at least some public places.[57] A few states ban the open carry of handguns, but not long guns (rifles and shotguns), while a few states ban the open carry of long guns, but not handguns.[58] Several states require a license to open carry and many impose other restrictions on the practice, such as limiting open carry in specified places or during certain hours of the day.[59]

Thus, in many jurisdictions, it is increasingly likely that firearms will be openly carried in public places, including in forums where public protests and demonstrations occur. The appearance of armed protesters at events such as the "Unite the Right" rally that took place in Charlottesville, Virginia, during the summer of 2017 has received significant attention.[60] But in fact, in some states and localities, firearms have been present at public protests and other events for many years.

Are Open Carry and Free Speech Inherently Incompatible?

In the context of public protests, many have asserted that free speech rights and the right to keep and bear firearms are inherently incompatible. Focusing specifically on the visibility of openly carried firearms, commentators have voiced concerns that public protest will be chilled or even eliminated as a result of the presence of firearms at public events.[61] Constitutional scholars have argued that exercising First Amendment rights of speech and assembly is both physically and theoretically incompatible with the open carrying of firearms at protests and demonstrations.[62] Shortly after the Charlottesville rally, the American Civil Liberties Union adopted a policy that it would no longer defend certain groups that demonstrate while openly carrying firearms.[63]

Thus, critics of open carry at public protests share a common concern that the presence of firearms will transform public protests into threatening, intimidating, and violent events.[64] They argue that the intimidation and threats of violence that accompany open carry at public protests chill the speech and other expressive activities of unarmed counter-protesters.[65] Professor Magarian argues that "insurrection short-circuits political debate."[66] He claims that "[e]ven keeping arms to enable insurrection would undermine debate by fostering a climate of mistrust and fear."[67] Professor Darrell Miller similarly argues that public display and use of firearms "must be tempered by other constitutional values, including the preservation of the social compact and democratic norms."[68] Miller contends that "the presence of a gun in public has the effect of chilling or distorting the essential channels of a democracy—public deliberation and interchange."[69] He reasons that "[v]alueless opinions enjoy an inflated currency if accompanied by threats of violence. Even if everyone is equally armed, everyone is deterred from free-flowing democratic deliberation if each person risks violence from a particularly sensitive fellow citizen who might take offense."[70]

These concerns have led to proposals to ban open carry at public protests. Under this view, the Free Speech Clause and the Second Amendment are in direct conflict with one another. We cannot have both, and we must choose either open carry or uninhibited and robust public debate.

The incompatibility argument rests on two fundamental premises. The first is that the mere presence of firearms at public protests is a form of intimidation that chills public speech by threatening violent suppression of protest. The second premise is that openly carrying a firearm conflicts with the democratic values served by freedom of speech (and other First Amendment rights). In essence, the claim is that allowing open carry at public protests elevates armed conflict over peaceful democratic discourse. This substitutes the brandishing of arms for counter-speech, which is the First Amendment's preferred response to protest and dissent.[71] According to Miller and Magarian, in the particular context of public protests, Second Amendment rights must give way to First Amendment rights and interests.[72]

There is a certain common sense appeal to the notion that the presence of armed protesters or counter-protesters will inhibit the exercise of First Amendment speech and assembly rights. At the least, the presence of firearms adds an element of potential danger to what can be crowded, rowdy, and contentious events. Rallies such as the one in Charlottesville suggest to some that free speech and firearms cannot co-exist.

On the other hand, it does not seem fair to assess the incompatibility argument with reference to the most combustible and violent events. When one thinks about the range of protest events that occur across the U.S., whether expression and firearms are *inherently* incompatible with one another becomes a much closer question.

The argument that we *cannot* have both First Amendment and Second Amendment rights at protests is factually incorrect. Anecdotally, in many places in the

U.S., firearms have been carried at public protests for some time.[73] In these jurisdictions, the open carrying of firearms seems not to have suppressed public speech.[74] Of course, some participants may have experienced subjective chill or inhibition at these events. Perhaps some failed to attend once they realized some protesters were armed. To understand the actual effect of open carry on public expression, we would need to empirically examine the psychological and actual physical impacts of public carry on public protest participants. We do not have that sort of data.

What we do have are anecdotal observations and accounts. Based on these, what we can say is that it is at least possible for free speech and firearms to co-exist at public protests. In fact, some scholars have assigned a positive free speech value to the open presence of firearms at protests. Professor Eugene Volokh argues that public carry might actually *facilitate* the exercise of First Amendment rights.[75] He argues that the right to openly carry firearms at public protests might "support public interchange, by assuring minority speakers that they can protect themselves against violent suppression."[76] Rather than view open carry as fatally undermining public discourse, Volokh suggests that it may level the playing field and encourage the communication of dissident and minority viewpoints. Some of the armed militia groups that participated in the Charlottesville rally sounded a similar note, claiming that they were present to ensure that all participants' First Amendment rights were respected.[77]

As noted earlier, most state legislatures and many courts have concluded that First Amendment and Second Amendment rights are not inherently in conflict with one another at public events. Laws protecting open carry, including in some public places, are politically popular. They suggest a political determination, bordering on consensus, that expression and firearms are *not* inherently incompatible. Of course, that does not mean tensions between these rights do not exist. It may mean, in some jurisdictions, officials will eventually move to ban protesting while armed or adopt measures aimed at reducing these tensions. Whether they can harmonize free speech and firearms will depend on how First Amendment and Second Amendment rights are interpreted in this context.

Open Carry and Freedom of Speech

Open carry at public protests may implicate both First Amendment and Second Amendment rights. However, in this context as in others previously discussed, reliance on the Free Speech Clause will not get us very far in terms of reconciling these rights.

The Free Speech Clause does not generally provide a basis for defending—or limiting—open carry at public protests. The scope and exercise of open carry rights in this context will depend primarily on how the Second Amendment, not the First Amendment, is interpreted.

In some very limited circumstances, the keeping and bearing of firearms might be sufficiently expressive to constitute speech covered by the Free Speech Clause. Symbolic acts—that is, those intended to convey messages that audiences, in particular contexts, are likely to understand—are considered to be speech under the First Amendment.[78] For example, the Supreme Court has held that burning a flag at a political protest qualifies as sufficiently expressive to warrant some coverage.[79] With respect to symbolic acts, context matters—particularly in terms of the likelihood that an audience will comprehend what a person seeks to communicate through conduct.

The clearest case in terms of *coverage* for open carry involves a situation in which individuals openly carry firearms *at a public rally for Second Amendment rights*. Assume that the jurisdiction otherwise allows open carry, but has banned the practice during protests and demonstrations. In this context, the act of openly carrying a firearm would likely be deemed expressive.[80] Indeed, open carry in this context would constitute a form of what Chapter 2 called "rights speech"—a communication about or concerning the recognition, scope, or exercise of a constitutional right. Open carry would itself convey support for the right to carry firearms openly, and the audience viewing a demonstration devoted to that right would likely understand this to be the case.

Assuming the open carry ban targets the act for safety reasons and is not based on content, whether there is a free speech right to openly carry a firearm would depend on whether government has an important interest in restricting open carry and whether its restriction is narrowly tailored to that interest.[81] The government would argue that temporarily disarming individuals during a public protest is tailored to its important interest in protecting public safety.

Some commentators have determined that on this basis, the hypothetical ban would be valid under free speech standards.[82] One problem with the argument is that subjective fear of violence, without more, is not considered a valid justification for prohibiting free speech.[83] Thus, the mere prospect or potential for violence from the carrying of firearms might be deemed too speculative. Of course, a locality might make a more concrete showing—perhaps, for example, by showing that there have been shootings at public protests in the locality or elsewhere.

In addition, the government would have to show that a temporary ban was necessary even though alternative means of ensuring safety—including protest policing and, as discussed below, the separation of firearms carriers from other protesters—were available. Contrary to the claims of some commentators, it is not crystal clear that the government would meet these burdens under the Free

Speech Clause.[84] So in this narrow context, there might be a free speech right to openly carry a firearm.

However, before Second Amendment proponents celebrate this conclusion, note that the Free Speech Clause has other serious limitations as a guarantor of open carry rights. Under the standards applicable to expressive conduct, described earlier, the free speech right likely extends only to the carrying of an *unloaded* firearm. The firearm itself is the expressive object, and whether it is loaded or unloaded seems to have no bearing on the communication of the message to a public audience. Thus, even if the First Amendment covers and indeed protects open carry in some limited circumstances, it likely does not protect the right to carry a fully functional weapon.

In terms of other limits, the Free Speech Clause does not protect threatening displays of firearms. Thus, there is no First Amendment right to brandish firearms in a manner that places an individual in fear of imminent bodily injury or death.[85] Nor can arms-carriers use words that incite others to engage in these kinds of actions, at least where the speaker intends that imminent lawless activity occur and there is a likelihood that it will imminently occur.[86] Law enforcement officers would have the power to arrest any armed protester who communicates to fellow arms-bearers that they should use their weapons to inflict immediate harm on those present or threaten others with imminent death or bodily injury. In short, even if the open carry of firearms is considered to be expressive in some cases, dangerous displays would not be covered by the First Amendment.

Further, outside the context of a political protest specifically relating to the right to carry firearms in public, the prospects for Free Speech Clause coverage are much dimmer. To be sure, gun rights proponents might argue that the act of keeping and bearing arms at *any* public protest is inherently expressive. They might argue that they intend to communicate the following: a willingness to defend themselves against private force; the importance of an armed citizenry to defend against an overreaching government; or support for Second Amendment rights. They might even argue that a firearm, like our national flag, is "pregnant with expressive content"—a symbol of rugged individualism, frontier values, and self-defense.[87]

The act of marching in a demonstration is a form of covered speech, as are the placards, banners, and songs marchers use to communicate their message.[88] Further, as the Supreme Court said with regard to a public parade, "a narrow, succinctly articulable message is not a condition of constitutional protection."[89] But the fact that the demonstration is a form of covered speech does not mean that *everything* one does in that context is automatically expressive. The act of carrying a stick, a pole, a rock, a container of mace, or any other item does not have any inherently expressive element. These acts seem no more inherently expressive than other public acts such as driving a car or recycling a plastic container. One might be expressing the virtues of driving or recycling, but the speech element is decidedly marginal and, what is more important, is not likely to be understood by an audience.[90] Finally, it seems unlikely that courts would treat a long rifle as akin to a national flag or other national symbol, in terms of inherent expressiveness.

As the Supreme Court has stated, conduct is not to be characterized as speech "whenever the person engaging in the conduct intends thereby to express an idea."[91] Further, the need for some explanatory speech to enable the audience to understand the intended message "is strong evidence that the conduct at issue . . . is not so inherently expressive that it warrants protection."[92] This principle would apply to most instances of open carry, which would require some explanation in order to convey an understandable message.

Given the weaknesses and limitations of the First Amendment argument, one might inquire whether reliance on free speech rights in this context should be characterized as "opportunistic."[93] In other words, is dressing what appears to be a Second Amendment claim up as one raising free speech issues an inappropriate use or misuse of the Free Speech Clause?

As I have argued throughout the book, assessing whether this sort of free speech claim is "opportunistic" requires both a close look at the competing claims and an understanding of the use of the Free Speech Clause in the broader context of constitutional movements. *Heller* recognized a right to keep and bear arms in the *home*, for self-defense and defense of one's family members.[94] As discussed further below, the decision does not specifically address recognition or exercise of Second Amendment rights in public places. Some lower courts have held that the Second Amendment protects a Second Amendment right to self-defense outside the home.[95] However, Second Amendment jurisprudence in this and other respects is in a state of flux. Some courts have upheld limits on the open carrying of firearms in public, while others have invalidated such laws.[96]

Thus, it is not clear that the Free Speech Clause claim is substantively weaker than a potential Second Amendment claim. Nor is it apparent that pursuing a free speech claim in this context is a *misuse* of the Free Speech Clause. Indeed, particularly in the context of a case involving the right to express support for Second Amendment rights, it seems entirely appropriate to invoke the Free Speech Clause. Freedom of speech protects core political speech of this nature, owing to its connection to self-government and the search for truth regarding matters of public concern. It seems no more "inappropriate" to invoke the Free Speech Clause in this context than it was to rely on it to facilitate recognition and exercise of equal protection, free exercise, abortion, and other rights.

Of course, concluding that it is not a misuse of the Free Speech Clause is not the same as saying it is preferable to focus on the expressive aspects of open carry rather than the substance of public Second Amendment rights. The Free Speech Clause does not address the central question: whether an individual has a right to openly carry a firearm in public places. It might provide some narrow, short-term, protection for open carry rights in specific cases. But in the long run, the Second Amendment issues must be addressed.

Just as it is unlikely that the Free Speech Clause will provide a strong basis for *protecting* open carry rights, so too is it unlikely that it will provide a basis for *restricting* open carry during public protests. As noted earlier, commentators have argued that the open visibility of firearms at public protests "chills" the exercise of free speech and other First Amendment rights.[97] For some individuals, protesting in the presence of armed counter-protesters heightens tensions, engenders fear, and intimidates. Some will either not participate in protests, or will trim their sails for fear that expression will lead to violent reactions from armed protesters. In light of these concerns, could protest participants invoke the First Amendment as a ground for *restricting* open carry rights?

Under current free speech precedents, concerns about "chilling" First Amendment rights at public protests do not provide a valid basis for banning open carry during public protests. Three separate considerations support this conclusion.

First, the Supreme Court has held that the mere prospect that speech will be chilled or inhibited by *governmental* action does not constitute a cognizable injury or harm under the First Amendment.[98] Thus, for example, the subjective fear or concern that government officials are subjecting speakers to surveillance does not provide a basis for challenging the surveillance on free speech grounds. In the context of public protests, subjective fears relating to the presence of firearms would not provide a basis for banning or limiting open carry.

Second, in the public protest context, the allegedly chilling activity comes not from government actors but from *private* firearms carriers. In the jargon of constitutional law, plaintiffs are generally limited to challenging "state action." While it is true in my hypothetical that the government has authorized the exercise of Second Amendment rights in public places, the alleged injury relates most directly to private decisions to openly carry firearms at public protests, and not to any unlawful act of government. This sort of expressive "chill" argument is thus likely not cognizable.[99]

Third, many things protest participants do and say can be intimidating or even speech-inhibiting. Protesters and counter-protesters yell, engage in demonstrative expressive conduct, and sometimes disobey legal restrictions on speech and assembly for disruptive purposes. Public events, particularly large protests and demonstrations, are not for the faint of heart. This reality also cuts against the conclusion that the mere subjective fear of violence, without more, is a valid justification for restricting or prohibiting open carry during public protests.

There is one potentially serious free speech concern relating to the regulation of open carry during public protests. This concern relates to protesters' rights *in general*, rather than just the rights of expressive arms-carriers. Suppose that instead of banning open carry during a public protest, government instead restricts all arms-bearers to specific areas or "open carry zones" on a parade route or protest venue.[100] Assume that the zones establish specific places at a protest or along a parade route where open carry would be permitted.

On its face, this kind of "place" regulation seems like it would be tailored to reduce the potential for violence at public protests, while it would still preserve the free speech rights of open carriers. Zoning is a very common regulatory tactic at public protests. Speakers are frequently confined to specific areas or spaces during public protests and demonstrations. Courts frequently reject free speech challenges to zones and other speaker displacements.[101]

One problem with the open carry zone is that it might *exacerbate*, rather than resolve, the government's public safety and expressive chill concerns. This would likely not be a concern if all those placed in the zone were advocates for open carry rights—as, for example, in the hypothetical discussed earlier. However, assuming other protesters and speakers were involved, zoning might bring armed protesters and counter-protesters together in the same small pen or zone. That would seem to make armed conflict *more*, rather than less, likely.

The zoning option also raises an important concern about trading away free speech rights in the context of armed protests. As officials seek to reduce the possibility of violence and intimidation, they might be tempted to take measures that negatively impact the free speech rights of protesters and counter-protesters. Thus, in order to reduce the potential for violence, they might reduce the number of protesters that are allowed in certain places or restrict spontaneous gatherings that are hard to police. In this sense, zoning may diminish, rather than protect, First Amendment rights.[102]

Depending on their construction and placement, open carry zones could limit armed speakers to certain out-of-the-way locations, where discharge of firearms is less likely to harm the general public. It might also make it less likely that those inside the zone will engage in robust expressive activities—both with one another and with those located outside the zone. If the concern at an open public protest is that speakers will trim their sails out of fear of armed reprisal, that sort of intimidation seems more likely to occur in the close quarters of an armed pen or zone. Thus, displacing protesters, whether armed or not, in an effort to reduce tensions or in furtherance of public safety may diminish the First Amendment rights of all protesters.

As the discussion shows, the intersection between free speech and firearms at public protests highlights some tensions between the First Amendment and Second

Amendment. The presence of firearms at public protests implicates both freedom of speech and the right to keep and bear arms. However, the analysis shows that the Free Speech Clause is mostly a distraction from the principal concern—whether and, if so, how the Second Amendment permits officials to regulate open carry at public protests.

The Second Amendment and Armed Protests

In answering the Second Amendment question, we are again taking the law as it currently exists. This includes a lack of Supreme Court precedent concerning public carry rights. If free speech and firearms are to be made more compatible in this context, officials will need to have some discretion and power to regulate. So what are the measures that authorities can take with the aim of reducing the tensions and concerns associated with open carry at public protests?

Before considering different sorts of regulations, we need to review the current interpretation of the Second Amendment as it relates to public carry rights. In *Heller*, the Supreme Court recognized an individual right to bear arms for the purpose of self-defense in the home. The Court emphasized that "[l]ike most rights, the right secured by the Second Amendment is not unlimited."[103] It does not, said the Court, protect "a right to keep and carry any weapon whatsoever in any manner whatsoever and for whatever purpose."[104] In a passage that has received a lot of attention and may affect the constitutionality of some public carry regulations, the Court wrote:

> Although we do not undertake an exhaustive historical analysis today of the full scope of the Second Amendment, nothing in our opinion should be taken to cast doubt on longstanding prohibitions on the possession of firearms by felons and the mentally ill, *or laws forbidding the carrying of firearms in sensitive places such as schools and government buildings*, or laws imposing conditions and qualifications on the commercial sale of arms.[105]

Although the Court did not specifically address public carry rights, *Heller* suggests that there might be some coverage for such rights. The Court concluded that the Second Amendment "guarantee[s] the individual right to possess and carry weapons in case of confrontation," which of course can occur outside the home.[106] The Court also observed that "the inherent right of self-defense" rests at the core of the Second Amendment.[107] Although the Court noted that the need for self-defense was "most acute" in the home, it did not expressly limit the scope of the Second Amendment to that place.[108]

Aside from these cryptic references, the Supreme Court has not specifically addressed whether or to what extent the right recognized in *Heller* extends to public places. Some lower courts have reached the conclusion that it does, and invalidated explicit or effective bans on the public carrying of firearms.[109] Other courts, relying in part on *Heller*'s acknowledgment that there is some historical support for restrictions on carrying firearms in public, have upheld public carry restrictions.[110] Some courts have recognized that the Second Amendment protects public carry rights, but subjected restrictions on such rights to a lower standard of judicial scrutiny owing to the fact that they do not restrict core firearms rights.[111]

The scope of the term "Arms" is also the subject of ongoing judicial and academic debate. *Heller* states that the term covers "Arms" that are "in common use at the time for lawful purposes like self-defense."[112] It seems clear that individuals cannot carry hand grenades and other weapons of war to public protests. However, which weapons are covered by the Second Amendment, and what standard of judicial review ought to be used to adjudicate limits on specific "Arms," remain open questions.

Given the gaps left by *Heller*, it is difficult to make solid predictions about which open carry regulations would survive Second Amendment challenges. But *Heller* appears to leave ample room for regulations that would restrict or perhaps, in some cases, effectively ban openly carrying firearms during public protests. I put to the side whether an explicit ban on public carry would survive Second Amendment scrutiny. My analysis addresses more tailored measures that officials in jurisdictions that currently allow some form of open carry could adopt or enforce.

States can likely ban certain *paramilitary groups* from carrying firearms at public protests. In *Presser v. Illinois* (1886), the Supreme Court observed that a state law prohibiting bodies of men to associate together as military organizations, or to drill or parade with arms in cities without authorization, would not violate the Second Amendment.[113] The statement is not authoritative, since as the Court acknowledged the Second Amendment had not yet been applied to the states.[114] However, in *Heller* itself, the Supreme Court interpreted *Presser* as standing for the proposition that the Second Amendment does not prevent states from prohibiting "private paramilitary organizations."[115]

As noted in the free speech discussion above, governments can ban firearms carriers from using their weapons in unlawful or intimidating ways. There is no right under the Second Amendment to unlawfully discharge a weapon or to threaten another with such discharge.[116] *Heller* makes clear that the Second Amendment right is not absolute. Application of criminal firearms laws would readily survive any Second Amendment challenge.

A few states have laws that prohibit carrying firearms "to the terror of the people."[117] In some others, going "armed to the terror of the people" has been a common law offense since the nineteenth century.[118] This particular crime, which prohibits a form of intimidation-by-firearm, has deep roots in English common law.[119] *Heller* suggests that state laws with long historical pedigrees are likely to be considered consistent with the Second Amendment. Thus, as in the case of armed paramilitary bans, the historical lineage would count in favor of sustaining these measures against Second Amendment challenges. In some recent instances, law enforcement officials in states allowing open carry have charged "going armed to the terror of the people" as a means of disarming both protesters and counter-protesters.[120]

"Armed to the terror of the people" laws prohibit a form of menacing-by-firearm, based on the subjective or objective fear of the public. There could be some constitutional problems associated with enforcing this limit on open carry. For instance, the laws and offenses may be deemed too vague to provide proper notice to arms-carriers as to whether they are in compliance. Further, insofar as application of these laws is based on bystanders' subjective fears of violence, the laws might not satisfy a Second Amendment requirement that they be based on and further important governmental interests. Some courts might view this offense as an overbroad regulation of public carry rights.

States and localities might also be able to enact and enforce place- or time-based bans on open carry. Laws and regulations could prohibit firearms in certain specific places where protests and demonstrations typically occur, such as in public parks or public plazas. Officials could justify such restrictions based on the Court's statement that the right to keep and bear arms does not extend to certain "sensitive places." Courts have held that physical places, including public parking lots and national parklands, constitute "sensitive places."[121] It is possible that public protest marches and demonstrations, which can often be tumultuous and difficult to police, might be considered "sensitive places" or perhaps "sensitive events" during which open carry is not permitted.

Heller may also permit limited time-based or event-specific bans on open carry. Thus, a regulation that bans open carry during the duration of a particular public protest or other permitted event may be valid under the Second Amendment. Some lower courts have applied a weaker degree of scrutiny to public carry restrictions. Thus, it may be possible to defend an event-related ban as a narrowly tailored time regulation furthering important interests in public safety.[122] Those interests can be characterized as particularly acute in the context of large-scale public protests and demonstrations. To be sure, review of such restrictions might raise the same sorts of problems addressed in the earlier free speech analysis. Thus, officials would need to convince a court that the temporary ban was adequately justified by public safety concerns.

A variety of even narrower regulations might also be used to defuse the tensions and concerns associated with the open presence of firearms at public protests. For instance, as discussed earlier, officials could adopt measures that physically separate speakers and arms-bearers from one another. Open carry zones would not ban firearms altogether, but rather restrict those carrying firearms to certain locations. As discussed earlier, open carry zones would not eliminate the danger of armed confrontation. Indeed, if they place armed protesters and counter-protesters in the same physical pen or zone, they could exacerbate the threat of violence. If it is possible to do so, authorities would need to establish separate zones for protesters and counter-protesters.

Zoning would not eradicate the potential for violent confrontation. However, it would address one of the central problems that affected competing rallies such as the one in Charlottesville—the considerable difficulties associated with policing armed individuals who are roaming freely among protest participants. As discussed earlier, officials would need to structure and place open carry protests in ways that minimize the impact on free speech and assembly rights. Whether zoning would satisfy Second Amendment standards depends, once again, on what standard of review applies and, more specifically, whether the government's public safety and policing interests outweigh the right to openly carry a firearm anywhere in the protest venue.

Officials could also adopt and enforce measures that restrict the *types of arms* participants are allowed to openly carry. In terms of the potential chilling of expression and public safety concerns, the open carrying of semi-automatic rifles may be of particular concern. *Heller* does not recognize a right to keep and bear *any* weapon one might want to carry in public places. Federal appeals courts have generally upheld bans on the sale and possession of AR-15s and other "assault rifles."[123] Thus, authorities can likely ban individuals from openly carrying certain particularly dangerous and intimidating firearms during public protests.

It may also be possible for officials to limit the carrying of firearms at public protests to *concealed* weapons. This limitation would not address all concerns about potential violence, but would diminish concerns about expressive chill owing to the lack of visible firearms at protests. Note, again, the proposal is not an outright ban on open carry, but rather a restriction on open carry during particular public events.

Finally, officials could permit firearms to be openly carried at public protests, but limit or burden their *use* in ways that further public safety interests. For example, laws could allow firearms carriers to keep ammunition on their persons, but require that any firearms remain *unloaded* during the protest. This kind of restriction would be difficult, though perhaps not impossible, to enforce. An ammunition restriction would not prevent the actual use of firearms for self-defense, which is the purpose *Heller* articulates, although it would make actually using a weapon more onerous and hence perhaps less likely. Another possibility is to allow for the presence of concealed firearms during public protests, but require that they remain holstered or secured. This would not prevent the discharge of firearms, but again might make it less likely to occur and would make violations easier to police.

Heller does not definitively resolve whether *any* of the foregoing proposals would violate the Second Amendment. That will depend on a number of factors: the scope of the Second Amendment in public places; the standard of review for Second Amendment regulations; and the definition and scope of "Arms."[124] However, all of the proposed restrictions have some grounding in statements made in *Heller* and current approaches to interpreting Second Amendment rights in the lower courts. All restrict open carry to some degree, but none ban the practice outright.

None of the proposed measures *guarantee* that public speakers will be free from intimidation or discomfort, or that firearms will not be used during public protests, demonstrations, and rallies. The question we started with was whether the exercise of free speech and firearms rights is *inherently* incompatible at public protests, demonstrations, and similar events. Anecdotally, the answer is no. Legally and constitutionally, there are measures governments can enact and enforce that would limit and mitigate the tensions associated with open carry at public events. As discussed further below, future experience may demonstrate incompatibilities that have not yet materialized. But based on current knowledge and practices, it is *possible* to have both free speech and firearms at public protests.

Make no mistake, the presence of firearms will likely change the tone, tenor, and experience of some public protests. Speakers and other participants are already expected to exhibit a measure of "civic courage" when they engage in public contention.[125] The presence of visible firearms will test this resolve. If we are to prevent open carry from doing serious harm to our public discourse, there will need to be some limits on the exercise of Second Amendment rights at public protests and demonstrations. The discussion above suggests that under current interpretations of the Second Amendment, authorities are far from powerless to preserve both free speech and firearms rights.

FIREARMS AND ACADEMIC FREEDOM

Another complicating aspect of the relationship between firearms and free speech has been the adoption in some states of campus carry laws. Some states permit, and a few even require, public colleges and universities to allow students and faculty to carry concealed weapons in certain areas of campus—including in classrooms.[126]

The presence of firearms at events such as campus protests could raise public safety and "chill" concerns similar to those addressed above, in the general context of public protests. However, the greater potential threats to freedom of speech and free speech interests relating to academic inquiry relate to classroom carry. The extension of concealed carry rights into the classroom raises the question whether the presence of firearms is compatible with the expressive and academic activities that occur in that special forum.

In this context, the Second Amendment intersects with First Amendment-based interests relating to "academic freedom."[127] In *Keyshian v. Board of Regents of the State of New York* (1967), which invalidated a state law that required professors to sign a certificate stating they were not and never had been Communists, the Supreme Court said the following with regard to freedom of speech and academic freedom:

> Our nation is deeply committed to safeguarding academic freedom, which is of transcendent value to all of us and not merely to the teachers concerned. That freedom is therefore a special concern of the First Amendment, which does not tolerate laws that cast a pall of orthodoxy over the classroom. . . . The classroom is peculiarly the "marketplace of ideas." The nation's future depends upon leaders trained through wide exposure to that robust exchange of ideas which discovers truth "out of a multitude of tongues, [rather] than through any kind of authoritative selection."[128]

In general terms, academic freedom shields academic institutions from certain interventions by the state, such as efforts to impose official viewpoints. It may also protect individual professors' autonomy to engage in pedagogical and research activities, and might be a defense to certain adverse employment actions.[129] Students may also possess academic freedom rights in some contexts. All of the qualifiers are notable, and necessary. Academic freedom is a complicated concept, and courts have made little progress in terms of clarifying the concept's substance and scope. Thus, for example, it remains an open question whether individual professors, who are among the most likely to be affected by classroom carry, have any enforceable academic freedom rights.[130]

Notwithstanding this uncertainty, professors have argued that the presence of firearms in classrooms violates their academic freedom rights to determine what materials to cover, in what manner, and under what circumstances. This includes, they have argued, determining whether firearms can be brought into the classroom. Professors have also argued that classroom carry chills debate, thereby undermining efforts to foster and facilitate a robust and sometimes uncomfortable exchange of ideas in the classroom.

These were the primary grounds upon which a group of liberal arts professors at the University of Texas challenged their state's campus carry law, which required that state universities permit licensed faculty and students to carry concealed firearms in the classroom. A federal district court rejected the professors' plea that the law be enjoined prior to taking effect, reasoning that the law did not directly regulate speech or impose any official orthodoxy on the professors.[131] The court subsequently dismissed the professors' complaint on a different ground, namely that they could not demonstrate a concrete injury from the mere presence of concealed weapons in their classrooms. The court concluded that the professors' claim that classroom discussion would be narrowed, truncated, or cut off by the presence of firearms was too speculative to be a cognizable legal harm.[132]

Although the decision will not likely be the last word on classroom carry and academic freedom, the case highlights some of the difficulties associated with managing classroom carry according to free speech and related concerns. As noted, it is not clear that individual professors have "academic freedom" rights. Even if they do, it is far from certain that they extend to making decisions concerning the presence of firearms in the classroom.[133] The argument that the presence of concealed firearms requires wholesale revision of syllabi or lesson plans seems farfetched.

Moreover, with regard to free speech rights, professors bear the burden of demonstrating that knowledge that some might be carrying concealed firearms in the classroom will disrupt teaching, chill debate, or interfere with academic inquiry. As in the protest context, subjective fear of firearms in the classroom is perhaps understandable. But demonstrating *objective* effects on professors' or students' communication of ideas or academic discourse will be more difficult. Indeed, there do not appear to have been any reported instances of firearms-related violence relating to classroom discussion, even though classroom carry has been in effect in some states for some time. Further, in general, classrooms are forums for robust, although managed and regulated, discussions. Although many faculty and students may not want or welcome classroom carry, it is far from clear that the introduction of concealed firearms into that environment will have the dire effects the Texas professors predict.

Thus, just as public protesters will not be able to exclude firearms from rallies and demonstrations based on concerns about their free speech rights, faculty will likely find that the Free Speech Clause and related academic freedom interests do not provide grounds for overturning classroom carry laws.

In most states, this matter has been determined with reference to interpretation of Second Amendment rights. In the classroom setting, the Second Amendment issue is rather simple to resolve. *Heller* strongly suggests that states can treat classrooms and other areas of campus as "sensitive places" where firearms can be banned. Most states have taken this approach. Their determinations that firearms do not have a place in classrooms, which may be in part related to academic freedom and free speech concerns, rest on solid Second Amendment footing.

But what about states that adopt a different interpretation of Second Amendment rights and allow classroom carry? Even if the Free Speech Clause does not provide a basis for reversing their laws, might it be of some general use in diminishing the tensions that campus carry produces?

One rather obvious free speech tie-in relates to opportunities to engage in counter-speech. In states where classroom carry must be permitted, are professors able to dissent from the state's policy? Certainly they have free speech rights to oppose classroom carry on their own time, as citizens speaking on matters of public concern. But states and campus administrations should also permit professors to try to explain, in their syllabi for example, why they feel concealed carry will detrimentally affect classroom discussion. This dissent cannot be communicated in a manner that acts as an effective ban on concealed carry. Nor can students' exercise of their right to carry in classrooms affect the grading of their performance in the class. However, just as professors may try to persuade their students not to use laptops in the classroom without banning them, professors ought to be given the opportunity to present arguments and evidence relating to the effect of classroom carry.

More generally, the core principles and values associated with freedom of speech could help in terms of navigating this intersection between firearms and free speech. Although many might be reluctant to do so, one possibility is for instructors, where it is germane to classroom discussion, to make the presence of firearms a topic of discussion. If the classroom is a "marketplace of ideas," the response to practices, beliefs, and ideas that cause discomfort should be more speech rather than silence.[134] Instructors could have an open and balanced dialogue about firearms, public safety, and perhaps even the exercise and intersection of constitutional rights. Highlighting rather than avoiding the subject might help demystify firearms.

This sort of affirmative engagement with firearms is not the only option. Another approach, also rooted in free speech values, is to exercise tolerance with regard to firearms. The Free Speech Clause has been defended on the ground that it encourages tolerance for even extreme points of view.[135] I am not suggesting that the concealed carrying of firearms is technically "speech," or that it communicates a viewpoint. Rather, the idea is to apply general tolerance principles to the *exercise* of a right that many find threatening or disruptive.

Tolerance encourages individuals to be open to different cultural and political perspectives. In the abstract, and again not as a constitutional matter, the carrying of firearms represents a perspective that being armed is necessary for self-defense and perhaps defense of others. On this view, firearms make campuses—including classrooms—safer.

To some, this represents an extreme and empirically incorrect view of the scope of Second Amendment rights—that is, only when firearms are everywhere will we all be safe. However, just as we have decided, as a society, to show tolerance to Nazi marchers in Skokie and protesters at military funerals, so too might we exercise a degree of tolerance for even the most extreme perspectives regarding firearms. In particular, we ought to check our impulse to exclude firearms on campuses and in other places because we do not agree with the ideas sometimes associated with their presence or, what is worse, because we do not like those who espouse such ideas.

The invocation of tolerance principles, particularly in this context, will undoubtedly draw objections. Some will resist treating the carrying of firearms as a perspective, viewing it instead as nothing more than a dangerous form of conduct.[136] Others will reject the premise that we ought to tolerate such a potentially dangerous perspective or activity, especially in university classrooms. Still others might argue that tolerance, in the sense suggested, actually *interferes with* academic discourse because it requires instructors to tolerate a form of extremism in their classrooms.

Without denying the genuineness of such concerns, it is worth considering whether our long experience with contentious forms of public discourse and our tolerance for different perspectives might help us come to terms with the reality of firearms in university classrooms.[137] Framing the issue as one of tolerance will at least challenge those who oppose firearms on campus to ask whether, or to what extent, their opposition is based on their disagreement with the argument that an armed populace will produce a safer society. Some campuses have welcomed firearms into their classrooms. For professors and students in those classrooms, finding constructive ways to mentally process this reality may help diminish the fears and concerns that this extension of Second Amendment rights has caused.

Encouraging engagement and tolerance does not entail limiting the rights of faculty, students, and others to speak out against campus concealed carry laws in other settings. Tolerance does not entail suppressing dissent, although it can produce moderation in social discourse. Tolerating Nazi uniforms and salutes in Skokie, Illinois, or Charlottesville, Virginia, has not entailed suppressing counter-speech or censoring moral outrage. Professors, administrators, student publications, and gun control organizations should all be free to express their points of view on the subject of campus carry. Indeed, University of Texas students found some clever ways to protest campus carry—including carrying sex toys on campus to demonstrate that while such harmless objects had been banned from campus, firearms had been legally permitted.

At this moment, the Second Amendment remains a white-hot focal point of political, cultural, and constitutional conflict. After *Heller*, and in the wake of mass murders at high schools and other places, many have a strong urge to restrict firearms in as many places as possible. As free speech and firearms continue to intersect, we will need to find ways to reconcile the rights that protect them. As in the context of public protests, the Second Amendment permits states broad leeway to regulate firearms on campus. In states that take the broadest view of firearms rights on campus, professors and students will need to devise ways to facilitate open discourse in the face of classroom carry. Free speech principles and values may be of some assistance in that endeavor.

The Once, and Future, Relationship between Free Speech and Firearms

Like other rights relationships discussed in the book, the relationship between freedom of speech and Second Amendment rights has been marked by periods of synergy and conflict. In terms of recognition and construction, the Free Speech Clause has likely taken the Second Amendment as far as it can. However, as the discussion of classroom carry suggests, that does not mean free speech has nothing to offer debates about firearms rights. Our long national experience with the construction and exercise of free speech rights may provide an invaluable window into how Second Amendment rights will be debated and developed.

SYNERGY AND SALIENCE

Since prior to formal ratification, the First Amendment and Second Amendment have been connected to one another through text and analogical reasoning. Professor Amar argued that initially, a collectivist Second Amendment and a collectivist Free Speech Clause provided overlapping structural protections against a newly powerful national government. Later, he observed, as a result of Reconstruction Era dynamics, the two provisions were transformed into the robust individual rights we recognize today.

This transformation was itself a product of the exercise of free speech rights. Freedom of speech facilitated the recognition of an individual right to keep and bear arms in multiple respects. It mediated a decades-long discourse concerning the nature, status, and scope of the Second Amendment. Civic organizations, litigants, scholars, and courts debated whether the Second Amendment, like the First Amendment, was a right worthy of the label "fundamental."

In *Heller*, the Supreme Court relied heavily on free speech history and doctrine to establish the fundamental status of the Second Amendment right. It also suggested that the scope of the Second Amendment could be determined on categorical grounds; just as the Free Speech Clause excludes certain categories of speech from its coverage, so too might the Second Amendment be interpreted to categorically exclude certain arms, locations, or arms-carriers. As discussed, lower courts and scholars have taken this analogy further, developing a "tiered scrutiny" approach that closely resembles and often relies explicitly on Free Speech Clause doctrine.

As I have argued, the Free Speech Clause has likely taken the Second Amendment as far as it can or should. Specific doctrines relating to concepts such as licensure and content-neutrality cannot be accurately grafted onto the Second Amendment. Moreover, as we have seen, relying on the Free Speech Clause to protect public carry or other Second Amendment rights will likely yield few meaningful victories for firearms proponents. Opponents of Second Amendment rights likewise will not likely be able to exclude firearms based on concepts such as expressive "chill."

As suggested in the earlier discussion of campus carry rights, the salience of the Free Speech Clause and freedom of speech for debates about the modern Second Amendment will likely take a different, more abstract, form. Take, for instance, the notion of *absolute* rights. The Free Speech Clause is written in absolutist terms—"Congress shall make no law . . ."—and yet there are myriad constitutional restrictions on the freedom of speech. Speakers do not have the right to communicate whatever they want, wherever they want, in any manner they desire. *Heller* plainly adopts a non-absolutist interpretation of the Second Amendment.

And yet, as it concerns the Second Amendment, political and social discourse on the right frequently adopts absolutist terms.[138] Thus, according to some Second Amendment proponents, *any* regulation of the right to keep and bear arms is simply intolerable and unconstitutional. This is an inaccurate, unrealistic, and shortsighted view. Like free speech advocates, Second Amendment proponents need to prepare themselves for a future in which persons do not have the right to carry any weapon they want, wherever they want, in any manner they desire.

As well, discourse on the left sometimes adopts the perspective that despite *Heller*, the right to keep and bear arms is illegitimate, or that firearms are inherently threatening and dangerous objects that deserve no constitutional protection. But as discussed below, this was once a prevalent attitude regarding the freedom of speech—particularly, although not exclusively, in public places. The expression of certain ideas was once considered a threat to public order, safety, and national security. American free speech history shows that notions of what is publicly or societally acceptable are subject to change.

As the free speech experience also shows, absolutist conceptions of the Second Amendment are also jurisprudentially short-sighted. The process of debating and establishing the limits of a right can help to clarify and even strengthen its core purposes and values. Thus, over time, debates about the "core" protections of the Free Speech Clause have assisted courts and scholars in identifying its principal justifications and values. For example, theories have been built around the concept of "political speech" as a core concern of the Free Speech Clause.[139]

Thus, understanding *why* we have a Free Speech Clause has contributed significantly to the robust protection and exercise of free speech rights. Second Amendment absolutists are foregoing this invaluable process in an ill-fated attempt to establish an absolute right to keep and bear arms. As the free speech example demonstrates, this process is perpetual and there will always be disagreements about what aspects of a right reside at its "core" and periphery. As this dynamic plays out in the context of the right to keep and bear arms, two things are likely to occur: first, the scope of the Second Amendment will become clearer, and, second, the "core" will be more readily defensible.

Another lesson from our free speech experience is that all of this will take time—lots of it. The modern Free Speech Clause was constructed over a period spanning more than a century. Interpretations of the Free Speech Clause have changed in response to episodes of social upheaval, political realignments, academic discourse, and judicial dynamics. Thus, as *Heller* appears to recognize, Second Amendment doctrine will not be established in a single decision or even a series of them. We will know what the Second Amendment means only after social, political, academic, and judicial processes have acted upon it. Again, as demonstrated by our experience with the Free Speech Clause, what the Second Amendment means today may be starkly different from what it will mean in the future.

As recounted throughout the book, the Free Speech Clause's history demonstrates that the frequency and nature of its interactions with other constitutional rights will influence the construction of the Second Amendment. In addition to the Free Speech Clause, the Second Amendment is likely to intersect with the Fourth Amendment, the Equal Protection Clause, and the Due Process Clause.[140] How firearms are policed, who is entitled to exercise them, whether Second Amendment rights must be recognized across state lines, and how free speech and firearms interact will all influence future understandings of Second Amendment rights.

These interactions may help clarify the rights that the Second Amendment intersects with. Interactions between the Free Speech Clause and the Second Amendment may illuminate the central justifications for freedom of speech. As Professor Magarian argues, we will need to think more carefully about the difference between revolution-by-words and revolution-by-arms. Similarly, how the Second Amendment interacts with search and seizure rights, and due process rights, will add to our understandings of these rights as well.

As we consider the future relationship between the Free Speech Clause and the Second Amendment, the most useful insights will result not from formal or explicit modeling of one based on the other, but from their shared experiences as fundamental rights. Although it is part of a system of rights, the Second Amendment will need breathing space to develop on its own, just as the Free Speech Clause has done over the past century.

THE PUBLIC SECOND AMENDMENT

The Supreme Court may eventually recognize some right to keep and bear arms outside the home. If *Heller* is any indication, such a decision will not settle the matter of public Second Amendment rights completely. Here, too, the free speech experience suggests how the public Second Amendment might develop in the years to come.

With regard to public speech and firearms rights, we ought to start by making a simple, but important, connection: The exercise of free speech and other First Amendment rights, like the public carrying of firearms, was once considered a threat to public order and security. Certain forms of public dissent were once treated much the same as many currently view the open carrying of firearms—as insurrectionist, intimidating, and criminal.

For instance, public speech critical of government was once considered inherently dangerous—a "clear and present danger," as the Court characterized it during the first quarter of the twentieth century.[141] Moreover, in the beginning, there was no recognized First Amendment right to use public places, including streets and parks, for expressive purposes.[142] It was not until the 1960s that the Supreme Court recognized broad rights to speak and assemble in public places.[143]

In the context of public protests and public campuses, many still view the display of firearms as a dangerous and unwelcome activity—essentially a form of intimidation. Arguments equating the public display of firearms with violence or unlawful activity are common. There is, of course, an obvious difference between speech and firearms in this regard: In general, unlike exercises of the right to speak, exercises of the right to openly carry firearms can have deadly consequences. However, that difference alone likely does not explain the urge to ban firearms in public places.

If this skepticism and fear is to be overcome, it will take more than a Supreme Court decision (or two) recognizing a right to public carry. As in the speech context, much will depend on how public firearms rights are policed and exercised. In the free speech context, the Supreme Court developed a set of "Roberts Rules of Order" for public speech rights.[144] In addition to being prohibited from inciting violence, communicating threats, or uttering "fighting words," speakers were subject to regulations that addressed threats to public safety, order, and competing uses of public property.[145] Free speech rights were subject to limits based on collective concerns.

In the case of the Second Amendment, these rules are being constructed primarily by state legislatures, many of which are eager to expand public carry rights. Legislative recognition of open carry rights has provided a valuable boost to the development of the public Second Amendment. However, although nearly all states provide some form of protection for open carrying of firearms, many states and localities impose restrictions resembling free speech time, place, and manner regulations. These limits will constitute the bulk of the "Roberts Rules" for public carry.

Such rules will assist with the policing of public carry, which will also influence its development. If the public First Amendment consisted of only mobs and mayhem, few would participate in or support public speech rights. Thus, the manner in which public speech rights have been regulated and policed has been critically important to the development of the public First Amendment. Although earlier periods were characterized by aggressive and even violent policing methods, the modern approach is for officials to "negotiate" with speakers in advance, at least where possible.[146] Of course, in the context of public protests, not all speakers wish to cooperate with law enforcement. But for the most part, today even large-scale demonstrations and marches are generally peaceful affairs.

Whether public Second Amendment rights can be effectively policed remains to be seen. Public protests are already challenging assignments for local and state law enforcement. Adding firearms to the mix will present additional and unique challenges. In addition to concerns about the unlawful use of firearms, police will have to confront the fact that they no longer have a monopoly on the display and potential use of firearms. They must also deal with the possibility of situational confusion arising from the uncertainty that comes with armed protests. Is the armed person a lawfully carrying protest participant or an active shooter?[147] Finally, police forces may need to be concerned about whether they have adequate firepower to resist or defend against armed protesters. These policing challenges will affect the scope and exercise of public Second Amendment rights.

How public rights are *exercised* also has a bearing on their scope and enforcement. In the free speech context, public speakers who mounted the earliest challenges to limits on expressive activities were not a rambunctious crowd. In fact, most were arrested and convicted even though they were engaged in peaceful, non-threatening forms of public expression.[148] The early exercises of free speech and assembly for which litigants sought protection mostly took the form of nonviolent communications—pamphleteering, proselytizing, and generally orderly public assemblies.

The law-abiding nature of speakers that came before the Court in the earliest cases set the stage for the future expansion of the public First Amendment. Over time, the First Amendment absorbed public speakers and speech that caused significant discomfort or raised safety concerns. The First Amendment now protects a wide range of potentially disruptive and intimidating public activities, including face-to-face proselytizing, picketing, flag burning, and funeral protesting.[149] In public places, audiences have been admonished to avert their eyes when confronted with speech they find upsetting or offensive.[150]

The lesson here may be that the manner in which early open carriers exercise their rights will have some bearing on the future public Second Amendment. In this respect, it is noteworthy that, at least to date, the violence and injuries sustained at public protests and demonstrations have not been related to the discharge of firearms. At the Charlottesville "Unite the Right" rally, a single weapons incident led to criminal charges.[151] Most of the violence occurred as protesters and counter-protesters clashed using sticks, batons, and other weapons.[152] So far, there have been very few reports of gun violence or unlawful brandishing of weapons at public protest events or on campuses.

Of course, this situation could change rather quickly. A mass murder or other catastrophic incident, for example at a public protest or in a college classroom, could change the tenor of the debate concerning open carry rights. So far, mass murders have not produced a wave of gun control measures.[153] But violence at public protests or in college classrooms might be seen as threatening aspects of American free speech culture in ways that demand some action. In sum, in certain respects, the future of the public Second Amendment is in the hands of those who exercise open carry rights at public protests and similar events.

Finally, as noted earlier, there is an important connection between free speech and firearms in terms of the need to establish the justifications for and values relating to these rights. Just as limits on public speech rights have been assessed with reference to the values and purposes of the Free Speech Clause, the constitutionality of specific restrictions on open carry will depend in part on the underlying values or purposes that the Second Amendment is intended to serve.[154]

Justifications for free speech rights have been debated and refined over the course of many decades. No single justification commands a consensus, in the sense that it is regarded as the definitive justification for protecting free speech.[155] Instead, the Supreme Court and most scholars have adopted a pluralistic approach to free speech justifications, relying on several—self-government, the search for truth, and speaker autonomy—to justify protection for speech rights in public places.[156]

Heller observes that the "core" or "central component" of the right to keep and bear arms is self-defense.[157] However, the decision does not purport to fully determine the normative justifications or values relating to Second Amendment rights in general, or open carry rights in particular. Does open carry serve autonomy values, much as freedom of speech does?[158] Does the Second Amendment embrace what some scholars have referred to as a "marketplace of violence," similar to the First Amendment's marketplace in ideas, which might justify open carry in terms of deterring threats?[159] Or does open carry protect a form of self-government, for example by deterring or preventing tyrannical government action?[160]

As the First Amendment example shows, open carry rights do not require a unitary theory or single justification. However, the normative values of the Second Amendment, as well as others that might relate to its "central component" of self-defense, could interact with open carry regulations in distinctive ways. A right based on autonomy or tyranny-deterrence might severely restrict the extent to which authorities could disarm or limit open carry at public protests. In contrast, a right based on narrower self-defense principles might allow authorities to limit open carry in certain respects, in order to further public interests in safety and order.

Right now, the Second Amendment lacks a clear and cogent set of normative values or principles. As the free speech example shows, those values will be critically important to constructing the public Second Amendment. Thinking them through now, for example in the context of controversies relating to arming public protests and campus carry, can help determine the scope of public Second Amendment rights. This effort may also help officials and courts harmonize the exercise of public free speech and firearms rights, which may sometimes need to be balanced against each other in cases of tension or conflict.

8

RIGHTS PLURALISM

RELYING ON THE book's findings and conclusions with regard to freedom of speech and its relation to other constitutional rights, this final chapter describes and defends a conception of the American system of constitutional rights that it refers to as "Rights Pluralism." The central premise of Rights Pluralism is that we must act to preserve a plural and diverse system of constitutional rights. This goal can be partly achieved through a leveraging of the Free Speech Clause's rights-related functions. But it also depends on maintaining conceptual and enforcement space between free speech and non-speech constitutional rights. The chapter offers several suggestions toward this end: protecting a robust constitutional rights discourse; reviving subordinated constitutional rights; educating the people about constitutional rights; and constructing pluralistic rights theories.

The System of Constitutional Rights

The Constitution explicitly provides for a pluralistic system of constitutional rights. The Founders' original plan was to rely on a system of *structural* checks and balances to protect constitutional liberty. However, they also proposed and ratified a system of constitutional rights. Part of that system—the first ten amendments to the Constitution—is generally referred to as our "Bill of Rights."[1] Subsequent generations

The Dynamic Free Speech Clause. Timothy Zick.

ratified additional rights protections, including the Fourteenth Amendment's Equal Protection Clause and Due Process Clause. These various provisions have interacted with one another, and with the Bill of Rights, across generations.

American constitutional rights are a product of two-plus centuries of discourse, debate, exercise, and enforcement. As the book has shown, we cannot fully understand the rights in our constitutional system in isolation from one another. Many of the Constitution's rights provisions have been participants in long-term, dynamic relationships. Free speech and non-speech rights, which have been the particular focus of this book, have developed and matured together. The process in which this has occurred, Rights Dynamism, has constructed not just individual rights protections but also a pluralistic *system* of intersecting, overlapping, and sometimes conflicting rights.

In this context, "pluralism" refers, in part, to the basic fact that there are more rights than one. As it pertains to constitutional rights, pluralism also connotes *diversity*—in terms of the substance of individual rights, and their different connections to constitutional democracy. Finally, in the context of constitutional rights, pluralism is also identified with normative arguments about the benefits of a strong and robust system of constitutional rights.[2]

Rights Pluralism facilitates one of the central purposes of constitutional rights, which is the attainment of liberty. In simple terms, a diverse and thriving system of rights facilitates the protection and enjoyment of constitutional liberty. The Constitution's system of overlapping and intersecting rights provisions envisions multiple checks on government. Governments operate within a system of multiple and diverse constraints. As they regulate, officials must act within the constraints imposed by various clauses and provisions that check and sometimes trump their power. When governments bear the burden of demonstrating that their actions comply with not just one but a system of rights, individual liberty is enhanced.

This is not simply an expression of the view that two (or three, or four) rights are better than one, although in terms of liberty there is something to that sentiment. As we have witnessed, in many instances, the sum of individual rights can be greater than its individual components. The combination of two or more rights can provide a basis for relief that each individual right, standing alone, might not afford. As discussed in Chapter 4, religious adherents have benefitted from the existence of both the Free Exercise Clause and the Free Speech Clause. The combination of these two provisions helped Jehovah's Witnesses and others obtain relief from oppressive and discriminatory laws. The Equal Protection Clause formally required equal treatment under law. But as Chapter 5 showed, the actual enjoyment of constitutional equality has depended significantly on rights guaranteed by the Free Speech Clause. One could multiply these examples. Thus, as discussed in Chapter 6, standing alone the

Due Process Clause may provide some coverage for the right to abortion. But recognition of abortion rights is also a product of free speech concepts and principles.

Rights Pluralism can also lead to mutual illumination of individual rights provisions. As noted in the Introduction, constitutional rights are a form of argument, rhetoric, and discourse. Thus, their meanings are partially and mutually clarified through comparisons—of texts, histories, doctrines, and principles. We have a better sense of what the Equal Protection Clause and Free Speech Clause mean owing to their frequent interactions. Similarly, as discussed in Chapter 7, placing Second Amendment rights and free speech rights in conversation with one another may sharpen our understanding of both.

Our system of constitutional rights does not invariably produce more expansive interpretations of individual rights.[3] When they are combined together, rights can limit as well as broaden one another's meanings. Again, interactions between the Free Speech Clause and Second Amendment provide an example. As discussed in Chapter 7, Second Amendment proponents may find that using the Free Speech Clause as a model will produce narrower firearms rights than they hope or expect. This realization may lead Second Amendment advocates to abandon free speech borrowing in favor of other approaches that can produce more expansive interpretations of the right to keep and bear arms. In this sense, understanding the limits of rights analogies can enhance or clarify understandings of constitutional liberty.

Rights Pluralism also serves a set of narrower and more pragmatic ends. Emphasizing the need to treat rights provisions as distinct guarantees can help avoid textual redundancies. Further, maintaining some separation between rights can help to clarify constitutional doctrines. For example, the separation of Free Speech Clause and Equal Protection Clause doctrines during the 1970s helped clarify the respective domains of the two provisions. Granted, to put things mildly, creating this separation has not always resulted in doctrinal coherence. However, one thing separation produced was opportunities for illumination and clarification that might not otherwise have materialized.

Treating constitutional rights as a system of rights also highlights the need to avoid having any one right become dominant or subordinating vis-à-vis other rights. Instead, the Constitution's rights ought to be treated as related—"cognate," "kaleidoscopic," and "stereoscopic"—protections.[4] As this conception of constitutional rights implies, the Free Speech Clause ought not to subordinate or dominate other rights in the system of rights. In terms of facilitating constitutional liberty, a central project is to continue to leverage the power of the Free Speech Clause to facilitate non-speech constitutional rights, while at the same time constraining its expansionist tendencies.

The Rights Functions of the Free Speech Clause

As we have seen throughout the book, freedom of speech has been critically important to Rights Pluralism. The Free Speech Clause has been invoked as a mobilizing mechanism, an analogy, and even a model for other constitutional rights. In our system of constitutional rights, it has been both a dynamic agent of change and an object of change.

With regard specifically to Rights Pluralism, freedom of speech has served a number of critical functions. As emphasized throughout the book, it has functioned as an *antecedent* guarantee. Without freedoms to think, believe, and communicate ideas, it is difficult to imagine the kinds of equality, free exercise, and other constitutional rights Americans enjoy today.

In many instances, as in the case of the civil rights and LGBT equality movements, rights advocates have turned *first* to the Free Speech Clause, and only much later to non-speech concerns.[5] Advocates for free exercise, equal protection, abortion, Second Amendment, and other rights all used the Free Speech Clause to create necessary breathing space for political mobilization and constitutional movements.[6] Indeed, this is the principal reason why I have expressed reservations about condemning free speech claims that relate to other constitutional rights as "opportunistic."[7] Where the Free Speech Clause is being invoked for the purpose of creating space for the initial recognition of another constitutional right, it is being used in a manner that furthers important free speech and non-speech values.

The Free Speech Clause has also facilitated Rights Pluralism by *mediating* public discourse about other constitutional rights. It has allowed proponents and opponents to debate and contest the meanings of constitutional rights. Among other things, free speech rules and doctrines have assured that rights advocates have access to public places, prohibited government from discriminating against political and other speech based on its content, and protected speakers from official compulsion with regard to speech.

Moreover, the Free Speech Clause has functioned as both sword and shield. It has advanced the cause of constitutional rights, while also ensuring that dissenters are not compelled to accept official orthodoxies about those rights. These and other framework principles have facilitated a "robust, uninhibited, and wide-open" discourse about constitutional rights, which in turn has allowed the people to determine largely for themselves the meaning and scope of constitutional rights in the American system of rights.

This is why, despite concerns about Americans' penchant for engaging in "rights talk," we must protect basic rights to debate, research, contest, and freely engage with the subject of constitutional rights. As discussed in Chapter 2, regulations of "rights speech"—communications about or concerning the recognition, scope, or exercise of constitutional rights—interfere with the mediating functions of the Free Speech Clause. Rights Pluralism depends on free and open discourse about and concerning constitutional rights. Regulations of ideological, informational, and consultative rights speech are suspect not only owing to their impact on free speech rights, but also because they compel or restrict communications that help determine how other constitutional rights are to be interpreted and exercised. In this sense, too, freedom of speech contributes to self-governance as it relates to the system of constitutional rights.

There is also an important connection between discourse about constitutional rights and the effective *enjoyment* of those rights. Time and again, we have seen that governmental restrictions on speech have negatively impacted the exercise of religious, equal protection, abortion, and other constitutional rights. Our system of constitutional rights depends on the free and voluntary flow of information about those rights. Freedom of speech assures the effective exercise of rights in that system.

To be sure, the Free Speech Clause does not always perform its facilitative and mediating functions evenly or effectively. The chapters have noted many shortcomings and complications in this regard. However, in general, the book has shown that freedom of speech functions as an effective facilitator of other constitutional rights and as a capable mediator of rights discourse. It is, of course, important to continue to support and improve the rights functions of the Free Speech Clause. Thus, for example, we need to ensure that there is adequate public space for rights discourse, and to work on further limiting government's power to dictate, suppress, or otherwise manipulate the content of rights discourse.

Rights Pluralism begins—but, as explained below, by no means ends—with preserving and improving the Free Speech Clause's rights functions. Free speech facilitation and mediation are necessary conditions for creating a diverse and effective system of rights. But these conditions alone are not sufficient to produce Rights Pluralism.

Diversity without Dominance

Rights Pluralism requires a system of rights that exhibits diversity without dominance. The Free Speech Clause undermines Rights Pluralism insofar as it dominates, subordinates, or supplants other constitutional rights. As we have seen in the preceding chapters, this is always a potential danger whenever freedom of speech interacts with other rights in the system. In some instances, these interactions have resulted in a troubling form of free speech expansionism.

For example, as discussed in Chapter 3, the Free Speech Clause has generally supplanted its textual neighbors—the Assembly Clause, Press Clause, and Petition Clause. These once "cognate" rights provisions are now treated as "ancillary" to the Free Speech Clause. They have all been subsumed into an atextual "Free Expression Clause."

In a more limited sense, the Free Exercise Clause has surrendered some conceptual and doctrinal territory to the Free Speech Clause. As explained in Chapter 4, this began to occur in the 1980s, when religious adherents turned to the Free Speech Clause to challenge governmental policies excluding religion. Supreme Court precedents established public forum doctrine as a baseline for religious inclusion in public programs. Other precedents treated religion as an expressive viewpoint, which suggests that it cannot be excluded from public programs and forums. As discussed, this free speech turn occurred in cases where the Free Exercise Clause itself provided a plausible basis for relief.

Although it did not completely supplant the Free Exercise Clause, heavy reliance on the Free Speech Clause created other problems. As explained in Chapter 4, it elided the ways in which exclusionary government policies harmed *religious* freedoms. Using the public forum doctrine as a general measure of rights to religious inclusion also complicated understandings of the Establishment Clause. The negative implications of the free speech turn for religious liberty were highlighted in *Christian Legal Society v. Martinez* (2010), in which the Supreme Court held that a public law school could compel a Christian student organization to accept members that did not share its religious beliefs as a condition of official recognition. Again, it was the public forum doctrine, not free exercise or religious association rights, that determined the case's outcome.

Chapter 6 discussed the extent to which abortion rights have been litigated in free speech terms. In this context, too, religious conservatives turned to the Free Speech Clause, this time to defend their efforts to limit access to abortion services and to advocate for such limits. Abortion clinic "free speech" controversies produced several important precedents; but remarkably, none of them ever mentioned that the controversies centered on the exercise of a constitutional right to abortion. Women were considered "patients" seeking "health care services." The Justices upheld or rejected various limitations on protesters' and sidewalk counselors' speech, with most (with the notable exception of Justice Scalia) never acknowledging the underlying right to abortion. The cases were reported in the press as "free speech" cases, which of course they were. But they were also about the Due Process Clause-based right to terminate a pregnancy. So were cases involving protests targeting the residence of abortion providers, threats communicated to abortion providers, and spending conditions that limited access to abortion services. Yet in all of these cases, as well, there was no mention at all of abortion rights.

Finally, as discussed in Chapter 7, scholars, litigants, and courts—including the Supreme Court—have long relied on analogies between the Free Speech Clause and the Second Amendment. This simple analogical reasoning has morphed into explicit modeling of Second Amendment rights on Free Speech Clause doctrines and principles. As in the case of the Free Exercise Clause, this approach would not result in the Free Speech Clause supplanting the Second Amendment. However, it would construct the right to keep and bear arms in the image of free speech rights. This borrowing ignores important historical, practical, and theoretical differences between free speech and firearms protections.

The only rights provision examined in prior chapters that did not experience some form of free speech domination was the Equal Protection Clause. It is true that for some time, the Supreme Court treated equal protection and free speech claims as essentially interchangeable. However, that treatment did not indicate a dominance of one provision over the other. As they pertain to Equal Protection Clause, free speech rights have primarily been used to facilitate and mediate recognition and mobilization, respectively. Proponents of constitutional equality did not seek to model equal protection rights on free speech principles or doctrines, or substitute free speech for equality rights. Instead, freedom of speech (like due process) was considered a means to an end, particularly in early stages of constitutional equality movements.

As the abortion and Second Amendment examples show, Free Speech Clause dominance can take many forms. The Free Speech Clause can supplant, subordinate, substitute for, and obscure other constitutional rights. In all of these forms, free speech dominance reduces the prospects for a robust and effective system of constitutional rights.

Outright expansionism, as in the case of the Assembly Clause, Press Clause, and Petition Clause, poses the gravest threat to Rights Pluralism.[8] This form of dominance supplants non-speech provisions, creates constitutional redundancies, and reduces the number of potential trumps on government. It subsumes several independent checks and fundamental trumps into a collective protection for "expressive rights."

Further, in all of its various forms, expansionism tends to *standardize* constitutional rights. In a system dominated by the Free Speech Clause, constitutional liberty is protected insofar as the regulated activity—assembly, publication, petition, prayer, etc.—can be characterized as "speech." This standardization reduces or eliminates the conceptual space between constitutional rights, which in turn reduces or eliminates opportunities for synergy and mutual illumination. When constitutional rights are standardized, opportunities to compare and contrast their distinct coverages, meanings, doctrines, and principles are lost.

We have a much better understanding of the scope and substance of the Free Exercise Clause, the Equal Protection Clause, and the Due Process Clause precisely because we have had some opportunities to see these provisions interact with one another, and with the Free Speech Clause, as independent guarantees. For this same reason, we also have a better understanding of the Free Speech Clause.

The magnetism and appeal of the Free Speech Clause has undermined the independent development of other constitutional rights. It has sometimes distracted litigants, scholars, and courts from considering or approving substantive changes to equal protection, free exercise, abortion, and other rights. Framing claims primarily or exclusively as free speech concerns has devalued non-speech rights and retarded their development.

When the Free Speech Clause supplants other constitutional rights, the subordinated provisions survive in name only. Litigation, academic, and other resources are directed to developing free speech principles and theories rather than the substance of assembly, press, free exercise, and other rights. Academic and judicial discourses are rerouted in the direction of the Free Speech Clause. In short, when the magnetic Free Speech Clause sucks all the oxygen from the room, other rights suffocate.

Expansionism has produced a rights-scape increasingly dominated by free speech doctrines and principles. To sustain Rights Pluralism, we will need to devote as much energy and attention to the substance of other rights provisions as we have to developing the Free Speech Clause. In short, we will need to leverage the facilitative and mediating powers of the Free Speech Clause, while restraining its tendency to dominate and colonize other rights.

Free speech dominance also impacts our constitutional discourse. A myopic focus on free speech rights obscures the importance and purposes of other constitutional rights.[9] Ignoring the non-speech implications of "free speech" controversies, such as those involving the right to abortion, skews debates about the health and vibrancy of other rights and the system of constitutional rights. Over time, over-focusing on free speech suggests that so long as we have free speech rights, we do not really need a system of diverse and independently enforceable constitutional rights.

In addition to these serious effects on non-speech rights, free speech dominance is ultimately bad for the Free Speech Clause and for free speech rights. The effort to characterize so many activities—assembling, accessing and publishing information, petitioning government, praying, etc.—as "speech" stresses the Free Speech Clause by forcing it to perform a wide range of non-speech functions. Information-gathering is certainly related to "speech," but this activity seems more plausibly covered by "press" rights. Similarly, not all gatherings and assemblies are "expressive."

The act of "petitioning" government is also expressive, but it is directed to a special audience—government officials. Finally, although it occurs through speech, prayer is a uniquely *religious* practice or ritual best preserved by ensuring a robust Free Exercise Clause.

In part owing to the stress placed on the Free Speech Clause, expansionism often complicates doctrines and principles on the free speech side of the relationship. Indeed, this was true in each of the rights relationships studied in previous chapters. To some degree, doctrinal complications are a natural consequence of Rights Dynamism. However, these complications are exacerbated by free speech expansionism. As Michael McConnell has demonstrated, courts and others can avoid some of these complications by constraining the inclination to rely on the Free Speech Clause. Thus, as McConnell argues, basing the Supreme Court's decision in *Citizens United* on the Press Clause would have avoided some of the complications occasioned by the Court's reliance on the Free Speech Clause.[10]

Finally, to some extent, expansionism may be detrimental to free speech rights themselves. Insofar as they devote insufficient energy to establishing and exercising other constitutional rights, people may be less able or willing to participate as full members of the political community. A speaker armed only with free speech rights is not as well-positioned to challenge governmental authority as one enjoying robust assembly, petition, free exercise, and other rights. Here, too, the relationship between free speech and other constitutional rights is bidirectional.

Surely, one might argue, there is some value in looking to the Free Speech Clause when considering the nature and scope of other constitutional rights. Imitation is the sincerest form of flattery. And as a fundamental right that has expanded individual liberty and inspired constitutional change, freedom of speech seems very much worth imitating.

Indeed, there are good reasons to imitate and borrow from the Free Speech Clause. For example, it seems appropriate to invoke the example of the Free Speech Clause to advocate in favor of recognition of a neighboring and seemingly equally fundamental right, like the right to keep and bear arms. However, it is quite a different thing to mechanically map the Free Speech Clause's doctrines and principles onto the Second Amendment.[11] As discussed in Chapter 7, recalling the history and experience of free speech rights can certainly inform the present and future scope of Second Amendment rights. But the Second Amendment needs space to develop on its own merits, rather than with regard to ill-fitting free speech concepts such as prior restraint, content neutrality, and public forum.

It seems rather obvious but, as this study demonstrates, nevertheless worth emphasizing that the Free Speech Clause is a necessary but radically insufficient guarantee of individual liberty. It does not provide oppressed minorities, assemblies, press institutions, religious adherents, gun owners, and others with anything close to the full coverage and protection afforded under a plural system of constitutional rights.

Relatedly, it also seems an obvious proposition that we need to maintain the independence of each of the (relatively few) individual rights provisions in the Constitution. Indeed, the Supreme Court has emphasized that constitutional provisions are not to be interpreted in ways that render them nullities or redundancies.[12] However, that is precisely how some of the rights in the Bill of Rights are currently interpreted. When one considers the vast powers granted to modern governments and the relatively few rights "trumps" in the Constitution, the subordination or effective loss of even one, much less a few, constitutional rights is cause for alarm.

Pursuing Pluralism

We have a vitally important and facilitative Free Speech Clause that sometimes exhibits expansionist tendencies. In light of these facts, what can be done to further the goals of Rights Pluralism? There are no simple fixes. Pursuing Rights Pluralism will take time and hard work, by all who are participants in our system of constitutional rights. This includes activists, litigators, judges, scholars, and the public at large. This final part proposes an agenda, based on the dynamic relationships examined in previous chapters, which will move us in the direction of a more pluralistic system of constitutional rights. Connecting the bookend themes of the study this agenda aims to convert Rights Dynamism into Rights Pluralism.

RIGHTS EDUCATION

Despite the frequency with which Americans invoke the Constitution in private and public discussions, relatively few have a rudimentary grasp of its rights provisions. If Americans are to appreciate and understand the importance of having a plural system of constitutional rights, they will need to learn more about the rights that comprise that system.

A recent survey found that more than one in three Americans (37 percent) could not name *a single right* protected by the First Amendment (never mind more "obscure" rights provisions such as the Equal Protection Clause or Due Process Clause). Of those who could do so, nearly half recalled freedom of speech. But only 15 percent recalled that the First Amendment protects freedom of religion. This shortcoming is not limited to constitutional rights. Basic knowledge concerning our system of government—for instance, the fact that the powers of the national government are divided into three branches or departments—is also vanishingly thin.[13]

These results will come as no surprise to political scientists and other scholars, who have long studied constitutional ignorance.[14] However, if the project is to revive and invigorate Rights Pluralism, this lack of knowledge is especially worrisome. Having and maintaining a robust system of constitutional rights presupposes that the beneficiaries of that system know something about its various components.

To be sure, as this book has shown, activists, lawyers, judges, and scholars—elites—are the primary participants in terms of bringing and assessing constitutional rights claims. Their functions in that regard are discussed below. However, as noted in the Introduction, rights are more than formal legal trumps. They are forms of rhetoric and power. In those respects, public knowledge and opinion are vitally important to the project of Rights Pluralism.

There are many possibilities in terms of providing public rights education. Basic civics education is an obvious place to start. Press institutions, which influence public understanding of constitutional rights, could better educate reporters on their substance and scope. Like the general public, American media tend to gravitate toward free speech contests and conflicts, while devoting far less attention to Fourth Amendment, due process, privacy, and other constitutional rights. This convention both reflects and reinforces the negative effects of free speech expansionism.

These basic educational initiatives will not produce a populace fully literate in constitutional rights. However, they might improve basic knowledge of our system of rights, and highlight the necessity of having plural checks on government.

RIGHTS DISCOURSE

Merely being *aware* of the system of constitutional rights is not enough to ensure that the system operates effectively. Individuals must also be free to discuss, publish information about, and resist official compulsion with regard to their discourse concerning constitutional rights. This part of the Rights Pluralism agenda relates specifically to freedom of speech.

Chapter 2 emphasized the importance of protecting rights to communicate about or concerning constitutional rights. One of the central functions of the Free Speech Clause is to ensure that there are open channels of communication about matters of public concern. This obviously includes discussions relating to the recognition, scope, and exercise of non-speech constitutional rights. Simply put, individuals must be free to discuss whether to recognize a constitutional right, what limits there ought to be on recognized rights, and the most effective means of exercising and enforcing those rights.

As indicated in Chapter 2, this is quite different from saying that Americans should characterize all of their arguments concerning policy and politics in constitutional rights terms. "Rights speech" addresses the more fundamental principle that the people ought to be free to discuss the nature and extent of limits on government.

Regulations of rights speech, which are more prevalent than one might assume, implicate both free speech and the underlying non-speech rights. They affect the ability to discuss, consider, and effectively exercise a range of constitutional rights. Thus, limiting governmental suppression or compulsion of rights speech can help protect the system of constitutional rights.

It is also important to Rights Pluralism that we protect the free flow of information concerning constitutional rights. Governmental interventions that restrict access to information about rights manipulate and skew rights discourse. Ensuring that people know what their various rights are, as well as when and how those rights can be enforced, is also part of the educative process described above.

RECOVERING RIGHTS IN EXILE

Educating the public about constitutional rights and protecting basic rights to communicate about constitutional rights will not be enough. We will also need to work to recover, to the extent possible, constitutional rights that the Free Speech Clause has subordinated or supplanted.

In the legal academy, serious efforts are underway to recover, revive, and rescue First Amendment assembly, press, and petition rights from the shadow of the Free Speech Clause. Scholars have proposed theories and approaches that seek to disaggregate free speech and other First Amendment rights.[15] If adopted, their approaches would at least partially revive or recover long-supplanted rights provisions. As discussed in Chapter 3, these rights have been downgraded to a status "ancillary" to the Free Speech Clause.

Disaggregating these provisions is a necessary first step toward recovering a suite of "corollary" and "kaleidoscopic" First Amendment rights.[16] If these approaches and interpretations find their way into judicial decisions and constitutional discourses, we may see a dynamic change in the rhetoric and power of First Amendment rights. If that is to occur, activists, civic institutions, academics, and courts will need to get involved in the recovery effort.

As scholars have recognized and this book confirms, the events that conspired to place these rights in exile spanned many decades. Combating this phenomenon will likely require a similar timetable.

PLURAL RIGHTS THEORIES

Although it may at first seem counter-intuitive, we also need to devote more intellectual energy to developing *relational* rights theories. In other words, we first need to disaggregate free speech and non-speech rights. We then need to re-connect those rights in ways that produce synergies and mutual benefits.

As noted in the book's Introduction, aside from the efforts of a few notable intratextualist scholars, constitutional rights tend to be treated as if they operate in segregated silos. However, as noted in Chapter 3, some scholars are working to change this perspective. Thus, with regard to First Amendment rights, Ashutosh Bhagwat and John Inazu have developed approaches that treat these rights provisions as "cognate" and "kaleidoscopic."[17] They have argued that free speech, assembly, press, and free exercise rights can and should be invoked, studied, and enforced in light of their democratic, pluralistic, and other *common* purposes. These approaches do not ignore differences between and among rights. However, they emphasize the common ties that bind these rights together and the synergies that occur when they are treated as companionate guarantees.

The relational treatment of rights in this book shows that this project can be extended beyond the rights in the First Amendment. Treating the Constitution's rights provisions as "cognate" and "kaleidoscopic" rather than hermetically segregated from one another can help to illuminate their common values and purposes. Placed in relational context, rights can illuminate one another's meanings in unexpected ways. Through Rights Dynamism, constitutional rights can form new combinations that enhance constitutional liberty.[18] Considering rights in clusters, or in dynamic duos, can help clarify how and why they are interpreted differently, but also how and why they might facilitate common objectives.[19]

Scholars are just beginning to devote more sustained attention to the relational aspects of our system of constitutional rights.[20] They are studying the effects of cumulative and aggregate constitutional rights claims, and developing interpretive theories that focus on the *sum* of the parts of our system of rights. As in the case of efforts to rescue individual rights provisions, it will be necessary to translate these new insights into tangible results.

Obergefell v. Hodges (2015), which rooted a right to marriage equality in both the Equal Protection Clause and Due Process Clause, demonstrates that synergistic and pluralistic approaches to constitutional rights can produce precedents. In terms of articulating the connections between equal protection and due process rights, *Obergefell* barely scratches the surface. The success of Rights Pluralism will depend, in part, on whether Rights Dynamism will reveal the relational attributes and powers of the Constitution's rights provisions.

Notes

INTRODUCTION

1. Palko v. Connecticut, 302 U.S. 319, 327 (1937).

2. Akhil Reed Amar, "First Amendment Firstness," 47 *U.C. Davis L. Rev.* 1015, 1027 (2014).

3. Steven H. Shiffrin, *What's Wrong with the First Amendment?* 4 (Cambridge Univ. Press, 2016).

4. See Akhil Reed Amar, *The Bill of Rights: Creation and Reconstruction* xi (Yale Univ. Press, 1998) ("Instead of being studied holistically, the Bill [of Rights] has been broken up into discrete blocks of text, with each segment examined in isolation.").

5. See Obergefell v. Hodges, 135 S. Ct. 2584 (2015).

6. Since the free speech/non-speech distinction is central to the book, a couple of preliminary comments concerning this terminology are in order. First, the distinction sets the Free Speech Clause and freedom of speech apart from other *First Amendment* rights that are typically described as "expressive." This group includes the right of peaceable assembly, freedom of the press, and the right to petition government for redress of grievances. Chapter 3 criticizes the collapse of all of these rights into the Free Speech Clause or what it refers to as a "Free Expression Clause." Second, although there is typically some overlap between free speech and non-speech rights, the book treats these rights provisions as distinct and independently enforceable. For example, as discussed in Chapter 4, the Free Exercise Clause protects certain kinds of religious speech that are also covered by the Free Speech Clause. However, these rights provisions differ in terms of their histories, texts, and substantive coverages. The book treats their overlapping qualities as part of the dynamics by which rights relate to and influence one another.

7. See generally Akhil Reed Amar, "Intratextualism," 112 *Harv. L. Rev.* 747 (1999).

8. For recent examples of scholarly work that focus on the relational nature of rights, see Kerry Abrams & Brandon L. Garrett, "Cumulative Constitutional Rights," 97 *B.U. L. Rev.* 1310 (2017) (discussing "cumulative," "hybrid," and "intersecting" constitutional rights claims); Michael Coenen, "Combining Constitutional Clauses," 164 *U. Pa. L. Rev.* 1067 (2016) (examining Supreme Court decisions that combine rights in various ways in order to resolve cases).

9. *The Federalist*, No. 48.

10. Jack M. Balkin, "Digital Speech and Democratic Culture: A Theory of Freedom of Expression for the Information Society," 79 *N.Y.U. L. Rev.* 1, 57 (2004).

11. Id.

12. Id.

13. See, e.g., Pamela S. Karlan, "Equal Protection, Due Process, and the Stereoscopic Fourteenth Amendment," 33 *McGeorge L. Rev.* 473 (2002) (examining the interactions between the Fourteenth Amendment's Due Process Clause and Equal Protection Clause).

14. Obergefell v. Hodges, 135 S. Ct. 2584 (2015).

15. Id. at 2593.

16. Id.

17. Id. at 2596.

18. See, e.g., United States v. Chester, 628 F.3d 673, 682 (4th Cir. 2010) (considering First Amendment doctrines as a general model for developing Second Amendment law); Mark Tushnet, "*Heller* and the Perils of Compromise," 13 *Lewis & Clark L. Rev.* 419, 421–23 (2012) (suggesting that First Amendment doctrines might provide a general template for adjudicating Second Amendment claims).

19. See generally Timothy Zick, "Rights Dynamism," 19 *U. Pa. J. Const. L.* 791 (2017).

20. *See* Amar, *The Bill of Rights*, supra note 4, at 235 (observing that Reconstruction Republicans frequently mentioned and invoked free speech rights in debates); Michael W. McConnell, "The Problem of Singling Out Religion," 50 *DePaul L. Rev.* 1, 16 (2000) (noting the connection between early struggles to publish religious tracts and freedom of the press); John Howard Yoder, "Response of an Amateur Historian and a Religious Citizen," 7 *J.L. & Religion* 417, 417 (1989) ("There was a long British Puritan history, from the age of Milton to the 1689 Bill of Rights, in the course of which the civil freedoms of speech, press, and assembly arose out of religious agitation, not the other way round.").

21. Amar, supra note 2, at 1027.

22. See, e.g., Carlos A. Ball, *The First Amendment and LGBT Equality: A Contentious History* (Harvard Univ. Press, 2017) (explaining how LGBT claimants used the Free Speech Clause to advance equality rights); Daniel Hildebrand, "Free Speech and Constitutional Transformation," 10 *Const. Comm.* 133 (1993) (discussing religious adherents' successful use of free speech and press claims during the 1930s and 1940s); Harry Kalven, Jr., *The Negro and the First Amendment* (Univ. of Chicago Press, 1965) (describing civil rights advocates' use of expressive rights to advance racial equality).

23. See Amar, supra note 2, at 1027 (observing that it would not be possible to have a robust constitutional democracy without expressive freedoms).

24. N.Y. Times Co. v. Sullivan, 376 U.S. 254, 279–80 (1964).

25. See, e.g., Robert C. Post & Reva B. Siegel, "Legislative Constitutionalism and Section Five Power: Policentric Interpretation of the Family and Medical Leave Act," 112 *Yale L.J.* 1943, 2030

(2003) (observing that "the First Amendment ensures that all Americans can express their beliefs about the Constitution").

26. See id. (noting the importance of freedom of speech to constitutional discourse).

27. Balkin, supra note 10, at 57.

28. See Amar, *The Bill of Rights*, supra note 4, at 235 (observing that Reconstruction Republicans frequently mentioned and invoked expressive rights in debates).

29. See Reva B. Siegel, "The Jurisgenerative Role of Social Movements in United States Constitutional Law," at 11 (for publication with the papers of the Seminario en Latino América de Teoria Constitucional y Politica (SELA), June 10–12, 2004, Oaxaca, México) (emphasizing the need each movement has "to express its values as public values" and to persuade citizens and officials to recognize claims).

30. Frederick Schauer, "The Boundaries of the First Amendment: A Preliminary Exploration of Constitutional Salience," 117 *Harv. L. Rev.* 1765, 1787–800 (2004).

31. See Leslie Kendrick, "First Amendment Expansionism," 56 *Wm. & Mary L. Rev.* 1199, 1200 (2015) (describing "expansionism" as the situation "where the First Amendment's territory pushes outward to encompass ever more areas of law").

32. See John Inazu, *Liberty's Refuge: The Forgotten Freedom of Assembly* (Yale Univ. Press, 2012); Ronald J. Krotoszynski, Jr., *Reclaiming the Petition Clause: Seditious Libel, "Offensive Protest," and the Right to Petition Government for a Redress of Grievances* (Yale Univ. Press, 2012); Sonja R. West, "First Amendment Neighbors," 66 *Ala. L. Rev.* 357 (2014).

33. See Employment Div. v. Smith, 494 U.S. 872 (1990).

34. See Mark Tushnet, "The Redundant Free Exercise Clause?," 33 *Loyola U. Chi. L. Rev.* 71 (2001).

35. See Schauer, supra note 30, at 1795 (discussing the rhetorical attractiveness of free speech arguments).

36. See, e.g., Frederick Schauer, "First Amendment Opportunism," in Lee C. Bollinger & Geoffrey R. Stone, *Eternally Vigilant: Free Speech in the Modern Era* (Univ. of Chicago Press, 2003).

37. See Frederick Schauer, "The Politics and Incentives of First Amendment Coverage," 56 *Wm. & Mary L. Rev.* 1613, 1635 (2015) (suggesting, among other possibilities, that opportunism may weaken searching judicial review of governmental decision-making and strict standards relating to punishment of certain categories of speech).

38. See Amanda Shanor, "The New *Lochner*," 2016 *Wisc. L. Rev.* 133 (2016).

39. See, e.g., Frederick Mark Gedicks, "Towards a Defensible Free Exercise Doctrine," 68 *Geo. Wash. L. Rev.* 925 (2000); Robert W. Tuttle, "How Firm a Foundation? Protecting Religious Land Use after *Boerne*," 68 *Geo. Wash. L. Rev.* 861 (2000).

40. For discussions of doctrinal borrowing in the Second Amendment context, see, e.g., Joseph Blocher, "Categoricalism and Balancing in First and Second Amendment Analysis," 84 *N.Y.U. L. Rev.* 375 (2009) (comparing the categorical and balancing approaches in the areas of speech regulation and gun control); Gregory P. Magarian, "Speaking Truth to Firepower: How the First Amendment Destabilizes the Second," 91 *Tex. L. Rev.* 49 (2012) (arguing that First Amendment theory and doctrine do not support a robust right to bear arms).

41. See generally Eugene Volokh, "Freedom of Speech and the Constitutional Tension Method," 3 *U. Chi. Roundtable* 223 (1996) (critiquing rights balancing).

42. See Nebraska Press Ass'n v. Stuart, 437 U.S. 539, 560–61 (1976) (noting that free press and fair trial rights sometimes clash, and that the press has an obligation to safeguard the fairness of trial proceedings); Bartnicki v. Vopper, 532 U.S. 514, 534 (2001) (holding that privacy interest in contents of private conversation gave way to public interest in dissemination of information on matters of public concern); Snyder v. Phelps, 562 U.S. 433 (2011) (holding that members of a church who protested at military funerals and conveyed messages such as "God Hates Fags" could not be held liable for the common law tort of intentional infliction of emotional distress). In one case, the right to vote managed to prevail in a balancing contest with freedom of speech. See Burson v. Freeman, 504 U.S. 191, 211 (1992) (plurality opinion) (upholding limits on political campaign speech near polling places).

43. See, e.g., Jeremy Waldron, *The Harm in Hate Speech* (Harvard Univ. Press, 2012).

44. See, e.g., Boy Scouts of America v. Dale, 530 U.S. 640 (2000) (recognizing a right not to associate with homosexual members).

45. See Ball, supra note 22, at 278 (noting the "duality of the [first] amendment's relationship to sexual equality").

46. See Karlan, supra note 13, at 474 (observing that "the ideas of equality and liberty expressed in the equal protection and due process clauses each emerge from and reinforce one another")

47. See, e.g., Robert Post, "Informed Consent to Abortion: A First Amendment Analysis of Compelled Physician Speech," 2007 *U. Ill. L. Rev.* 939 (2007) (discussing compelled speech doctrine as applied to mandatory abortion disclosures); Kent Greenawalt, "Viewpoints from Olympus," 96 *Colum. L. Rev.* 697 (1996) (criticizing Supreme Court's content-neutrality analysis in religious speech cases).

48. For some examples of these approaches, see generally Amar, "Intratextualism," supra note 7; David Strauss, *The Living Constitution* (Oxford Univ. Press, 2010); Jack M. Balkin, *Living Originalism* (The Belknap Press of Harv. Univ. Press, 2011); David Cole, *Engines of Liberty* (Basic Books, 2015); Mark V. Tushnet, "The Constitution Outside the Courts: A Preliminary Inquiry," 26 *Val. L. Rev.* 427 (1992).

49. See Timothy Zick, "Rights Speech," 48 *U.C. Davis L. Rev.* 1 (2014).

50. See Post & Siegel, supra note 25, at 2030 (noting the importance to social and constitutional movements of free and uninhibited discourse about constitutional rights).

51. DeJonge v. Oregon, 299 U.S. 353, 364 (1937).

52. See, e.g., Toni M. Massaro, "Gay Rights, Thick and Thin," 49 *Stan. L. Rev.* 45, 63 (1996) ("As an all-encompassing metaphor or a complete theory of constitutional rights for gays, lesbians, and bisexuals, [freedom of expression] falls short.").

CHAPTER 1

1. See, e.g., Ashutosh Bhagwat, "The Democratic First Amendment," 110 *Nw. U. L. Rev.* 1097 (2016) (arguing that the "democratic rights protected by the First Amendment are not independent points, but rather are deeply interrelated and overlapping").

2. See Timothy Zick, "Rights Speech," 48 *U.C. Davis L. Rev.* 1 (2014) (observing that freedom of speech intersects with a number of constitutional rights, including abortion and Second Amendment rights); Kerry Abrams & Brandon Garrett, "Cumulative Constitutional Rights," 97 *B.U. L. Rev.* 1310 (2017) (arguing that constitutional rights frequently intersect and combine in ways that inform constitutional remedies).

3. See Abrams & Garrett, supra note 2 (focusing on remedial concerns).

4. See Michael Coenen, "Combining Constitutional Clauses," 164 *U. Pa. L. Rev.* 1067, 1078–83 (2016) (examining how the Supreme Court sometimes combines constitutional provisions to decide cases).

5. See generally Timothy Zick, "Rights Dynamism," 19 *U. Pa. J. Const. L.* 791 (2017).

6. Jack M. Balkin, "Digital Speech and Democratic Culture: A Theory of Freedom of Expression for the Information Society," 79 *N.Y.U. L. Rev.* 1, 55 (2004).

7. Id.

8. See, e.g., Ronald Dworkin, *Taking Rights Seriously* (Harv. U. Press, 1978); John Finnis, *Natural Law and Natural Rights* (Oxford Univ. Press, 1980); Jeremy Waldron, ed., *Theories of Rights* (Oxford Univ. Press, 1984).

9. Ronald Dworkin, "Rights as Trumps," in Waldron, supra note 8, at 153–67.

10. Balkin, supra note 6, at 57.

11. Id.

12. Id.

13. See Randy E. Barnett, *Restoring the Lost Constitution: The Presumption of Liberty* (Princeton Univ. Press, 2004); John Hart Ely, Democracy and Distrust: A Theory of Judicial Review (Harvard Univ. Press, 1980); Cass R. Sunstein, Democracy and the Problem of Free Speech (Free Press, 1995).

14. See Akhil Reed Amar, "Intratextualism," 112 *Harv. L. Rev.* 747 (1999).

15. See David Strauss, *The Living Constitution* (Oxford Univ. Press, 2010).

16. See, e.g., David Cole, *Engines of Liberty* (Basic Books, 2015) (emphasizing role of civil society organizations in constitutional change); Jack M. Balkin, *Living Originalism* (The Belknap Press of Harv. Univ. Press, 2011) (describing a process of "living originalism" that relies on historical understandings of the text, but also posits that changes in constitutional meaning are the product of dynamic, evolutionary, and public processes involving a multitude of participants); Larry D. Kramer, *The People Themselves: Popular Constitutionalism and Judicial Review* (Oxford Univ. Press, 2005) (examining popular constitutionalism); Reva B. Siegel, "The Jurisgenerative Role of Social Movements in United States Constitutional Law," at 11 (for publication with the papers of the Seminario en Latino América de Teoria Constitucional y Politica (SELA), June 10–12, 2004, Oaxaca, México) (focusing on the processes and challenges of constitutional movements).

17. See, e.g., Adarand Constructors, Inc. v. Pena, 515 U.S. 200, 227 (1995) (describing equal protection as a "personal" right).

18. See, e.g., Balkin, *Living Originalism*, supra note 16, at 237 (explaining how subsequent amendments relating to the right to vote, including the Nineteenth, Twenty-Fourth, and Twenty-Sixth Amendments, "interact with" the Fifteenth Amendment).

19. See Michael W. McConnell, "The Problem of Singling Out Religion," 50 *DePaul L. Rev.* 1, 16 (2000) (noting the connection between early struggles to publish religious tracts and freedom of the press); John Howard Yoder, "Response of an Amateur Historian and a Religious Citizen," 7 *J.L. & Religion* 417, 417 (1989) ("There was a long British Puritan history, from the age of Milton to the 1689 Bill of Rights, in the course of which the civil freedoms of speech, press, and assembly arose out of religious agitation, not the other way round.").

20. See Bhagwat, supra note 1, at 1099–1100 (observing that expressive rights are connected by a common concern with democratic participation).

21. See Balkin, *Living Originalism*, supra note 16, at 222 (explaining that Section One of the Fourteenth Amendment was originally intended to prohibit caste legislation).

22. See Griswold v. Connecticut, 381 U.S. 479, 484 (1965) (articulating a "penumbral" approach to privacy that relied on a number of different individual rights, including First Amendment rights).

23. Obergefell v. Hodges, 135 S. Ct. 2584, 2593 (2015).

24. Laurence H. Tribe, "Equal Dignity: Speaking Its Name," 129 *Harv. L. Rev. Forum* 16 (2015).

25. See Kenji Yoshino, "A New Birth of Freedom?: Obergefell v. Hodges," 129 *Harv. L. Rev.* 147, 148–71 (2015) (discussing long-term cross-doctrinal developments that contributed to recognition of marriage equality right).

26. See Pamela S. Karlan, "Equal Protection, Due Process, and the Stereoscopic Fourteenth Amendment," 33 *McGeorge L. Rev.* 473, 474 (2002) (observing that "the ideas of equality and liberty expressed in the equal protection and due process clauses each emerge from and reinforce one another").

27. See generally Akhil Reed Amar, *The Bill of Rights: Creation and Reconstruction* (Yale Univ. Press, 1998). See also Strauss, supra note 15, at 53 ("The central principles of the American system of freedom of expression . . . are not the product of a moment of inspired constitutional genius 200-plus years ago. We owe those principles, instead, to the living, common law Constitution.").

28. See Strauss, supra note 15, at 62 (observing that the process of interpreting freedom of speech principles "developed over fifty years, often through trial and error"); Balkin, *Living Originalism*, supra note 16, at 229 ("Interpreting the Equal Protection Clause today means interpreting it after the New Deal, after the civil rights revolution, and after the second wave of American feminism.").

29. See, e.g., Ry. Express Agency v. New York, 336 U.S. 106 (1949) (raising both due process and equal protection challenges to municipal ordinance that restricted commercial advertising).

30. See David Cole, *Engines of Liberty* Part II (Basic Books, 2015).

31. See, e.g., Karlan, supra note 26, at 474–75 (describing scholars' contributions to the shift in LGBT cases from the Due Process Clause to the Equal Protection Clause).

32. See Samuel Warren & Louis Brandeis, "The Right to Privacy," 4 *Harv. L. Rev.* 193 (1890).

33. See Harry Kalven, Jr., *The Negro and the First Amendment* (Univ. of Chicago Press, 1965).

34. See, e.g., Karlan, supra note 26, at 474 (observing that "the ideas of equality and liberty expressed in the equal protection and due process clauses each emerge from and reinforce one another").

35. See, e.g., Carey v. Brown, 447 U.S. 455, 471–72 (1980) (Stewart, J., concurring) (arguing that the Free Speech Clause, rather than the Equal Protection Clause, was the proper grounds for invalidating a content-based picketing restriction).

36. See Karlan, *supra* note 26, at 480–83 (suggesting that the Due Process Clause has sometimes limited the scope of the Equal Protection Clause).

37. See Obergefell, 135 S. Ct. at 2593 (discussing relationship between Due Process Clause and Equal Protection Clause, as it relates to same-sex marriage).

38. See Employment Div. v. Smith, 494 U.S. 872, 878–89 (1990) (recognizing the "hybrid" constitutional claim). But see Michael W. McConnell, "Free Exercise Revisionism and the *Smith* Decision," 57 *U. Chi. L. Rev.* 1109, 1122 (1990) (criticizing the concept of "hybrid" rights).

39. See Palko v. Connecticut, 302 U.S. 319, 327 (1937) (incorporating the Free Speech Clause).

40. See Akhil Reed Amar, *The Bill of Rights: Creation and Reconstruction* 235 (Yale Univ. Press, 1998) (observing that Reconstruction Republicans frequently mentioned and invoked expressive rights in debates).

41. See generally Daniel Hildebrand, "Free Speech and Constitutional Transformation," 10 *Const. Comment.* 133 (1993) (examining the Hughes Court decisions of the 1930s and 1940s, which elaborated on free speech, free press, and free exercise rights).

42. See, e.g., Police Dept. of Chicago v. Mosley, 408 U.S. 92, 100 (1972) (invalidating under Equal Protection Clause restriction on picketing near schools).

43. See Stephen Brown, *Trumping Religion: The New Christian Right, the Free Speech Clause, and the Courts* (Alabama Univ. Press, 2008) (examining Christian Right's free speech litigation strategy during the 1980s and 1990s).

44. See, e.g., Gregory P. Magarian, "Speaking Truth to Firepower: How the First Amendment Destabilizes the Second," 91 *Tex. L. Rev.* 49 (2012); Joseph Blocher, "Categoricalism and Balancing in First and Second Amendment Analysis," 84 *N.Y.U. L. Rev.* 375 (2009); Alan Brownstein, "Protecting Religious Liberty: The False Messiahs of Free Speech Doctrine and Formal Neutrality," 18 *J.L. & Pol.* 119, 131–33 (2002); Nan D. Hunter, "Life after *Hardwick*," 27 *Harv. C.R.-C.L. L. Rev.* 531 (1992); Richard Delgado, "Words That Wound: A Tort Action for Racial Insults, Epithets, and Name-Calling," 17 *Harv. C.R.-C.L. L. Rev.* 133 (1982).

45. See Wollschlaeger v. Governor of Florida, 797 F.3d 859, 900 (11th Cir. 2015) (upholding state law prohibiting physicians from asking patients about firearms ownership unless medically appropriate); Planned Parenthood of Se. Pa. v. Casey, 505 U.S. 833, 884 (1992) (plurality opinion) (upholding compelled abortion disclosure provision).

46. See Bhagwat, supra note 1, at 1 ("The rest of the First Amendment—the Press, Assembly, and Petition Clauses—might as well not exist.").

47. See, e.g., Frederick Schauer, "First Amendment Opportunism," in Lee C. Bollinger & Geoffrey R. Stone, *Eternally Vigilant: Free Speech in the Modern Era* (Univ. of Chicago Press, 2002). See also Leslie Kendrick, "First Amendment Expansionism," 56 *Wm. & Mary L. Rev.* 1199, 1200 (2015) (describing "expansionism" as the situation "where the First Amendment's territory pushes outward to encompass ever more areas of law").

CHAPTER 2

1. See generally Timothy Zick, "Rights Speech," 48 *U.C. Davis L. Rev.* 1 (2014); Timothy Zick, "Professional Rights Speech," 47 *Ariz. St. L.J.* 1 (2016).

2. I am grateful to one of my manuscript reviewers for suggesting that I distinguish among the different types of rights speech.

3. Central Radio Co., Inc. v. City of Norfolk, 776 F.3d 229 (4th Cir. 2015), aff'd in part, rev'd in part, and remanded, 811 F.3d 625 (4th Cir. 2016).

4. Subsequent to the Fourth Circuit's decision, the Supreme Court invalidated a sign code that was very similar to Norfolk's, on the ground that it was based on subject matter and failed to satisfy strict scrutiny. See Reed v. Town of Gilbert, 135 S. Ct. 2218 (2015). The Fourth Circuit case was on appeal to the Supreme Court when *Reed* was decided, and was remanded to the Fourth Circuit in light of the Court's decision.

5. Central Radio Co., 776 F.3d at 242 (Gregory, J., dissenting).

6. Id.

7. See, e.g., Madsen v. Women's Health Center, Inc., 512 U.S. 753, 757 (1994) (invalidating broad bubble provision that banned all unwanted physical approaches, but upholding 36-foot buffer zone and other injunctive provisions); Hill v. Colorado, 530 U.S. 703, 725 (2000) (upholding state law restricting certain unwanted approaches near abortion clinics).

8. See, e.g., S.D. Codified Laws § 34-23A-10.1(1)(c) (2011). See also Planned Parenthood Minn. v. Rounds (Rounds II), 686 F.3d 889, 906 (8th Cir. 2012) (en banc) (upholding mandatory script that required, among other things, that physician inform woman that abortion would affect "human being"); Tex. Med. Providers Performing Abortion Servs. v. Lakey, 667 F.3d 570, 577 (5th Cir. 2012) (rejecting physicians' compelled speech challenge to mandatory abortion disclosure law); Planned Parenthood of Ind., Inc. v. Comm'r of Ind. State Dep't of Health, 794 F. Supp. 2d 892, 916, 918 (S.D. Ind. 2011) (upholding requirement that physicians inform abortion patients that "human physical life begins when a human ovum is fertilized by a human sperm").

9. See Planned Parenthood of the Columbia/Willamette, Inc. v. Am. Coal. of Life Activists, 290 F.3d 1058, 1086 (9th Cir. 20020 (en banc) (upholding imposition of civil liability for distribution of "Wanted" posters and operation of "Nuremberg Files" website that identified specific abortion providers).

10. See, e.g., Frisby v. Schultz, 487 U.S. 474, 488 (1988) (upholding restriction on "targeted picketing" outside residence of abortion provider).

11. See Rust v. Sullivan, 500 U.S. 173, 196 (1991) (upholding federal funding restrictions on abortion counseling by physicians at federally funded programs).

12. See Evergreen Ass'n v. City of New York, 740 F.3d 233, 249–50 (2d Cir. 2014) (invalidating pregnancy center services disclosure provision under strict and intermediate scrutiny); Greater Balt. Ctr. for Pregnancy Concerns, Inc. v. Mayor of Balt. (*Greater Balt. Ctr. I*), 683 F.3d 539, 555 (4th Cir. 2012) (invalidating mandatory pregnancy center disclosures under strict scrutiny). *But see* Fargo Women's Health Org., Inc. v. Larson, 381 N.W.2d 176, 182 (N.D. 1986) (upholding mandatory disclosures).

13. See Frye v. Kan. City Mo. Police Dep't, 375 F.3d 785, 792 (8th Cir. 2004) (holding that a restriction allowing demonstrators to display signs depicting abortion images further from a busy road was narrowly tailored to serve a compelling interest in public safety); Tatton v. City of Cuyahoga Falls, 116 F. Supp. 2d 928, 934 (N.D. Ohio 2000) (finding that officers who had ordered protester to cease displaying images of aborted fetuses were entitled to qualified immunity against free speech claims); St. John's Church in the Wilderness v. Scott, 296 P.3d 273, 283–85 (Colo. App. 2012) (upholding an injunctive provision banning protesters from displaying signs with images of aborted fetuses near a church); and Operation Save Am. v. City of Jackson, 275 P.3d 438, 461 (Wyo. 2012) (suggesting that injunction against display of images of aborted fetuses might be valid if there was sufficient evidence regarding injury or potential injury such as irreparable harm to children).

14. Choose Life Ill., Inc. v. White, 547 F.3d 853, 866 (7th Cir. 2008) (finding that Illinois prohibition of pro-choice license plates but not pro-life ones was reasonable because "[t]o the extent that messages on specialty license plates are regarded as approved by the State, it is reasonable for the State to maintain a position of neutrality on the subject of abortion").

15. In four decisions, the Eleventh Circuit considered, under different standards of scrutiny, a Florida law restricting physician inquiries concerning firearms possession. See Wollschlaeger v. Governor of Fla. (*Wollschlaeger I*), 760 F.3d 1195, 1220 (11th Cir. 2014), vacated and superseded on reh'g, Wollschlaeger v. Governor of Fla. (*Wollschlaeger II*), 797 F.3d 859 (11th Cir. 2015),

vacated and superseded on reh'g, Wollschlaeger v. Governor of Fla., 814 F.3d 1159 (11th Cir. 2015) (*Wollschlaeger III*), vacated and superseded on reh'g en banc, Wollschlaeger v. Governor of Fla. (*Wollschlaeger IV*), 848 F.3d 1293 (11th Cir. 2017).

16. See Jim Malewitz, "Lawmakers Move Swiftly to Block Release of Gun Permit Records," *Stateline* (Mar. 7, 2013), http://www.pewstates.org/projects/stateline/headlines/lawmakers-move-swiftly-to-block-release-of-gun-permit-records-85899457096 (discussing recent enactments in Maine, Virginia, Arkansas, and Mississippi).

17. See Kelsey M. Swanson, "The Right to Know: An Approach to Gun Licenses and Public Access to Government Records," 56 *UCLA L. Rev.* 1579, 1623-25 (2009) (addressing arguments against disclosure of gun records).

18. See "OC Student Ordered to Remove NRA T-Shirt Because it Promotes Gun Violence," CBS Los Angeles, Oct. 2, 2013, available at http://losangeles.cbslocal.com/2013/10/02/oc-high-school-student-ordered-to-remove-nra-t-shirt-because-it-promotes-gun-violence/; Kevin Dolak, "W. Va. Teen Arrested After "Almost Starting Riot" Wearing NRA Shirt to School," abcnews.com, Apr. 22, 2013, available at http://abcnews.go.com/US/west-virginia-teen-arrested-wearing-nra-shirt-school/story?id=19017896#.UXai76KG3To. See also Newsom v. Albemarle County Sch. Bd., 354 F.3d 249 (4th Cir. 2003) (granting student injunction against school prohibition on wearing NRA hunting t-shirt).

19. See FIRE, "First Amendment Rights Trampled by Pittsburgh College after Student Advocates for Concealed Carry of Firearms on Campus," May 27, 2009, available at http://www.thefire.org/first-amendment-rights-trampled-by-pittsburgh-college-after-student-advocates-for-concealed-carry-of-firearms-on-campus/.

20. See Kan. Stat. Ann. § 75-6705 (West 2014) (prohibiting local officials from using state funds to lobby for or against gun control at the state level).

21. See Arthur L. Kellermann & Frederick P. Rivara, "Silencing the Science on Gun Research," 309 *J. Am. Med.* Ass'n. 549 (2013).

22. See Harper v. Poway Unified Sch. Dist., 445 F.3d 1166 (9th Cir. 2006) (upholding against free speech challenge school officials' decision to prohibit student from wearing T-shirt conveying anti-gay message, in part on ground that gay students' self-worth was negatively affected); Riccio v. New Haven Bd. of Ed., 467 F. Supp.2d 216 (D. Conn. 2006) (fact issues precluded summary judgment on claims of same-gender harassment based on sexual orientation).

23. See *Revised Resolution Rule 8.4: Misconduct*, Am. Bar Ass'n, http://www.americanbar.org/content/dam/aba/administrative/professional_responsibility/final_revised_resolution_and_report_109.authcheckdam.pdf (last visited October 15, 2016) (proposing extended protection for transgender individuals and including gender identity in definition of protected groups).

24. See, e.g., Lexington Fayette Urban Cty. Human Rights Comm'n v. Hands on Originals, Inc., No. 2015-CA-000745-MR (Ky. Ct. App. May 12, 2017) (refusal to print T-shirt promoting gay pride festival did not violate anti-discrimination ordinance). Cf. Hurley v. Irish-American Gay, Lesbian, and Bisexual Group of Boston, 515 U.S. 557 (1995) (application of anti-discrimination law to require parade organizers to allow LGBT group to march in parade violated organizers' right not to be compelled to speak). In these cases, which have also sometimes involved bakers, photographers, and others who challenge requirements that they participate in same-sex marriage ceremonies, there is an antecedent question whether there is any compulsion of speech. In the event speech is compelled, it is arguably a form of rights speech—communications that advocate, favor, or accept the equality of LGBT persons.

25. See King v. Governor of N.J., 767 F.3d 216, 240 (3d Cir. 2014) (rejecting Free Speech Clause challenge to New Jersey's ban on sexual orientation change efforts (SOCE) for minor patients); Pickup v. Brown, 740 F.3d 1208, 1231 (9th Cir. 2014) (rejecting Free Speech Clause challenge to California's SOCE ban).

26. There have been a number of cases involving abortion speech in public schools and at colleges and universities. See, e.g., Taylor v. Roswell Indep. Sch. Dist., 713 F.3d 25, 34 (10th Cir. 2013) (upholding restriction on distribution of rubber fetus dolls, owing to concerns about disruption); Heinkel ex rel. Heinkel v. Sch. Bd. of Lee County, 2005 WL 1571077 (M.D. Fla. July 1, 2005) (upholding school's restriction on student distribution of literature addressing alternatives to abortion, based primarily on concerns about disruption); O'Neal v. Falcon, 668 F. Supp. 2d 979, 985–87 (W.D. Tex. 2009) (holding that instructor's decision not to allow student in speech class to discuss abortion did not violate the Free Speech Clause).

27. Walker v. Texas Div., Sons of Confederate Veterans, 135 S. Ct. 2239 (2015).

28. See generally Mary Ann Glendon, *Rights Talk: The Impoverishment of Political Discourse* (The Free Press, 1993); Joseph Blocher, "Gun Rights Talk," 94 *B.U. L. Rev.* 813 (2014).

29. See Akhil Reed Amar, "First Amendment Firstness," 47 *U.C. Davis L. Rev.* 1015, 1027 (2014).

30. See Akhil Reed Amar, *The Bill of Rights: Creation and Reconstruction* 235 (Yale Univ. Press, 1998) (observing that Reconstruction Republicans frequently mentioned and invoked expressive rights in debates).

31. See Reva B. Siegel, "The Jurisgenerative Role of Social Movements in United States Constitutional Law," at 11 (for publication with the papers of the Seminario en Latino América de Teoria Constitucional y Politica (SELA), June 10–12, 2004, Oaxaca, México) (emphasizing the need each movement has "to express its values as public values" and to persuade citizens and officials to recognize claims).

32. N.Y. Times Co. v. Sullivan, 376 U.S. 254, 279–80 (1964).

33. See, e.g., Robert C. Post & Reva B. Siegel, "Legislative Constitutionalism and Section Five Power: Policentric Interpretation of the Family and Medical Leave Act," 112 *Yale L.J.* 1943, 2030 (2003) (observing that "the First Amendment ensures that all Americans can express their beliefs about the Constitution").

34. 515 U.S. 557 (1995).

35. 530 U.S. 640 (2000)

36. See Post & Siegel, supra note 33, at 2030.

37. Obergefell v. Hodges, 135 S. Ct. 2584, 2596 (2015).

38. See Linda Greenhouse & Reva B. Siegel, "Before (and After) *Roe v. Wade*: New Questions about Backlash," 120 *Yale L.J.* 2028 (2011) (surveying arguments about *Roe*'s effect on social and political discourse regarding abortion rights); Reva B. Siegel, "The Right's Reasons: Constitutional Conflict and the Spread of Women-Protective Antiabortion Argument," 57 *Duke L.J.* 1641 (2008) (noting the recent shift toward protection of women as a justification for abortion restrictions).

39. See Alexander Meiklejohn, *Political Freedom: The Constitutional Powers of the People* 24–25 (Harper, 1960) (discussing self-government and other democratic values associated with freedom of speech).

40. Robert Post, *Constitutional Domains: Democracy, Community, Management* 166 (Harvard Univ. Press, 1995).

41. Regarding the concept of speech marketplaces and the search for truth by means of free speech, see Abrams v. United States, 250 U.S. 616, 630 (1919) (Holmes, J., dissenting), and John Stuart Mill, *On Liberty* 16-20 (Hackett Pub. Co., 1978).

42. See Caroline Mala Corbin, "Compelled Disclosures," 65 *Ala. L. Rev.* 1277, 1292–98 (2014) (discussing marketplace-based objections to compelled abortion disclosures).

43. See Bigelow v. Virginia, 421 U.S. 809, 822 (1975) (invalidating restriction on abortion advertising in part because "the activity advertised pertained to constitutional interests").

44. See Corbin, supra note 42, at 1259–58.

45. First Nat'l Bank of Bos. v. Bellotti, 435 U.S. 765, 783 (1978).

46. See Planned Parenthood of Se. Pa. v. Casey, 505 U.S. 833, 883 (1992).

47. See Carol Sanger, "Seeing and Believing: Mandatory Ultrasound and the Path to a Protected Choice," 56 *UCLA L. Rev.* 351, 360–61 (2008) (asking "when or to what extent may the state persuade a person not to exercise a constitutional right?").

48. See Post & Siegel, supra note 33, at 2030 ("the First Amendment ensures that all Americans can express their beliefs about the Constitution").

49. See McCullen v. Coakley, 134 S. Ct. 2518, 2536 (2014) ("Petitioners are not protesters. They seek not merely to express their opposition to abortion, but to inform women of various alternatives and to provide help in pursuing them.").

50. See, e.g., Children of the Rosary v. City of Phoenix, 154 F.3d 972 (9th Cir. 1998) (upholding rejection of pro-life advertisement from city transit spaces).

51. See Rust v. Sullivan, 500 U.S. 173 (1991) (upholding federal regulations prohibiting fund recipients from discussing abortion with patients); Rumsfeld v. Forum for Academic and Institutional Rights, 547 U.S. 47 (2006) (upholding federal condition requiring equal access for military employers to law school campuses). For criticism of the FAIR decision, see Dale Carpenter, "Unanimously Wrong," 2006 *Cato Sup. Ct. Rev.* 217, 246; Erwin Chemerinsky, "Why the Supreme Court Was Wrong about the Solomon Amendment," 1 *Duke J. Const. Law & Pub. Poly.* 259, 275–76.

52. See generally Zick, "Professional Rights Speech," supra note 1.

53. See Lowe v. SEC, 472 U.S. 181, 232 (1985) (White J., concurring) ("Where the personal nexus between professional and client does not exist, and a speaker does not purport to be exercising judgment on behalf of any particular individual with whose circumstances he is directly acquainted, government regulation ceases to function as legitimate regulation of professional practice . . . ; it becomes regulation of speaking or publishing as such, subject to [the First Amendment].").

54. See id. ("One who takes the affairs of a client personally in hand and purports to exercise judgment on behalf of the client in the light of the client's individual needs and circumstances is properly viewed as engaging in the practice of a profession"); Planned Parenthood of Se. Pa. v. Casey, 505 U.S. 833, 884 (1992) (acknowledging that physician's free speech rights were "implicated" by mandatory abortion disclosure law, but "only as part of the practice of medicine, subject to reasonable licensing and regulation by the State . . .").

55. Casey, 505 U.S. at 804 (joint opinion).

56. Kathleen Sullivan, "Intersection of Free Speech and the Legal Profession: Constraints on Lawyers' First Amendment Rights," 67 *Fordham L. Rev.* 569, 571 (1998).

57. See In re Primus, 436 U.S. 412, 412 (1978) (invalidating state anti-solicitation rule as applied to an ACLU lawyer seeking to represent a woman in a forced sterilization case); NAACP

v. Button, 371 U.S. 415, 428–29 (1963) (invalidating Virginia law that restricted solicitation of clients for purposes of challenging racial segregation in public schools); Gentile v. State Bar, 501 U.S. 1030, 1034 (1991) (describing lawyer's press conference statements as "classic political speech . . . critical of the government and its officials").

58. See Frederick Schauer, "First Amendment Opportunism," in Lee C. Bollinger & Geoffrey R. Stone, *Eternally Vigilant: Free Speech in the Modern Era* (Univ. of Chicago Press, 2002).

59. S.D. Codified Laws § 34-23A-10.1(1)(b) (2011).

60. Id. § 34-23A-10.1(1)(c).

61. See Planned Parenthood Minn. v. Rounds, 686 F.3d 889, 906 (8th Cir. 2012) (en banc); Planned Parenthood Minn. v. Rounds, 530 F.3d 724, 738 (8th Cir. 2008) (en banc) (vacating preliminary injunction); Planned Parenthood of Ind., Inc. v. Comm'r of Ind. State Dep't of Health, 794 F. Supp. 2d 892, 918 (S.D. Ind. 2011) (upholding requirement that physicians inform abortion patients that "human physical life begins when a human ovum is fertilized by a human sperm").

62. See N.C. Gen. Stat. Ann. § 90-21.85(a)(2), (a)(4) (West 2011); Tex. Health & Safety Code Ann. § 171.012(a)(4)(C), (D) (West 2011); LA. Rev. Stat. Ann. § 1299.35.2(D)(2)(a) (2012).

63. See Caroline Mala Corbin, "Abortion Distortions," 71 *Wash. & Lee L. Rev.* 1175, 1190-94 (2014) (discussing courts' failure to apply strict scrutiny to physicians' compelled speech in the abortion disclosure context). See also Jennifer M. Keighley, "Physician Speech and Mandatory Ultrasound Laws: The First Amendment's Limit on Compelled Ideological Speech," 34 *Cardozo L. Rev.* 2347, 2389 (2013); Robert Post, "Informed Consent to Abortion: A First Amendment Analysis of Compelled Physician Speech," 2007 *U. Ill. L. Rev.* 939, 959–62 (2007).

64. See generally Jesse Hill, "The First Amendment and the Politics of Reproductive Health Care," 50 *Wash. U. J. L. & Pol'y* 103 (2016).

65. For general commentary on professional speech, see Robert C. Post, *Democracy, Expertise, Academic Freedom: A First Amendment Jurisprudence for the Modern State* (Yale Univ. Press, 2012); Daniel Halberstam, "Commercial Speech, Professional Speech, and the Constitutional Status of Social Institutions," 147 *U. Pa. L. Rev.* 771 (1999); Claudia Haupt, "Professional Speech," 125 *Yale L.J.* 1150 (2015); Robert Kry, "The 'Watchman for Truth': Professional Licensing and the First Amendment," 23 *Seattle U. L. Rev.* 885 (2000). For works that examine speech restrictions relating to specific professionals, such as lawyers or physicians, see Paula Berg, "Toward a First Amendment Theory of Doctor-Patient Discourse and the Right to Receive Unbiased Medical Advice," 74 *B.U. L. Rev.* 201 (1994); Sanger, supra note 47; Sullivan, supra note 56.

66. Lowe, 472 U.S. at 232 (White, J., concurring in the result).

67. Halberstam, supra note 65, at 812.

68. Id.

69. Post, supra note 65, at 61.

70. Halberstam, supra note 65, at 815.

71. See Helen Norton, "The Equal Protection Implications of Government's Hateful Speech," 54 *Wm. & Mary L. Rev.* 159 (2012) (addressing equal protection limits on government speech regarding homosexuality and gay rights); Deborah Hellman, "The Expressive Dimension of Equal Protection," 85 *Minn. L. Rev.* 1 (2000) (discussing equal protection concerns relating to laws regarding homosexuality). See also Elizabeth S. Anderson & Richard H. Pildes, "Expressive Theories of Law: A General Restatement," 148 *U. Pa. L. Rev.* 1503, 1531–51 (2000) (focusing on equal protection and religious non-establishment limits on government speech).

72. See, e.g., Rust v. Sullivan, 500 U.S. 172, 175 (1991) (upholding regulations prohibiting physicians at government-funded health care facilities from counseling patients regarding abortion services).

73. See Pleasant Grove City v. Summum, 555 U.S. 640, 647 (2009) ("[I]f the government is engaging in [its] own expressive conduct, then the Free Speech Clause has no application.").

74. See Walker v. Texas Division, Sons of Confederate Veterans, 135 S. Ct. 2239 (2015).

75. U.S. Const., amend IX.

76. Summum, 555 U.S. at 647.

77. See Maher v. Roe, 432 U.S. 464, 474 (1977) (government may "make a value judgment favoring childbirth over abortion, and . . . implement that judgment by the allocation of public funds"); Planned Parenthood of Se. Penn. v. Casey, 505 U.S. 833, 877–78 (1992) (joint opinion) (holding that government is permitted to seek to persuade women not to exercise their constitutional right to choose to terminate a pregnancy, so long as it does not coerce women or otherwise unduly interfere with the abortion decision). See also Sanger, supra note 47, at 360–61 (asking "when or to what extent may the state persuade a person not to exercise a constitutional right?").

78. See Michael Dorf, "Same-Sex Marriage, Second-Class Citizenship, and Law's Social Meaning," 97 *Va. L. Rev.* 1267, 1293–98 (2011) (discussing equality concerns relating to official enactments regarding sexual orientation). See also Norton, supra note 71 (addressing equal protection limits on government speech regarding homosexuality and gay rights); Hellman, supra note 71 (discussing equal protection concerns relating to laws regarding homosexuality).

79. See Nelson Tebbe, "Government Nonendorsement," 98 *Minn. L. Rev.* 648, 692 (2013) (arguing that government speech regarding constitutional rights, including equality and abortion rights, is subject to First Amendment free speech limits under a principle of "government nonendorsement"); Dorf, supra note 78, at 1300 (observing that "[s]ome of the constitutional harm done by a requirement that people wear a badge of inferiority sounds in freedom of expression").

80. See Dorf, supra note 78.

81. Id. at 1278.

82. Id. at 1275.

83. Id.

84. Id. at 1298.

85. See id. at 1344 (arguing that same-sex marriage bans should be subject to heightened scrutiny "because the members of an identifiable victim group reasonably understand those laws as branding them and their relationships as second-class").

86. Tebbe, supra note 79, at 653.

87. See id. at 650 (government nonendorsement principle "cuts across multiple provisions—including equal protection, due process, and free speech itself—and it brings them together to prohibit any endorsement that abridges full and equal citizenship in a free society"). However, not everyone agrees that the First Amendment is implicated in these contexts. See, e.g., Abner S. Greene, "Government Endorsement: A Reply to Nelson Tebbe's Government Nonendorsement," 98 *Minn. L. Rev.* 87, 90 (2013) ("None of this has anything to do with the freedom of speech.").

88. Tebbe, supra note 79, at 666.

89. Id. at 667.

90. Id. at 667–68.

91. Id. at 676.

92. Id. at 676–77.

93. Id. at 677 n.107. Tebbe does not pursue the free speech objection more fully, he says, "because it involves mainly private speech." Id. However, if the First Amendment has a constraining role, it would seem that part of its function would be to limit government's ability to structure even private speech about something as significant as marital rights. In any event, it is not appropriate to characterize such speech—which is a central aspect of social discourse—as narrowly private or not touching upon matters of public concern.

94. Id.

95. Id. at 704–05.

96. See James E. Fleming & Linda C. Mcclain, *Ordered Liberty: Rights, Responsibilities, and Virtues* 4 (Harvard Univ. Press, 2013) (arguing that the state should use its persuasive powers to "help persons develop their moral capacities for self-government and, in that sense, live good lives"); Corey Brettschneider, *When the State Speaks, What Should it Say? How Democracies Can Protect Expression and Promote Equality* 73 (Princeton Univ. Press, 2012) (arguing that the state "should non-neutrally express and promote the values of free and equal citizenship"); Greene, supra note 87, at 88 ("With a few limits, the state, as a representative of the people in their capacity as citizens, may and should take distinctive positions on contested issues to achieve certain public goods, and to teach what the state believes to be true.").

97. See Brettschneider, supra note 96, at 71–72 (proposing a concept of "value democracy" for government communications, which is grounded in the Free Speech Clause).

98. See, e.g., Stephen Gey, "Why Should the First Amendment Protect Government Speech When the Government Has Nothing to Say?", 95 *Iowa L. Rev.* 1259 (2010).

CHAPTER 3

1. Michael W. McConnell, "Reconsidering *Citizens United* as a Press Clause Case," 123 *Yale L.J.* 412, 416 (2013).

2. See, e.g., John D. Inazu, *Liberty's Refuge: The Forgotten Freedom of Assembly* (Yale Univ. Press, 2012); Ronald J. Krotoszynski, Jr., *Reclaiming the Petition Clause: Seditious Libel, "Offensive" Protest, and the Right to Petition the Government for a Redress of Grievances* (Yale Univ. Press, 2012).

3. See, e.g., Zechariah Chafee, "Book Review," 62 *Harv. L. Rev.* 891, 898 (1949); Thomas Emerson, "Colonial Intentions and Current Realities of the First Amendment," 125 *U. Pa. L. Rev.* 737 (1977).

4. See generally Jud Campbell, "Natural Rights and the First Amendment," 127 *Yale L.J.* 246 (2017) (concluding, based on natural law understandings, that freedom of speech and freedom of press comprised distinctive guarantees).

5. See David A. Anderson, "The Origins of the Press Clause," 30 *UCLA L. Rev.* 455, 465 (1983) (observing that of the early state constitutions, only Pennsylvania's contained a free speech provision).

6. See id. at 473.

7. See Leonard Levy, *Legacy of Suppression: Freedom of Speech and Press in Early American History* 5–6 (Harvard Univ. Press, 1960).

8. Anderson, supra note 5, at 533.

9. Levy, supra note 7, at 5.

10. Sonja R. West, "Awakening the Press Clause," 58 *UCLA L. Rev.* 1025, 1038 (2011) (footnotes omitted).

11. See Melville Nimmer, "Introduction—Is Freedom of the Press a Redundancy: What Does It Add to Freedom of Speech?", 26 *Hastings L.J.* 639, 640 (1975).

12. See Campbell, supra note 4.

13. Id.

14. See Inazu, supra note 2, at 21–35 (tracing the early history of the constitutional right to peaceably assemble).

15. See Krotoszynski, supra note 2, at 153 ("the right to petition for redress of grievances predates both the derivative rights of speech and assembly; it once held an importance that equaled, if not exceeded them, and retained that status for well over a hundred years after giving birth to the secondary freedoms of speech and press").

16. Anderson, supra note 5, at 478.

17. Id. at 474.

18. Id. at 484.

19. See id. at 488 ("[T]he notion of an interrelated complex of protections for thought, belief, and expression, is a modern concept. To impose it retrospectively on the framers is anachronistic.... The Framers began not with a general theory of intellectual freedom, but with specific solutions to concrete grievances.").

20. See Akhil Amar, *The Bill of Rights: Creation and Reconstruction* 20–26 (Yale Univ. Press, 1998) (discussing free speech and free press); id. at 26–32 (discussing assembly and petition).

21. See id. at 223–24.

22. Anderson, supra note 5, at 509.

23. Levy, supra note 7, at 214–15 ("freedom of the press was everywhere a grand topic for declamation").

24. Amar, supra note 20, at 237.

25. Id.

26. See id. at 244–46.

27. Ashutosh Bhagwat, "The Democratic First Amendment," 110 *Nw. L. Rev.* 1097, 1098–99 (2016) (emphasis added).

28. As discussed below, scholars have offered separate accounts of the history and current understandings of the Assembly Clause, Press Clause, and Petition Clause. However, these studies do not holistically or comparatively consider the dynamics that produced the "Free Expression Clause." This chapter synthesizes accounts of individual clauses and seeks to explain how the First Amendment's suite of "expressive" rights intersect and relate.

29. An early example is Thomas I. Emerson, "Toward a General Theory of the First Amendment," 72 *Yale L.J.* 877, 878 (1963) ("The fundamental purpose of the first amendment was to guarantee the maintenance of an effective system of free expression.").

30. See, e.g., Schenck v. United States, 249 U.S. 47 (1919); Abrams v. United States, 250 U.S. 616 (1919).

31. See Schenck, 249 U.S. at 52 ("The question in every case is whether the words used are used in such circumstances and are of such a nature as to create a clear and present danger that they will bring about the substantive evils that Congress has a right to prevent.").

32. See John Stuart Mill, *On Liberty* (John W. Parker & Son, 1859); John Milton, *Aeropaegetica* (The Grolier Club, 1890).

33. E.g., Abrams, 250 U.S. at 619 (referring to "freedom of speech and of the press").

34. Id. at 627 (Holmes, J., dissenting).

35. Id.

36. Id. at 630.

37. Whitney v. California, 274 U.S. 357, 375 (1927) (Brandeis, J., concurring). See Inazu, supra note 2, at 50 (discussing the influence of assembly in Brandeis's concurrence).

38. See Whitney, 274 U.S. at 376 ("To justify suppression of free speech there must be reasonable ground to fear that serious evil will result if free speech is practiced."); id. at 376 ("But even advocacy of violation, however reprehensible morally, is not a justification for denying free speech where the advocacy falls short of incitement and there is nothing to indicate that the advocacy would be immediately acted on."); id. at 377 ("no danger flowing from speech can be deemed clear and present, unless the incidence of the evil apprehended is so imminent that it may befall before there is opportunity for full discussion. If there be time to expose through discussion the falsehood and fallacies, to avert the evil by the processes of education, the remedy to be applied is more speech, not enforced silence."); id. at 378 ("The fact that speech is likely to result in some violence or in destruction of property is not enough to justify its suppression.").

39. See, e.g., N.Y. Times Co. v. Sullivan, 376 U.S. 254, 270 (1964) (referring to Brandeis's *Whitney* concurrence as the "classic formulation" of free speech principles); H. Jefferson Powell, *A Community Built on Words: The Constitution in History and Politics* 194 (Univ. of Chicago Press, 2002).

40. Sullivan, 376 U.S. at 270.

41. See generally Alexander Meiklejohn, *Political Freedom: The Constitutional Powers of the People* (Harper, 1960) (discussing the relationship between free speech and self-government).

42. See generally Thomas I. Emerson, *The System of Freedom of Expression* (Vintage Books, 1971).

43. Bradley C. Bobertz, "The Brandeis Gambit: The Making of America's 'First Freedom,' 1909–1931," 40 *Wm. & Mary L. Rev.* 557, 560 (1999).

44. Inazu, supra note 2.

45. See United States v. Cruikshank, 92 U.S. 542, 552 (1875); Presser v. Illinois, 116 U.S. 252, 267 (1886).

46. See Jason Mazzone, "Freedom's Associations," 77 *Wash. L. Rev.* 639, 712–13 (2002).

47. See Inazu, supra note 2, at 22–25.

48. See id. at 40-44 (discussing state court decisions, treatises, and other sources that adopted a broader definition of assembly).

49. Id. at 50.

50. See id. at 57–59.

51. Id. at 61.

52. Id.

53. See generally id., chs. 3, 4.

54. Id. at 63.

55. DeJonge v. Oregon, 299 U.S. 353, 364 (1937).

56. 357 U.S. 449 (1968).

57. Id. at 460.

58. See Inazu, supra note 2, at 81–82.

59. See id. at 85.

60. Id. at 87–88.

61. See id. at 94–96.

62. Id. at 96.

63. Id. at 97.

64. Id. at 115–16 (discussing intellectual influences on legal culture).

65. See id. at 119–24.

66. Runyon v. McCrary, 427 U.S. 160, 168 (1976).

67. Id. at 176.

68. See Griswold v. Connecticut, 381 U.S. 479, 483 (1965).

69. Inazu, supra note 2, at 132.

70. 468 U.S. 609, 617–18 (1984).

71. Id. at 627.

72. Id. at 623.

73. New York State Club Ass'n v. City of New York, 487 U.S. 1, 13 (1988).

74. Christian Legal Soc'y v. Martinez, 561 U.S. 661 (2011).

75. See, e.g., Timothy Zick, "Recovering the Assembly Clause," 91 *Tex. L. Rev.* 375, 398 (2012) ("Assembly is protected in its own right; it stands on its own bottom.").

76. See Cox Broadcasting Corp. v. Cohn, 420 U.S. 469, 496–97 (1975). Even in *Cohn*, the Court referred at times to "freedom of expression" or "the First Amendment" in a more generic sense.

77. See C. Edwin Baker, "The Independent Significance of the Press Clause under Existing Law," 35 *Hofstra L. Rev.* 955, 956 (2007) ("The Court has never explicitly recognized that the Press Clause involves any significant content different from that provided to all individuals by the prohibition on abridging freedom of speech."). See also Richmond Newspapers, Inc. v. Virginia, 448 U.S. 555 (1980) (invalidating trial court closure order on grounds that public and press have a right to attend trial proceedings).

78. See, e.g., David Lange, "The Speech and Press Clauses," 23 *UCLA L. Rev.* 77, 88–90, 92–96 (1975) (discussing colonists' conceptual understanding of free speech and free press).

79. David A. Anderson, "Freedom of the Press," 80 *Tex. L. Rev.* 429, 430 (2002).

80. 4 W. Blackstone, *Commentaries on the Laws of England* 151–52 (Oxford, 1769).

81. See Leonard Levy, *Freedom of the Press from Zenger to Jefferson* lv–lvi (Bobbs-Merrill Co., 1966); Levy, *Legacy of Suppression*, supra note 7.

82. See Patterson v. Colorado, 205 U.S. 454 (1907) (suggesting that First Amendment protection was limited to invalidating prior restraints).

83. 1 Zechariah Chafee, Jr., *Government and Mass Communication* (Univ. of Chicago Press, 1947).

84. Id. at 34

85. See 2 Thomas M. Cooley, *Constitutional Limitations* 883–86, 937–44 (Little, Brown & Co., 8th ed. 1927); Robert McCormick, *The Freedom of the Press* 1 (D. Appleton-Century, 1936).

86. Anderson, supra note 79, at 448.

87. See, e.g., Zechariah Chafee, *Three Human Rights in the Constitution of 1787* (University of Kansas Press, 1956). Professor Chafee led a U.S. delegation to the United Nations that advocated for, among other things, the adoption of free speech and press rights.

88. E.g., Grosjean v. Am. Press Co., 297 U.S. 233, 251 (1936).

89. See Miami Herald Pub. Co. v. Tornillo, 418 U.S. 241 (1974).

90. See Leathers v. Medlock, 499 U.S. 439, 447 (1991) (interpreting press taxation cases as based on free speech principles).

91. See, e.g., Time, Inc. v. Hill, 385 U.S. 374 (1967) (analyzing judgment against magazine as abridgment of the rights of free speech and press).

92. See Sullivan, 376 U.S. at 256 ("We are required in this case to determine for the first time the extent to which the constitutional protections for speech and press limit a State's power to award damages in a libel action brought by a public official against critics of his official conduct."). The Supreme Court used some version of the formulation "freedoms of speech and press" throughout its opinion. See, e.g., id. at 265.

93. See David A. Anderson, "Freedom of the Press in Wartime," 77 *U. Colo. L. Rev.* 49, 73 (2006).

94. See RonNell Anderson Jones, "The Dangers of Press Clause Dicta," 48 *Ga. L. Rev.* 705, 718–19 (2014).

95. See David A. Yalof & Mark Kenneth Dautrich, *The First Amendment and the Media in the Court of Public Opinion* 10 (Cambridge Univ. Press, 2002).

96. West, supra note 10, at 1036.

97. See id. at 1028 ("Because the freedoms to publish and to disseminate speech are also protected by the Free Speech Clause, the Press Clause has been left with nothing to do.").

98. See, e.g., Jerome Barron, "Access to the Press—A New First Amendment Right," 80 *Harv. L. Rev.* 1641 (1967); David Lange, "The Role of the Access Doctrine in the Regulation of the Mass Media: A Critical Review and Assessment," 52 *N.C. L. Rev.* 1 (1973).

99. See Belotti, 435 U.S. 765, 799–800.

100. David Lange, "The Speech and Press Clauses," 23 *UCLA L. Rev.* 77, 88 (1975).

101. Id.

102. See, e.g., Branzburg v. Hayes, 408 U.S. 665, 704 (1972) (observing that defining the press for purposes of evidentiary privileges "would present practical and conceptual difficulties of a high order").

103. Address by Mr. Justice Stewart, Yale Law School Sesquicentennial Convocation, November 2, 1974, reprinted in Stewart, "Or of the Press," 26 *Hastings L.J.* 631 (1975).

104. Melville Nimmer, "Introduction—Is Freedom of the Press a Redundancy: What Does It Add to Freedom of Speech?," 26 *Hastings L.J.* 639 (1975).

105. See generally Bruce J. Schulman, *The Seventies: The Great Shift in American Culture, Society, and Politics* (Da Capo Press, 2002).

106. As Sonja West has noted, "[t]he justices' understandable desire to avoid favoring an elite group has led them to allow the Speech Clause to swallow the Press Clause." West, supra note 10, at 1031.

107. As RonNell Jones has observed, the Court's rhetoric concerning the democratic values of press freedom is "one of the most consistent, defining characteristics of the U.S. Supreme Court's media law jurisprudence in the last half century." Jones, supra note 94, at 707. See, e.g., Leathers v. Medlock, 499 U.S. 439, 447 (1991) ("The press plays a unique role as a check on government abuse."); Mills v. Alabama, 384 U.S. 214, 219 (1966) ("The Constitution specifically selected the press, which includes not only newspapers, books, and magazines, but also humble leaflets and circulars, to play an important role in the discussion of public affairs.").

108. 408 U.S. 665 (1972).

109. See Mary-Rose Papandrea, "Citizen Journalism and the Reporter's Privilege," 91 *Minn. L. Rev.* 515, 546 & nn.175, 176 (2007) (collecting statutory citations).

110. See Annenberg Public Policy Center, University of Pennsylvania, "Americans Are Poorly Informed about Basic Constitutional Provisions," https://www.annenbergpublicpolicycenter.org/americans-are-poorly-informed-about-basic-constitutional-provisions?utm_

source=news-release&utm_medium=email&utm_campaign=2017_civics_survey&utm_term=survey&utm_source=Media&utm_campaign=e5f213892a-Civics_survey_2017_2017_09_12&utm_medium=email&utm_term=0_9e3d9bcd8a-e5f213892a-425997897 (Sept. 12, 2017) (last visited Oct. 13, 2017). See also Elisabeth Zoller, "The United States Supreme Court and the Freedom of Expression," 84 *Ind. L.J.* 885, 886 (2009) (observing that "freedom of expression" is frequently used by the Court because "[f]reedom of speech and freedom of the press are so united in American culture today that, in practice, the Court makes almost no distinction between the two").

111. See Yalof & Dautrich, supra note 95, at 11–19 (explaining the decline in media trust after 1970).

112. First Nat'l Bank v. Bellotti, 435 U.S. 765, 800 (1978) (Burger, J., concurring).

113. See Elizabeth Zoller, "The United States Supreme Court and the Freedom of Expression," 84 *Ind. L.J.* 885, 886 (2009).

114. See Citizens United v. FEC, 558 U.S. 310, 431 (2010) (Stevens, J., concurring) (challenging Justice Scalia's claim that the Press Clause does not support special treatment for corporate media).

115. See, e.g., West, supra note 10.

116. Id. at 109.

117. Id.

118. Stephen H. Higginson, "A Short History of the Right to Petition Government for a Redress of Grievances," 96 *Yale L.J.* 142, 142 (1986).

119. See United States v. Cruikshank, 92 U.S. 542, 552 (1876) ("The very idea of a government, republican in form, implies a right on the part of its citizens to meet peaceably for consultation in respect to public affairs and to petition for a redress of grievances.").

120. See, e.g., Adderley v. Florida, 385 U.S. 39, 52 (1966) (Douglas, J., dissenting) ("We do violence to the First Amendment when we permit this 'petition for redress of grievances' to be turned into a trespass action . . .").

121. McDonald v. Smith, 472 U.S. 479, 482 (1985).

122. Wayte v. United States, 470 U.S. 598, 610 n.11 (1985).

123. Borough of Duryea v. Guarnieri, 564 U.S. 379, 388 (2011).

124. Krotosyynski, supra note 2, at 121.

125. Id. at 127.

126. See Cox v. Louisiana, 379 U.S. 536, 545 (1965) (invalidating conviction of leader of civil rights group arising from public protest); Hurley v. Irish-American Gay, Lesbian and Bisexual Group of Boston, 515 U.S. 557, 569–70 (1995) (concluding that parade was expressive).

127. Gary Lawson & Guy Seidman, "Downsizing the Right to Petition," 93 *Nw. L. Rev.* 739, 739 (1999).

128. See, e.g., Frederick Schauer, "Principles, Institutions, and the First Amendment," 112 *Harv. L. Rev.* 84, 88–91 (1998) (critiquing analytical structure of press cases decided under free speech doctrines).

129. See, e.g., McConnell, supra note 1.

130. See, e.g., Randall P. Bezanson, "Whither Freedom of the Press?," 97 *Iowa L. Rev.* 1259, 1261 (2012) ("[T]o an interpreter of the Constitution, it is awkward to read the free press guarantee out of the First Amendment.").

131. See Inazu, supra note 2 (assembly); West, supra note 10 (press); Krotoszynski, supra note 2 (petition).

132. Inazu, supra note 2, at 150.

133. See id. at 2–4 (critiquing "expressive association" and advocating an alternative right of assembly).

134. See West, supra note 10, at 1033–41. See also Bezanson, supra note 130, at 1273 ("We need a guarantee of freedom of the press distinct from freedom of speech.").

135. West, supra note 10, at 1069–70.

136. Bezanson, supra note 130, at 1273.

137. West, supra note 10, at 1056–70 (defining and defending a narrow definition of "the press").

138. Bezanson, supra note 130, at 1273.

139. See, e.g., Eugene Volokh, "Freedom of the Press as an Industry, or for the Press as a Technology? From the Framing to Today," 160 *U. Penn. L. Rev.* 459, 538–39 (2012) (arguing that the Press Clause has been understood throughout American history to guarantee "equal treatment to [all] speakers without regard to whether they are members of the press-as-industry").

140. Krotoszynski, supra note 2.

141. Id. at 155.

142. Id. at 166.

143. Id. at 162–73.

144. See RonNell Anderson Jones & Sonja West, "The Fragility of the Free American Press," 112 *Nw. Univ. L. Rev.* 567, 572–84 (2017) (discussing the various "pillars" that protect freedom of the press).

145. See Bezanson, supra note 130, at 1262–63 ("Indeed, I know of no scholar of the First Amendment and press freedom who has taken the view that the press consists only of an 'institutional' character, and certainly not only a corporation formally so designated.").

146. McConnell, supra note 1, at 416.

147. See id. ("But the most important flaw . . . was to analyze the case under the wrong clause of the First Amendment.").

148. Id. at 416–17, 419.

149. See Krotoszynski, supra note 2, at 156 ("[T]he Petition Clause should secure a baseline right of access to a particular intended audience, access that the other First Amendment expressive freedom guarantees have thus far failed to provide.").

150. This is, incidentally, how the Supreme Court *used to* describe these rights. See De Jonge v. Oregon, 299 U.S. 353, 365–66 (1937). See also Thomas v. Collins, 323 U.S. 516, 530 (1945).

151. Bhagwat, supra note 27, at 1118.

152. Id.

153. Id. at 1113.

154. Professor Bhagwat sets the Free Exercise Clause to one side, on the ground that the history suggests a different role for religious freedom. I discuss the intersection between the Free Speech Clause and the Free Exercise Clause in Chapter 4.

155. John D. Inazu, "The Four Freedoms and the Future of Religious Liberty," 92 *N.C. L. Rev.* 787, 788 (2014).

156. Id.

157. As Professor Inazu notes, there is also serious confusion over how each of the First Amendment rights ought to be analyzed separately—giving rise, as he observes, to "the worst of both worlds." See id. at 808.

158. Id. at 809.

CHAPTER 4

1. See John D. Inazu, "The Four Freedoms and the Future of Religious Liberty," 92 *N.C. L. Rev.* 787, 791 (2014) ("The First Amendment's freedoms of speech, press, religion, and assembly once reinforced one another").

2. See Mark Tushnet, "The Redundant Free Exercise Clause?," 33 *Loy. U. Chi. L.J.* 71, 73 (2001) ("Contemporary constitutional doctrine may render the Free Exercise Clause redundant.").

3. See U.S. Const. amend. I ("Congress shall make no law respecting an establishment of religion, or prohibiting the free exercise thereof. . . .").

4. Ashutosh Bhagwat, "The Democratic First Amendment," 110 *Nw. U. L. Rev.* 1097, 1100 (2016).

5. I use the term "expressive" owing to its currency in judicial and academic analyses of the First Amendment. For the reasons examined in Chapter 3, I reject the modern approach, which collapses speech, assembly, press, and petition rights into a fictional "Free Expression Clause."

6. See Michael W. McConnell, "The Problem of Singling Out Religion," 50 *DePaul L. Rev.* 1, 16 (2000) (noting the connection between early struggles to publish religious tracts and freedom of the press).

7. John Howard Yoder, "Response of an Amateur Historian and a Religious Citizen," 7 *J.L. & Religion* 417, 417 (1989) ("There was a long British Puritan history, from the age of Milton to the 1689 Bill of Rights, in the course of which the civil freedoms of speech, press, and assembly arose out of religious agitation, not the other way round.").

8. See Inazu, supra note 1, at 799–801 (discussing the framers' "pluralist" vision, which resulted in the combining of speech, assembly, press, petition, and free exercise rights in the First Amendment).

9. For a description of the cases, see Stephen M. Feldman, "The Theory and Politics of First Amendment Protections: Why Does the Supreme Court Favor Free Expression over Religious Freedom?," 8 *U. Pa. J. Const. L.* 431, 443–51 (2006); Daniel Hildebrand, "Free Speech and Constitutional Transformation," 10 *Const. Comment.* 133, 150–59 (1993).

10. See generally Shawn Francis Peters, *Judging Jehovah's Witnesses: Religious Persecution and the Dawn of the Rights Revolution* (Univ. Press of Kansas, 2000).

11. See, e.g., Lovell v. City of Griffin, 303 U.S. 444 (1938).

12. Court records from this era have only recently been made available. See Barry Cushman, "The Hughes Court Docket Books: The Early Terms, 1929–1933," 40 *J. Sup. Ct. Hist.* 103 (2015).

13. See Murdock v. Pennsylvania, 319 U.S. 105, 115 (1943) ("Freedom of press, freedom of speech, freedom of religion are in a preferred position.").

14. Prince v. Massachusetts, 321 U.S. 158, 164 (1944).

15. 310 U.S. 296 (1940).

16. Id. at 310.

17. See Inazu, supra note 1, at 805.

18. See John D. Inazu, *Liberty's Refuge: The Forgotten Freedom of Assembly* 58 (Yale U. Press, 2012).

19. See Inazu, supra note 1, at 806–07.

20. See Feldman, supra note 9, at 448 (observing that the Hughes Court typically relied on freedom of speech and press rationales).

21. See id. ("Without the support of free expression, religious freedom claims inevitably failed.").

22. See Eric Michael Mazur, *The Americanization of Religious Minorities: Confronting the Constitutional Order* 50 (Johns Hopkins Univ. Press, 1999).

23. 319 U.S. 624 (1943).

24. See Vincent Blasi & Seana V. Shiffrin, "The Story of *West Virginia State Board of Education v. Barnette*: The Pledge of Allegiance and the Freedom of Thought," in *First Amendment Stories* 115 (Richard W. Garnett & Andrew Koppelman eds., Foundation Press, 2012).

25. Feldman, supra note 9, at 432 (arguing that "the transition from republican to pluralist democracy practically turned the First Amendment concepts of free expression and religious freedom on their heads").

26. Id. at 455–56.

27. Id. at 470–72.

28. Id. at 473.

29. See generally David Rabban, *Free Speech in Its Forgotten Years 1870–1920* (Cambridge Univ. Press, 1999).

30. See Reynolds v. United States, 98 U.S. 145, 167 (1878).

31. See, e.g., Stromberg v. California, 283 U.S. 359, 369 (1931) (invalidating flag desecration law).

32. See, e.g., Bridges v. California, 314 U.S. 252 (1941) (holding that courts generally may not hold speakers in contempt for commenting on pending litigation and criticizing judges).

33. See DeJonge v. Oregon, 299 U.S. 353, 364 (1937) (describing right of assembly as "cognate" to those of free speech and free press).

34. See, e.g., Thomas Emerson, *Toward a General Theory of the First Amendment* ix (Random House, 1966) (noting that the influential early treatise on the First Amendment would not address the Religion Clauses).

35. See generally Stephen Brown, *Trumping Religion: The New Christian Right, The Free Speech Clause, and the Courts* (Univ. of Alabama Press, 2008) (examining Christian Right's free speech litigation strategy).

36. Id. at 5.

37. Id. at 10.

38. See Stephen Gey, "When Is Religious Speech Free Speech?," 2000 *U. Ill. L. Rev.* 379, 381 (quoting religious rights advocate concerning strategic use of Free Speech Clause).

39. See Sherbert v. Verner, 374 U.S. 398 (1963).

40. See Christopher L. Eisgruber & Lawrence G. Sager, *Religious Freedom and the Constitution* 42 (Harvard Univ. Press, 2007) (observing that courts were not actually applying strict scrutiny in religious rights cases).

41. 494 U.S. 872 (1990).

42. The political backlash against *Smith* was swift and resounding. Two years after the decision, Congress unanimously enacted the Religious Freedom Restoration Act (RFRA), which restored pre-*Smith* standards. Pub. L. No. 103-141, 107 Stat. 1488 (November 16, 1993), codified at 42 U.S.C. § 2000bb through 42 U.S.C. § 2000bb-4. The Supreme Court invalidated RFRA as applied to the states. Boerne v. Flores, 521 U.S. 507 (1997). However, many states have enacted

"mini-RFRA" laws that require strict scrutiny when government actions substantially burden religious exercise.

43. See Church of the Lukumi Babalu Aye v. City of Hialeah, 508 U.S. 520 (1993).

44. 454 U.S. 263, 277 (1981).

45. Id. at 269.

46. Id. at 269–70.

47. See Lamb's Chapel v. Center Moriches Union Free Sch. Dist., 508 U.S. 384 (1993); Rosenberger v. Rector and Visitors of the Univ. of Virginia, 515 U.S. 819 (1995); Good News Club v. Milford Cent. Sch., 533 U.S. 98 (2001).

48. See Alan Brownstein, "Protecting Religious Liberty: The False Messiahs of Free Speech Doctrine and Formal Neutrality," 18 *J.L. & Pol.* 119, 131–33 (2002) (observing that equal access restrictions plainly violated the Free Exercise Clause, yet were challenged only on free speech grounds).

49. Gustav Niebuhr, "Conservatives' New Frontier: Religious Liberty Law Firms," *N.Y. Times*, July 8, 1995, at A1.

50. See Eisgruber & Sager, supra note 40, at 42.

51. See, e.g., Engel v. Vitale, 370 U.S. 421 (1962) (invalidating official prayer in public schools).

52. See Perry Educ. Ass'n v. Perry Local Educators' Assn., 460 U.S. 37, 46 (1983) (summarizing public forum doctrine).

53. See, e.g., Geoffrey R. Stone, "Content Neutrality and the First Amendment," 25 *Wm. & Mary L. Rev.* 189 (1983).

54. See Carey v. Brown, 447 U.S. 455 (1980).

55. See United States v. O'Brien, 391 U.S. 367, 376 (1968); Spence v. Washington, 418 U.S. 405, 410 (1974).

56. Smith, 494 U.S. at 878–89.

57. See Church of the Lukumi Babalu Aye v. City of Hialeah, 508 U.S. 520 (1993).

58. See generally Tushnet, supra note 2.

59. See, e.g., Schneider, 301 U.S. at 160 (holding that municipality had to allow religious speakers to access public streets on equal terms with other speakers).

60. See Lovell, 303 U.S. at 668–69 (invalidating restrictions on distribution of literature in public places).

61. See, e.g., Cantwell, 310 U.S. at 307–08 (invalidating solicitation ban on free exercise grounds); Follett v. Town of McCormick, 321 U.S. 573, 576 (1944) (invalidating tax on religious activities).

62. Schneider v. State of New Jersey, 308 U.S. 147, 160 (1939).

63. Cantwell, 310 U.S. at 304.

64. Id. at 307.

65. Id.

66. See id. at 305–06.

67. See Smith, 494 U.S. at 881–82 (recognizing "hybrid" rights).

68. See, e.g., Michael W. McConnell, "Free Exercise Revisionism and the *Smith* Decision," 57 *U. Chi. L. Rev.* 1109, 1122 (1990) (criticizing the concept of "hybrid" rights).

69. See Tilton v. Richardson, 403 U.S. 672, 678 (1971) (plurality opinion) ("candor compels the acknowledgment that we can only dimly perceive the boundaries of permissible government activity in this sensitive area").

70. See, e.g., Zobrest v. Catalina Foothills Sch. Dist., 509 U.S. 1 (1993 (allowing public school district to provide sign-language interpreter to student at Catholic high school under a federal program for the disabled).

71. See, e.g., Comm. for Public Ed. v. Nyquist, 413 U.S. 756, 780 (1973) ("In the absence of an effective means of guaranteeing that the state aid derived from public funds will be used exclusively for secular, neutral, and non-ideological purposes, it is clear from our cases that direct aid in whatever form is invalid").

72. See, e.g., Lamb's Chapel, 508 U.S. at 392 (analyzing access by religious group to public school property under public forum doctrine).

73. Public forum doctrine imposes strict protections for free speech in "traditional" public places such as streets and parks, similar protections in public places "designated" for expressive activities, and far less speech protection in "limited" public fora—essentially, places neither traditionally nor by designation opened to expressive activities. See Perry Educ. Ass'n, 460 U.S. at 46 (summarizing public forum doctrine).

74. 515 U.S. 819 (1995).

75. Id. at 831.

76. Id. at 840.

77. Id. at 840–42.

78. Id. at 843.

79. Id. at 863 (Souter, J. dissenting).

80. Id. at 885.

81. Id. at 889.

82. Id.

83. 515 U.S. 753 (1995).

84. Pinette, 515 U.S. at 770.

85. See id.

86. In subsequent cases, the Court has declined to extend this public- forum-establishment framework to contexts in which no public forum is present or public forum principles are considered to be out of place. See Locke v. Davey, 540 U.S. 712, 720 & n.3 (2004) (holding that state was not required to permit individuals to use public funds for religious education); Pleasant Grove City v. Summum, 555 U.S. 460, 478 (2009) (holding that municipality was permitted to select permanent monuments for a public park without regard to public forum principles).

87. 137 S. Ct. 2012 (2017).

88. Id. at 2024.

89. See Hildebrand, supra note 9, at 133 (observing that "a coherent First Amendment tradition honoring the centrality of rich public debate began as early as the 1930s").

90. See Davis v. Massachusetts, 167 U.S. 43 (1897).

91. Hague v. Comm. for Indus. Org., 307 U.S. 496, 515 (1939).

92. See Schneider, 308 U.S. at 151 (observing that "the streets are natural and proper places for the dissemination of information and opinion").

93. See Hildebrand, supra note 9, at 156–58.

94. See Cox v. New Hampshire, 312 U.S. 569, 576 (1941).

95. See, e.g., Cantwell, 310 U.S. at 307.

96. See Chaplinsky, 315 U.S. at 573 (discussing "fighting words" category).

97. See Cantwell, 310 U.S. at 310.

98. See Schneider, 308 U.S. at 164 (discussing prohibition on suppression of certain views).

99. See Martin v. City of Struthers, 319 U.S. 141, 143 (1943) (freedom to distribute information "necessarily protects the right to receive it").

100. See id. at 147 (noting that householders have "the full right to decide whether [they] will receive strangers as visitors").

101. See Cantwell, 310 U.S. at 310 (noting that speakers sometimes resort "even to false statement" in political and religious debates).

102. Jamison v. Texas, 318 U.S. 413, 416 (1943).

103. West Va. State Bd. of Ed. v. Barnette, 319 U.S. 624, 642 (1943).

104. See, e.g., Abrams v. United States, 250 U.S. 616, 630 (Holmes, J. dissenting) (discussing marketplace justifications for free speech); Alexander Meiklejohn, *Free Speech and Its Relation to Self-Government* (Harper Bros., 1948) (articulating a theory of self-government focused on political speech).

105. See Cantwell, 310 U.S. at 310 ("The essential characteristics of these liberties is, that under their shield many types of life, character, opinion and belief can develop unmolested and unobstructed.").

106. See, e.g., Rosenberger, 515 U.S. at 830 (describing student activities fund as "metaphysical" public forum).

107. See Abner S. Greene, "The Concept of the Speech Platform: *Walker v. Texas Division*," 68 *Ala. L. Rev.* 338, 349 (2016) (arguing that the viewpoint discrimination prohibition in the limited public forum context has only been applied to benefit religious speakers).

108. Martinez, 561 U.S. at 697.

109. Id. at 680.

110. See, e.g., Inazu, supra note 1, at 821–22 (arguing that *Martinez* undermines both free association and free exercise rights of groups).

111. See Summum, 555 U.S. at 478 (upholding exclusion of monument from public park space).

112. Id. at 478.

113. Id.

114. See generally Gey, supra note 38.

115. See, e.g., Kent Greenawalt, "Viewpoints from Olympus," 96 *Colum. L. Rev.* 697, 697 (1996) ("The core of the Court's opinion [in *Rosenberger*] is unconvincing because it fails to elaborate a plausible account of what constitutes viewpoint discrimination.").

116. See Lehman v. Shaker Heights, 418 U.S. 298, 302 (1974) (upholding public transit rule barring political advertisements from city bus advertising spaces, but allowing commercial advertisements).

117. See Nelson Tebbe, "Excluding Religion," 156 *U. Pa. L. Rev.* 1253, 1308–18 (2008) (discussing exclusion of worship under free speech principles).

118. Barnette, 319 U.S. at 642.

119. Inazu, supra note 1, at 789.

120. See United States v. O'Brien, 391 U.S. 367, 376 (1968) (applying intermediate level of scrutiny to laws that incidentally burden expression).

121. See Brownstein, supra note 48, at 147–64 (examining application of free speech standards to religious zoning, expression, and conduct). See also Robert W. Tuttle, "How Firm a Foundation? Protecting Religious Land Uses after *Boerne*," 68 *Geo. Wash. L. Rev.* 861 (2000) (arguing that the Free Speech Clause protects rights of religious adherents in land use area).

122. See Tushnet, supra note 2. Cf. Inazu, supra note 18 (making similar point about the right of assembly and its relationship to free speech).

123. See Leslie Kendrick, "First Amendment Expansionism," 56 *Wm. & Mary L. Rev.* 1199, 1200 (2015) (describing "expansionism" as the situation "where the First Amendment's territory pushes outward to encompass ever more areas of law").

124. See Inazu, *supra* note 1, at 789 (lamenting that the "unified distinctiveness" of expressive and religious rights have been replaced "with an undifferentiated free speech framework").

125. Brownstein, supra note 48, at 185.

126. Id. at 169.

127. Id. at 167–68 (discussing Religious Land Use and Institutionalized Persons Act (RLUIPA)).

128. See id. at 175–76.

129. See Spence v. Washington, 418 U.S. 405, 409–11 (1974) (requiring for purposes of Free Speech Clause coverage that a speaker intend to communicate a message through action and that an audience be likely to understand the message).

130. See, e.g., Locke v. Davey, 540 U.S. 712, 721 (2004) (holding that state could exclude students seeking to use public scholarship funds for pursuit of devotional theology degree).

131. Inazu, supra note 1, at 826.

132. Cf. id. at 791 (arguing that First Amendment rights—speech, press, religion, and assembly—function most effectively as part of a pluralistic system of constitutional protections).

133. Id. at 790.

134. See Inazu, supra note 18; Bhagwat, supra note 4.

135. See Inazu, supra note 1, at 849 ("A thicker commitment to the kind of pluralism embodied in the Four Freedoms would at least have required the [*Martinez*] Court to evaluate each of these constitutional claims.").

136. Michael Coenen, "Combining Constitutional Clauses," 164 *U. Pa. L. Rev.* 1067, 1078–83 (2016).

137. Id. at 1103.

138. See id. at 1006 (arguing that "increased acceptance of combination analysis might carry with it the salutary, transparency-promoting effect of better aligning the public reasoning of judges' opinions with the internal thought processes of the judges themselves").

139. See id. at 1104–05 (explaining how combining constitutional clauses can lead to narrower decisions).

140. See Widmar, 454 U.S. at 269 n.6. See also Bronx Household of Faith v. Bd. of Ed. of the City of New York, 650 F.3d 30, 36–37 (2d Cir. 2011) (holding that exclusion of worship services from public school building did not constitute forbidden viewpoint discrimination under the Free Speech Clause).

141. See, e.g., Elane Photography v. Willock, 309 P.3d 53 (N.M Sup. Ct. 2013) (holding that application of New Mexico public accommodations law to photographer who opposed providing service to gay couple did not violate photographer's free speech or free exercise rights).

142. See Widmar, 454 U.S. at 274.

143. See Tebbe, supra note 117, at 1308–14 (discussing free speech issues related to worship exclusion).

144. See Bronx Household of Faith v. Bd. of Ed. of the City of New York, 750 F.3d 184 (2d Cir. 2014) (holding that worship exclusion did not violate Free Exercise Clause or Establishment Clause).

145. See, e.g., Rosenberger, 515 U.S. at 839 (noting that the Court has repeatedly "rejected the position that the Establishment Clause even justifies, much less requires, a refusal to extend free speech rights to religious speakers who participate in broad-reaching government programs neutral in design").

146. See, e.g., Craig v. Masterpiece Cake Shop Inc., 370 P.3d 272 (Colo. Ct. App. 2015) (rejecting free speech and free exercise claims).

147. Barnette, 319 U.S. at 640–41.

148. Id. at 642.

149. See Burwell v. Hobby Lobby Stores, Inc., 134 S. Ct. 2751, 2778 (2014) (recognizing as substantial burden on religion "facilitating the commission of an immoral act by another").

CHAPTER 5

1. References to the "Equal Protection Clause" refer both to the Fourteenth Amendment provision and the Fifth Amendment's Due Process Clause, which has been interpreted to include an equal protection component. See Bolling v. Sharpe, 347 U.S. 497, 499 (1954).

2. This chapter, like the rest of the book, focuses on constitutional rather than statutory rights. But of course, the two are related. Thus, for instance, recognition of constitutional equality rights facilitated passage of the Civil Rights Act of 1964. In recognition of this connection, the chapter includes some references to statutory equality rights.

3. Although it is primarily about the claims of gay men and lesbians, the chapter refers generally to lesbian, gay, bisexual, and transgender ("LGBT") equality and the "LGBT equality movement." However, as they relate to the intersection between freedom of speech and constitutional equality, the discrete claims and concerns of transgender persons are given separate treatment at the end of the chapter.

4. See Akhil Reed Amar, *The Bill of Rights: Creation and Reconstruction* 235 (Yale Univ. Press, 1998). Abolitionist speech had been outlawed and prosecuted prior to the Civil War, especially in the American South. See, e.g., State v. Worth, 52 N.C. 488 (1860); Richard R. John, "Highland Hall's 'Report on Incendiary Publications': A Forgotten Nineteenth Century Defense of the Freedom of the Press," in 41 *American Journal of Legal History* (1997).

5. See Palko v. Connecticut, 302 U.S. 319, 327 (1937) (incorporating the Free Speech Clause).

6. Other groups have invoked the Free Speech Clause to serve similar purposes. For example, feminists and gender equality advocates also invoked and exercised free speech and other First Amendment rights to facilitate their cause. This chapter focuses solely on the race and LGBT equality movements.

7. Recall from Chapter 3 that by this time, the Supreme Court was still occasionally mentioning the Assembly Clause, Press Clause, and Petition Clause in published decisions. By and large, however, these rights had all essentially been collapsed into the Free Speech Clause. During the civil rights era, litigants invoked the Assembly Clause and Press Clause as well. However, the Supreme Court generally treated these claims as arising under the Free Speech Clause and did not, in any event, develop any specific doctrines relating to other clauses.

8. See generally Harry Kalven, Jr., *The Negro and the First Amendment* (Univ. of Chicago Press, 1966).

9. See, e.g., Cox v. Louisiana, 379 U.S. 536, 545 (1965) (invalidating conviction of leader of civil rights group seeking to protest racial segregation); N.Y. Times Co. v. Sullivan, 376 U.S. 254, 270 (1964) (invalidating state libel laws); Edwards v. South Carolina, 372 U.S. 229, 238 (1963) (invalidating breach of peace convictions against civil rights protesters); NAACP v. Button, 371 U.S. 415, 429 (1963) (invalidating Virginia law that restricted solicitation of clients for purposes of challenging racial segregation in public schools); Garner v. Louisiana, 368 U.S. 157, 163 (1961) (invalidating on procedural due process grounds breach of peace convictions in sit-in case).

10. See Kenneth L. Karst, "Equality as a Central Principle in the First Amendment," 43 *U. Chi. L. Rev.* 20, 26 (1975) (observing that there is a "principle of equal liberty of expression . . . inherent in the First Amendment").

11. See generally Anthony Lewis, *Make No Law* (Vintage Press, 1992) (discussing the importance of developments in libel law to the Civil Rights Movement).

12. Carlos Ball, *The First Amendment and LGBT Equality: A Contentious History* 1 (Harvard Univ. Press, 2017).

13. Id. at 7.

14. See William N. Eskridge, Jr., *Gaylaw: Challenging the Apartheid of the Closet*, ch. 3 (Harvard Univ. Press, 1999) (discussing early cases involving free speech, association, and press rights).

15. See, e.g., Bowers v. Hardwick, 478 U.S. 186 (1986) (upholding criminal sodomy conviction), overruled by Lawrence v. Texas, 539 U.S. 558 (2003) (invalidating state same-sex sodomy statute).

16. Ball, supra note 12, at 3.

17. Robert C. Post & Reva B. Siegel, "Legislative Constitutionalism and Section 5 Power: Policentric Interpretation of the Family and Medical Leave Act," 112 *Yale L J.* 1943, 2030 (2003).

18. See generally Reva B. Siegel, "Constitutional Change: The Case of the De Facto ERA," 94 *Cal. L. Rev.* 1323 (2006).

19. N.Y. Times Co. v. Sullivan, 376 U.S. 254, 270 (1964).

20. See NAACP v. Ala. ex rel. Patterson, 357 U.S. 449, 462 (1958) (recognizing right to engage in anonymous expressive activity).

21. See, e.g., Taylor Branch, *Parting the Waters: America in the King Years 1954–63* (Simon & Schuster, 1988); Tomiko Brown-Nagin, *Courage to Dissent: Atlanta and the Long History of the Civil Rights Movement* (Oxford Univ. Press, 2011).

22. See Michael J. Klarman, *From Jim Crow to Civil Rights: The Supreme Court and the Struggle for Racial Equality* 440–41 (Oxford Univ. Press, 2004) (noting the rise in public sympathy for civil rights causes after violent scenes were televised); Bruce Ackerman, *We the People: The Civil Rights Revolution, Vol. 3* 95 (Harvard Univ. Press, 2014) (noting that "television made all the difference, transforming the terrible scenes into an ugly symbol that shocked viewers throughout the nation").

23. See generally Ackerman, supra note 22 (examining the complex institutional and other dynamics that led to the Civil Rights Act of 1964 and other landmark civil rights enactments).

24. Dale Carpenter, "Expressive Association and Anti-discrimination Law after *Dale*: A Tripartite Approach," 85 *Minn. L. Rev.* 1515, 1525 (2001).

25. See Eskridge, supra note 14, at 145.

26. Id. at 112.

27. Id. at 203.

28. See id. at 118.

29. Id. at 112.

30. See Ball, supra note 12, at 130–49.

31. See Doe v. Reed, 561 U.S. 186, 200 (2010) (rejecting facial First Amendment challenge to public records law that required disclosure of signatures for referendum measure denying full marriage equality). See id. at 228 (Scalia, J., concurring).

32. Obergefell v. Hodges, 135 S. Ct. 2584, 2596 (2015).

33. Id. at 2625 (Roberts, C.J., dissenting) ("By deciding this question under the Constitution, the Court removes it from the realm of democratic decision. There will be consequences to shutting down the political process on an issue of such profound public significance. Closing debate tends to close minds.").

34. Kalven, supra note 8, at 132.

35. See Garner v. Louisiana, 368 U.S. 157, 163 (1961) (invalidating breach of peace convictions not on free speech but procedural due process grounds).

36. See, e.g., Adderley v. State of Florida, 385 U.S. 39, 46 (1966) (holding that trespass convictions based on protest near county jail did not violate the Free Speech Clause).

37. See Brown v. Louisiana, 383 U.S. 131, 143 (1966) (overturning protesters' conviction for disturbing the peace).

38. See Eskridge, supra note 14, at 113–16.

39. See Ball, supra note 12, at 18.

40. Eskridge, supra note 14, at 196. See also Ball, supra note 12, at 36–41 (discussing early cases in the Supreme Court dealing with "physique" magazines).

41. See Ball, supra note 12, at 41–49.

42. See Eskridge, supra note 14, at 362–71 (collecting data on state "no promo homo" educational and other anti-LGBT policies).

43. Id. at 196. See also David Cole & William N. Eskridge, Jr., "From Hand-Holding to Sodomy: First Amendment Protection of Homosexual (Expressive) Conduct," 29 *Harv. C.R.-C.L. L. Rev.* 319 (1994).

44. See, e.g., Rowland v. Mad River Sch. Dist., 730 F.2d 444, 449 (6th Cir. 1984) (overturning damages judgment in favor of public school teacher who was dismissed for discussing her bisexuality with students); Childers v. Dallas Police Dept., 513 F. Supp. 134, 139 (N.D. Tex. 1981) (upholding dismissal of officer based in part on his open homosexuality and public gay activism); Acanfora v. Bd. of Educ., 359 F. Supp. 843, 853–57 (D. Md. 1973), aff'd 359 F.3d 498 (4th Cir. 1974) (upholding dismissal of public school teacher who disclosed that he was gay and commented in the media on his subsequent dismissal). As Professor Ball notes, some plaintiffs did prevail on the free speech argument. But in those cases, the employee was typically engaged in more than simple self-outing; he was also engaged in public expression about issues relating to homosexuality. Moreover, as Ball notes, even plaintiffs who managed to convince courts of the merits of their free speech arguments did not always obtain relief from adverse employment decisions. See Ball, supra note 12, at 100–12.

45. President Bill Clinton's administration adopted the "Don't Ask, Don't Tell" policy, which allowed gay service members to remain in military service so long as they did so in secrecy. The policy was codified at 10 U.S.C. § 654 (b) (repealed). Under the policy, any statement by a service member that indicated he was gay created a rebuttable presumption of intent to engage in homosexual activity—a dischargeable offense. For courts of appeals cases rejecting the First Amendment argument, see Able v. United States, 155 F.3d 628 (2d Cir. 1998); Holmes v. Cal.

Army Nat'l Guard, 124 F.3d 1126 (9th Cir. 1997); Richenberg v. Perry, 97 F.3d 256 (8th Cir. 1996); Able v. United States, 88 F.3d 1280 (2d Cir. 1996); Thomasson v. Perry, 80 F.3d 915 (4th Cir. 1996) (en banc); Steffan v. Perry, 41 F.3d 677 (D.C. Cir. 1994) (en banc); Pruitt v. Cheney, 963 F.2d 1160 (9th Cir. 1991); Woodward v. United States, 871 F.2d 1068 (Fed. Cir. 1989); and Ben-Shalom v. Marsh, 881 F.2d 454 (7th Cir. 1989). The "Don't Ask, Don't Tell" policy was repealed in 2010. See Don't Ask, Don't Tell Repeal Act of 2010, Pub. L. No. 111-321, 124 Stat. 3515 (2010) (providing for repeal sixty days after report by secretary of defense and certification by the president and military officials).

46. Frederick Schauer, "First Amendment Opportunism," in *Eternally Vigilant: Free Speech in the Modern Era* 174, 175 (Lee C. Bollinger & Geoffrey Stone eds., Chicago Univ. Press, 2002).

47. See Leslie Kendrick, "First Amendment Expansionism," 56 *Wm. & Mary L. Rev.* 1199, 1200 (2015) (describing "expansionism" as the situation "where the First Amendment's territory pushes outward to encompass ever more areas of law").

48. Schauer, supra note 46, at 184.

49. See id. at 185 (discussing alternative constitutional arguments).

50. Id. at 184.

51. Id. at 184–85.

52. See Timothy Zick, "Restroom Use, Civil Rights, and Free Speech 'Opportunism,' " 78 *Ohio St. L.J.* 963 (2017).

53. See, e.g., Nan D. Hunter, "Identity, Speech, and Equality," 79 *Va. L. Rev.* 1695, 1716 (1993); Cole & Eskridge, supra note 45; Toni M. Massaro, "Gay Rights, Thick and Thin," 49 *Stan. L. Rev.* 45, 63 (1996); Tobias Barrington Wolff, "Political Accountability and Representation under Don't Ask, Don't Tell," 89 *Iowa L. Rev.* 1633, 1649–50 (2004); Ball, supra note 12, at 126–30.

54. See Cole & Eskridge, supra note 43.

55. See Schauer, supra note 46, at 184 (describing free speech claim as "slightly less doctrinally dubious" than other claims and "slightly plausible"). It is not clear whether Professor Schauer was claiming that the expressive challenges to "no promo homo" policies were an actual *misuse* of the First Amendment.

56. See id. at 187 (observing that identity claims may have been successful in the longer term by "associating the persuasive power of the First Amendment with the movement to recognize the moral and constitutional rights of the homosexual community"). *See also* Hunter, *supra* note 53, at 1703 (describing how "no promo homo" policies produced a shift in judicial analysis from seeing homosexuality as conduct to consideration of gay speech "as the advocacy of ideas" about homosexuality).

57. See Beauharnais v. Illinois, 343 U.S. 250 (1952).

58. See R.A.V. v. City of St. Paul, 505 U.S. 377, 382 (1992). See also Matal v. Tam, 137 S. Ct. 1744, 1764 (2017) ("Speech that demeans on the basis of race, ethnicity, gender, religion, age, disability, or any other similar ground is hateful; but the proudest boast of our free speech jurisprudence is that we protect the freedom to express 'the thought that we hate.' ") (quoting United States v. Schwimmer, 279 U.S. 644, 655 (1929) (Holmes, J., dissenting)).

59. See Snyder v. Phelps, 562 U.S. 443, 459 (2011).

60. See, e.g., Richard Delgado & Jean Stefancic, *Must We Defend Nazis? Hate Speech, Pornography, and the New First Amendment* (N.Y.U. Press, 1997); Richard Delgado, "Words

That Wound: A Tort Action for Racial Insults, Epithets, and Name-Calling," 17 *Harv. C.R.-C.L. L. Rev.* 133 (1982).

61. See Jeremy Waldron, *The Harm in Hate Speech* (Harvard Univ. Press, 2012).

62. See West Va. Bd. of Ed. v. Barnette, 319 U.S. 624, 641–42 (1943) (invalidating compulsory flag salute laws).

63. Hurley v. Irish-American Gay, Lesbian and Bisexual Group of Boston, 515 U.S. 557 (1995).

64. Boy Scouts of America v. Dale, 530 U.S. 640, 653–54 (2000).

65. Christian Legal Society v. Martinez, 130 S. Ct. 2971 (2010).

66. Id. at 2980.

67. Id. at 2993.

68. Rumsfeld v. Forum for Academic and Institutional Rights, 547 U.S. 47, 70 (2006).

69. Dale, 530 U.S. at 654.

70. See Ball, supra note 12, ch. 4 (discussing LGBT activism outside the courts and beyond First Amendment litigation).

71. See Michael Dorf, "Same-Sex Marriage, Second-Class Citizenship, and Law's Social Meaning," 97 *Va. L. Rev.* 1267, 1293–98 (2011) (discussing free speech concerns relating to official enactments regarding sexual orientation); Nelson Tebbe, "Government Nonendorsement," 98 *Minn. L. Rev.* 648, 692 (2013) (arguing that government speech regarding constitutional rights, including equality rights, may be subject to First Amendment free speech limits under a principle of "government nonendorsement").

72. Helen Norton, "The Equal Protection Implications of Government's Hateful Speech," 54 *Wm. & Mary L. Rev.* 159 (2012) (addressing equal protection limits on government speech regarding homosexuality and gay rights); Deborah Hellman, "The Expressive Dimension of Equal Protection," 85 *Minn. L. Rev.* 1 (2000) (discussing equal protection concerns relating to laws regarding homosexuality).

73. See Romer, 517 U.S. at 632 (concluding that "the amendment seems inexplicable by anything but animus toward the class it affects"); Lawrence v. Texas, 539 U.S. 558, 575 (2003) ("When homosexual conduct is made criminal by the law of the State, that declaration in and of itself is an invitation to subject homosexual persons to discrimination both in the public and in the private spheres"); United States v. Windsor, 133 S. Ct. 2675, 2693 (2013) ("The avowed purpose and practical effect of the law here in question are to impose a disadvantage, a separate status, and so a stigma upon all who enter into same-sex marriages made lawful by the unquestioned authority of the States").

74. See generally Karst, supra note 10. See also Geoffrey R. Stone, "Fora Americana: Speech in Public Places," 1974 *Sup. Ct. Rev.* 233, 274–80.

75. Not all commentators have greeted this as a welcome development. See, e.g., Robert C. Post, "Equality and Autonomy in First Amendment Jurisprudence," 95 *Mich. L. Rev.* 1517 (1997).

76. See, e.g., Carey v. Brown, 447 U.S. 455, 471 (1980) (invalidating, based on the Equal Protection Clause, content-based picketing restriction).

77. See Sullivan, 376 U.S. at 273.

78. See Alexander Meiklejohn, *Political Freedom: The Constitutional Powers of the People* (Harper, 1960) (discussing the relationship between free speech and self-government).

79. Kalven, supra note 8, at 6.

80. See, e.g., Dennis v. United States, 341 U.S. 494, 511 (1951) (rejecting free speech defense to charges of communist conspiracy).

81. See Hague v. Comm. for Ind. Org., 307 U.S. 496, 515 (1939) (recognizing a right of access to public streets).

82. See Daniel Hildebrand, "Free Speech and Constitutional Transformation," 10 *Const. Comm.* 133, 150–59 (1993) (describing the Jehovah's Witnesses' Supreme Court free speech cases).

83. See, e.g., Harry Kalven, Jr., "The Concept of the Public Forum: *Cox v. Louisiana*," 1965 *UCLA L. Rev.* 1, 12–13 (describing civil rights cases and their influence on public forum doctrine).

84. See Cox, 379 U.S. at 545 (invalidating conviction of leader of civil rights group seeking to protest racial segregation); Edwards, 372 U.S. at 238 (invalidating breach of peace convictions against civil rights protesters).

85. See Timothy Zick, *Speech Out of Doors: Preserving Expressive Liberties in Public Places* 106–10 (Cambridge Univ. Press, 2009) (discussing the influence of civil rights protests on rights of public presence and contention).

86. NAACP v. Ala. ex rel. Patterson, 357 U.S. 449, 462 (1958).

87. Talley v. California, 362 U.S. 60 (1960). See also McIntyre v. Ohio Elections Comm'n, 515 U.S. 334, 341–42 (1995) (affirming right to publish information anonymously).

88. See NAACP, 357 U.S. at 462 (recognizing right of expressive association).

89. Doe v. Reed, 561 U.S. 186, 201 (2010).

90. NAACP, 357 U.S. at 462 (recognizing right of anonymous association).

91. See generally John D. Inazu, *Liberty's Refuge: The Forgotten Freedom of Assembly* (Yale Univ. Press, 2012) (discussing the importance of rights of assembly and association).

92. For criticisms of the Court's treatment of associational rights, see id.; Andrew Koppelman, "Signs of the Times: *Dale v. Boy Scouts of America* and the Changing Meaning of Nondiscrimination," 23 *Cardozo L. Rev.* 1819 (2002).

93. Koppelman, supra note 92.

94. See New York State Club Ass'n, Inc. v. City of New York, 487 U.S. 1, 13 (1988) (invalidating racially discriminatory exclusion policies); Bd. of Directors of Rotary Int'l v. Rotary Club of Duarte, 481 U.S. 537, 544 (same). See also Roberts v. U.S. Jaycees, 468 U.S. 609, 628–29 (1984) (holding that application of state anti-discrimination law to require Jaycees to admit women as full voting members did not violate the First Amendment).

95. See Dale, 530 U.S. at 653.

96. Christian Legal Soc'y v. Martinez, 561 U.S. 661, 680 (2010).

97. See, e.g., Ashutosh Bhagwat, "Associations and Forums: Situating *CLS v. Martinez*," 38 *Hastings Const. L.Q.* 543, 549 (2011) (arguing that the Court essentially ignored freedom of association rights).

98. See West Va. v. Barnette, 319 U.S. 624, 641–42 (1943) (invalidating compulsory flag salute laws).

99. See generally Joseph Blocher, "Rights To and Not To," 100 *Cal. L. Rev.* 761 (2012).

100. See Hurley v. Irish-American Gay, Lesbian, and Bisexual Group of Boston, 515 U.S. 557, 574 (1995). See also Dale, 530 U.S. at 654 (citing *Hurley* as "illustrative").

101. Rumsfeld v. Forum for Academic and Institutional Rights, 547 U.S. 47, 61–62 (2006).

102. Id.

103. Id.

104. Kalven, supra note 8, at 66.

105. Eskridge, supra note 14, at 111. See also Rhonda Rivera, "Our Straight-Laced Judges: The Legal Position of Homosexual Persons in the United States," 30 *Hastings L.J.* 799, 908–34 (1979).

106. 347 U.S. 483 (1954).

107. Romer v. Evans, 517 U.S. 620, 632 (1996).

108. See cases cited supra, note 94.

109. Newman v. Piggie Park Enters., 390 U.S. 400 (1968).

110. Id. at 403 n.5.

111. See Heart of Atlanta Motel, Inc. v. United States, 379 U.S. 241(1964) (upholding application of Civil Rights Act of 1964 to public accommodations on basis of Congress's power to regulate interstate commerce).

112. See Timothy Zick, "Property As/And Constitutional Settlement," 104 *Nw. U. L. Rev.* 1361 (2010).

113. NAACP, 357 U.S. at 462.

114. See, e.g., Wooley v. Maynard, 430 U.S. 705 (1977) (First Amendment protects right not to be compelled to display state messages on license plate).

115. See City of Cleburne v. Cleburne Living Ctr., 473 U.S. 432, 442 (1985) (discussing tiered scrutiny approach).

116. See generally Zick, supra note 52.

117. See Clyde Haberman, "Beyond Caitlyn Jenner Lies a Long Struggle by Transgender People," *N.Y. Times*, June 14, 2015 (discussing change in public attitudes toward transgender persons).

118. Obergefell, 135 S. Ct. at 2593 (emphasis added).

119. Toni M. Massaro, "Gay Rights, Thick and Thin," 49 *Stan. L. Rev.* 45, 63 (1996).

CHAPTER 6

1. Planned Parenthood of Se. Penn. v. Casey, 505 U.S. 833, 876–77 (1992) (joint opinion) (explaining "undue burden" standard).

2. 410 U.S. 113, 153 (1973).

3. 381 U.S. 479 (1965).

4. The Ninth Amendment states: "The enumeration in the Constitution, of certain rights, shall not be construed to deny or disparage others retained by the people."

5. Id. at 484.

6. Id. at 483–84.

7. Casey, 505 U.S. at 848–52.

8. See, e.g., Lawrence v. Texas, 539 U.S. 558, 562 (2003) ("Liberty presumes an autonomy of self that includes freedom of thought, belief, expression, and certain intimate conduct."); Obergefell v. Hodges, 135 S. Ct. 2584, 2593 (2015) (observing that the Constitution protects "a liberty that includes certain specific rights that allow persons, within a lawful realm, *to define and express their identity*").

9. Recall, as discussed in Chapter 3, that by the 1960s free press and assembly rights had generally been collapsed into the Free Speech Clause.

10. See Reva B. Siegel, "The Jurisgenerative Role of Social Movements in United States Constitutional Law," at 11 (for publication with the papers of the Seminario en Latino América de Teoria Constitucional y Politica (SELA), June 10–12, 2004, Oaxaca, México). See also Reva B. Siegel, "Constitutional Culture, Social Movement Conflict and Constitutional Change: The Case of the De Facto ERA," 94 *Cal. L. Rev.* 1323 (2006).

11. See Reva B. Siegel, "*Roe*'s Roots: The Women's Rights Claims That Engendered Roe," 90 *B.U. L. Rev.* 1875, 1880–86 (2010) (describing protests, assemblies, and speeches that advanced

non-medical values in support of the right to abortion). The history of abortion litigation leading up to *Roe v. Wade* is recounted in *Before* Roe v. Wade: *Voices That Shaped the Abortion Debate before the Supreme Court's Ruling* (Linda Greenhouse & Reva B. Siegel eds., Kaplan Publishing, 2010).

12. Siegel, supra note 10, at 1881.

13. Id. at 1882.

14. See Reva B. Siegel, "Sex Equality Arguments for Reproductive Rights: Their Critical Basis and Evolving Constitutional Expression," 56 *Emory L.J.* 815, 827–29 (2007).

15. For a discussion of pre-*Roe* rhetoric and claims, see, e.g., Mary Ziegler, "Beyond Backlash: Legal History, Polarization, and *Roe v. Wade*," 71 *Wash & Lee L. Rev.* 969 (2014). See also Caitlin E. Borgmann, "*Roe v. Wade*'s 40th Anniversary: A Moment of Truth for the Anti-Abortion-Rights Movement?," 24 *Stan. L & Poly Rev.* 245 (2013).

16. See Reva B. Siegel, "Dignity and the Politics of Protection: Abortion Restrictions under *Casey/Carhart*," 117 *Yale L.J.* 1694 (2008); Reva B. Siegel, "The Right's Reasons: Constitutional Conflict and the Spread of Woman-Protective Anti-Abortion Argument," 57 *Duke L. J.* 1641 (2008); Jeannie Suk, "The Trajectory of Trauma: Bodies and Minds in Abortion Discourse," 110 *Colum. L. Rev.* 1193 (2010).

17. See Act of March 3, 1873, ch. 258, § 217 Stat. 599 (1873) (an Act designed "for the suppression of trade in and circulation of obscene literature and articles of immoral use").

18. See Valentine v. Chrestensen, 316 U.S. 52, 55 (1942) (holding that commercial handbill was not covered by the Free Speech Clause).

19. See Va. State Bd. of Pharmacy v. Va. Citizens Consumer Council, Inc., 425 U.S. 748, 771–72 (1976).

20. 421 U.S. 809 (1975).

21. Id. at 822.

22. See generally Robert D. Goldstein, "Reading Casey: Structuring the Woman's Decision-making Process," 4 *Wm. & Mary Bill Rts. J.* 787 (1996).

23. See Harris v. McRae, 448 U.S. 297, 315–17 (1980) (rejecting challenges to the Hyde Amendment, which barred payments even for most medically necessary abortions); Maher v. Roe, 432 U.S. 464, 480 (1977) (upholding denial of Medicaid funds for abortion services).

24. Maher, 432 U.S. at 474.

25. Casey, 505 U.S. at 877–78.

26. Gonzales v. Carhart, 550 U.S. 124, 127–28 (2007).

27. See, e.g., City of Akron v. Akron Ctr. for Reprod. Health, Inc. (*Akron I*), 462 U.S. 416, 444–45 (1983) (invalidating information and informed consent provisions).

28. Casey, 505 U.S. at 884 (joint opinion).

29. Id.

30. Id. at 872.

31. Goldstein, supra note 21, at 802.

32. Id. at 791.

33. See Caroline Mala Corbin, "Compelled Disclosures," 65 *Ala. L. Rev.* 1277, 1324–28 (2014) (discussing mandatory abortion disclosure laws).

34. See, e.g., Rebecca Dresser, "From Double Standard to Double Bind: Informed Choice in Abortion Law," 76 *Geo. Wash. L. Rev.* 1599, 1602–04 (2008) (discussing informed consent requirement under common and statutory law).

35. For commentary on compulsory abortion disclosures, see generally Corbin, supra note 33; Jennifer M. Keighley, "Physician Speech and Mandatory Ultrasound Laws: The First Amendment's Limit on Compelled Ideological Speech," 34 *Cardozo L. Rev.* 2347, 2389 (2013); Robert Post, "Informed Consent to Abortion: A First Amendment Analysis of Compelled Physician Speech," 2007 *U. Ill. L. Rev.* 939, 959–62 (2007); and Carol Sanger, "Seeing and Believing: Mandatory Ultrasound and the Path to a Protected Choice," 56 *UCLA L. Rev.* 351, 399–400 (2008).

36. 500 U.S. 173 (1991).

37. See id. at 196.

38. Id. at 180 ("[I]n implementing the statutory prohibition by forbidding counseling, referral, and the provision of information regarding abortion as a method of family planning, the regulations simply ensure that appropriate funds are not used for activities, including speech, that are outside the federal program's scope.").

39. Id. at 192.

40. See id. at 200.

41. Rosenberger v. Rector and Visitors of the Univ. of Virginia, 515 U.S. 519, 533 (1995).

42. Lower courts have upheld a similar set of restrictions with regard to the funding of *international* family planning projects. *See* DKT Mem'l Fund Ltd. v. Agency for Int'l Dev., 887 F.2d 275, 288 (D.C. Cir. 1989) (upholding government's refusal to fund abortion speech by international organizations). See also Nina J. Crimm, "The Global Gag Rule: Undermining National Interests by Doing unto Foreign Women and NGOs What Cannot Be Done at Home," 40 *Cornell Int'l L.J.* 587, 601 n.98 (2007).

43. See Joshua C. Wilson, *The Street Politics of Abortion: Speech, Violence, and America's Culture Wars* (Stanford Univ. Press, 2013).

44. See id.

45. See Timothy Zick, *Speech Out of Doors: Preserving First Amendment Liberties in Public Places* 118–21 (Cambridge Univ. Press, 2009) (discussing abortion clinic protests).

46. See, e.g., Madsen v. v. Women's Health Ctr., Inc., 512 U.S. 753, 757 (1994) (invalidating broad bubble provision that banned all unwanted physical approaches, but upholding thirty-six-foot buffer zone and other injunctive provisions); Hill v. Colorado, 530 U.S. 703, 725 (2000) (upholding state law restricting certain unwanted approaches near abortion clinics).

47. Hill, 503 U.S. at 716.

48. See Timothy Zick, "Justice Scalia and Abortion Speech," 15 *First Am. L. Rev.* 288, 315-16 (2017).

49. See McCullen v. Coakley, 134 S. Ct. 2518, 2536 (2014).

50. Id. at 2537.

51. See Frisby v. Schultz, 487 U.S. 474, 488 (1988).

52. 18 U.S.C. § 248 (2012). In one case, the Supreme Court held that federal racketeering laws could not be applied to abortion protesters. See Scheidler v. Nat'l Org. for Women, Inc., 537 U.S. 393, 405 (2003).

53. See 18 U.S.C. § 248(a) (2012) .

54. Planned Parenthood of the Columbia/Willamette, Inc. v. Am. Coal. of Life Activists, 290 F.3d 1058, 1086 (9th Cir. 2002) (en banc).

55. Id. at 1062.

56. See id. at 1079–80.

57. See id. at 1086.

58. See id. at 1088 (Reinhardt, J., dissenting); id. at 1092–95 (Kozinski, J., dissenting).

59. Id. at 1092 (Kozinski, J., dissenting).

60. Id. at 1100.

61. See Va. State Bd. of Pharmacy v. Va. Citizens Consumer Council, Inc., 425 U.S. 748, 771–72 (1976).

62. See, e.g., N.Y. Times Co. v. Sullivan, 376 U.S. 254, 266 (1964).

63. Bigelow, 421 U.S. at 822.

64. See Central Hudson Gas & Elec. Corp. v. Public Svc. Comm'n of New York, 447 U.S. 557, 562–63 (1980) (announcing an "intermediate scrutiny" standard for commercial speech regulations).

65. Madsen v. v. Women's Health Ctr., Inc., 512 U.S. 753 (1994); Schenck v. Pro-Choice Network, 519 U.S. 357, 386 (1997).

66. Schenck, 519 U.S. at 765.

67. Madsen, 512 U.S. at 793 (Scalia, J., concurring in part and dissenting).

68. Id. at 785 (Scalia, J., concurring in the judgment in part and dissenting).

69. Id. at 815.

70. See Daniel A. Farber, "Playing Favorites? Justice Scalia, Abortion Protests, and Judicial Impartiality," 101 *Minn. L. Rev. Headnotes* 23, 31 (2016).

71. Id.

72. Texas v. Johnson, 491 U.S 397, 411–12 (1989).

73. Hill, 530 U.S. at 719.

74. See Hill, 530 U.S. at 742–48 (Scalia, J., dissenting) (arguing that the Colorado law was content-based). See also Alan K. Chen, "Statutory Speech Bubbles, First Amendment Overbreadth, and Improper Legislative Purpose," 38 *Harv. C.R.-C.L. L. Rev.* 31, 31 (2003) (observing that *Hill* has been "condemned by progressive and conservative legal scholars alike"); Jamin B. Raskin & Clark L. LeBlanc, "Disfavored Speech about Favored Rights: *Hill v. Colorado,* the Vanishing Public Forum and the Need for an Objective Speech Discrimination Test," 51 *Am. U. L. Rev.* 179, 199 (2001) (arguing that "the majority fell head over heels for the seductive Colorado statute"); Colloquium, "Professor Michael W. McConnell's Response," 28 *Pepp. L. Rev.* 747, 747 (2001) (suggesting that the justices were voting based on their support or opposition to the speakers); Colloquium, supra, at 750 (quoting Harvard law professor Laurence Tribe as describing *Hill* as "slam-dunk simple" and claiming the Court got it "slam-dunk wrong").

75. Hill, 530 U.S. at 742.

76. Id. at 750, 742.

77. Id. at 720 (citation omitted).

78. 134 S. Ct. 2518 (2015).

79. Id. at 2543.

80. Id. at 2548–49.

81. See, e.g., Cohen v. California, 403 U.S. 15, 25 (1971) ("Surely the State has no right to cleanse public debate to the point where it is grammatically palatable to the most squeamish among us.").

82. See id. at 21–22.

83. Schenck, 519 U.S. at 386 (Scalia, J., dissenting).

84. Id.

85. McCullen, 134 S. Ct. at 2535–37 (holding that statute suppressed more speech than necessary and explaining value in face-to-face communications).

86. Id. at 2541 (Scalia, J., concurring).

87. Id.

88. See generally Timothy Zick, "Justice Scalia and Abortion Speech," 15 *First Am. L. Rev.* 288 (2017).

89. See generally Timothy Zick, "Professional Rights Speech," 47 *Ariz. St. L.J.* 1 (2016).

90. See, e.g., Pickup v. Brown, 740 F.3d 1208, 1228 (9th Cir. 2014) (discussing *Casey*'s treatment of professional speech rights in the context of a review of restrictions on licensed therapists).

91. See Rosenberger v. Rector and Visitors of the Univ. of Virginia, 515 U.S. 819, 833 (1995) (recognizing that "when the government appropriates public funds to promote a particular policy of its own it is entitled to say what it wishes").

92. See Pleasant Grove City v. Summum, 555 U.S. 460, 481 (2009) (government speech is not limited by the Free Speech Clause).

93. Casey, 505 U.S. at 872.

94. See Lee Epstein, Christopher M. Parker &, and Jeffrey Segal, *Do Justices Defend the Speech They Hate? In-Group Bias, Opportunism, and the First Amendment* (2014), available at http://papers.ssrn.com/sol3/papers.cfm?abstract_id=2300572 (2014) ("In a nutshell, justices are opportunistic free speechers, willing to turn back regulation of expression when the expression conforms to their values and uphold it when the expression and their preferences collide.").

95. N.C. Gen. Stat. § 90–21.85 (2011).

96. Id.

97. As this book goes to print, one such measure is being reviewed by the Supreme Court. See Natl. Inst. of Fam. & Life Advocates v. Becerra, 839 F.3d 823 (9th Cir.), cert. granted, 138 S. Ct. 464 (2017).

98. Stuart v. Camnitz, 774 F.3d 238, 246 (4th Cir. 2014).

99. Id. at 246.

100. Id. at 250.

101. See Linda Greenhouse & Reva B. Siegel, "*Casey* and the Clinic Closings: When 'Protecting Health' Obstructs Choice," 125 *Yale L.J.* 1428 (2016).

102. See, e.g., Whole Woman's Health v. Hellerstedt, 136 S. Ct. 2292 (2016) (invalidating admitting privileges and surgical center requirements as applied to abortion providers); Jackson Women's Health Org. v. Currier, 760 F.3d 448 (5th Cir. 2014) (invalidating state law requiring abortion providers to secure admitting privileges at local hospitals).

CHAPTER 7

1. See U.S. Const., amend. 2 ("A well regulated Militia, being necessary to the security of a free State, the right of the people to keep and bear Arms, shall not be infringed.").

2. 554 U.S. 570 (2008).

3. Eugene Volokh, "The First and Second Amendments," 109 *Colum. L. Rev. Sidebar* 97 (2009).

4. See, e.g., Commonwealth v. Blanding, 20 Mass. 304, 314 (1825) ("The liberty of the press was to be unrestrained, but he who used it was to be responsible in case of its abuse; like the right to keep fire arms, which does not protect him who uses them for annoyance or destruction.").

5. 1 William Blackstone, Commentaries 144.

6. See Akhil Reed Amar, *The Bill of Rights: Creation and Reconstruction* chs. 2, 3 (Yale Univ. Press, 1998).

7. See id. at 231–46 (discussing post-Reconstruction expressive rights); 257–68 (discussing post-Reconstruction right to keep and bear arms).

8. See United States v. Miller, 307 U.S. 174 (1939) (interpreting Second Amendment as protecting a collective right relating to arming militias).

9. See David Cole, *Engines of Liberty* Part II (Basic Books, 2015).

10. United States v. Miller, 307 U.S. 174 (1939).

11. The individual rights argument was considered and rejected in the following cases: United States v. Johnson, 497 F.2d 548, 550 (4th Cir. 1974); Stevens v. United States, 440 F.2d 144, 149 (6th Cir. 1971); Quilici v. Village of Morton Grove, 695 F.2d 261, 270 (7th Cir. 1982); United States v. Nelsen, 859 F.2d 1318, 1320 (8th Cir. 1988); Fresno Rifle and Pistol Club, Inc. v. Van de Kamp, 746 F. Supp. 1415, 1418 (E.D. Cal. 1990); Vietnamese Fishermen's Ass'n v. Knights of the Ku Klux Klan, 543 F. Supp. 198, 210 (S.D. Tex. 1982).

12. United States v. Tot, 131 F.2d 261, 266 (3d Cir. 1942), rev'd on other grounds, 319 U.S. 463 (1943).

13. See Carl T. Bogus, "The History and Politics of Second Amendment Scholarship: A Primer," 76 *Chi.-Kent. L. Rev.* 3, 8 (2000) (reporting the notable increase in individualist articles during the period 1970–1989).

14. See id. at 14 (noting NRA financial support for Second Amendment scholarship).

15. See Sanford Levinson, "The Embarrassing Second Amendment," 99 *Yale L.J.* 637 (1989).

16. Id. at 650–51.

17. See Akhil Reed Amar, "The Bill of Rights and the Fourteenth Amendment," 101 *Yale L.J.* 1193, 1205–11, 1261–62 (1992); Akhil Reed Amar, "The Bill of Rights as a Constitution," 100 *Yale L.J.* 1131, 1162–75 (1991).

18. Amar, "The Bill of Rights as a Constitution," supra note 17, at 1164.

19. See William Van Alstyne, "The Second Amendment and the Personal Right to Arms," 43 *Duke L.J.* 1236, 1250–51, 1255 (1994).

20. See Laurence H. Tribe, 1 *American Constitutional Law* (3d ed. Foundation Press, 2000).

21. See generally Joseph Blocher, "Gun Rights Talk," 94 *B.U. L. Rev.* 813 (2014); Dan Kahan, "The Gun Control Debate: A Culture-Theory Manifesto," 60 *Wash & Lee L. Rev.* 3 (2003).

22. Heller, 554 U.S. at 592; 625–26.

23. Id. at 582.

24. Id. at 595.

25. Id. at 635.

26. Id. at 628 n.27.

27. See generally David Klein & Neal Devins, "Dicta, Schmicta: Theory versus Practice in Lower Court Decision Making," 54 *Wm. & Mary L. Rev.* 2021 (2013) (observing that empirical evidence shows that lower courts do not draw sharp distinctions between narrow holdings and broad dicta in Supreme Court decisions).

28. See, e.g., United States v. Chester, 628 F.3d 673, 682 (4th Cir. 2010) (considering First Amendment law as a model for developing Second Amendment standards of review); United States v. Marzzarella, 614 F.3d 85, 89 n.4 (3d Cir. 2010) ("the structure of First Amendment doctrine should inform our analysis of the Second Amendment").

29. E.g., Glenn Harlan Reynolds, "Guns and Gay Sex: Some Notes on Firearms, the Second Amendment, and 'Reasonable Regulation,'" 75 *Tenn. L. Rev.* 137, 149 (2007).

30. See, e.g., Eugene Volokh, "Implementing the Right to Keep and Bear Arms for Self-Defense: An Analytical Framework and a Research Agenda," 56 *UCLA L. Rev.* 1443 (2009) (arguing that courts should not adopt rigid tiers of scrutiny, but rather should consider different categories of justification for restricting rights).

31. See, e.g., Joseph Blocher & Darrel A.H. Miller, "Lethality, Public Carry, and Adequate Alternatives," 53 *Harv. J. Legis.* 279, 291–93 (2016) (suggesting that lower courts are using a variation of the free speech "time, place, and manner" test in reviewing certain public arms restrictions); Joseph Blocher, "Firearms Localism," 123 *Yale L.J.* 82 (2013) (basing approach to Second Amendment regulations in part on obscenity doctrine).

32. See Darrell A.H. Miller, "Guns as Smut: Defending the Home-Bound Second Amendment," 109 *Colum. L. Rev.* 1278, 1280 (2009).

33. Volokh, supra note 3, at 98. Professor Miller authored a brief reply. See Darrell A.H. Miller, "A Short Reply to Professor Volokh," 109 *Columbia L. Rev. Sidebar* 105 (2009).

34. See Volokh, supra note 30, at 1514 (defending right of noncitizens to bear arms); Joseph Blocher, "The Right Not to Keep or Bear Arms," 64 *Stan. L. Rev.* 1, 18–48 (2012) (discussing rights not to speak and parallel Second Amendment rights).

35. See Christopher A. Chrisman, "Mind the Gap: The Missing Standard of Review under the Second Amendment (and Where to Find It)," 4 *Geo J.L. & Pub. Pol'y* 289, 327 (2006) (arguing that Second Amendment doctrine should import prior restraint doctrine from First Amendment); Calvin Massey, "Guns, Extremists, and the Constitution," 57 *Wash. & Lee L. Rev.* 1095, 1128–29 (2000) (proposing adoption of First Amendment rules barring arbitrary licensing).

36. See id. at 55–56.

37. Id. at 56–57.

38. Id. at 57–58.

39. Id. at 63–64.

40. See id. at 66 ("Not even the most ardent advocate of gun regulations suggests that moral considerations alone compel prohibitions on carrying guns in public.").

41. See id. at 69–70 (rejecting prior restraint analogy).

42. Id. at 70.

43. See Joseph Blocher & Darrell A.H. Miller, "What Is Gun Control? Direct Burdens, Incidental Burdens, and the Boundaries of the Second Amendment," 83 *U. Chi. L. Rev.* 295, 302 (2016) (discussing autonomy and "marketplace in violence" theories of the Second Amendment).

44. See id. at 73 ("Debates about the purpose of free speech protection reveal a compelling ground for treating the Second Amendment right as embodying a collectivist rather than an individualist purpose . . .").

45. See id. at 87.

46. See Joseph Blocher, "Categoricalism and Balancing in First and Second Amendment Analysis," 84 *N.Y.U. L. Rev.* 375, 381–83 (2009) (explaining distinction between categoricalism and balancing approaches).

47. See id. at 378.

48. Id. at 428.

49. See id. at 413 ("Second Amendment doctrine will eventually become, like First Amendment doctrine, a patchwork of balancing and categorical tests").

50. See Mark Tushnet, "*Heller* and the Perils of Compromise," 13 *Lewis & Clark L. Rev.* 419, 421–22 (2009).

51. Id. at 430. Professor Tushnet is quick to add that the doctrinal category of free speech laws subject to "time, place, and manner" review—content-neutral laws—appear to have no equivalent under the Second Amendment. See id. at 431 ("gun regulations are 'about,' well, guns").

52. See Gregory P. Magarian, "Speaking Truth to Firepower: How the First Amendment Destabilizes the Second," 91 *Tex. L. Rev.* 49, 79–83 (2012) (reviewing free speech justifications).

53. Id. at 87–88.

54. Id. at 95.

55. See Brandenburg v. Ohio, 395 U.S. 444 (1969) (adopting a narrow definition of what constitutes uncovered "incitement" to unlawful action).

56. See McDonald v. City of Chicago, 561 U.S. 742, 767 (2010 (explaining that "individual self-defense is 'the central component' of the Second Amendment right").

57. For a 50-state survey of current laws relating to the open and concealed carrying of firearms, see Giffords Law Center To Prevent Gun Violence, "Open Carry: State by State," http://lawcenter.giffords.org/gun-laws/state-law/50-state-summaries/open-carry-state-by-state/. Only California, Florida, and Illinois ban the open carry of firearms in public places.

58. Id.

59. Id.

60. See David M. Shapiro, "Guns, Speech, Charlottesville: The Semiotics of Semiautomatics," 106 *Geo L. Online* (2017); Katlyn E. DeBoer, "Clash of the First and Second Amendments: Proposed Regulation of Armed Protests," 45 *Hastings Const'l L. Q.* 333 (Winter 2018).

61. See, e.g., David Frum, "The Chilling Effects of Openly Displayed Firearms," *The Atlantic* (Aug. 16, 2017) ("Within metropolitan areas, there is no reason—zero—that a weapon should ever be carried openly. The purpose is always to intimidate—to frighten others away from their lawful rights, not only free speech and lawful assembly, but voting as well,"); John Feinblatt, "Ban the Open Carry of Firearms," *N.Y. Times* (Aug. 17, 2017) (op-ed arguing for ban on open carry at public protests and in public places).

62. See Magarian, supra note 52, at 95 ("Even keeping arms to enable insurrection would undermine debate by fostering a climate of mistrust and fear."); Miller, supra note 32, at 1310 (arguing that "the presence of a gun in public has the effect of chilling or distorting the essential channels of a democracy—public deliberation and interchange").

63. Joe Palazzolo, "ACLU Will No Longer Defend Hate Groups Protesting With Firearms," *Wall St. Journal* (Aug. 17, 2017).

64. See McDonald, 561 U.S. at 891 (Stevens, J., dissenting) ("*[y]our* interest in keeping and bearing a certain firearm may diminish *my* interest in being and feeling safe from armed violence").

65. See Shapiro, supra note 60, at 2 (citing the "threat that the gun will chill the speech of others, such as counter-protesters"); DeBoer, supra note 60, at 340 (urging states "to enact regulation of armed protests in order to stop the intimidation and fear that armed protests engender, as well as the threat of violence and chilling of opposing viewpoints that inevitably ensure from it").

66. Magarian, supra note 52, at 95.

67. Id.

68. See Miller, supra note 32, at 1308.

69. Id. at 1310.

70. Id.

71. See Whitney v. California, 274 U.S. 357, 375 (1927) (Brandeis, J. concurring) ("the fitting remedy for evil counsels is good ones").

72. This sort of rights balancing is not uncommon. See, e.g., Burson v. Freeman, 504 U.S. 191, 211 (1992) (plurality opinion) (balancing free speech and voting rights and upholding limits on political campaign speech near polling places); Bartnicki v. Vopper, 532 U.S. 514, 534 (2001) (holding that privacy interest in contents of private conversation must give way to public interest in dissemination of information of public concern).

73. Eugene Volokh, "The First and Second Amendments," 109 *Colum. L. Rev. Online* 97, 102–03 (2009).

74. See id. (claiming that New Hampshire, Vermont, and Washington, which have long imposed few restrictions on carrying guns, enjoy the same level of robust political discourse as more restrictive states like Hawaii, Maryland, and New York).

75. Id. at 102.

76. Id.

77. See Paul Duggan, "Militiamen came to Charlottesville as neutral First Amendment protectors, commander says," *Wash. Post* (Aug. 13, 2017).

78. See United States v. O'Brien, 391 U.S. 367, 376 (1968); Spence v. Washington, 418 U.S. 405, 409 (1974).

79. Texas v. Johnson, 491 U.S. 397, 405 (1989).

80. See Shapiro, supra note 60, at 2 (arguing that open carry at the Charlottesville rally was sufficiently expressive); DeBoer, supra note 60, at 346–47 (concluding that open carry at a rally for Second Amendment rights is expressive).

81. O'Brien, 391 U.S. at 376–77.

82. E.g., Shapiro, supra note 60, at 5; DeBoer, supra note 60, at 355.

83. See, e.g., Tinker v. Des Moines Indep. Comm. Sch. Dist., 393 U.S. 503, 508 (1969) ("But, in our system, undifferentiated fear or apprehension of disturbance is not enough to overcome the right to freedom of expression").

84. One commentator has reached the opposite conclusion. See DeBoer, supra note 60, at 350–56 (arguing that prohibition on open carry during public protests would satisfy Free Speech Clause standards). The author's argument is based on the premise that government can justify a prohibition on open carry at public protests by pointing generally to crime-prevention and safety interests. For the reasons stated, it is not clear whether these general interests would satisfy free speech standards.

85. See Watts v. United States, 394 U.S. 705, 708 (1969) (holding that "true threats" are not covered by the Free Speech Clause); Virginia v. Black, 538 U.S. 343, 360 (2003) ("Intimidation in the constitutionally proscribable sense of the word is a type of true threat, where a speaker directs a threat to a person or group of persons with the intent of placing the victim in fear of bodily harm or death.").

86. See Brandenburg v. Ohio, 395 U.S. 444, 446 (1969) (defining uncovered incitement as speech that advocates unlawful action that is both imminent and likely to occur).

87. Johnson, 491 U.S. at 405 ("Pregnant with expressive content, the flag as readily signifies this Nation as does the combination of letters found in 'America.' "); DeBoer, supra note 60, at 343–48 (examining messages open carry might communicate).

88. Hurley v. Irish-Am. Gay, Lesbian & Bisexual Group of Bos., 515 U.S. 557, 569 (1995).

89. Id.

90. See Rumsfeld v. Forum for Academic and Institutional Rights, 547 U.S. 47 (2006) (rejecting symbolic conduct claim and upholding federal condition requiring that law schools send emails and provide other forms of equal access for military employers).

91. O'Brien, 391 U.S. at 376.

92. Forum for Academic and Institutional Rights, 547 U.S. at 66.

93. See Frederick Schauer, "First Amendment Opportunism," in Lee C. Bollinger & Geoffrey R. Stone, *Eternally Vigilant: Free Speech in the Modern Era* (Univ. of Chicago Press, 2002).

94. Heller, 554 U.S. at 628 ("[T]he inherent right of self-defense has been central to the Second Amendment right.").

95. See, e.g., Moore v. Madigan, 702 F.3d 933, 937 (7th Cir. 2012) (recognizing that a Second Amendment right to carry a gun for self-defense logically extends beyond the home).

96. Compare Kachalsky v. Cty. of Westchester, 701 F.3d 81, 101 (2d Cir. 2012) (rejecting a challenge to New York's restriction of concealed carry licenses to individuals demonstrating "proper cause") with Peruta v. Cty. of San Diego, 742 F.3d 1144, 1172 (9th Cir. 2014) (invalidating San Diego's concealed carry permit scheme).

97. For discussions of the concept of expressive chill, see Frederick Schauer, "Fear, Risk and the First Amendment: Unraveling the Chilling Effect," 58 *B.U. L. Rev.* 685, 692 (1978); Henry P. Monaghan, "Constitutional Fact Review," 85 *Colum. L. Rev.* 229, 268 (1985); Daniel J. Solove, "The First Amendment as Criminal Procedure," 82 *N.Y. U. L. Rev.* 112, 142 (1997); Leslie Kendrick, "Speech, Intent and the Chilling Effect," 54 *Wm. & Mary L. Rev.* 1633, 1649–50 (2013).

98. See Laird, 408 U.S. at 11 (holding that subjective chill is not a cognizable injury).

99. See Monica Youn, "The Chilling Effect and the Problem of Private Action," 66 *Vand. L. Rev.* 1474, 1477 (2013) (proposing that private chill is properly attributable to government only where the state has violated some rule or "trespassed constitutional norms").

100. See Shapiro, supra note 60, at 5 (proposing "open carry zones").

101. See Timothy Zick, "Speech and Spatial Tactics," 84 *Tex. L. Rev.* 581, 591-606 (2006) (discussing use and effects of speech zoning and other spatial restrictions).

102. See id. (discussing various harms to free speech from zoning and other spatial tactics).

103. Heller, 554 U.S. at 626.

104. Id.

105. Id. at 626–27.

106. Id. at 592.

107. Id. at 628.

108. Id. See also McDonald, 561 U.S. at 767 (explaining that "individual self-defense is 'the central component' of the Second Amendment right" without any indication that the right is limited to the home).

109. See, e.g., Peruta v. Cty. of San Diego, 742 F.3d 1144, 1179 (9th Cir. 2014); Moore v. Madigan, 702 F.3d 933, 937 (7th Cir. 2012) (concluding that the right to self-defense extends beyond the home).

110. See Heller, 554 U.S. at 626. See also, e.g., Drake v. Filko, 724 F.3d 426, 430 (3d Cir. 2013) ("It remains unsettled whether the individual right to bear arms for the purpose of self-defense extends beyond the home."); Kachalsky v. Cty. of Westchester, 701 F.3d 81, 101 (2d Cir. 2012) (upholding New York law restricting concealed carry to those who could demonstrate "proper cause").

111. See, e.g., United States v. Masciandaro, 638 F.3d 458, 471 (4th Cir. 2011) ("[W]e conclude that a lesser showing is necessary with respect to laws that burden the right to keep and bear arms outside of the home.").

112. Heller, 554 U.S. at 627.

113. Presser v. Illinois, 116 U.S. 252, 254–65 (1886).

114. Id. at 265.

115. Heller, 554 U.S. at 675.

116. See Watts v. United States, 394 U.S. 705, 708 (1969) (holding that "true threats" are not covered by the Free Speech Clause).

117. See, e.g., S.C. Code § 22-5-150 (prohibiting any person from going "armed offensively, to the terror of the people").

118. See State v. Huntly, 25 N.C. 418, 418 (1843); State v. Staten, 32 N.C. App. 495, 496-97 (1977); Simpson v. State, 13 Tenn. (5 Yer.) 356 (1833); O'Neill v. State, 16 Ala. 65, 67 (1849). See also Saul Cornell, "The Right to Keep and Carry Arms in Anglo-American Law: Preserving Liberty and Keeping the Peace," 80 *Law & Cont. Prob.* 11 (2017) (discussing early common law concerning public arms-bearing).

119. See 4 William Blackstone, Commentaries on the Laws of England 148–49 (1769) ("The offence of riding or going armed with dangerous or unusual weapons is a crime against the public peace, by terrifying the good people of the land; and is particularly prohibited by the statute of Northampton."). Under the common law rule, because carrying a dangerous weapon (such as a firearm) in populated public places naturally terrified the people, it was a crime against the peace—even if unaccompanied by a threat, violence, or any additional breach of the peace. See Chune v. Piott, 80 Eng. Rep. 1161, 1162 (K.B. 1615) ("Without all question, the sheriffe hath power to commit . . . if contrary to the Statute of Northampton, he sees any one to carry weapons in the high-way, in terrorem populi Regis; he ought to take him, and arrest him, notwithstanding he doth not break the peace in his presence.").

120. See Dahlia Lithwick & Olivia Li, "Can You Bring a Gun to a Protest?," *Slate* (Oct. 17, 2017) (discussing state enforcement of the offense of "going armed to the terror of the people").

121. See, e.g., United States v. Dorosan, 350 Fed. Appx. 874, 875–76 (5th Cir. 2009) (positing that a parking lot belonging to the USPS was a sensitive place); United States v. Masciandaro, 648 F. Supp. 2d 779, 790 (E.D. Va. 2009) ("Although Heller does not define 'sensitive places,' the examples given—schools and government buildings—plainly suggest that motor vehicles on National Park land fall within any sensible definition of a 'sensitive place.'").

122. See DeBoer, supra note 60, at 367–70 (arguing that armed protest bans satisfy current Second Amendment standards).

123. See, e.g., Kolbe v. Hogan, 849 F.3d 114, 121 (4th Cir. 2017) (upholding Maryland's ban on assault rifles and noting that four other sister circuits had also upheld similar bans).

124. See id. at 293–99 (examining Second Amendment theories as they might relate to restrictions on carrying lethal weapons).

125. Doe v. Reed, 561 U.S. 186, 228 (2010) (Scalia, J., concurring).

126. See Shaundra K. Lewis, "Crossfire on Compulsory Campus Carry Laws: When the First and Second Amendment Collide," 102 *Iowa L. Rev.* 2109, 2113–17 (2017) (discussing campus carry laws).

127. See Robert M. O'Neil, "Academic Freedom and the Constitution," 11 *J.C. & U.L.* 275, 281 (1984).

128. 385 U.S. 589, 603 (1967). See also Sweezy v. New Hampshire, 354 U.S. 234, 250 (1957) (finding that the government's inquiry into the subject matter of a University of New Hampshire lecturer's presentations "unquestionably was an invasion [of the lecturer's] liberties in the areas of academic freedom and political expression—areas in which government should be extremely reticent to tread").

129. David M. Rabban, "A Functional Analysis of 'Individual' and 'Institutional' Academic Freedom under the First Amendment," 53 *Law & Contemp. Probs.* 227, 231 (Summer 1990).

130. For a general discussion concerning the relationship between academic freedom and the First Amendment, see William W. Van Alstyne, "Academic Freedom and the First Amendment in the Supreme Court of the United States: An Unhurried Historical Review," 53 *Law & Contemp. Probs.* 79 (1990).

131. See Glass v. Paxton, 2016 WL 8904948, _ F. Supp. 3d __ (W.D. Tex. 2016).

132. Glass v. Paxton, 2017 WL 4506806, __ F. Supp. 3d. __ (W.D. Tex. 2017).

133. Professor Lewis makes the opposite argument, namely that academic freedom outweighs any legal right to keep and bear arms in the classroom. See Lewis, supra note 126, at 2134 (arguing that in the event of a conflict between academic freedom and the right to bear arms in the classroom, the "First Amendment predominates"). Lewis's perception of the strength of academic freedom rights, at least in this context, differ markedly from my own.

134. Regarding the marketplace concept, see Abrams v. United States, 250 U.S. 616, 630 (1919) (Holmes, J., dissenting); John Stuart Mill, *On Liberty* 15–16 (Wiley-Blackwell, 1895).

135. See generally Lee C. Bollinger, *The Tolerant Society* (Oxford Univ. Press, 1988).

136. See Lewis, supra note 126, at 2112–23.

137. See generally John D. Inazu, *Confident Pluralism: Surviving and Thriving through Deep Difference* (Univ. of Chicago Press, 2016).

138. See Blocher, supra note 21.

139. See Alexander Meiklejohn, *Political Freedom: The Constitutional Powers of the People* 24–25 (Harper, 1960) (discussing self-government and other democratic values associated with freedom of speech).

140. See generally Jeffrey Bellin, "The Right to Remain Armed," 93 *Wash. U. L. Rev.* 1 (2015) (discussing the impact of Fourth Amendment rights on Second Amendment rights). Restrictions on arms possession by certain classes of individuals may violate the Equal Protection Clause. Limits on the mobility of firearms carriers and Second Amendment rights may implicate the Due Process Clause and the right to travel.

141. See Schenck v. United States, 249 U.S. 47 (1919); Abrams v. United States, 250 U.S. 616 (1919); Debs v. United States, 249 U.S. 211 (1919).

142. See Tabatha Abu El-Haj, "The Neglected Right of Assembly," 56 *UCLA L. Rev.* 543, 580-84 (2009) (discussing evolution of courts' approach to public forums).

143. See Cox v. Louisiana, 379 U.S. 536, 545 (1965) (invalidating conviction of leader of civil rights group seeking to protest racial segregation); Perry Educ. Assn. v. Perry Local Educators' Assn., 460 U.S. 37, 46 (1983) (describing categorical approach to expressive rights in public places).

144. See Harry Kalven, Jr., *The Concept of the Public Forum*: Cox v. Louisiana, 1965 SUP. CT. REV. 1, 12 (describing Court's evolving time, place, and manner doctrine as establishing a Roberts Rules for public expression).

145. See Brandenburg, 395 U.S. 448 (holding that incitement is not covered speech), Watts, 394 U.S. at 708 (holding that true threats are not covered speech); Chaplinsky, 315 U.S. 573 (holding that fighting words are not covered speech).

146. See Timothy Zick, *Speech Out of Doors: Preserving First Amendment Liberties in Public Places* 59 (Cambridge Univ. Press, 2009) (discussing "negotiated management" policing strategies).

147. See Molly Hennessy-Fiske, "Dallas police chief: Open carry makes things confusing during mass shootings," *L.A. Times* (Jul. 11, 2016) (reporting on sniper shooting in Dallas, Texas that claimed the lives of several police officers).

148. See Timothy Zick, "Managing Dissent," 95 *Wash. U. L. Rev.* __ (forthcoming, 2018) (discussing early free speech and assembly cases).

149. See Cantwell v. Connecticut, 310 U.S. 296 (1940) (invalidating breach of peace conviction stemming from public proselytizing); McCullen v. Coakley, 134 S. Ct 2518 (2014) (invalidating abortion clinic buffer zones that suppressed speech of sidewalk counselors); Johnson, 491 U.S. at 405 (invalidating conviction for flag desecration); Snyder v. Phelps, 562 U.S. 443 (2011) (overturning civil tort judgment against protesters at military funeral).

150. See Cohen v. California, 403 U.S. 15, 21 (1971).

151. See Jonah Engel Bromwich & Alan Blinder, "What We Know About Alex Fields, Driver Charged in Charlottesville Killing," *N.Y. Times* (Aug. 13, 2017).

152. See Sheryl Gay Stolberg & Brian M. Rosenthal, "Man Charged After White Nationalist Rally in Charlottesville Ends in Deadly Violence," N.Y. Times (Aug. 12, 2017) (describing violent clashes between protesters and counter-protesters).

153. See Sheryl Gay Stolberg, "Why the Push to Ban Rifle 'Bump Stocks' Has Slowed," *N.Y. Times* (Nov. 8, 2017) (discussing legislative gridlock on gun control efforts in the wake of mass shooting in Las Vegas).

154. See Blocher & Miller, supra note 31, at 293-99 (examining Second Amendment theories as they might relate to restrictions on carrying lethal weapons); Joseph Blocher & Darrell A.H. Miller, "What Is Gun Control? Direct Burdens, Incidental Burdens, and the Boundaries of the Second Amendment," 83 *U. Chi. L. Rev.* 295, 347-53 (2016) (discussing Second Amendment theories.

155. See generally Frederick Schauer, *Free Speech: A Philosophical Enquiry* (Cambridge Univ. Press, 1982) (examining various theories that are said to justify protection for freedom of speech).

156. See Alexander Meiklejohn, *Political Freedom: The Constitutional Powers of the People* 24-25 (Harper, 1960) (discussing self-government and other democratic values associated with freedom of speech); Abrams v. United States, 250 U.S. 616, 630 (1919) (Holmes, J., dissenting); John Milton, *Areopagitica: A Speech for the Liberty of Unlicensed Printing* 45 (MacMillan 1959) (H.B. Cotterill, ed.) (originally published 1644) ("Let her and falsehood grapple; who ever knew Truth put to the worse in a free and open encounter?"); C. Edwin Baker, *Human Liberty and Freedom of Speech* (Oxford Univ. Press, 1989); Martin H. Redish, "The Content Distinction in First Amendment Analysis," 34 *Stan. L. Rev.* 113 (1981).

157. See Heller, 554 U.S. at 599, 630 (recognizing the core self-defense justification).

158. See Blocher & Miller, supra note 31, at 294 (examining application of autonomy theory to Second Amendment).

159. Id. at 295.

160. Id. at 299.

CHAPTER 8

1. Gerard Magliocca, *The Heart of the Constitution: How the Bill of Rights Became the Bill of Rights* (Oxford Univ. Press, 2017).

2. For arguments connecting Rights Pluralism to strong normative or conceptions of political and constitutional pluralism, see generally John D. Inazu, *Confident Pluralism: Surviving and Thriving Through Deep Difference* (Univ. of Chicago Press, 2016); John D. Inazu, "The Four Freedoms and the Future of Religious Liberty," 92 *N.C. L. Rev.* 787, 788 (2014).

3. See Pamela S. Karlan, "Equal Protection, Due Process, and the Stereoscopic Fourteenth Amendment," 33 *McGeorge L. Rev.* 473 (2002) (examining the bidirectional relationship between the Fourteenth Amendment's Due Process Clause and Equal Protection Clause).

4. See DeJonge v. Oregon, 299 U.S. 353, 364 (1937) (describing the right of assembly as "cognate" to those of free speech and free press). See also Ashutosh Bhagwat, "The Democratic First Amendment," 110 *Nw. L. Rev.* 1097, 1098–99 (2016) (describing freedom of speech, press, and assembly as "kaleidoscopic" rights).

5. See, e.g., Carlos A. Ball, *The First Amendment and LGBT Equality; A Contentious History* (Harvard Univ. Press, 2017).

6. They also formally relied on assembly, press, and petition rights. However, as explained in Chapter 3, those rights have generally been treated as "ancillary" to the Free Speech Clause.

7. See generally Frederick Schauer, "First Amendment Opportunism," in Lee C. Bollinger & Geoffrey R. Stone, *Eternally Vigilant: Free Speech in the Modern Era* (U. of Chicago Press, 2003).

8. See Leslie Kendrick, "First Amendment Expansionism," 56 *Wm. & Mary L. Rev.* 1199, 1200 (2015) (describing "expansionism" as the situation "where the First Amendment's territory pushes outward to encompass ever more areas of law").

9. Frederick Schauer, "The Boundaries of the First Amendment: A Preliminary Exploration of Constitutional Salience," 117 *Harv. L. Rev.* 1765, 1787–800 (2004).

10. See Michael W. McConnell, "Reconsidering *Citizens United* as a Press Clause Case," 123 *Yale L.J.* 412 (2013).

11. See, e.g., Darrell A.H. Miller, "Guns as Smut: Defending the Home-Bound Second Amendment," 109 *Colum. L. Rev.* 1278, 1280 (2009); Gregory P. Magarian, "Speaking Truth to Firepower: How the First Amendment Destabilizes the Second," 91 *Tex. L. Rev.* 49 (2012).

12. See Marbury v. Madison, 5 U.S. (1 Cranch) 137, 174 91803) ("It cannot be presumed that any clause in the constitution is intended to be without effect; and therefore such construction is inadmissible, unless the words require it.").

13. See Annenberg Public Policy Center, University of Pennsylvania, "Americans Are Poorly Informed About Basic Constitutional Provisions" (Sept. 12, 2017), https://www.annenberg publicpolicycenter.org/americans-are-poorly-informed-about-basic-constitutional-provisions?utm_source=news-release&utm_medium=email&utm_campaign=2017_civics_survey&utm_term=survey&utm_source=Media&utm_campaign=e5f213892a-Civics_survey_2017_2017_09_12&utm_medium=email&utm_term=0_9e3d9bcd8a-e5f213892a-425997897 (last visited Oct. 13, 2017).

14. See generally Ilya Somin, *Democracy and Political Ignorance: Why Smaller Government Is Smarter* (2d ed. Stanford Univ. Press, 2016).

15. See John Inazu, *Liberty's Refuge: The Forgotten Freedom of Assembly* (Yale Univ. Press, 2012); Ronald J. Krotoszynski, Jr., *Reclaiming the Petition Clause: Seditious Libel, "Offensive Protest," and the Right to Petition Government for a Redress of Grievances* (Yale Univ. Press, 2012); Sonja R. West, "First Amendment Neighbors," 66 *Ala. L. Rev.* 357 (2014).

16. See Bhagwat, supra note 4, at 1098–99.

17. See generally id. See also Inazu, supra note 2, at 788.

18. See Obergefell v. Hodges, 135 S. Ct. 2584 (2015) (recognizing a right to marriage equality, rooted in both the Eual Protection Clause and Due Process Clause). See also Laurence H. Tribe, "Equal Dignity: Speaking Its Name," 129 *Harv. L. Rev. Forum* 16 (2015).

19. See Akhil Reed Amar, "Intratextualism," 112 *Harv. L. Rev.* 747 (1999).

20. See, e.g., Michael Coenen, "Combining Constitutional Clauses," 164 *U. Pa. L. Rev.* 1067 (2016) (examining how the Supreme Court sometimes combines rights in order to reach constitutional decisions); Kerry Abrams & Brandon Garrett, "Cumulative Constitutional Rights," 97 *B.U. L. Rev.* 1310 (2017) (arguing that constitutional rights frequently intersect and combine in ways that inform constitutional remedies).

Index